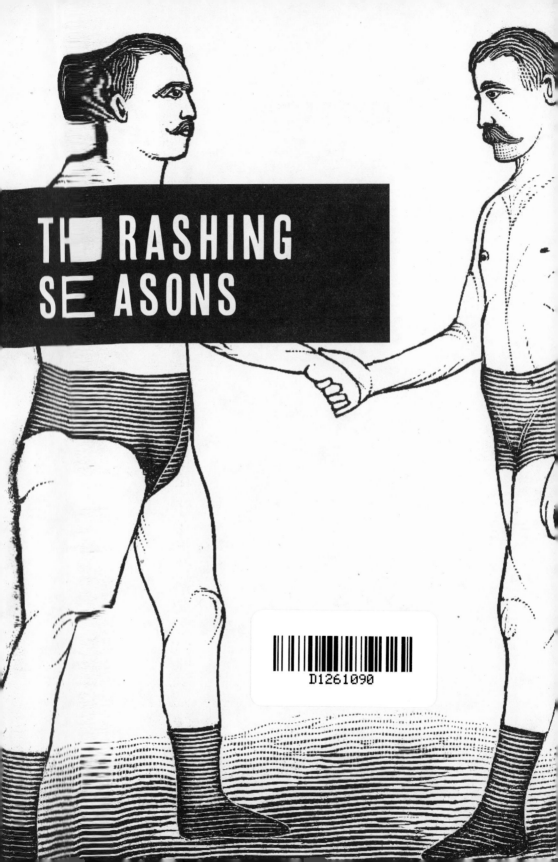

THRASHING
SEASONS

THRASHING SEASONS

SPORTING CULTURE IN MANITOBA AND THE GENESIS OF PRAIRIE WRESTLING

C. Nathan Hatton

To Ryan,
One of my dearest
friends in the
world.
Migwiich!

UMP
University of Manitoba Press

University of Manitoba Press
Winnipeg, Manitoba
Canada R3T 2M5
uofmpress.ca

Printed in Canada
Text printed on chlorine-free, 100% post-consumer recycled paper

20 19 18 17 16   1 2 3 4 5

Cover design: Mike Carroll
Interior design: Jess Koroscil
Cover image: Tom Connors, *The Modern Athlete* (1890)

Library and Archives Canada Cataloguing in Publication

Hatton, C. Nathan, 1978–, author
Thrashing seasons : sporting culture in Manitoba and the genesis
of prairie wrestling / C. Nathan Hatton.

Includes bibliographical references and index.
Issued in print and electronic formats.
ISBN 978-0-88755-800-9 (pbk.)
ISBN 978-0-88755-497-1 (pdf)
ISBN 978-0-88755-495-7 (epub)

1. Wrestling—Manitoba—History. 2. Wrestling—Social aspects—
Manitoba—History. 3. Wrestlers—Manitoba—History. I. Title.

GV1198.15.M35H38 2016   796.812097127   C2015-908001-0
                                               C2015-908002-9

This book has been published with the help of a grant from the Federation for the
Humanities and Social Sciences, through the Awards to Scholarly Publications Program,
using funds provided by the Social Sciences and Humanities Research Council of Canada.

The University of Manitoba Press gratefully acknowledges the financial support
for its publication program provided by the Government of Canada through the Canada
Book Fund, the Canada Council for the Arts, the Manitoba Department
of Culture, Heritage, Tourism, the Manitoba Arts Council,
and the Manitoba Book Publishing Tax Credit.

THIS WORK IS DEDICATED TO RANDY ROSTECKI

Contents

Illustrations

1. Pugilist Ed McKeown, pictured in this 1889 engraving, was actively involved in Winnipeg's early sports scene, including with professional wrestling. Despite frequent run-ins with the law, his connections with the Liberal Party of Canada later netted him a position as a secret police officer during the Klondike Gold Rush. Source: Winnipeg *Siftings*, 16 February 1889. / *pg. 44*

2. Swedish-born middleweight Charles Gustafson was Winnipeg's most prominent professional mat artist in the decade before World War I and claimed the Canadian Middleweight Title. Source: Manitoba *Free Press*, 26 February 1910. / *pg. 71*

3. Ernest (Ernie) Sundberg stands at attention. Like his counterpart Charles Gustafson, Sundberg hailed from Sweden and had a large local following in Winnipeg. Source: Manitoba *Free Press*, 5 February 1910. / *pg. 73*

4. Alex Stewart, a professional featherweight, took on many different roles in wrestling during the 1910s and 1920s, serving as an athlete, coach, and referee. Source: Manitoba Sports Hall of Fame and Museum, MS2011.25.261. / *pg. 91*

5. American wrestler Walter Miller, featured in this newspaper action shot, enjoyed a following within the province's Polish community as a result of his ethnic heritage. Source: Manitoba *Free Press*, 29 September 1913. / *pg. 110*

6. Winnipeg YMCA Wrestling Club, 1908–1909. Back row: H. Black, Jas. J. Bowskill, R.G. Bacon, R.J. Thompson, C.S. Judson, George Akins, H.R. Hadcock (Phys. Dir.). Middle row: P.F. Kennedy, Ray La Have, Christie Akins, Thomas Dickinson (Instructor), W. Bates, P.H. Dilts, A. Lockley. Front Row: John S. Honsberger, John A. MacDonald (Chairman), A.J. Mitchell, A.V. Ashley. Source: Manitoba Sports Hall of Fame and Museum, MS2013.21.1. / *pg. 126*

7. George Washington Akins, an early amateur wrestling standout in Manitoba. Source: Manitoba Sports Hall of Fame and Museum, MS2011.25.259. / *pg. 131*

8. Wrestler Patsy Picciano was one of a small handful of non Anglo-Canadian wrestlers who achieved amateur championship laurels in Manitoba during the prewar era. During the early part of the Great War he wrestled professionally as Patsy Bachant, but as the conflict in Europe escalated, public demand for professional wrestling declined in the province. Source: Manitoba Sports Hall of Fame and Museum, MS2014.25.12. / *pg. 147*

9. Wrestling matches on horseback, such as this one staged by members of the Canadian Expeditionary Forces during July 1916, were regular attractions at military sporting events. Library and Archives Canada, PA-000221. / *pg. 151*

10. Winnipeg Police Officer and CEF veteran Tom Johnstone was instrumental in reviving professional wrestling in Manitoba after the Great War. Source: Manitoba *Free Press*, 5 October 1920. / *pg. 165*

11. A playbill from Brandon's Willis Theatre, advertising a match between Harry McDonald and the "Terrible Swede" Charles Olson. Source: Brandon *Sun*, 12 February 1921. / *pg. 167*

12. Unrivalled as a talent in western Canada during the first half of the 1920s, Canadian-born Jack Taylor ushered in "big time" heavyweight professional wrestling to Winnipeg in 1922 and appeared in communities of all sizes through-out the Prairies. Source: Glenbow Archives, NA-5602-59. / *pg. 173*

13. Playbill for a March 1928 Amateur Boxing and Wrestling card. The Win-nipeg Police Athletic Association was an avid promoter of amateur wrestling during the 1920s. Source: Manitoba *Free Press*, 5 March 1928. / *pg. 204*

14. The working-class One Big Union enthusiastically promoted the quality of the facilities that they offered to their membership. Source: OBU *Bulletin*, 11 September 1924. / *pg. 210*

15. Winnipeg City Policeman William Loyd (W.L.) McIntyre, who won numerous local, provincial, national, and international amateur titles during the late 1920s and early 1930s. Source: Manitoba Sports Hall of Fame and Museum, MS2011.25.262. / *pg. 218*

INTRODUCTION

Tuesday night.

Showtime.

A pair of electric lamplights, strung pendulously from the board ceiling, cast their glow on the scene unfolding below in Winnipeg's Industrial Exhibition (Board of Trade) Building on 3 April 1923. Below the lights, approximately 2,000 people were gathered in the convention hall, one of several facilities housed in the impressive-looking (though rather shoddily constructed) edifice located at the corner of Main and Water Streets in the city's downtown centre. Most of those present were seated on wooden folding chairs. Some, almost exclusively located in the back rows of the two separate balconies situated one above the other, stood for a better view. A small number also perched in the hall's wide wooden rafters, accessible from the walls in the upper balcony, seeking to obtain the highest spot from which to see the show. At seventy degrees Fahrenheit, the room was a comfortable temperature, far removed from the sweltering heat experienced in the same facility, at a similar event, eight months earlier. Since it was still too warm to wear an overcoat for an extended period, many in attendance also used the rafters as makeshift coat racks. A sign reading "No Smoking" affixed to the top balcony was as much a precautionary measure against setting the wooden interior ablaze and ensuring orderly behaviour as it was an effort to preserve public health. Directly below, those without the benefit of rafters draped their jackets over the plank railing in front of the bottom balcony. Several rows of seating also filled the convention hall floor, and most of them, but by no means all, were occupied. In particular, chairs located in the back-most row remained vacated since people exercised their option to be as close to the action as possible. The crowd ranged considerably in age, from the adolescent to the elderly. Overwhelmingly, however, they were men clad in suit and tie. Still, conspicuous by their presence, were perhaps no more than a dozen women, who, in their rolled-brim hats, had decided to partake in the predominantly masculine spectacle.

Anyone who listened closely enough would have noted that the hum of voices, even if similar in tenor, were not singing the same song. Native-born English, though loudest that evening, mixed with a pastiche of other accents, and in some sections different languages altogether could be heard through the din. Winnipeg was a multicultural city, and what was about to transpire was a multicultural spectacle. It had been this way for nearly a quarter century. Most of the men in attendance had dressed well for their public outing, but not all of them had the finest of clothes available to them. Some came from the city's North End, and the occasional frayed sleeve and collar betrayed their working-class roots. Others, seated farther in front of them, with shirts starched and pressed, came from more prosperous areas to the south, close to the Assiniboine River. Many in attendance, however, wore more than their clothing that night. They wore their identities. The combative spectacle that they were about to witness was symbolic of greater conflicts being waged on the factory floors and in the streets, community halls, immigrant sheds, and boarding rooms throughout a city where ethnic and class divisions shaped the fabric of daily existence. When the show began, there were no clear-cut lines between good and bad, hero and villain, even if certain members of the public wished it to be that way. For a moment, all eyes turned forward, and a hush settled in.

Near the room's centre stood a raised rectangular wooden platform. An apron, frayed in places, shielded its underside from public view. On the apron were hung handwritten placards, one saying "Tribune" and the other "Athletic Commission," indicating the privileged positions allocated for the press and civic authorities at the event. A square ring had been constructed on the platform, equidistant from the rectangular structure's shortest sides. Four unpainted wooden posts and three horizontal ropes held in place by metal eye bolts demarcated the periphery of the ring. Stains mottled the middle rope, which, wrapped in white tape, hinted at contact with sweat and skin. A single canvas sheet layered the inside of the ring, under which only a thin veneer of padding shielded those above from the unyielding boards below. If the ring ropes hinted at the source of their discoloration, the strikingly irregular pattern of blotches on the mat spoke unequivocally of contact with dirt, sweat, and blood. Some of the blotches were by-products of the three boxing matches staged earlier in the evening, though reminders of past contests certainly accented the uneven hue.

Inside the ring in one corner was Alex Stewart, a Scottish immigrant of diminutive stature, whose tailored suit hid an athletic physique. As the referee, Stewart was to ensure that the participants in the night's performance did not extend themselves too far beyond his already liberal enforcement of the written rules. Behind the next post, located to Stewart's left, a second man, his hair parted in the middle, stood with a thick robe draped over his right arm. In a moment, he would pull the wooden folding chair in front of him out of the ring. To Stewart's right, in the third corner, a second robe and a clean white towel were flopped casually over the top rope, left there by a burly figure with a shaved head and columnar neck.

Near the ring's centre, two large men, shirtless, their right hands grasped in salutary embrace, eyed one another with steely glares. The first of the pair, Paul Martinson, was an American of Danish descent and recently arrived in the city. At five feet ten inches in height, and weighing 237 pounds, Martinson was bulky, with dark hair, short neck, broad chest, and thick waist. On his left elbow, a white bandage provided tentative shielding for an abrasion incurred when skin made swift and pressured contact with coarse canvas. Left uncared for, the wound could become infected and lead to serious complications. Nonetheless, a day earlier, Winnipeg physician William Black had declared him medically fit to wrestle. It was certainly not the first time that Martinson had sustained such an injury, and, necessity overriding caution, it was possible that he would sustain another that night. Wearing only dark shorts, his bare knees bore testimony to similar scrapes, incurred under similar circumstances, throughout his adult life. Sparing the arches of his feet as well as his toe knuckles from similar abuse were a pair of tightly fitting, ankle-high, black leather shoes. With thin soles, they granted the skin a measure of protection while simultaneously ensuring that the foot itself retained its tactile sensitivity to the external environment.

At the other end of Martinson's grasp stood Jack Taylor, a Canadian by birth and well known to the Winnipeg public. Physically, the Canadian bore little resemblance to the Dane. At six feet one inch in height and 216 pounds, Taylor sported a freshly shaven head atop a lean muscular torso that, several years prior to the rise of Charles Atlas to fame, had earned the Canuck grappler the title of World's Most Perfectly Developed Man. Still impressive, his physique was not, if one looked closely, as striking as it once had been. At thirty-six, Taylor was not a young man for his chosen vocation, nor was Martinson. Although not as thickly built as his counterpart, Taylor possessed rounder shoulders, larger biceps, and enormous forearms that testified to his ability to perform various feats of grip strength for the amazement of onlookers. On any given day, he could be seen walking about the city's streets, squeezing a pair of racket balls that he carried continually in his pockets, ensuring that the tendons in his hands remained like steel.

Clothing also differentiated the Canadian from the Dane. Covering Taylor's legs were wool tights, onto which were sewn padding to protect his knees. The tights, however, like his leather shoes, served a double purpose, allowing for sweat absorption and an unyielding grip once his legs were secured around their selected target. In spite of the marked differences in their appearances, the men shared one physical trait: a pronounced deformation of the external ear caused by repeated hard blows. Whether fully clothed or in their present state, this condition, medically termed traumatic auricular hematoma, more colloquially termed cauliflower ear, identified them as professional wrestlers. Over the course of sixty minutes and thirty seconds following the handshake, they would showcase their skills to the enthusiastic crowd that surrounded them in the convention hall.[1]

When Paul Martinson and Jack Taylor met in Winnipeg's Industrial Exhibition Building, they were participating in a form of cultural expression beloved, for a host of reasons, by thousands of people living in Manitoba.[2] On a grander scale, it was an activity whose basic origins extended beyond the sparse veneer of time deemed fruitful by historians for study. Born deep in humankind's paleolithic prehistory, wrestling has survived, in innumerable forms and in virtually all cultures, to the present day. That it has done so speaks to the widespread propensity for human beings to attach meaning to expressions of physicality that, at their core, necessitate the struggle of one person to gain mastery over another.[3] This study, far more limited in both temporal and geographic scope, examines wrestling in Manitoba up to the early years of the Great Depression, with particular emphasis on the years after 1896. Although wrestling is my focus throughout, my aim is to illuminate the larger social context in which the activity took place. The study is therefore not merely an analysis of the sport itself but also an attempt, using wrestling as a lens, to garner a greater understanding of the values and attitudes held by people living in Manitoba, especially after 1896, when western Canada became a major destination for immigrants. The historical significance of a match in 1923 between a Dane and an Anglo-Canadian, refereed by a Scot, and staged in the west's biggest and wildest city in front of a multicultural and multi-occupational crowd can be understood only by interrogating the deeper meanings attached to wrestling in the Prairies.

Guiding my enquiry are several key questions. Which groups within Manitoba society participated in wrestling, and what purpose(s) did they attach to it? Did various groups, demarcated by variables such as class and ethnicity, attach their own meanings to the sport? How, if at all, did public attitudes toward wrestling change during the period under study, and which factors affected these changes? Was public support for wrestling always contingent on its adherence to specific social norms, and did violation of these norms result in a decline in the sport's popularity? Far from being simply an amusing pastime, as I will show, wrestling was a social phenomenon that echoed larger, and fluid, debates over sport's "proper" purpose, expressions of masculinity, respectable public conduct, and the position of immigrant and minority communities in a predominantly Anglo-Protestant society.

An additional question, one of definition, likewise requires consideration. What are the delimitations regarding the central subject? Unlike broader etymological categorizations such as sport, wrestling has received little scholarly attention in terms of articulating explicitly what is meant by it.[4] Since wrestling is a near-universal cultural practice, an understanding of the term, similar to "sport," might seem to be implicit. Yet even a cursory survey will reveal massive variation in how wrestling is practised across the globe. Arnold W. Umbach and Warren R. Johnson, in confronting the ubiquity and variety of wrestling, have likened it to language: "All peoples possess the ability to speak; but the way in which they speak depends upon where they happen to be born.... Similarly, wrestling has taken different forms in different parts of the world. Also, as with language, some countries have produced more than one type of wrestling."[5] Uniting all wrestling forms, however, are certain commonalities. All involve individuals physically manipulating their opponents to manoeuvre them into a position that signifies termination of the contest. This broad definition makes considerable allowance for variations in rules and therefore includes systems whose express goal is to throw opponents to the ground, pin them, force them to concede to a submission hold, force them out of an enclosed space, gain positional advantage for which points are awarded, or any combination thereof. Additionally, it permits the use of specialized clothing (for example, a belt in Icelandic glima or a *gi* in Japanese jiu-jitsu), if agreed upon within the customary rules, to gain victory. Such a liberal characterization allows for the type of inclusive analysis befitting a multicultural region such as Manitoba. However, though this study is intended to be a wide-ranging examination of wrestling, by the 1880s and 1890s the catch-as-catch-can system, one of several styles with historical ties to the British Isles, was fast becoming the most common in Manitoba and elsewhere in North America. Because most matches in the province were conducted under catch-as-catch-can rules, the term "wrestling" will be synonymous with that style unless specified otherwise. The style's key features are outlined in Chapter 1.

With respect to wrestling, two other terms require specific attention: "contest" and "match." Typically, both are used in reference to wrestling, whereas "game" is not (the exception being the colloquial term "mat game" used synonymously with "wrestling"; the colourful expression is also employed in this study). Sociologist Harry Edwards, in examining the distinction between contest/match and game, suggests that "contests typically pivot around the demonstration of individual excellence in speed, endurance, accuracy, strength, coordination, and/or mental acuity." Although acknowledging that at least one of these qualities is present in sports commonly classified as games, Edwards further clarifies that "in the contest it is the outcome for the individual that assumes most immediate priority."[6] Since wrestling typically involves individuals engaged directly in competition with one another, his definition, though potentially problematic with respect to common usage, is adequate for the purpose of this study.[7] Therefore, specific instances in which individuals engage in wrestling are referred to as either contests or matches. A third term, "bout," is used interchangeably with contest and match. One expression omitted from this study in reference to wrestling, however, is "fight." Writers have applied it in recent years to wrestling matches, but such was rarely the case in the late nineteenth century and early twentieth century, when that term was reserved, in a sporting context, for activities such as boxing.[8] Accordingly, in keeping with traditional usage, it is not applied to wrestling here.

Since the effort here is to present a broad-ranging history of the sport before the 1930s, both amateur and professional wrestling are examined. Commonly, if both are mentioned in the same instance, it is merely to differentiate the contest (amateur wrestling) from the scripted exhibition (professional wrestling).[9] If one examines contemporary professional wrestling, it certainly does not meet the criteria established for sport because, even though its practitioners frequently display incredible athletic skill, the outcome of each match, even to the untrained eye, is wholly predetermined. However, earlier in the twentieth century, it was not necessarily easy to make such a distinction because the technical character of matches did not always overtly betray whether or not they were completely "fixed." Debates concerning professional wrestling's competitive legitimacy as well as its transition to a fully prearranged endeavour are nevertheless regular parts of discussions that centre on the period.[10]

Although the matter is not ignored here, the focus is less on whether each match staged in Manitoba was, in fact, "on the level" and more on public perceptions of professional wrestling, which invariably included debates about its sporting "purity." My intention, therefore, is not to provide a specific analysis of professional wrestling's inner workings, and I deliberately exclude many terms peculiar to the business.[11] Further, far more than any source written to date, this study attempts to examine both professional and amateur wrestling, their relation to one another, and what it says of western Canadian society during the period. By subjecting professional and amateur wrestling to completely separate analyses, historians create a simplistic dichotomy that fails to account for the rather more nuanced association between the two that persisted through much of the late nineteenth century and early twentieth century. Prior to the 1930s, professional and amateur wrestling enjoyed a far closer relationship than in later decades, and as I and other authors have previously noted, skilled professionals often provided the impetus for amateur wrestling's growth.[12] This theme, along with others concerning the interrelationship between amateur and professional wrestling, is explored in greater detail in the ensuing chapters.

Because wrestling is a sport requiring little, if any, specialized equipment and the presence of no more than two individuals wishing to test one another's physical skills, undoubtedly tens of thousands of impromptu wrestling matches, or perhaps more, occurred in Manitoba's homes, schoolyards, wheat fields, barns, saloons, and factories over the years prior to the Great Depression.[13] In some cases, records remain of such encounters, particularly if they resulted in some sort of unfortunate accident.[14] Although conceding historian and sociologist Allen Guttman's assertion that sport does not necessarily require an audience, I emphasize here, particularly when addressing the years after 1870, organized, competitive wrestling and training, not casual, unpremeditated bouts that sprang spontaneously from everyday human interactions.[15] Since residents of Manitoba during the post-Confederation period allotted limited leisure time to participating in or patronizing formally structured wrestling classes and contests, it is through organized encounters that the greatest depth of public interest and the greatest volume of documentation and commentary pertaining to wrestling's significance to them can be found.

Despite wrestling's ancient pedigree and worldwide practice, there have been few English-language historical studies devoted to the subject. In particular, the period prior to the popularization of television has been largely neglected by professional historians seeking to gain a better understanding of the sport's social importance. Moreover, there has been little attempt to "survey the field" with respect to published sources on the subject, so commentary on it, however brief, is warranted.

As early as the 1930s and intermittently thereafter, popular historians, several of whom had long-standing connections to wrestling, began to chronicle its development. The early studies were of varying strength with regard to factual accuracy, few offered social contexts to accompany their narratives, and their focus strayed only marginally from professional wrestling as conducted in the United States. Nevertheless, they remain among the few published surveys of the major individuals and events associated with the sport in North America prior to the Great Depression.[16] Particularly significant among early works was Marcus Griffin's *Fall Guys: The Barnums of Bounce* (1937), which presented a then novel examination of wrestling. In addition to supplying the seemingly obligatory overview of wrestling's historical roots across the globe, Griffin, a New York sports editor, attempted to "lift the veil" on the largely successful efforts of a small cadre of promoters to control the outcomes of professional heavyweight wrestling matches throughout the United States in the years following the First World War.[17] In contrast to previous works, which had directed attention mainly toward professional wrestling's pre-eminent athletes and better-known matches, Griffin's treatise also presented the public with backgrounds on American promoters, who, operating throughout North America, had remained largely anonymous outside their own regions up to that time. *Fall Guys* also gave insight into the rivalries and alliances forged among promoters, the various clandestine arrangements made among them, and the efforts by some wrestlers to resist their machinations. Although Griffin's exposé poses its own unique difficulties for historians looking for a factually accurate account of wrestling's past,[18] its primary value lies in understanding, in broad strokes, how professional heavyweight wrestling began to evolve into the business that we recognize today, and therefore it serves to inform, in particular, Chapter 6 of this work.

After a modest proliferation of published sources related to wrestling history in the 1930s, followed thereafter in the 1950s and 1960s by a smattering of notable texts, few works were released. Popular historians nevertheless continued to enthusiastically collect and disseminate their research findings, made possible after the rise of the Internet largely through resources such as J. Michael Kenyon's online *WAWLI Papers* (an acronym for Wrestling As We Liked It), devoted primarily to professional wrestling between 1915 and 1962.[19] The past several years have witnessed, along with an explosion of books related to wrestling's more recent past, a modest resurgence of enthusiasm for works concerning wrestling's history prior to the Great Depression. Foremost among authors is Mark S. Hewitt, whose *Catch Wrestling: A Wild and Wooly Look at the Early Days of Professional Wrestling in America* (2005) and *Catch Wrestling Round Two: More Wild and Wooly Tales from the Early Days of Pro Wrestling* (2007) provide biographical backgrounds on professional wrestlers in all weight categories in conjunction with episodic accounts of various matches staged in the United States, Canada, and Great Britain.[20] In contrast to earlier treatments of the subject, Hewitt's books evidence scrupulous effort toward ensuring factual accuracy, and supporting documentation is well cited. Tim Hornbaker's *National Wrestling Alliance: The Untold Story of the Monopoly that Strangled Pro Wrestling*, released shortly before Hewitt's second book, continued the trend toward providing well-written and well-researched popular histories. In many ways an extension of the institutional history offered in *Fall Guys*, Hornbaker's book recounts the formation and growth of the National Wrestling Alliance, a trust made up of promoters from across North America who controlled professional wrestling on the continent after the Second World War. Although focusing primarily on the postwar period, Hornbaker's work, more attentively researched and less fancifully written than Griffin's, likewise delves into attempts made during the 1920s to monopolize the sport and thus, along with its predecessor, provides critical background for Chapter 6 of this book.[21] Most recently, Jonathan Snowden's *Shooters: The*

Toughest Men in Professional Wrestling has continued the tradition begun by Griffin in casting a critical eye on the often dubious practices associated with professional wrestling.[22]

The efforts of Hewitt, Hornbaker, and Snowden, like those that preceded them, focused primarily, but not exclusively, on the United States. Western Canadian wrestling history has been illuminated largely by Vern May (better known as Vance Nevada), whose reference-oriented *The Central Canadian Professional Wrestling Almanac* (1999), and far more intensively researched and detailed *Wrestling in the Canadian West* (2009), survey the numerous wrestling promotions that have operated in western Canada.[23] Like Hornbaker, Nevada focuses primarily on providing an institutional history of the professional wrestling industry, and, though his 1999 work contains greater background on wrestling in Manitoba during the pre-Depression period, *Wrestling in the Canadian West* is currently without peer as a reference text focused on a single region anywhere in North America.[24] A handful of reference and biographically oriented manuscripts likewise testify to the labours undertaken by popular historians to document professional wrestling's more distant past.[25]

In a few instances, wrestlers themselves have written and published memoirs. Yet, compared with the recent rash of largely ghost-written autobiographies, athletes of earlier generations were characteristically silent concerning their exploits.[26] Clarence Eklund, who wrestled in the Prairies before the First World War, fortunately was among the few who did so, and his self-published *Forty Years of Wrestling* (1947) and edited collection *Wyoming's Wrestling Rancher: Life and History of Clarence Eklund, Champion Wrestler* (1993), published by his daughter Hazel Eklund-Odegard, provide rare insights into professional wrestling in the region during the pre-First World War years.[27]

Any study of professional wrestling owes a considerable debt to popular historians' work on gathering and disseminating information on the sport's past. Academic investigation of the subject has been far more lacking, and to date fewer than half a dozen significant studies have been published addressing wrestling during the pre-Depression period. Glynn A. Leyshon's *Of Mats and Men: The Story of Canadian Amateur and Olympic Wrestling from 1600 to 1984* (1984), one of the earliest works of this nature, focused on the even more understudied realm of amateur wrestling.[28] Leyshon's seminal work surveyed the institutional and organizational development of Canadian wrestling, including difficulties faced by the sport's early proponents in conducting and organizing competitions as well as important competitive achievements by Canadian athletes. Significantly, *Of Mats and Men* provided an overview of the sport's social and cultural significance among Aboriginal peoples in pre-Confederation Canada. Immigrant cultures' early wrestling practices (particularly those of British lineage), as well as the role of professional wrestling in helping to shape the early amateur wrestling movement, also received attention. Leyshon's work did not delve extensively into wrestling's social impacts, how the sport reflected larger tensions or trends in Canadian society with respect to masculinity, class, or ethnicity, and how these issues changed over time. To date, however, it remains one of the few published academic studies devoted to early Canadian wrestling and is required reading for those seeking an overview of the sport's growth as a competitive enterprise in the country.

By the late 1980s, American social historians were beginning to direct their attention to the mat game, and one theme that immediately emerged in their analyses was the importance of nationalism in wrestling. J.J. Mondak's 1989 article on the subject, "The Politics of Professional Wrestling," examined wrestling's cyclical nature within the context of international politics, contending that the sport provided a medium through which complex ideas related to American foreign relations could be simplified into power plays between "good" and "evil."[29] A decade later Matthew Lindaman further explored this thread in his article "Wrestling's Hold on the Western World before the Great War." Through his analysis of heavyweight champion Frank Gotch's career, Lindaman drew a link between wrestling and American nationalism.[30] Ideas about wrestling and masculinity proved to be a second important theme in the emergent academic literature. John Rickard's "'The Spectacle of Excess': The Emergence of Modern Professional Wrestling in the United States and Australia" likewise placed early wrestling exhibitions within the context of a growing physical culture movement that celebrated male muscular development.[31] Masculinity also featured in Lindaman's examination the following year, which placed wrestling matches, and specifically Gotch's exploits on the mat, within the framework of concerns over corroding masculinity in a modern industrial age.[32]

The efforts of a few academic historians, through published articles, to provide some social context for understanding professional wrestling did not precipitate a flowering of monographs. To date, Scott M. Beekman's *Ringside: A History of Professional Wrestling in America* (2006) remains the only scholarly monograph devoted to the subject. It is intended to be a survey of American wrestling from its earliest times to the date of publication, but its strongest analysis is fortunately of the pre-Depression period. Although the events illustrated in his narrative do not stray considerably from those already recalled by authors such as Fleischer, Griffin, and Chapman, Beekman provides social context for understanding the sport's development lacking in previous works. He argues that professional wrestling's emergence as a popular spectator pastime in the post-Civil War era was closely linked to the growth of industrial capitalism, urbanization, and advances in communication and transportation technologies.[33] Drawing on Rickard's and Lindaman's earlier analyses, Beekman likewise explores wrestling's popularity in conjunction with widespread ideas about the human (and specifically male) body, race, and nationalism.[34] Such themes are similarly central in my work. Although a significant landmark in studying professional wrestling's growth and social significance, *Ringside*, as "the first nonpictorial history of wrestling," necessarily attempts to provide only the broadest overview, and in doing so it neglects several critical avenues of inquiry.[35]

In following the narrative on American professional wrestling established by previous popular historians, Beekman perpetuates the notion that the sport's past can be encapsulated by (and was synonymous with) the activities conducted within the heavyweight division's upper echelon. *Ringside* does not account for the sport's regional peculiarities, nor does it address the point that, despite the fame accorded to heavyweight matmen during the period, wrestling's survival was typically ensured by local talent who, not always drawn from the heavyweight division, catered, among other things, to specific ethnic, nationalist, and civic interests in the regions where they operated. Although acknowledging the importance of factors such as nationalism and ethnicity to wrestling, Beekman fails to address, among other things, how wrestling reflected changing public perceptions of immigration, its role in illustrating interethnic and interregional rivalries, and its importance as a medium for highlighting unique cultural perspectives of various immigrant communities, all of which are themes in my work.

Although American wrestling had a profound influence on developments in Canada, *Ringside*, as a distinctly American-based history, likewise does not examine wrestling's relation to events unique to the Canadian experience. Additionally, as his title implies, Beekman examines only professional wrestling and, as a result, eliminates several potentially fruitful lines of investigation that can be better explored by examining both professional and amateur branches of the sport during the pre-Depression period, particularly with regard to the contrasting values believed by many to be intrinsic to both movements.

Despite the paucity of academic historical examinations devoted to wrestling, a rich body of literature on sport and its relationship to masculinity, class, and ethnicity helps to further inform an understanding of wrestling in Manitoba. Morris Mott's doctoral dissertation, "Manly Sports and Manitobans: Settlement Days to World War One," is a necessary starting point for any study of early sporting practices in Manitoba, especially in relation to sport's function in promoting a vision of masculinity largely cultivated by members of the province's Anglo-Canadian middle class, most of whom had come from Ontario.[36] Subsequent authors have similarly stressed the pre-eminent role played by middle-class men, generally of Anglo-Protestant extraction, in shaping the nation's sporting practices and values. In particular, they were aided in this endeavour by their institutions, including religious, recreational, and broad-reaching "amateur" sports organizations, of which I will say substantially more in the ensuing chapters.[37] Works by authors such as Elliott Gorn, Kevin B. Wamsley, David Whitson, Robert S. Kossuth, and Colin D. Howell provide additional insights into sport, male (particularly working-class) culture, and aggressive masculinity, to which the world of wrestling, particularly before the First World War, was frequently linked.[38]

It would be misleading, however, to assert that masculinity can be reduced purely to violence. As demonstrated in literature spanning the past quarter-century, masculinity is a socially, as opposed to genetically, derived notion whose meaning can vary according to time, location, and social station.[39] Although masculinity as a construct was (and remains) ubiquitous in society, as Canadian historian Mike O'Brien argues, a universally agreed standard has never existed, and its definition has been "eminently open to contestation even within a single historical context."[40] Accordingly, I stress that many people saw value in wrestling aside from its merit as a purely aggressive undertaking. Wrestling, in fact, was frequently "contested territory" around which there was considerable debate related to, among other things, appropriate male conduct on and off the mat. Informed by Colin D. Howell's *Northern Sandlots: A Social History of Maritime Baseball* (1995) and Bruce Kidd's analysis in *The Struggle for Canadian Sport* (1997), the notion of contested territory is an important element in my study, extending not only to gender but also to how various groups and individuals in society attempted, through wrestling, to further their own unique ethnic, occupational, and class interests in the half century after Confederation.[41] On occasion, however, cooperation could coexist with conflict, and through an analysis of wrestling we see that various groups frequently at odds with one another could also demonstrate the ability to work together to achieve common goals. Wrestling, therefore, highlights that social interactions among groups were frequently less monolithic, and more complex, than a model stressing either antagonism or alliance would imply.

Two central factors make Manitoba a valuable and compelling place to situate a regional examination of wrestling. First, Manitoba was the first province in western Canada to enter into Confederation, receive a large number of settlers, and experience significant urbanization. As I will show, extensive settlement in the province occurred contemporaneously with a rising and widespread interest in sport in Canada. As the province grew from a sparsely populated region, whose financial base was largely linked to the dwindling fur and hide trade, into a bustling agricultural powerhouse with an increasingly diversified economy, so did sport, in multiple forms, emerge from the social margins to become relevant in many people's lives. Accordingly, it is possible to trace the growth of both wrestling and Manitoba from their mutual infancy along parallel courses. Second, Manitoba is an ideal site for examining ideas related to wrestling and ethnicity because, more than central and eastern Canada, it saw the influx of settlers from many nations outside the English-speaking world.[42] Concomitantly, in wrestling, because of its one-on-one nature, ethnicity and race were far more apparent than they were in team sports, allowing for acute examination of the subject.

Although Manitoba's sporting culture owed much to central Canada, it was also shaped by the peculiarities of western Canadian life, which included a larger proportion of non-English immigrants than in Ontario. This diversity, coupled with the fact that many immigrants were familiar with wrestling before arriving in Canada, makes Manitoba, through the lens of wrestling, an ideal location for investigating themes related to ethnic rivalry, nativism, racism, and assimilation.[43] Since Winnipeg quickly emerged as the dominant metropolitan centre of the Prairies and the unchallenged economic, social, cultural, and transportation centre of Manitoba, it looms large in my study. I also examine wrestling in the province's smaller population centres, but as in other matters Winnipeg was where the most events occurred and with the greatest frequency.[44]

Research on wrestling's history in Manitoba inevitably necessitated reading and examining the sports reports in the province's many newspapers.[45] Of additional value were advertisements (typically playbills) as well as photographs printed in the newspapers, the latter of which were specifically relevant for understanding ideas related to the male physical form. In a number of instances, letters from wrestlers and members of the public who attended wrestling matches also appeared in newspapers, giving insight into their views concerning the sport.

Although newspapers are vital for studying wrestling because they are one of the few extant primary sources providing regular documentation on the subject (particularly professional wrestling), there are intrinsic flaws to relying on newspapers to the exclusion of other records. Intended for commercial consumption as opposed to posterity, the details chronicled in their pages were frequently hastily gathered, with concern over looming deadlines trumping desire for complete factual accuracy and measured reflection on an incident's importance. Undoubtedly, reports in newspapers also reflected editorial biases concerning what should be included in, or excluded from, the limited space available, and such decisions often served to marginalize certain segments of the population according to political affiliation, language, occupation, and ethnicity. Yet, as American historian Jerry W. Knudson contends, newspapers, as commercial documents, also had to present information in ways that were culturally intelligible and relevant to their audiences or face economic hardship. Newspaper commentary, particularly during a period with limited alternative media, such as in the late nineteenth century and early twentieth century, could strongly inform public opinion.[46] A broad reading of newspaper commentary related to wrestling across time and publication aided me in differentiating incidental remarks from themes with wider resonance, and to this end I drew on non-English-language publications such as Le Manitoba, La Presse, Czas, and labour-oriented papers such as the Winnipeg Voice and One Big Union Bulletin. Through observations on matters such as attendance numbers, venues for matches, audience composition, behaviour, and public reaction to the events unfolding at wrestling matches, I gained insights on where the sport took place, who patronized it, and what value they saw in it. Supplemented extensively by sources such as Winnipeg's Henderson's Directories, the Canada

Census, Records of the Department of National Defence, Winnipeg City Police Court Records, and Winnipeg Police Commission Books, newspapers were likewise crucial in ascertaining the names, ethnic backgrounds, occupations, and personal activities of those who participated as athletes or boosters.

Another important body of information related to wrestling in Manitoba came from institutional records produced by various organizations that sponsored wrestling programs, including the Scottish Athletic Association, Young Men's Christian Association, Winnipeg City Police Athletic Association, One Big Union, Department of National Defence (specifically, within the context of the Great War, the Canadian Expeditionary Forces), and Amateur Athletic Union of Canada and its Manitoba affiliate. From them can be ascertained, among other things, the reasons for supporting wrestling programs, membership composition, conditions for participation, costs associated with staging events, and relationships with other institutions and individuals in the province. Although a periodical, the One Big Union *Bulletin*, as the official organ for the organization, also proved to be a valuable source, particularly in regard to interaction with other clubs in the city and views on sport's "appropriate" purpose. Unfortunately, records from the many commercial clubs that operated, often briefly, in Manitoba have not survived, nor have private records produced by professional wrestling promoters, so much of the information on them must be gleaned from newspapers.

Among other significant sources were City of Winnipeg bylaws and municipal manuals as well as the Statutes of Manitoba and Journals of the Legislative Assembly of Manitoba, which provided information on efforts to regulate the sport, respectively, at local and provincial levels. A number of instructional and technical manuals related to physical fitness and wrestling, published during the period under study and widely available throughout North America, supplied background on ideas related to wrestling, exercise, and the male physical form during the decades bookending the nineteenth and twentieth centuries. A small number of photographs, not published in newspapers, also proved to be useful.

In this book, I adopt a chronological approach to examining wrestling's history in Manitoba, placing significant events in the sport within the context of a society whose values, ethnic composition, and interaction with the larger world were ever in flux. Although matters such as masculinity, class, respectability, nationality, and ethnicity were always important elements of life in Manitoba, as similarly noted by social historian Joy Parr, any one element, depending on time and place, could assume centre stage while others simultaneously dropped to the background.[47] Accordingly, each chapter gives varying emphasis to themes whose significance, and character, were subject to changing historical forces.

Before the bell rings, let me show you around the canvas. The story of wrestling in Manitoba begins by exploring the nature of and cultural meanings associated with the wrestling and wrestling-related activities undertaken, first, by the Indigenous people who occupied the regions that would later constitute the province of Manitoba and, second, by the mixed-blood and European fur-trading cultures. Confederation, representing a distinct break from the past, saw the regrafting of an Anglo-Protestant culture with strong ties to Ontario onto the Prairies. The new settlers brought with them not only their own wrestling practices but also, more importantly, competing ideas (frequently class based but never universal to any one class) about the sport's "appropriate" purpose in the new province. I also place wrestling's growth within the framework of advances in transportation and communication technologies that, in addition to facilitating ties to culture in Ontario and Britain, initiated the development of links to American sporting culture. Building on these themes, I then tackle professional wrestling's growth in Manitoba between 1896 and 1914, situating it within a public discourse that both extolled wrestling as a worthwhile physical, moral, and civic enterprise and condemned it for encouraging and showcasing inappropriate (and at times unscrupulous) behaviour. Next I consider wrestling in light of the remarkable demographic changes that occurred in the Prairies after 1896. Far more than in the past, ethnicity took on heightened significance in the sport as various groups, already acquainted with wrestling in their homelands, attached their own meanings to it. Although wrestling, as a commercial enterprise, often capitalized on ethnic divisiveness in the increasingly multicultural province, the chapter also illustrates its role in fostering community cohesion within particular ethnic groups in the province. I then shift the discussion from professional wrestling to amateur wrestling, which developed considerably in the seven years prior to 1914. Placed within the context of an expanding nation-wide amateur sporting movement and guided by the philosophical tenets outlined by the Young Men's Christian Association, the chapter investigates amateur wrestling's frequently ambiguous relationship with professional wrestling as well as its geographic, class, and ethnic composition during its formative years. Having covered the decade and a half bookending the nineteenth and twentieth centuries, I then tighten my hold to focus on wrestling during the Great War, neglected until relatively recently as a period for studying Canadian sport. I examine wrestling's function in reinforcing masculine, militarist, and imperialist values as well as its position as a forum for challenging specific class-based stereotypes of professionalism. The decade after the First World War, coming as it did in the wake of unprecedented carnage and loss of life on European battlefields, marked an important new era for sport. Turning to the 1920s, I therefore tangle with professional wrestling and its adaptation to the changing values witnessed during the decade. I pay particular attention to professional wrestling as a site for capitalizing on mounting anti-"foreigner" sentiment, expanding consumer-based values, and the sport's growing connection to the U.S. professional heavyweight wrestling market. Next I explore amateur wrestling's continued growth during the 1920s, its expansion beyond its previously narrow class, ethnic, and geographic confines, and the continuities that persisted from the pre-Great War period because of ongoing adherence to a rigid amateur code. With the footlights ready to dim, I conclude by looking at professional wrestling's final transformation into a form of melodramatic athletic entertainment within the context of emergent social and technological forces driving that change.

Wrestling has a long though largely unexplored history in Manitoba. It was a sport enjoyed by thousands of people from a variety of ethnic and occupational backgrounds who attached meaning to participating in matches, organizing clubs and tournaments, attending events, or otherwise keeping abreast of the latest developments in the mat game both in the province and in the larger world. What follows is a matside people's history of the sport's many hues and contours in western Canada's oldest province.

Chapter 1

BEFORE THE BOOM
WRESTLING TO 1896

Wrestling's origins in the regions that would later comprise the province of Manitoba predate the widespread European settlement that occurred during the last three decades of the nineteenth century. First Nations, mixed-blood peoples, and European traders participated in various forms of the sport long before Confederation, each group imbuing it with a distinct social purpose. After 1870, society in Manitoba underwent a radical transformation as large numbers of settlers, the vast majority of whom were of British Canadian extraction, came to the province. These settlers, who formed the ethnic majority by the decade's end, did not create a wholly new society in the Prairies but sought to shape the province according to their pre-existing customs and beliefs. British Canadians brought with them to Manitoba a rich sporting tradition that included wrestling. In the ensuing years, wrestling increased in popularity as improvements in the province's communication and transportation infrastructure assisted in integrating Manitoba into a larger culture of sport that, by the 1880s, spanned the English-speaking world. During the late nineteenth century, wrestling experienced its most remarkable growth in Winnipeg, which emerged as the region's dominant metropolitan centre following Confederation. Although popular, wrestling was also highly controversial, for it was predominantly associated with Winnipeg's bachelor sporting culture, a group whose interests and activities often ran counter to reform-minded members of the middle class who sought to shape wrestling according to their own values of "manly" respectability. Tension between these two sets of values was often evident in the press, which simultaneously criticized the sport on moral grounds while capitalizing on its commercial appeal, and among wrestlers themselves, who both cultivated and defied an image of respectability.

WRESTLING PRIOR TO 1870

Prior to Confederation, First Nations and mixed-blood peoples, both in the Red River settlement and in the regions of the Canadian northwest that later fell within Manitoba's borders, participated in displays of ritualized combat that affirmed important values associated with masculine identity. Written records of wrestling among First Nations peoples are rare, partly because those with sufficient literacy levels in the northwest, among them priests and explorers, were concerned more with documenting activities directly related to their work in the region than with detailing the day-to-day activities of the people whom they encountered.[1] A notable exception in this regard can be found in Samuel Hearne's writings.

Hearne, an explorer employed with the Hudson's Bay Company (HBC), travelled extensively throughout the northwest between 1769 and 1772, primarily in search of copper deposits.[2] In 1771, he commented that, among the Chipewyan, male youth regularly engaged in wrestling contests in which both combatants usually grasped the other by the hair until one had been dragged to the ground, signalling the end of the contest.[3] Undoubtedly, there was some level of skill involved in these matches, but beyond Hearne's brief mention little can be said about the technical character of the encounters. There is no evidence to indicate that the wrestling practised by Chipewyan boys was taught to them in any systematic fashion, and it is unlikely that formalized instruction occurred. Psychologist Clare Brant notes, in his observations on wide-reaching Native ethics and principles, that traditional teaching transpired in an environment in which practices were modelled to the young until they felt sufficiently competent to undertake the activities themselves. Brant contrasts this "modelling" method to the more rigidly structured, operant "shaping" method commonly applied in Western societies whereby overt instruction is undertaken, and rewards are commonly given, for successively improved attempts.[4] Furthermore, the Aboriginal principle of non-interference in another individual's affairs, particularly important among the Chipewyan, ensured that children were given wide latitude to make choices concerning their everyday activities.[5] It is therefore unlikely that either adults or adolescents took concerted efforts to ensure that they learned wrestling skills.

Although clearly a common practice among Chipewyan youth, wrestling served purposes besides being a simple recreational diversion. As a strenuous physical endeavour, it both tested and displayed many of the physical qualities associated with hunting.[6] Similar observations might be generalized to virtually any culture wherein hunting is an important element of survival, but the extreme physical challenges imposed by the northern environment in which the Chipewyan people lived added gravity to the necessity for hunting prowess. Although game could be plentiful at times, its acquisition tended to be more sporadic because of the migratory patterns associated with critical animals in the food economy, particularly caribou.[7] Communities were therefore frequently forced to confront famine conditions because of the inherently cyclical character of the hunt.[8] In times of scarcity, a hunter's ability to secure game became a matter of acute consequence. Developing physical attributes essential to the hunt was therefore of dire importance to the Chipewyan.

Wrestling also took on social meaning that extended far beyond the inculcation, and celebration, of hunting ability. The Chipewyan also engaged in the culturally distinct practice of wife wrestling. Hearne observed that "it has ever been the custom among those people for the men to wrestle for any woman to whom they are attached, and of course, the strongest party always carried off the prize."[9] At least one Chipewyan man echoed his commentary, declaring decades later to David Thompson that "the strong men take the Women when they want them; certainly the strong men have the right to the Women."[10] Within Chipewyan culture, the ability to take more than one wife was symbolic of a man's strength and social status.[11] Obtaining a wife through wrestling matches also often served immediately practical ends. Hearne observed, for example, that, if considerable physical work needed to be done, a man might wrestle to obtain a wife for the labour.[12]

Wife wrestling was neither a rare nor an isolated occurrence among the Chipewyan. Hearne noted that "this custom prevails throughout all their tribes" and happened with considerable frequency.[13] Adolescent interest in wrestling, which mimicked the adult matches in technical terms, was considered to be an investment in future marital stability, since skill in wrestling could prevent a wife from being taken from a husband.[14] For husbands at the other end of the life cycle, however, the question naturally arises about how they were able to retain their wives in the face of diminishing physical abilities. Hearne offered no direct commentary on the matter. Nevertheless, at least with regard to some older members of society, remarks in his journals, combined with a broader understanding of Chipewyan culture, provide important clues.

Hearne noted that some older men were highly influential in their communities and effectively able to persuade younger men to moderate their zeal for wife wrestling. In particular, elderly men considered to have skill in "conjuration" held sway over others.[15] Although physical strength was clearly an important attribute in Chipewyan society, it was only one way in which individuals gained, and exercised, social capital. Supernatural abilities were another important source of power. Chipewyan belief structures held that the physical and spiritual worlds were manifestations of the same unified reality.[16] The supernatural could therefore have a direct impact on the physical. Some were considered more skilled than others in manipulating the spiritual realm in order to have tangible effects on the environment around them, including people. Chipewyan spirituality was of a highly practical nature, and those who demonstrated their gifts by producing specific outcomes were considered to be powerful.[17] Shamans were the most adept in this regard, but all individuals had spiritual abilities, so it was critical that others be respected lest they use that power against them.[18] Older men, weak in physical power but strong in spiritual power, presumably would have been able to apply the same influence that they had in the larger community to challenges to their marriages. For male members of the community who lacked demonstrable power, spirituality provided a possible recourse. Widely held beliefs within Aboriginal societies, including the Chipewyan, stressed that spirits took mercy on individuals with meagre social standing and few resources at their disposal.[19] Accordingly, indigent husbands might have had some measure of supernatural protection against losing their wives.

Hearne's recollections provide additional clues to at least one other category of people exempted from the potentialities of wife wrestling. He remarked that "a weak man, unless he be a good hunter and well-beloved, is seldom permitted to keep a wife that a stronger man thinks worth his notice."[20] John West, an Anglican missionary who lived in the Red River Colony between 1820 and 1823, and travelled through Chipewyan territory to and from York Factory, similarly commented that "[the Chipewyan] may permit a weak man, if he be a good hunter to keep the object of his choice; but otherwise he is obliged to yield his wife to a stronger man."[21] Since hunting was of paramount importance to collective survival, it is little surprise that those skilled in it, but otherwise short on physical strength, would be held in high esteem and accorded some reprieve.

Men whose social standing gave them no exemption from engaging in a wrestling match used clever methods to ensure that they did not come out on the losing end of it. Hearne observed that some participants would secretly shave their heads and grease their ears immediately before a match. Emerging from his dwelling, the man would rush his opponent and throw him to the ground.

Since the typical technique was to grip the hair, removing the customary handle and greasing the ears afforded a weaker man the ability to triumph over a much stronger adversary, retaining his wife in the process.[22] As I will discuss in Chapter 2, "greasing" tactics were also adopted by European Canadian wrestlers more than a century later, though prevailing sentiments about the practice differed markedly from those held by the Chipewyan.

Although wrestling was a male-only endeavour, consideration must be accorded to the role of women, given that they were so often the foci of the contests. Wife wrestling was a rather unique custom and has accordingly attracted interest and debate among both observers and academic theorists. Hearne, in providing the most detailed historical account of wife wrestling, did not do so with a neutral eye. The explorer, who admired the Chipewyan people for their incredible ingenuity, commenting in one instance that their craftwork was "not to be excelled by the most expert mechanic, assisted with every tool he could wish," nevertheless brought his European cultural biases to his observations concerning wrestling. He found the bouts "very unpleasant" and felt "pity" for the "wretched victims" of them.[23] He related, in graphic terms, how women were torn, often brutally, from their former husbands: "I have seen them won, perhaps, by a man they mortally hated. On those occasions their grief and reluctance to follow their new lord has been so great, that the business has often ended in the greatest brutality; for, in the struggle, I have seen the poor girl stripped quite naked and carried by main force to their new lodgings."[24] The image presented by Hearne suggests that wrestling served as a means of buttressing, through force, an extreme form of patriarchal privilege. Cultural anthropologist Henry S. Sharp has observed that such practices among the Chipewyan people serve as a "fly in the ointment" to prevailing views stressing the separate, but equally valued, roles of men and women in Aboriginal society.[25] Academic examinations, including Wendell H. Oswalt's classic treatise *This Land Was Theirs: A Study of the North American Indian* (1966), reinforce the idea of one-sided subjugation among the Chipewyan. Discussing life during the late eighteenth century and early nineteenth century, Oswalt opined that "females were subordinated to men in every way, and the men were oppressive. Women were held in gross contempt by the men."[26] Subsequent scholarship, however, coupled with further analysis of Hearne's accounts, challenges such one-sided views.

The ability to take more than one wife carried with it prestige, but the decision to do so was not entirely a matter of cementing one's personal standing within the community. Husbands, in some cases, appear to have been not only cognizant of but also sympathetic to the extreme burdens that heavy labour placed on their wives. A stronger man would often claim a weaker man's wife if he thought that his own wife or wives were already overburdened with furs or provisions.[27] Women, too, were likely able to ply their own influence over a husband. Wife wrestling matches were almost exclusively contested over young women. In Chipewyan culture, the youngest wife was required to do most of the heavy work, so senior wives were able to exercise their own agency by urging their husbands to take on another wife to reduce their own labours.[28] Additionally, as Sharp suggests, it is highly likely that women, fully aware of the conventions of wife wrestling, could arrange to be "wrestled away" from untenable marital situations.[29] Although their voices on the subject are absent, Hearne's recollection of a "fine girl" shedding a perfunctory tear and letting out a whimper after being lost by a husband whom she did not like hints that the public image of female powerlessness might have been, at least in small part, artifice.[30] At minimum, interpretations of wife wrestling as a form of simple chattelhood wherein women possessed no social capital should be considered with caution.

Despite Eurocentric attitudes toward Chipewyan wrestling, the custom was clearly an effective form of social arbitration. Although unequivocal in his abhorrence of the custom, Hearne never observed any act of violent revenge within the community, save for the matches themselves, none of which ever resulted in injury. Indeed, he noted that murder was virtually unknown, being "shunned and detested by all the tribes."[31] Likewise, wrestling contests, from his experience, never escalated to the point where other individuals, including close family members, interfered in the proceedings except to warn a weaker but game combatant that protracted conflict might result in physical harm.[32] John West, who also viewed the matches as "barbarous," conceded, as Hearne did, that they substituted for more serious violence.[33] This point, however, did not prevent European traders from intervening in contests, which they viewed as an affront both to their own notions of male chivalry and to their monogamous worldview. In one instance, David Thompson chased away the winner of a wrestling match, and in another he defended a man who, more in keeping with encroaching European practices, shot his conqueror after losing a bout.[34] Thompson was heavily criticized for his decision to shield the perpetrator and was told by a member of the Chipewyan community that "on no account whatever ought the ground to be made red with man's blood" over marital disputes.[35]

Farther north, among the Inuit, wrestling was also common, and travel journals from the region note its prevalence.[36] Here, too, wrestling matches were often useful in resolving disagreements between two individuals. Specifically among the Netsilik, ritualized unarmed combat in which both men would strike one another on the forehead or shoulder until one capitulated served a similar function. Thereafter, the grievance would be considered settled. Formal wrestling or striking matches prevented aggression from escalating and potentially ruining favourable relationships within the community.[37] Additionally, wrestling partnerships were formed among pairs of Netsilik men from different bands as part of a complex dyadic social ritual that also involved wife and food sharing.[38] Although written over thirty years after Manitoba's entry into Confederation, reports in the Winnipeg *Voice* give further insight into wrestling's practice among the Inuit. In 1901, the paper noted that, "next to gambling, the Esquimo men like to wrestle. The usual way of doing this is a test rather of strength than skill. The wrestlers sit down on the floor or in any convenient place, side by side, and facing in opposite directions, say with right elbows touching. Then they lock arms, and each strives to straighten out the other's arm."[39] Difficulties arise in determining how widespread this specific type of wrestling was among the Inuit, for writings on Indigenous peoples who lived outside European settlement areas frequently generalized specific occurrences to be indicative of wider cultural practices.[40] The report is nevertheless instructive since it describes not only the sport's apparent prevalence but also its unique attributes. Inuit wrestling often took place indoors, a point also noted by ethnologist Diamond Jenness, who observed that wrestling occurred primarily in the winter months, once the summer migrations and hunting expeditions were at an end and more time became available for recreational pursuits.[41] Additionally, the emphasis on strength, rather than skill, in wrestling had direct relevance to the hunt, in which the ability to drag, carry, and haul animals was of paramount importance. Strong wrestlers were accordingly granted high social standing within Inuit communities.[42]

Among the voyageurs who traversed Canada's northwest interior long before extensive European settlement in the late nineteenth century, physical strength, endurance, and courage were central elements of their identity. Carolyn Podruchny argues that, in their inherently transient, physically arduous, and exclusively male work environment, alcohol consumption, explicit acts of bravery, and fighting earned voyageurs "masculine capital" among their peers.[43] So important were such themes to voyageur existence that Daniel Harmon, a trader with the North West Company, remarked that he had little interest in conversing with the "illiterate ignorant Canadian[s]" because "all of their chat [was] about Horses, Dogs, Canoes and Women, and strong Men who [could] fight a good battle."[44] Harmon's attitude, much like observations made by Europeans concerning First Nations peoples, betrays the extent to which an accurate understanding of a people's cultural practices can be distorted when commentators from outside that culture apply their own values and social expectations in assessing the group's behaviour. Nevertheless, the importance of physicality, including fighting prowess, to voyageur culture is widely documented, regardless of the disdain that it garnered among bourgeois fur-trade officials.[45]

Detailed descriptions of voyageur fighting practices, though rare, indicate that contests were more violent and unstructured than those engaged in by either the Chipewyan or the Inuit. An account in the Montreal *Gazette* vividly describes one nineteenth-century encounter. Combatants employed not only wrestling tactics but also, "with the ferociousness of bull-dogs," attempted to disfigure one another's face and gouge eyes from their sockets.[46] At Fort William, such bouts were common during the annual rendevouz, and the ultimate winner would be crowned "champion" of the fort, a title that carried with it a high degree of "masculine capital" in a culture that put pre-eminent stock in fighting prowess.[47] The chaotic nature of the contests, part boxing, part wrestling, and part brawling, can be attributable in part to the liminal nature of voyageur existence. A series of transitions characterized voyageur life as men continually moved from one geographic area to another and back and forth between European and First Nations cultures. Living such a transient lifestyle allowed a greater degree of freedom and experimentation in cultural practices than would be permitted in a social setting with long-established customs and social mores.[48]

Decades earlier in Virginia, a remarkably similar form of combat was practised by members of mid-eighteenth-century planter society. Although more settled than the voyageur world, with an established gentry who formed a social elite, Virginian society during the period was nevertheless characterized by what historian Rhys Isaac termed "a perpetual struggle for advantage ... constantly wrenching against the confines of settled community and the fixities of hereditary land tenure."[49] Since social status in mid-eighteenth-century Virginian society was in a constant state of negotiation, men were acutely concerned with maintaining, or seeking to improve, their place among their peers through exorbitant betting, audacious boasts, and brutal fighting. Perceived insults to one's status commonly instigated fights.[50] However, as historian Elliott Gorn has observed, such contests became far more rare in Virginian society by the end of the century as landed gentry, who had participated in these intensely violent spectacles, instead sought to emulate British aristocratic customs (including pistol duelling) as a means of distinguishing themselves from those perceived to be their social inferiors.[51]

By the beginning of the nineteenth century, the violent and unstructured fighting practices in the eastern state had migrated to the less-settled American backcountry. Practised by what Gorn terms "gamblers, hunters, herders, roustabouts, rivermen, and yeomen farmers," it became known as rough-and-tumble fighting. There, too, as widespread settlement encroached, its practice fell into disfavour.[52] The voyageurs' economic pursuits covered a wide swath of North American territory, including not only present-day Canada but also the southern Great Lakes, the Ohio and Illinois region, and along the Mississippi River.[53] Members of the highly mobile voyageur culture inevitably came into contact with the rough-and-tumble fighting practices of the American backcountry, and it is therefore of little surprise that similar methods were witnessed among them. Further linking mid-eighteenth-century Virginia, the backcountry of the American territories, and the fur-trading world of the voyageurs was the precarious nature of life and work, which included the ever-present danger of horrific injury or death. Their tenuous existence conditioned the men living in these regions to accept violence more readily than people in more stable environments, so chaotic and frequently disfiguring brawls found a receptive audience.[54]

Similar to the voyageurs, among the HBC York boat tripmen who transported furs and supplies among the Red River Colony, Norway House, and York Factory from the end of the eighteenth century to the middle of the nineteenth century, courage, physical strength, and fighting prowess were held in high regard. Like that of the voyageurs, the work of the tripmen was transient and dangerous as they passed from the Red River Colony on the plains south of Lake Winnipeg and from Fort Edmonton far to the west, through frequently treacherous waterways, to the boreal forests and marshlands that marked the territory of the company's northern posts. Their voyages, which lasted approximately nine weeks round trip, were conducted in large, slow-moving vessels known as York boats, first introduced to the region after 1797. The boats held roughly seventy-five packets weighing 100 pounds each, and considerable physical power and endurance were needed to load and unload the boats during the many portages along the route. Joseph James

Hargrave, an early Red River historian and a long-time resident of the northwest, in observing their work, noted admiringly that "the facility with which such pieces can be handled by the muscular tripmen is perfect."[55]

The physical prowess of the tripmen was also put to use in their recreational pursuits. When various brigades converged at Norway House and York Factory, bare-knuckle fights were customarily staged among the respective brigade champions to determine overall supremacy.[56] Few details of the tripmen's encounters have survived. As a result, it is difficult to ascertain the precise physical and technical nature of their matches. However, the York boat period coincided with both the growth of rough-and-tumble fighting on the American frontier and the popularization of bare-knuckle boxing in Great Britain. Although it is not strictly known which customs presided among the tripmen, neither form of combat exempted wrestling from its repertoire. Modern boxing's first rules, formulated by British boxing champion Jack Broughton in 1743, outlawed few tactics save hitting a man when he was down and letting other parties interfere with a fight.[57] His rules remained the sport's most common code of conduct until they were superseded in 1838 by the London Prize Ring Rules, which more explicitly outlined foul tactics. Although biting, scratching, gouging, kicking, and using foreign objects such as stones in the hands and spikes on the boots were declared unacceptable, wrestling was not.[58] Many matches from the period featured much stand-up wrestling, and published technical manuals on the sport provided detailed instructions on wrestling in addition to striking.[59] It was not until publication of the Marquis of Queensberry Rules in 1867, which gradually supplanted the London Prize Ring Rules over the next two decades, that wrestling was removed entirely from boxing matches.

York Factory, on the southwestern shore of Hudson Bay, was the key nexus of cultural contact between Great Britain and the Canadian northwest. It was from this point that considerable material, cultural as well as physical, flowed into the interior. Accordingly, whereas historians such as Donald Creighton, in positing his Laurentian thesis, have stressed the importance of the eponymous east-west waterway corridors in Canada's early development, W.L. Morton, in looking specifically at the Canadian west and present-day Manitoba prior to Confederation, has viewed the region's development in north-south terms.[60] It is therefore tenable that the fighting practices adopted by the tripmen were influenced by the direct and sustained contact with Great Britain through York Factory. W. Cornwallis King, an HBC clerk who arrived from England in 1862, described a contest that he saw during his first night at York Factory as "the cleverest and most skilful boxing that I have ever witnessed."[61] What transpired upon his arrival in North America was readily recognizable. King's account therefore suggests that the familiar methods of the London Prize Ring (or a close approximation thereof), and not simply unrestrained brutality, were in use by the mid-century tripmen.

J.J. Gunn also provides evidence of more direct sporting contact between British and New World combatants. In chronicling the York boat workers' combative exploits, he notes, for instance, that one of the great contests of the period was staged at York Factory against a "big English sailor" from the *Prince of Wales* ship.[62] Such exchanges, and there were likely more than the one incident illustrated by Gunn, offer a hint of the early intercontinental links between combative sports in Great Britain and the Canadian northwest during the fur-trade era.

Modern bare-knuckle boxing was a British innovation, but the York boat tripmen and their champions were overwhelmingly of Métis and First Nations extraction. Within the fur-trade society of the Canadian northwest, the tripmen were also typically drawn from the lower social orders. Hargrave, who worked as Governor William McTavish's private secretary and whose father had served as HBC chief factor, noted in referring to the Red River-based Portage la Loche tripmen that they "rank very low in the colony" and that "their priests profess a certain influence over them, but they confess their flock is disreputable."[63] The fur-trading elite, among them Hargrave, might have looked upon the tripmen remonstratively, particularly in light of ongoing labour disputes with the HBC during the period, but such perceptions were not universal. The champion fighters were men of considerable popular appeal. Prior to disembarking, it was well known which champions would be travelling with the brigades, and upon returning people would line the riverbanks to hear word of the outcomes of the contests.[64]

History has recorded the names of several brigade champions, including Michael Lambert, renowned for his speed, and the physically powerful Poulet (Paulet) Paul, who earned folk hero status within western Canada's Métis community.[65] However, by the beginning of the twentieth century, Gunn commented that "some few [tripmen] still remain to tell of the glories of a calling that dwindled away before steamboats and railways, and is now completely unknown as though it had never been."[66] His remarks, applied to only one class of men working in the northwest, capture the essence of the transformation under way in and around the former Red River Colony during the last three decades of the nineteenth century. Following Manitoba's entry into Confederation with passage of the Manitoba Act in July 1870, the largely French-speaking and mixed-blood society was replaced, both in number and in influence, by Anglo-Canadian settlers who brought with them their social norms and customs. Combative sports, specifically wrestling, which had a long history in the region, took on new forms and meanings in the burgeoning Manitoba society.

ANGLO-CANADIAN CULTURE IN THE PRAIRIES

During the first half of the nineteenth century, popular perception among residents and officials in the United Provinces of Canada held that the prairie region, then controlled by the HBC, was generally unsuitable for farming and large-scale settlement. By the late 1850s, however, views began to change as prominent Canadian scientists, politicians, and businessmen re-evaluated the west in terms of both its agricultural merit and its prescient role in fostering a "new Britannic empire on [the] American shores."[67] Anglo-Canadian cultural imperialism also fused with more immediately practical considerations to drive interest in the region. Much of the viable farmland in Canada West (the region previously known as Upper Canada) was already under cultivation by mid-century, leading to inflated land prices, concerns over future resource scarcity, and reduced interest in settlement among prospective immigrants. Additionally, apprehension about American annexation, particularly by the end of the Civil War in 1865, provided an incentive for rapid western settlement.[68]

After prolonged negotiations with the HBC, the Dominion of Canada secured title in 1870 to the area known as Rupert's Land. Between 1870 and 1877, and again in 1884–85, the federal government quelled Métis resistance to Canadian expansion in, respectively, the Red River settlement and North West Territories. It also negotiated a series of treaties with the region's First Nations peoples in order to extinguish their title to Manitoba's lands and make way for widespread European settlement.[69] Following ratification of the Dominion Lands Act in 1872, settlers slowly began to arrive, with the goal of transplanting British Canadian (specifically Ontario) Protestant culture to the Manitoba grasslands and supplanting the fur-trade-based economy of the Métis and First Nations with grain farming. Within the decade, they succeeded in achieving numerical, economic, and cultural dominance.[70] Social transformation occurred not only with the tacit consent of central Canadian authorities but also with their explicit forceful support. The Mounted Constabulary Force (later the

Manitoba Provincial Police Force), established under federal jurisdiction after Confederation, emerged as a symbol of the changes under way in Manitoba during the decade after Confederation.[71] Since the force was established under federal authority, like the North West Mounted Police (NWMP) who later served the North West Territories, it was aimed not only at preventing the notorious (and often exaggerated) lawlessness of the American frontier but also at extending central Canadian authority into the region.[72]

The police presence, however, was not the only visual indication of Manitoba's growing connection to central Canada. During the period, a large number of sporting pastimes, including team sports such as cricket, lacrosse, soccer, rugby, curling, and rowing, and individual sports such as pedestrianism and snowshoeing, already practised in Ontario, appeared in Manitoba.[73] The widespread popularity of sports in the province reflected larger trends seen throughout the English-speaking world during and after the 1870s, when many members of society increasingly came to view sports not only as enjoyable endeavours but also as vehicles for positive social change. Specifically, sports were looked at as a medium through which to teach desirable "manly" values to young men. Much of this had to do with prevailing definitions of masculinity among the increasingly influential Protestant middle class and the rapid shift away from an agrarian-based rural economy to urban industrialism.

SPORT AND MASCULINITIES

During the decades surrounding Confederation, ideas of appropriate manhood underwent a fundamental shift within Protestant English-speaking society in large part because of the growing influence of the middle class in virtually all realms of human interaction. Early in the nineteenth century, Protestantism generally placed pre-eminent value on moral qualities such as piety, gentleness, community service, and domesticity.[74] Physical prowess, from a middle-class perspective, had little to do with a man's worth as a Christian. Methodism's powerful influence on Upper Canada's residents during the Second Great Revival bolstered this view by promoting an anti-materialist conception of Christianity, stressing one's direct spiritual relationship with God, and rejecting the material world, seen as an expression of humanity's fall from divine grace. However, by the middle of the 1800s, Christian reformers, in increasing numbers, began to reject the internally oriented conception of Christianity in favour of one that stressed physicality.[75] Although the impetus for this change is attributable to a number of sources, prominent theologians and writers, including Charles Kingsley and Thomas Hughes, were among its most vocal and articulate advocates.

Kingsley, who drew inspiration for his ideas from a variety of earlier sources, including the classical Greek works of Plato, saw a direct connection between the previously separate physical and spiritual realms, arguing that proper Christianity entailed serving God with one's entire being. Direct physical action, not just personal reflection and prayer, could bring an individual closer to God and assist in inculcating proper Christian values.[76] His doctrine, popularly termed Muscular Christianity, quickly gained wide acceptance, spurred on in large part by the commercial success of Thomas Hughes's novel *Tom Brown's School Days.*[77] Through participation in sports, Tom Brown, the protagonist, not only gains greater physical prowess but also learns moral lessons that shape his character and make him a proper model of Christian manhood. Many middle-class Protestants had viewed participation in sports as largely a waste of time that distracted them from more important business and spiritual matters. However, the doctrine of Muscular Christianity gave new meaning to these previously frivolous activities.[78] In fact, far from being an unnecessary indulgence, sport now became an important vehicle for preparing young men for success in public life, including business, for it taught critical traits such as team work, determination, healthy competitiveness, and playing by the rules, all of which were seen as critical in a burgeoning capitalist economy.[79] Sport served as an efficient means to achieve higher ends. Hughes's work gained widespread acclaim, and by the 1880s it was included on both the Ontario and the Manitoba supplementary reading lists for Protestant schoolteachers.[80] Muscular Christianity's precepts became so pervasive that even Jesus Christ was recast as a physically robust model of ideal manliness.[81]

Despite manhood's growing association with physicality, such ideas never achieved universal acceptance. As historian Janet Guildford contends, conceptions of masculinity were not exclusively shaped by men. Instead, women, through their own ideas regarding what constituted appropriate manhood, helped to shape male self-identity and behaviour.[82] As her analysis of mid-Victorian literature suggests, many middle-class women were ambivalent, at best, toward "vaunted" attributes such as male physical strength, instead advocating qualities such as generosity, a capacity for passion tempered by self-control, and a genuine interest in cultural pursuits.[83] Some segments of the male population, including prominent Christian leader Samuel J. May and the more secularly minded transcendentalist Walt Whitman, believed that men could best be served by removing the social and political barriers that separated them from women (and in the process adopting many so-called feminine traits), not by emphasizing physical strength as the path to self-actualization.[84]

TAVERNS AND COMMERCIAL SPORT

Although it never gained complete hegemony, Muscular Christianity gave tremendous impetus to legitimating sport. Yet, even as interest in sport grew, the idea that its sole purpose was to cultivate Christian morality did not garner universal acceptance. By the mid-nineteenth century, many sporting pastimes, including wrestling, had long-standing associations in Canada with taverns. In Upper Canada, taverns were found in communities of all sizes.[85] In addition to providing alcohol, meals, and lodging, taverns offered a huge array of amusements for their patrons.[86] In some instances, wrestling matches occurred without apparent prearrangement as part of a larger pattern of social interaction that generally condoned convivial roughhousing in taverns. Impromptu contests of this nature gave men a chance to enhance their social standing by showcasing valued physical attributes such as speed and strength.[87] Wrestling matches also proved to be exciting spectacles for those who witnessed them. However, both the keepers and the patrons valued taverns as public spaces that facilitated orderly interactions, and a host of informal but well-understood social customs ensured that wrestling bouts did not escalate to the point where either the individuals or the taverns involved were harmed.[88] Although Upper Canadian tavern-goers were familiar with wrestling, it is not clear how many contests were deliberately arranged ahead of time for patrons' amusement. The subject, beyond the scope of my investigation, nevertheless warrants detailed research. Similar customs around orderly (albeit rough) interactions, including wrestling, were reproduced in Manitoba's drinking establishments and could still be observed as late as the turn of the twentieth century.[89]

The gradual shift from an agricultural to an industrial economy, which began during the mid-nineteenth century, aided wrestling's development as a commercial undertaking. Industrialization facilitated the growth of urban centres, and in turn urban taverns grew to service the rapidly expanding towns and cities. Eventually, tavern proprietors, who had long permitted friendly wrestling bouts in their establishments during the pre-industrial period, also recognized that formally staged contests could be lucrative, for they would draw people into their taverns, and those people could be charged to watch the matches.[90] In Britain, where industrial development long predated its counterpart in Canada, wrestling matches were organized by tavern owners in London as early as the 1820s.[91] Matches staged in Lancashire county were regularly sponsored by taverns such as the Humphrey in Cheetham, the Bay Horse in Bolton, and the Roebuck Inn in Oldham. Bowling greens, which commonly abutted the properties, served as sites for contests.[92] As urban centres in Canada grew in size, tavern owners and other entrepreneurs, recognizing the widespread interest in commercial sport, expanded their activities into larger venues.[93] By the early 1870s, an enthusiastic sporting community with a keen interest in wrestling was already evident in Canada. In July 1873, for instance, a match in Troy, New York, between American John McMahon (a well-known wrestler with close ties to New York City tavern owner Harry Hill) and Thomas A. Copeland, described as "champion of Canada" and "representative champion of the British provinces," took place in Harmony Hall. Reports described the hall as "crowded with sporting men from all over the United States and Canada."[94] One notable feature of the contest, ubiquitous in all similar affairs, was gambling on the outcome.

By the 1870s, gambling had a well-established connection to tavern life, and this carried over into commercial sport. Although not all tavern-goers gambled, the practice of placing bets on the outcomes of games and amusements (whether in the form of money or by "treating" someone to a drink) was long-standing.[95] Individuals could gain esteem among their peers and, with a sufficient level of skill, generate income by participating in sporting endeavours at which money rested on the results.[96] Additionally, individuals who lacked the requisite skills to excel in sports could nevertheless profit from them by placing bets.[97] The emphasis on sport as a money-making enterprise stood in stark contrast to middle-class Muscular Christian doctrines that prescribed sport primarily as a character builder. Many bourgeois sports enthusiasts frowned on mixing sport with money, in part, because of a worldview that equated financial success with hard work. Mainstream Protestant denominations in Canada (whose members likewise were among the country's leading Muscular Christians) generally condemned gambling as selfish and wasteful, and the quick money that could be made from competing for prize money or betting on an event's outcome contravened their work ethic.[98] The presence of money in sport, many argued, could also lead to behaviour that completely contradicted ideas of middle-class respectability, including rule breaking or outright fixing in sporting events. As

Manitoba entered Confederation in mid-1870, both the middle-class Protestant-based ideas of Muscular Christian sport and the commercial, profit-oriented model were familiar to the Anglo-Protestants who were to settle there. It was the latter vision of sport, far more than the former vision, that provided the framework for the advance of wrestling in Manitoba until the early twentieth century. Wrestling also depended, however, on a number of other interrelated factors for its growth.

COMMUNICATION, TRANSPORTATION, URBANIZATION, AND WRESTLING

Improvements in communication and transportation technology, as well as rapid urban expansion, were vital factors in the development of wrestling. Although it would be erroneous to describe either the Red River settlement or other regions of the northwest as "cut off" from Canadian and British civilization, the existing communication infrastructure made regular contact with the outside world problematic. The HBC's presence throughout the northwest ensured ongoing communication with the English-speaking world during the fur-trading era, with much of the information that arrived in the region funnelled through York Factory. Newspapers and popular journals arrived on supply ships during the ice-free season at the post and were distributed to subscribers located at the numerous inland trading posts. Letter writing also allowed for current events to be further disseminated throughout the region.[99]

By 1870, mail from Canada was directed through Minnesota and into Manitoba. Arriving at Pembina, on the international border, it was shipped by boat up the Red River to Winnipeg and again by river to scattered settlements in the province. At the time, there were only six postal outlets across the Prairies.[100] In the summer of 1871, the dominion government gave approval to the North-Western Telegraph Company to construct a telegraph line between Lower Fort Garry and the Minnesota border, and it was completed later that year.[101] Although early services were not always reliable, the arrival of telegraphic communication symbolized an epochal shift for Manitoba, for it precipitated the transition from what Gerald Friesen has termed the "textual-settler" era to the "print-capitalism" stage of western Canadian development.[102] Just as the arrival of thousands of new settlers in the ensuing decades changed Manitoba's demographic and ethnic composition, so too the telegraph changed the means by which those in the province interacted with others and understood the world around them, vastly accelerating the interchange of information and diminishing the degree to which time and space were impediments to the region's integration into Canadian and North American society.[103] Between 1874 and 1887, telegraph lines were constructed and linked central Canada to Manitoba and other areas of the northwest.[104] The province's burgeoning newspaper industry benefited more than any other commercial enterprise from telegraphic services, for it was now able to provide increasingly detailed and topical reports on events of regional, national, and international significance.[105] As Manitoba's population increased fivefold in the decade and a half after Confederation, consumer demand for newspapers expanded accordingly. In 1874, two newspapers, the Manitoba *Free Press* and *Nor'Wester,* began daily publication.[106] Over the next decade, various other newspapers appeared that went to print on a daily or weekly basis.[107]

Manitoba's entry into the "print-capitalism" era corresponded with sport's rapid growth in urban centres across the continent.[108] Wrestling benefited from both developments, albeit not immediately. Evidence suggests that, if organized wrestling matches were staged in the province during the 1870s, they did not garner any significant media attention.[109] Likewise, bouts held in the United States and central Canada rarely occasioned mention in the daily press.[110] However, during the 1880s, indicative of wrestling's growing popularity, newspaper coverage of wrestling matches expanded dramatically. Advances in communication technology, including introduction of the telegraph, allowed Manitobans to acquaint themselves with prominent wrestlers, keep abreast of upcoming matches and the financial stakes associated with them, and become familiar with various wrestling styles and methods, all from hundreds and even thousands of kilometres away. Readers were given regular accounts of contests, only days after they occurred, from various centres, such as New York City, Buffalo, Boston, Cleveland, Toledo, Detroit, St. Louis, Chicago, and San Francisco.[111] This coverage ultimately helped to create a popular audience for wrestling in Manitoba that, even with the absence of locally staged matches, could feel connected to the goings-on elsewhere.

Improvements in transportation infrastructure supplied the next important component for the development of wrestling. In December 1878, the province's first railway commenced operation, linking St. Boniface, on the east shore of the Red River across from Winnipeg, to Emerson on the Manitoba-Minnesota border, making existing steamboat operations along the north-south Red River corridor obsolete. The railway gave settlers a direct connection to St. Paul, Minnesota, facilitating the flow of both people and commercial goods.[112] Continuous railway service reduced the time and inconvenience of travel and gave athletes new access to population centres in the United States.

Communication and transportation technology allowed unprecedented levels of contact with the larger world. Rapid urban population growth simultaneously aided and was aided by these developments. In Manitoba, and indeed in the entire prairie region, Winnipeg emerged as the dominant metropolitan centre. In the fifteen years after Confederation, it had mushroomed from a tiny settlement at the junction of the Red and Assiniboine Rivers with two dozen buildings and between 100 and 200 residents to a city of 20,000.[113] This rapid growth produced an overwhelming sense of optimism among its residents. In December 1879, Mayor Alex Logan encapsulated the general mood of the city: "Winnipeg has grown from a little village into a city which is making progress by leaps and bounds. Today nearly one thousand dwelling houses stud the plain, where ten years ago they could be counted on the fingers of two hands. That Winnipeg is destined to be a great distributing centre of the Northwest is now no empty figure of speech for it admits of no denial. It is now all but an accomplished fact."[114] During the early 1880s, the city experienced even more rapid growth because of the decision to build the transcontinental Canadian Pacific Railway (CPR) through it. The details of Winnipeg's successful bid to become the western hub of the transcontinental railway and the subsequent property and construction boom that it initiated, have been well documented by Canadian historians.[115] Significant to wrestling are not just the raw numbers associated with Winnipeg's population explosion during its early years but also the demographic characteristics.

Census records from 1881 indicate that, between the ages of twenty-one and thirty-one, men living in Winnipeg (Selkirk District) far outnumbered women. Concurrently, the number of married men in the same age range was smaller than the number of married women. As Alan F.J. Artibise notes, however, the census failed to adequately account for the large "floating" population in the city, which, overwhelmingly male, might have been double that recorded in official reports.[116] A disproportionately large segment of the community's population during this period consisted of young, unattached, male labourers, many of whom, as described by W.L. Morton, were "of the roughest kind." Although a police presence helped to curtail violent crimes, particularly those involving guns, a large number of hotels, taverns, gambling dens, and prostitution houses emerged to provide services to the predominantly male population. Fighting was common, and police courts frequently levied fines for prostitution and public intoxication.[117] Winnipeg's national reputation as a vice-ridden community was so widespread that, as early as 1876, the Toronto Young Men's Christian Association (YMCA) deemed that, in the entire dominion, only Barrie, Ontario, could match the Manitoba capital in depravity. At the annual YMCA convention, prayers were offered for both cities.[118] Despite appeals to the Almighty, Winnipeg retained its reputation as a "vice city" for many years.[119]

PROFESSIONAL WRESTLING'S EARLY YEARS IN MANITOBA

Among the large male population, interest in individual tests of physical strength and skill ran high, and it is little surprise that wrestling, which the press was already covering in detail by the early 1880s, became popular among Winnipeg's young men. As Morris Mott notes, virtually any organized sport in Manitoba can trace its origins to Winnipeg.[120] Wrestling is no exception. Although impromptu wrestling matches undoubtedly took place throughout the city, by the early 1880s local commercial entrepreneurs began to capitalize on the sport's popularity. During this period, a relationship was established that would remain important well into the twentieth century: organized wrestling maintained close ties to Winnipeg's hotels and liquor establishments. As noted, this connection had existed for years in the taverns of Great Britain, Ontario, and the eastern United States, and like many customs it was recreated by settlers in the west. In the spring of 1882, Winnipeg's first known wrestling gym, one of many that would spring briefly into existence over the next four decades, opened at the Winnipeg Hotel when two individuals named Barnes and Tilley began offering instruction in the sport to the public along with sparring and club swinging.[121] Thomas Montgomery, proprietor of the Winnipeg Hotel, evidently took an active interest in the sport himself and was not reluctant to demonstrate his skills in his own establishment. In 1884, while engaged in a "friendly" bout in the hotel's bar, he accidentally injured Mr. Nott, co-proprietor of a local plumbing, steam, and gas fitting firm. Nott fractured his leg when he was thrown awkwardly to the ground, requiring a surgeon's attention to set the bone.[122]

Although wrestling invited potential injury, the risk of physical harm did not, by itself, generate controversy for the sport. Indeed, among middle-class reformers, wrestling had the potential to inculcate many desirable traits, and contemporary accounts frequently spoke of its benefits. Among young boys, wrestling was encouraged as a positive, "natural" activity that exercised all of the body's muscles.[123]

Some commentators even advocated it for men in their advanced years, stating that "two old men living in a city can get excellent exercise by wrestling in a large, light room," but of course, because of their age, "there must be more gentleness displayed in the struggle than two 12 year old boys would observe."[124]

Even more important was its efficacy as a character builder for young men. Part of wrestling's perceived value was its effectiveness in combatting effeminacy. Wrestling, along with other combative sports, could help a boy to avoid a reputation as a "milksop" or "sissy" among his peers. By the late nineteenth century, effeminate behaviour carried the potential for social scorn among one's age cohort, but it was also viewed as a moral failing in its own right. The soft, weak body became indicative of a soft, weak character. With little physical capital, the effeminate man might resort to more devious means to achieve goals. Physical training, particularly in combative sports, offered an antidote to effeminacy that could also teach boys to stand up for themselves in an honourable and respectful fashion—a habit that would be of benefit to future businessmen.[125] As Judge Henry A. Shute opined, "let your boys learn to box, to wrestle, to fence, and so develop every muscle. I never yet saw a boy who knew how to box strike with a club, a stone or a dangerous weapon."[126]

Although a safer and more morally uplifting alternative to solving personal disputes with weapons, wrestling injuries did occur. Yet injuries occurred in many sports. Playing rugby, for example, which assisted in developing so many of Tom Brown's "manly attributes" and was the conscious creation of middle-class British educators, commonly resulted in injuries and even deaths. Such tragedies were tolerated, if never fully accepted, because of the moral qualities that aggressive sports imbued in their participants.[127] With regard to wrestling, of greatest concern to middle-class reformers was not its danger but the fact that matches were generally associated with less reputable activities such as gambling, rowdy behaviour, and alcohol consumption. Individuals prominently involved in the sport also constituted less "respectable" members of society whose behaviour was not in keeping with the tenets of Muscular Christianity. Additionally, many of the wrestling matches held in the province were not seen to serve "higher" purposes.

Newspapers sporadically reported the problems associated with professional wrestling. On 22 March 1882, for instance, the Manitoba *Free Press* carried a report from Pueblo, Colorado, of a match at a local theatre in which a defeated wrestler's supporters threatened the referee with pistols. A general fight erupted among the spectators, resulting in one man being rendered unconscious and another being injured severely.[128] Such reports contributed to wrestling's growing reputation as a dubious commercial undertaking, and local newspapers occasionally took on the role of moral guardian for the community. The Winnipeg *Sun*, in commenting on British-born wrestlers Duncan C. Ross and Edwin Bibby, warned that "if Winnipeg is ever threatened with an eruption of this fraternity the Sun will light up some of the dark corners of these contests. The Sun man has been there."[129] With the growing population of young men and the subsequent proliferation of other "less respectable" entertainments, however, wrestling became one of the many commercial amusements offered in the city.

By early 1884, the sport, along with boxing, was evidently popular among Winnipeg's residents, and matches were being staged in the various variety theatres that had been quickly erected to meet growing demands for entertainment. In April 1884, the Winnipeg *Sun*, reporting on a recent boxing match at the Theatre Comique, noted that "pugilistic encounters and wrestling matches are the latest dodges resorted to by the proprietors of these places, and prove 'drawing cards.'"[130] The report's derisory tone reflected the widespread sentiment that had grown among many members of the press, in addition to a large segment of Winnipeg's population, that the city's variety theatres were an offence to public decency. Liquor sales accounted for most of the theatres' revenues, and alcohol-fuelled rowdiness among the all-male spectators, in addition to the lewd nature of many of the acts, drew the scorn of reform organizations, including the Women's Christian Temperance Union and Blue Ribbon Society, as well as several members of Winnipeg City Council.[131] Wrestling's close association with the city's generally disreputable variety theatre business certainly did not help its standing. Nevertheless, such entertainments had wide appeal among men that transcended class boundaries, and even well-to-do citizens often attended the shows, while other people of the same social station decried them.[132]

The athletes most directly associated with wrestling at the local level during the 1880s also helped to shape its reputation. A closer examination of their lives provides further insight not only into wrestling's image among middle-class reformers but also into the nature of Winnipeg's male sporting culture during this period. During the 1880s, the most prominent athletes were the McKeown brothers. As noted by long-time resident Joe Fahey, who later founded Winnipeg's North End Athletic Club, "the McKeown boys, Edward [Ed], John [Jack], and Peter, were always at the fore with anything that was going on [in sport]."[133]

The McKeowns immigrated to Winnipeg from Simcoe County, Ontario, during the city's growth period in the late 1870s and early 1880s.[134] Although it is difficult to ascertain when each arrived, by the early 1880s all three were living in the city and heavily immersed in local sports. A fourth brother, James, likewise joined them in Winnipeg but was less athletically inclined. Although Peter, a railway policeman, was a gifted sportsman who competed in field athletics such as hammer throwing and caber tossing, Jack (the eldest) and Ed (the youngest) were most associated with wrestling.[135] Jack and Ed were all-round athletes, competing in a variety of events and often doing so for money.[136] In addition to wrestling, Jack, an expressman by trade, participated for gate receipts and side bets in pedestrian racing, a sport that enjoyed great popularity in the late 1870s and early 1880s in many Canadian urban centres.[137] Ed was best known as a pugilist and fought several well-publicized bouts in Winnipeg.[138] For several years, he was the proprietor of the Nickel Plate Hotel at 589 Main Street, where he also taught Indian club and dumbbell exercises, in addition to boxing lessons, in an adjoining gym.[139] Boxing and wrestling were frequently staged together, and Ed served as a referee or master of ceremonies for matches.[140] Evidently, he was held in high enough regard within the local sporting community to be called on to serve in official capacities for other events in which prize money played a role.[141]

The McKeowns demonstrate professional wrestling's frequent connection to a larger culture of criminality and violence in nineteenth-century Winnipeg. During the 1880s and 1890s, the three brothers appeared in local police court dozens of times. Often the charges were minor, including arrests and fines for being drunk or disorderly in the street.[142] However, many of their offences were of a more serious nature. In mid-September 1884, Peter was arrested and pled guilty to assault and beating.[143] John faced similar charges on at least one occasion in August 1887 in addition to resisting arrest.[144] Ed, though, appears to have been the most prone to violence.

Since prize fighting was illegal under the Criminal Code of Canada, Ed McKeown's charges sometimes stemmed from activities associated with boxing. Following his fight with Ike Fullerton on 25 January 1885, both contestants were placed under arrest, but neither appears to have been convicted. Less than a month later, on 18 February, Ed was once again arrested, this time for going into training for a prize fight. Eleven witnesses were sworn in and examined, including his brothers John (Jack) and Peter. Ed was convicted and released on his own recognizance for $500. The hefty bond does not appear to have been much of a deterrent, because on 31 March he was once again taken into court by the police for engaging in a prize fight a week earlier. However, the charges were withdrawn.[145] Although his pugilistic pursuits invited repeated censure, they were not the sole source of his legal difficulties.

Between 1884 and 1907, Ed appeared in Winnipeg courts on at least twelve occasions for offences such as assault, assault and beating (eight times), felonious assault (once), aggravated assault (once), malicious wounding (once), and intimidating a witness by threats (once).[146] He did not always get away from confrontations unscathed. During a visit to Olympic Hotel in St. Paul, Minnesota, in 1886, for example, after an argument, Ed was pistol-whipped, knocked to the ground, kicked repeatedly, and then later robbed of a $325 pin and a watch.[147] He also took an active part in animal blood sports such as cock and dog fighting during his sporting career. He owned a large number of dogs, and railway links to the United States facilitated his ability to take them to Minnesota for fights. His champion was a bull terrier named Spring, which he claimed to be "the best in the Northwest."[148] Although records do not indicate that Ed or any other member of the McKeown clan ever faced legal action for being involved in animal blood fights, arrests did occur.[149]

Residents who wished to purge Winnipeg of its more disreputable entertainments carried with them a mandate for social reform already backed by law. Yet some members of the public continued to defy attempts to impose moral censure. Many in the emergent working class, drawing on traditions that predated intensive urbanization and industrialization, persisted in celebrating forms of manhood tied to bloodshed and violence. Irrespective of (or perhaps even, in part, because of) brushes with the law, the McKeowns undoubtedly enjoyed a measure of fame and adulation among many Manitobans. With their ability to influence the world around them through raw physical force and daring, they were tangible and powerful symbols of resistance to hegemonic and oppressive authority in an increasingly regulated society.

The case of the McKeowns and late nineteenth-century Winnipeg also illustrates a reality in which social values were not exclusively disseminated from "on high," to be absorbed by those with less social and economic capital. In some circumstances, they also filtered upward.[150] It is therefore incorrect to assume that even the bloodiest and most brutal events were frequented only by individuals of poor social standing. As in the case of variety theatre, men of many different stations took great interest in "disreputable" activities such as animal blood sports. Many of Winnipeg's most prominent citizens were reportedly at ringside in January 1889 when members of the city's sporting fraternity staged "the biggest cock fight ever held in this country," involving over forty birds wearing two-and-a-half-inch steel spurs. Hundreds of dollars were wagered on the matches, but the participants escaped detection by the city police. The event was said to be just one of several planned for that winter.[151] Similarly, members of St. George Snowshoe Club, one of the city's most popular sporting clubs, with "a membership that include[d] nearly every able-bodied Winnipegger of active and alert disposition," also held cock fights, along with wrestling and various other entertainments, following their "tramps."[152] Since even the goriest pastimes crossed class boundaries, professional wrestling cannot be viewed soley as a spectacle enjoyed by the lower social orders.

Well-known sportsmen with connections to professional wrestling in Manitoba likewise did not travel exclusively in social circles that left them divorced from mainstream "respectable" activities, including involvement in local and national electoral politics. Ed McKeown was an ardent Liberal Party supporter who took an active role in the political campaigns of parliamentarians such as Winnipeg's "Fighting Joe" Martin, a staunch defender of Ontario-style culture in the Prairies.[153] Additionally, Ed's frequent forays into court in no way negated his propensity for selfless courage, demonstrated most notably when, during a fire at the Nickel Plate Hotel, he wrapped himself in a blanket and ran through the flames to rescue a missing child, suffering burns to his face in the process.[154] As the case of Ed McKeown demonstrates, society was often far more dynamic and fluid, and individuals more ethically complex, than a simple dichotomy categorizing them as wholly respectable or wholly disreputable. Naturally, however, not all members of Manitoba society took an interest in professional wrestling, nor did they advocate the practices and behaviours that often surrounded it.

Newspaper reports frequently looked with disapproving eyes on wrestling and the larger sporting culture in which it was situated, yet, despite their admonitions and criticisms, coverage steadily grew during the 1880s and 1890s. Publishers' apparently duplicitous decision to give increasing column space to sporting activities that they, and many reform-minded (and highly influential) citizens, found distasteful stemmed largely from economic imperatives. By the early 1880s, it was increasingly evident that detailed sports coverage could considerably boost a paper's circulation. In the United States, a number of weekly journals had vastly expanded their readership and circulation by emphasizing

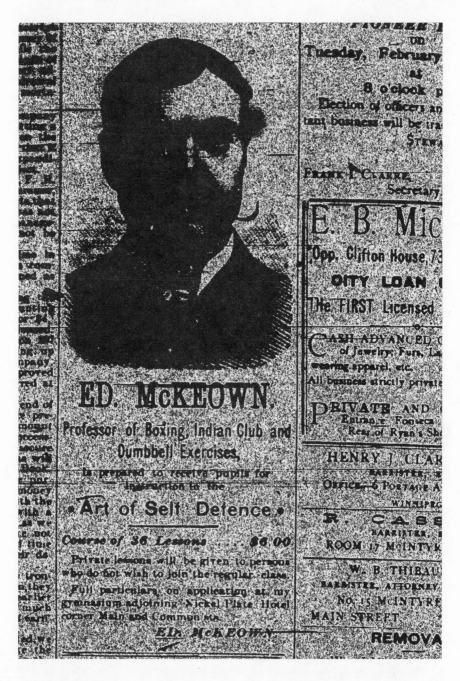

1. Pugilist Ed McKeown, pictured in this 1889 engraving, was actively involved in Winnipeg's early sports scene, including with professional wrestling. Despite frequent run-ins with the law, his connections with the Liberal Party of Canada later netted him a position as a secret police officer during the Klondike Gold Rush. Source: Winnipeg *Siftings*, 16 February 1889.

sports reporting. The most notable in this regard were the New York *Clipper* and *National Police Gazette*. The *Police Gazette* in particular proved that interest in commercial sports such as boxing and wrestling extended far beyond the individuals and spectators immediately involved in the contests. Prior to 1880, the *Police Gazette* focused primarily on lurid tales of crime and sex. However, when its owner, Richard Kyle Fox, noticed that the paper's coverage of important prize fights significantly boosted sales, he began to focus on sports reporting. Circulation, which averaged 150,000 in 1880, later rose to over 1 million.[155] In Canada, newspaper publishers expanded their sports coverage both to attract readers and to lure advertisers. During the late nineteenth century, newspapers became increasingly dependent on advertising revenue. Wood pulp-based newsprint, which came into use during the last two decades of the nineteenth century, reduced the cost of newspaper production, allowing larger papers to be produced. Larger papers, in turn, allowed for more advertising space to be sold. By offering news items that appealed to a broad readership, newspapers could increase circulation, allowing them to attract more advertisers and to charge higher prices for advertising space.[156]

Fed by changing technology and the new economic opportunities that it created, the 1880s and 1890s represented the genesis of what has been termed by sociologist Sut Jhally "the sports/media complex": a symbiotic relationship in which sport boosted newspaper sales and newspaper sales created further interest in sport.[157] Yet, as the case of professional wrestling in Manitoba makes abundantly clear, the relationship during the period was not straightforward. Instead, an acute tension between moral imperatives and a simple desire to "boost" the sport (and by extension sales) was continually evident, especially around matches staged at the local level.

In Manitoba, as in the rest of Canada, newspaper publishers recognized that public demand for sports reporting included coverage of local, national, and international events.[158] Particularly interesting to the public, however, was that the confluence of communication and transportation technology allowed athletes with national or international fame to visit the region. As the largest population centre in the Prairies and the region's major railway hub, Winnipeg was the first centre to entertain famous wrestlers. The earliest and most significant wrestler of international reputation to visit the city was Matsuda Sorakichi, who engaged in two local matches in August 1886. Sorakichi was the first Japanese wrestler to gain prominence in North America. He arrived on the continent in 1883 and had his first match in New York City on 14 January 1884 against British-born Edwin Bibby. Over the next several years, he engaged in numerous tours throughout the United States, facing virtually all of the country's top wrestlers.[159] In Manitoba, Sorakichi, often referred to simply as "the Jap," received considerable attention in the press, and he was well known by Winnipeg's residents prior to his arrival.[160] His two matches in the city illustrate many of the features endemic to wrestling matches not only in the 1880s but also in the decades thereafter.

Sorakichi's first match was against local grappler John Blackey. Given the Japanese native's international reputation as a superb wrestler, it was agreed that Sorakichi would wrestle with a handicap, consenting to pin Blackey three times in an hour. Handicap matches were common when one opponent possessed either greater skill or greater size than the other, and they ensured public interest in what might otherwise have been a mismatch. Additionally, they created favourable conditions for betting, for they allowed money to be wagered on more even terms. Considerable wagering preceded the match between Sorakichi and Blackey, and the Winnipeg man's supporters were willing to back Blackey into the hundreds of dollars.[161] As evidence of a growing interest in quantification among the sports-minded public, the night prior to their contest both men were carefully weighed, Sorakichi weighing in at 160 pounds and Blackey at 148 pounds. Additionally, unlike during the era when voyageurs plied their physical skills in the Canadian northwest, wrestling matches were now being contested according to specific rules.[162] By the 1880s, Winnipeg was already becoming integrated into what historians Richard Gruneau and David Whitson term "the world of sports": a far-reaching culture of common practices and standardized sporting forms well known among the general public throughout North America.[163] In the case of the Sorakichi-Blackey match, the contest adhered to the established conventions of catch-as-catch-can wrestling.

Catch-as-catch-can wrestling, which originated in Lancashire, England, was already practised in Ontario by the 1870s.[164] However, the art gained further prominence throughout North America following the arrival of several outstanding wrestlers from Lancashire between 1880 and 1883, notable among them the aforementioned Edwin Bibby, later joined by Joe Acton, Tom Cannon, and Tom Connors.[165] Unlike the French Greco-Roman system, in which all wrestling occurred from the waist up, catch-as-catch-can allowed grips on both the upper and the lower body. Matches consisted of both standing and ground wrestling, and a win (often called a fall) was scored when one contestant had his shoulders pinned to the mat or conceded defeat. Custom permitted virtually any hold but typically prohibited tactics such as suffocation, scratching, and ear twisting, all deemed to be unfair.[166] The Sorakichi-Blackey bout was Manitoba's first significant catch-as-catch-can contest, and as elsewhere on the continent the local sporting community was concerned to see that the sport's conventions were followed. Governance of the match was therefore entrusted to a third party in the form of a referee.

The referee's role as arbiter in wrestling matches was an important convention that distinguished combative sports in the post-Confederation era from informal customs that had prevailed in the region. Although the idea of a single official to oversee a combative sporting contest is taken for granted today, early rule sets, including boxing's Broughton Rules, permitted one referee to be chosen by each side. In Cornish wrestling, a system of jacketed wrestling originating in its eponymous British county, three referees, termed "sticklers," were traditionally employed to oversee matches.[167] Although detailed information on earlier conventions around Lancashire wrestling is lacking, as in boxing the custom of employing a single referee to officiate matches was well established by the mid-nineteenth century.[168] The referee's role in catch-as-catch-can wrestling matches was vital in ensuring that the sport's customs were followed, but the equitable enforcement of rules was more than a matter of being fair to the combatants. Because of the prominent role played by gambling, the inequal application of rules, or general incompetence of the referee, could have wide-reaching consequences. The absence of formal governing bodies to oversee and regulate wrestling meant that the responsibility for selecting officials fell directly on the athletes and their backers. Much wrangling therefore frequently surrounded the selection of a referee, and it was sometimes difficult to find somebody who would fill the role. Written rules from the period, including those published by Lancashire's Tom Connors in his treatise *The Modern Athlete* (1890), therefore set forth provisions for selecting a referee in the event that one could not be agreed upon.[169]

A second official appointed for the Sorakichi-Blackey match, the timekeeper, imposed further order on the proceedings.[170] That it was a timekeeper who joined the referee to form the slim cohort presiding over wrestling matches was not inconsequential. In a society increasingly regulated and disciplined by the rigid requirements of industrial production, which called, among many things, for clearly defined work hours and rigid transportation schedules, wrestling also came to be ruled by the clock. Time limits, and equally as important the times when falls were scored in a match, became a matter of considerable interest.

The presence of both a referee and a timekeeper implied the imposition of order and discipline on the match itself, but it was not enough to sway public opinion regarding the event as a worthwhile enterprise. Sporting conventions, after all, were not the sole concern of wrestling's detractors. Respectability remained their primary interest, and criticisms on this ground were rarely confined to the match itself. Commenting on the Sorakichi-Blackey meeting, the *Free Press* noted that it was late in commencing, an immediate affront to the notion of social interactions proceeding according to a strict, and already delineated, timetable. In the meantime, the *Free Press* opined, "there were several attempts made by the various persons to make the time pass rapidly. Boys who should have been in bed put on gloves and slugged one another around the room for the amusement of men. Had the police stopped the disgusting sight, their actions would have been approved of."[171] Gratuitous violence carried out for the amusement of a mature audience was not the only problem. Evidently, there was also a strong suspicion that the larger and more experienced Japanese grappler was carrying his local opponent. The reporter noted that "when the Jap got tired of playing tricks for the amusement of the crowd he threw his opponent, thus terminating the match."[172]

The second match pitted Sorakichi against Winnipeg's most prominent wrestler, Jack McKeown, for a side bet of fifty dollars. The *Free Press* reports did not contain the same degree of moral commentary that followed the previous engagement, perhaps in part because it was considered a more even contest. The Japanese wrestler "looked a veritable dwarf beside the man he was to throw being nine or ten inches shorter and sixty or seventy pounds lighter," and as a result "McKeown's great size and strength prevented the Jap from using any of his customary tricks."[173] Of particular interest, however, is that public enthusiasm for the match remained high, despite moral criticisms of the previous one. In fact, much of the tremendous fervour that spectators brought to the Sorakichi-McKeown bout stemmed precisely from their anticipation of a rough spectacle. As Joe Fahey later recalled, "how the good people did fight that night ... to get seats to see the killing take place ... and the noise and excitement fairly shook the building as the contest progressed."[174] The keen reception of the match by the public, in addition to the motives that many people held in attending it, were further indications that middle-class, reform-minded values concerning sport's appropriate purpose had not yet achieved hegemony among Winnipeg's predominantly male sport-loving citizenry. On the strength of his appearance against Sorakichi in Winnipeg, Jack McKeown began to engage in wrestling matches outside the city. Completion of the CPR meant that athletes now had rapid access not only to American centres but also to Canadian cities, and in the fall of 1887 Jack travelled to Vancouver and Victoria to engage in a series of matches against Charles Barr, all of which received detailed coverage in the Winnipeg press.[175]

During the late 1880s, wrestling lost some of its earlier popularity among Winnipeg's residents. Although the reasons for its decline in public standing are not directly apparent, allegations surfaced in August 1888 that Ed McKeown had conspired to fix a boxing match with Len McGregor, a boxing and wrestling instructor from Marquette, Michigan. McGregor, in a sworn affidavit to officials in Selkirk County, stated that upon arriving in Winnipeg to arrange a boxing contest he had met McKeown in front of his saloon and that the local man had told him that "a square fight was not much good in Winnipeg as he had a business here and it would kill him in the town to get done up."[176] The Michigan man then detailed an elaborate scheme devised by McKeown to generate interest in their match. Ed's trainer, "Jack," was also implicated in the affidavit. Although not mentioned by surname, he was presumably Ed's older brother.[177] McGregor's statement also suggested that McKeown's actions were not isolated to this incident but reflective of common practice. The allegations, which simultaneously incriminated Winnipeg's most well-known boxer and wrestler, likely soured public sentiment toward patronizing wrestling matches.

Wrestling limped along through 1890 but garnered little public support. Reflective of both prevailing uninterest during this period and ongoing concerns over the sport's respectability, the *Free Press* commented that a match between John Richardson of London, who claimed the "Championship of Canada," and G. Perrie, "Champion of the Pacific Coast," attracted "[neither] a very large nor a very select audience" to the Princess Theatre in early November 1890.[178] The condition of the referee, Ed McKeown, was an additional concern. Following the match, a man at ringside offered to back the pugilist for $100 against either contestant. McKeown declined, stating that in addition to lacking the requisite skill he was far too drunk at the time to undertake the task.[179]

The presence of alcohol had been a central concern among Winnipeg's reform-minded citizens during the campaigns against variety theatres during the

1880s, and by the early 1890s the temperance movement was a powerful political force in Manitoba.[180] Of the many theatres that had opened in the city during the early 1880s, only the Princess Theatre remained in operation by 1890, in part because it had been able to escape much of the criticism levelled against its competitors. The large facade, spacious interior, and comfortable seating gave it an aura of grandeur more commonly associated with European opera houses and symbolized, for Winnipeg's residents, the city's transition from a frontier town to a stable, respectable community.[181] The Princess Theatre was described as the finest facility of its kind west of Chicago, and "as pretty a little opera house ... as any on the continent," and its management encouraged patrons to avoid many of the activities more commonly associated with less respectable establishments, such as smoking, dangling one's legs over the balcony railings, and overindulging in alcohol.[182] McKeown's inebriated condition contravened such policies, certainly offended the large number of prohibition-minded residents in the province, and likely did little to boost the reputation of the theatre or, by extension, the respectable image of the city.

THE WINNIPEG GYMNASIUM
AND THE ORIGINS OF AMATEUR WRESTLING

Although professional wrestling had clearly fallen into widespread disrepute by 1890, wrestling's merit as a physical endeavour was still recognized by Manitobans, particularly those associated with the Winnipeg Gymnasium. As an institution, it linked physical training in the newly settled west to far more ancient traditions dating from classical antiquity. Greek philosophers such as Plato viewed gymnastic training, coupled with musical instruction, as essential components of developing well-rounded citizens. However, gymnastic exercise was not valued exclusively for its role in promoting physical improvement, contrasted to music, which enhanced the mind. Instead, Plato argued, "teachers of both have in view chiefly the improvement of the soul."[183] Thus, both music and gymnastic exercise contributed to moral improvement.[184] As early as the 1820s, gymnasiums were being constructed in the English-speaking world with the express goal of harmonizing body and mind through physical activity. Their credibility in this regard was further enhanced by medical authorities such as Dr. William P. Dewes, who, by 1823, had promoted their moral merit in the *Journal of Health*.[185] With Muscular Christianity popularized after mid-century, millennia-old ideas surrounding exercise as a morally uplifting experience gained further credibility, and gymnasiums proliferated.

Interest in gymnasiums during the nineteenth century also originated from outside the English-speaking world. Germany, in particular, must be credited with enriching the general public's appreciation of gymnasiums and what the activities carried out within their walls could accomplish. The German "turner" (national gymnastic) movement, and the physically robust specimans of manhood that it produced, were closely linked to the nation's rise in international prominence. Upon arriving in North America, German immigrants also constructed many facilities in their new communities, and others were undoubtedly inspired by their example.

By the 1850s, gymnasiums also received a degree of formal state sanction in Canada. In Ontario, Methodist preacher and reformer Egerton Ryerson, who became the province's first superintendent of education, emerged as a staunch advocate of physical training within the school system. It was only later that physical education became a curricular activity, and few schools had the resources to construct gymnasiums at the time, but the province's first teacher training facility, the Toronto Normal and Model School, had "play sheds" constructed on site in 1853.[186] By 1882, secondary schools in Ontario were required to have gymnasiums in order to be designated as "collegiates."[187] Settlers who relocated to Manitoba brought with them an invigorated enthusiasm for the age-old institution, and as early as 1883 physical training classes were operated out of Wesley Hall under the auspices of the Winnipeg Athletic Club.[188] The club was replaced four years later by the Winnipeg Gymnasium, which opened in November 1887 and conducted public exhibitions throughout the remainder of the decade in the Wesley Hall training quarters.[189]

By 1891, wrestling showed some signs of recovery in Winnipeg, not as a stand-alone amusement, but as one of many athletic endeavours being offered by the Winnipeg Gymnasium. In early March 1891, the club staged an ambitious program at the Princess Theatre that, in addition to a wrestling demonstration between two men named Smith and Baird, showcased hand balancing, horizontal bar, trapeze and ring work, tumbling, club swinging, and bayonet exercises. Also included in the show were "fancy bicycle riding" and several non-athletic acts, including orchestra music, comedy sketches, and recitations.[190] Press reports were enthusiastic, as was public patronage, the *Free Press* noting that "a local entertainment has not for a long time past drawn a better audience."[191]

During the remainder of the winter, the club staged at least one well-attended competitive program at Wesley Hall, which included wrestling.[192] Following a visit to the club in early 1892, a *Free Press* reporter expressed fond admiration not only for its programs but also for its underlying principles. Its president, H.C. Rowley, explained that an effective gymnasium program "involve[d] a great deal of careful diet and abstinence." Students were encouraged to abstain from excessive use of tobacco and alcohol and likewise cautioned to avoid "late nights and other unwholesomeness." The *Free Press* representative applauded the institution's efforts, stating that "the gymnasium is an effective factor on the side of temperance and virtue." Winnipeg's citizens were therefore encouraged to "visit this meritorious institution" if they had not already done so.[193] Through sport, the Winnipeg Gymnasium aided in developing values that many members of the middle class saw as intrinsic to appropriate "manliness."[194] However, as the report shows, the institution was tasked not only with inculcating moral virtue (similar to how the Greeks had understood the gymnasium) but also with *preventing* moral vice. Reformers from the period were acutely concerned with the many "unwholesome" diversions available to young men in rapidly expanding cities. In New York, gymnasiums were revived as early as the 1830s and 1840s explicitly to fight what historian John R. Britts termed "the perils of urban comfort," and clearly similar considerations were in play in Winnipeg by 1891.[195]

The club's emphasis on temperance and moderation offered an apparent contrast to professional wrestling in the city, perceived among certain reform-minded segments of the population to be associated with violence, alcohol, and rowdiness. An additional element that separated it from its professional counterpart was financial compensation. Unlike in other wrestling bouts staged in the city, competitors did not receive financial rewards for their performances in the form of either gate receipts or side bets. They did receive, however, medals for their performances.[196] The club's decision not to allow monetary compensation reflects its adherence to the middle-class doctrine of amateurism.

Like many elements of Manitoban culture during the late nineteenth century, amateurism originated among central Canadians of Anglo-Canadian extraction. The ideas behind amateurism were first articulated in Canada by members of the middle class, most of whom lived in Montreal and Toronto and held occupations of high social standing.[197] The doctrine's early definitions displayed a distinct class bias, explicitly excluding labourers from membership in many clubs on the basis of their occupations.[198] After 1884, Canadian amateur organizations increasingly focused on the issue of monetary compensation in defining who could be considered an amateur. For acolytes of amateurism, by the late nineteenth century, money was considered to be at the root of many of the problems associated with sport, and as a result amateur organizations, in formulating their constitutions, sought to exclude individuals who had competed for prize money, competed against someone who had accepted prize money, or offered their services at a fee.[199] Class undertones remained implicit in such definitions, since the individuals who did not (or could not) meet the amateur criteria and decided to play for money had traditionally come from society's lower echelons.[200] During the 1890s, Manitoba did not have a central governing body to oversee and enforce the amateur code. Nevertheless, amateurism's tenets were well understood, and many organizations in the province, including the Winnipeg Gymnasium, explicitly defined themselves as amateur.[201] Despite the widespread stigma attached to professionalism in the province, amateur wrestling remained embryonic in Manitoba during the nineteenth century, and by the fall of 1892 professional wrestling was once more on the ascent. Curiously, the Winnipeg Gymnasium provided the initial impetus for its rejuvenation.

PROFESSIONALISM RETURNS

In September 1892, the newly formed Winnipeg Athletic Association, an umbrella organization for various clubs, including the Winnipeg Gymnasium, Prairie City Athletic Club, and Winnipeg Lacrosse Club, hired E.W. Johnston as its athletic instructor.[202] His appointment coincided with renovations to the Wesley Hall gymnasium, and considerable fanfare heralded his arrival. A native of Barrie, Ontario, Johnston held numerous athletic records throughout his long career, including in the standing long jump, standing high jump, and tossing the caber. In addition to competitive athletics, his advance publicity testified to his previous service as an instructor at a number of institutions, among them the New York Athletic Club, Brooklyn Athletic Club, Toronto Gymnasium, and Mechanics Institute in Belleville. Johnston arrived in Winnipeg "at the request of a number of the local amateur athletes for the purposes of training a club" and operated classes out of the Winnipeg Gymnasium.[203] Although claiming expertise in a number of sports, Johnston took "special pride" in wrestling and "advanced as he [was] in years he [was] yet willing to meet anyone in an all round wrestling contest."[204]

Quick response to the news of his arrival in Winnipeg demonstrates integration of the western metropolis into the wider North American communication infrastructure and "world of sport" by 1892. Little more than a week later, the *Free Press* received the following letter from W.H. Quinn of Cornwall, Ontario, dated 6 September:

> To the Sporting Editor of the Free Press.
>
> Sir, -- I see by the Montreal and Toronto papers that E.W. John-ston is posing as a wrestler in the Prairie City. Now, I challenged him some time ago and his backers posted a small forfeit, and after all arrangements were made, hall hired and billing matter out, Mr. Johnston got ill, very ill, and could not wrestle. Again I challenged him to meet me in Toronto which he agreed to do and he very suddenly finds urgent business at Winnipeg. Now I am anxious to arrange a match with Johnston, and have forwarded $100 to Mr. Herriman of your city, who will act for me and will arrange a five style match or any kind of match that may suit Mr. Johnston; give or take $50 for expenses.
>
> *W.H. Quinn*
> Champion of Canada[205]

Public challenges, such as that offered by Quinn, had their origins among Britain's landed gentry. Aggrieved individuals would challenge other men to duels by writing letters, also called "defis," in which they would declare their desire to engage in combat. Within tavern culture, a similar custom existed, though it usually took the form of an oral declaration. With interest growing in sport during the late nineteenth century, newspapers began to publish wrestlers' challenges.[206] Both athletes and publishers found the arrangement to be mutually beneficial. For the former, it gave them an opportunity to gain public recognition as athletes and generate interest in upcoming matches, and for the latter it provided another commercial incentive for the sport-hungry public to buy their newspapers. The prevalence of newspaper challenges also indicates that certain values associated with sport, including honour and bravery, were becoming marketable commodities by the late nineteenth century.[207] During the 1880s, newspaper challenges did not play a significant role in professional wrestling in Manitoba. However, beginning in the fall of 1892, they became a regular fixture in the sport. The custom lasted for roughly the next thirty years, continuing on long after most other sports had abandoned challenges in favour of league-scheduled or prearranged meets.

Soon after Quinn's newspaper defi, other athletes began to make similar overtures. Writing from Napinka, Manitoba, John D. McPherson (also spelled MacPherson), who had previous athletic dealings with Johnston, offered to wrestle for $100 a side, catch-as-catch-can, and to meet him in either a caber tossing match or an all-round Caledonian Games contest.[208] Athletes of the period were keenly aware of the connections among respectability, professionalism, and gambling in sport in Canada. In this instance, the Winnipeg Athletic Association's new trainer was clearly cognizant that his new employers and clientele were not entirely receptive to professional sport and its accompanying histrionics. His response represents an attempt to distance himself from the often disreputable world of professionalism and, in doing so, cultivate a respectable image. On 14 September, Johnston wrote that "those who know me, know that I would never consider it any honour to meet such men as [Quinn and McPherson]. Before I came to Winnipeg I made up my mind not to be drawn into any contest while engaged as a servant of such an honourable body as the Winnipeg Athletic [A]ssociation. I wish it to be distinctly understood that I shall not pay attention to any challenge unless by the full consent of the association whom I am a servant."[209] His challengers were nevertheless persistent. McPherson's subsequent reply questioned Johnston's personal qualities and abilities as an athlete, calling Johnston "cowardly and unsportsmanlike." McPherson stated that Johnston possessed "unlimited gall" in calling himself "champion all-around athlete of the world" and that "the people of Winnipeg [would] soon have him sized up for what he really [was]."[210]

Johnston did not acquiesce to either Quinn or McPherson. However, newspaper challenges continued to appear, and by late 1893 several professional wrestlers and would-be professional wrestlers were residing in Manitoba, including C.J. Currie, F.H. Joslin, J.W. Moffatt, Elwood Rourke, and John Allen. Fred Plaisted, the prominent American sculler, who opened a gymnasium in Winnipeg in November, also became involved in the sport, staging wrestling exhibitions as part of his gym's public performances.[211] Plaisted soon became embroiled in the ongoing challenges, eventually agreeing to wrestle Joslin. The match unfortunately had to be cancelled because, on 14 December, Plaisted received serious injuries after being attacked and struck in the head with a frozen goose by an unknown assailant. The well-known athlete was confined to his bed for several days.[212]

Although Johnston and Currie did perform a wrestling demonstration as part of the Dominion Day celebrations at Brandon in 1893, publicity related to professional wrestling appears to have far exceeded the actual amount of wrestling in the province.[213] However, as the year came to a close, Johnston finally agreed to a mixed match according to Cumberland-Westmoreland and catch-as-catch-can rules against Joslin for a $100 side bet and gate receipts.[214] By 1893, despite frequently ambivalent attitudes, the local press was also beginning to move beyond simply reporting on wrestling events to taking an active role in them. Indicating a growing willingness to cater to professional wrestling, the *Free Press* sporting editor appointed Fred Plaisted as the referee.[215] The wrestling contest provided the main entertainment of an ensemble program that included high jumping, club swinging, boxing exhibitions, singing, whistling, and impersonations. Having been fed by months of debate and publicity, the all-male, "decidedly sporting crowd" demonstrated an "intense" interest in the match, and "long before the 'ball' opened a medium-sized gathering occupied the benches."[216] Despite their demonstrable enthusiasm, the spectators, numbering between 250 and 300, remained "most orderly."[217] Nevertheless, the event and its patrons did not entirely escape criticism. The most glaring concern centred on excessive tobacco consumption, "not a man being present who was not smoking or chewing."[218] As a result, the floors were slippery with tobacco juice, and a perception arose that the atmosphere, thick with smoke, impaired some of the athletic performances.[219]

Regardless of such concerns, Winnipeg's wrestling fans, as the Johnston-Joslin match clearly illustrates, were active and vocal participants in the city's burgeoning sporting community. When the wrestlers appeared on stage, "the audience was in a [state] of expectancy and all rose to their feet." Ultimately, Joslin was victorious, winning the second bout under Cumberland-Westmoreland rules and the third bout according to the edicts of catch-as-catch-can. Some concern arose within the audience during the final match over whether Johnston had actually been pinned. The *Free Press*, siding with the man whom it had appointed, argued that "the referee's position on the stage would give him a better chance to judge, and his decision was accepted as correct."[220] Capitalizing on public controversy, however, Johnston began a campaign for a rematch. Joslin's response to Johnston "blowing his horn on the streets" exhibited characteristics similar to the exchanges between Johnston and McPherson months earlier. Joslin's reply, printed four days after their match, juxtaposed the respectability of the referee and by extension that of the *Free Press*, which had appointed him, against Johnston's character: "[His accusation] is a very poor squeal to make, as the referee, though named by the Free Press, was really the man that Johnston wanted. It is a well-known fact that Mr. Johnston and Mr. Plaisted travelled a number of years together in an athletic troupe, and are firm friends, while I was only a stranger to Mr. Plaisted, but that gentleman demonstrated the part that he could not be cajoled or bought into anything that was not fair and honourable. The above facts should be sufficient to shame Mr. Johnston for intimating the least against Mr. Plaisted's decision."[221] Ultimately, Joslin and Johnston met at the *Free Press* office to draft an agreement for a rematch. Plaisted was once more agreed upon by both parties as the referee. However, on the night of their match, he refused to assume the role because of the accusations against him, and after an hour and a half was spent trying to find a suitable replacement "the audience dispersed not a little disappointed over the termination of the affair."[222]

This ending, though unsatisfactory, did not extinguish public interest in wrestling. With numerous wrestlers in the province and various challenges bandied back and forth, a tournament was finally arranged for 22 February 1894 to decide the heavyweight champion of Manitoba. R.H. Dunbar, a local bartender and prominent athlete in varied sports such as track and field, bicycle racing, and curling, lent his patronage to the event by offering a gold medal emblematic of the provincial title.[223] Five men, John Blackey, E.W. Johnston, F.H. Joslin, W.J. Moffitt, all of Winnipeg, and Elwood Rourke, of Emerson, ultimately contested for the championship. Indicative of wrestling's growing appeal in Manitoba's other burgeoning communities and the widespread attention that the event generated, John Allen of Brandon and John Sullivan of Rat Portage also signalled their desire to participate.[224] The tournament, staged according to mixed styles, was well attended by the public, and after a series of matches Joslin emerged victorious. Plaisted once again acted as referee after Ed McKeown declined the role. The matches were all contested according to the rules and elicited none of the controversy associated with January's bout between Johnston and Joslin.[225] Still, concerns alluding to the respectability of the event and its patrons were voiced once again, particularly by the *Free Press*. Following boxing bouts described as "two preposterous exhibitions of juvenile sparring," there was an extended wait before the wrestling contests commenced. In the interim, "the audience was left ... to amuse themselves with the foul language and absurd behaviour of a drunken man." Indicating that the management was not entirely acquiescent to such behaviour, however, the man was eventually ejected by the referee.[226] Excessive tobacco smoke was once again an issue, the paper commenting that, following a musical rendition of "MacManus' Suit o'Clothes" by Harry Logrenin in which the audience asked for an encore, "the singer found the smoky atmosphere too much for his lungs and had to withdraw."[227] The report's general tenor suggested that, even if the wrestlers were competent athletes, the event itself was poorly organized, and the behaviour of the clientele was considered, in several instances, less than respectable. Despite such concerns, it is clear that professional wrestling had a strong public appeal, and by 1894 other communities in the province, including Brandon, were also staging shows.[228]

The heavyweight wrestling tournament for the championship of Manitoba was the pinnacle event for the sport during 1894. By July, the public was evidently growing sceptical of the wrestling events being staged by the province's grappling contingent. On 1 July, Johnston held a variety athletic show in Winnipeg that cast doubt on his heralded athletic reputation. Voicing general suspicion of the event, the *Nor'Wester* commented that "the exhibition of sparring, wrestling, etc. which was given by E.W. Johns[t]on et. al. of Winnipeg on Dominion Day might be termed a fake."[229] Likewise, a few weeks later it was reported that "Two Fakirs," Johnston and Joslin, were visiting Fort William for a series of matches.[230] The precise source of the suspicion around Joslin is not known, but it is clear that, by the middle of 1894, professional wrestling was entering a period of decline. Amateur wrestling, which remained in the shadows of its professional counterpart, also suffered from a lack of public favour by mid-1894.[231] By 1895, it appears that Johnston, the much-heralded director of the Winnipeg Athletic Association, had left the city.[232] Nevertheless, newspaper challenges persisted, and wrestlers, including Joslin, continued to engage in matches occasionally.[233]

CONCLUSION

Although wrestling had lost some of its public appeal, by the closing years of the nineteenth century it was a well-established sport in Manitoba. In the quarter century after Confederation, what had once been a cultural ritual among First Nations peoples, voyageurs, and York boat men of mixed-blood descent took on new forms and meanings as large numbers of British Canadian settlers immigrated to the province. Members of the new majority consciously transferred many of their existing customs and institutions, including wrestling, in an effort to recreate their cultural heritage on the western plains. Vast improvements to the province's communication infrastructure during the period gave the public unprecedented access to local, national, and international information about the sport. Developments in transportation infrastructure likewise gave athletes rapid and convenient access to Winnipeg and later other centres in Manitoba. Wrestling's growth in the province did not occur, however, without difficulty. British Canadians did not possess a homogeneous worldview, and competing conceptions of wrestling's appropriate social purpose often helped to shroud the sport in controversy and disrepute. On one end of the spectrum were middle-class reformers who viewed wrestling as vehicle for "manly" physical improvement and character building. On the other end were members of the province's large bachelor population. As both participants in and spectators of wrestling, they were often affiliated with taverns, variety theatres, and various illicit activities, including blood sports and gambling, that engendered controversy among reform-minded segments of the population. However, Manitoba society was not always so easily dichotomized. Newspapers, driven by both reform and profit motives, alternately criticized the sport and those associated with it and granted it considerable column space. Likewise, wrestlers, while frequently embroiled in controversy, often attempted to appropriate for themselves an image of middle-class respectability. Such issues did not disappear in the ensuing years, and, with sport's growing appeal in the province by the turn of the twentieth century, professional wrestling became an even more popular, and simultaneously controversial, activity.

Chapter 2

MANITOBA'S PROS
PROFESSIONAL WRESTLING DURING THE WESTERN BOOM, 1896-1914

After much activity in Manitoba between 1893 and 1895, professional wrestling entered an interlude of relative dormancy that lasted until the early twentieth century. Winnipeg was the central transportation hub for the Prairies, and professional wrestlers invariably passed through it en route to other parts of Canada and the United States, and challenges sometimes accompanied their arrival in the city. Likewise, wrestlers, including Brandon's W.H. West, continued to reside in the province and expressed their willingness to engage in competitive matches.[1] Nevertheless, few professional wrestling contests appear to have been staged in Manitoba during the period. The denouement in local wrestling activity might have been partly attributable to the controversies surrounding prominent athletes such as E.W. Johnston and F.H. Joslin. However, it is likely that the Klondike gold rush, which began in the summer of 1897, also redirected many professional athletes' attention away from Manitoba and other regions and toward the far northwest. Many wrestlers and boxers from across North America made the long trek to the Yukon Territory, and both sports became a regular form of entertainment in mining camps and communities such as Dawson City over the next four years.[2] Members of Manitoba's sporting fraternity were similarly lured away to Canada's new mining frontier, including Ed McKeown, who took part ownership of a freight-hauling operation on the rivers north of Whitehorse.[3] Although the Klondike gold rush might have assisted in temporarily stifling wrestling in Manitoba, it ultimately served to bring a great deal of international attention to Canada, and the discovery of vast quantities of gold helped to provide economic stimulus to both international markets and the Canadian economy.[4] By the turn of the century, numerous settlers were arriving in the Canadian west, and during the next fourteen years Manitoba's population increased by over 80 percent. This population growth was impressive, but even more remarkable was the growth in overall popularity of sports during this period. Virtually all sports experienced what Morris Mott termed an "explosion of activity" prior to the Great War as both participation in sport grew and a wider variety of sporting activities became available to the public for the first time.[5]

Solidly in accord with larger trends, professional wrestling saw a dramatic rise in popularity during the first decade and a half of the twentieth century as a growing number of athletes appeared in ever more frequent events staged not only in Winnipeg and Brandon but also in communities throughout the province. As a popular spectator activity, professional wrestling, even more than during previous years, became a terrain riddled with varied and frequently competing meanings. In many instances, the sport and those who participated in it were heralded as exemplars of ideal human physical form, masculinity, and scientific progressivism. Simultaneously, wrestling also satisfied the demands of many members of the public for rough physical spectacles and expressions of aggressive masculinity. On a more basic level, wrestling also prospered in Manitoba because many athletes, exhibiting some or all of these desirable traits, were seen to represent the communities or regions in which they lived. However, the ongoing association with money ensured that wrestling remained perpetually embroiled in controversy as excessive violence, poor sportsmanship, inconclusive endings to matches, and evidence of outright fixing regularly threatened to "kill" its popularity among all segments of the public. Wrestling, however, continued to thrive in spite of its problems, and in the four years before the Great War it attracted some of the sport's most well-known athletes to the province's largest and most prestigious public venues.

WRESTLING AND THE MALE PHYSICAL FORM

Between 1900 and 1904, professional wrestling matches were periodically staged in centres such as Winnipeg and Brandon, but the sport remained largely out of public favour. After 1905, however, wrestling entered a period of sustained popularity that lasted until the Great War. Public interest in wrestling can naturally be attributed, in part, to the overall rise in attention accorded to all sports. Wrestling rode the momentum that many other sports experienced in Manitoba during the same era. However, increased interest in wrestling was more than a by-product of the "explosion" that affected other athletic disciplines. Part of the public's fascination with professional wrestling derived from the fact that many practitioners were popularly heralded as exemplars of perfect male physical development. Much more than other prominent sports, such as hockey and baseball, wrestling allowed not only for the expression of athletic skill but also for a visual display of the ideal physical form. Whereas athletes in most other sports wore uniforms that covered much of their bodies, a wrestler's apparel typically consisted either of shorts or of long wool tights that prevented abrasions to the knee. Generally, wrestlers performed with leather shoes, though some chose to perform barefoot. Almost without exception, wrestling took place with both contestants stripped to the waist, completely displaying the upper torso. Underneath the theatre stage lights, spectators were therefore able to gain a full estimation of their physical development. The fact that wrestlers performed according to these conditions was not inconsequential, since both the press and the attendant public displayed keen appreciation for a wrestler's aesthetic qualities.

As already noted, the second half of the nineteenth century witnessed a re-orientation among many members of the middle class toward embracing a more physical expression of Christianity. Although interest in sport stemmed, in part, from theological considerations, there was also a growing concern among many reform-minded members of the population that the modern, urban lifestyle, characterized by long hours of sedentary work and mechanization, robbed men of their physical strength and vigour. By the time Manitoba entered Confederation in 1870, health reformers were already espousing the notion that members of industrialized society were physically inferior to their more physically active predecessors. Over the next several decades, the idea continued to gain wide circulation, and a growing body of literature related to health and fitness repeatedly emphasized the correlation between modernity and physical degeneracy.[6] In Manitoba, as elsewhere, these ideas received widespread articulation. The Portage la Prairie *Weekly Review*, for example, reporting on a recent meeting of the British Medical Association, noted concerns regarding "the danger to the nation's health, owing to the changed habits of the past half-century, which had led to marked muscular degenerations."[7] Similarly, the *Free Press* stressed that the modern office worker faced the lamentable dilemma of possessing an overworked mind and an underworked body: "The modern business man moves as carefully and carries his head as level as if he was carrying a well filled bowl of water. He walks from his easy chair to his carriage, from his carriage to his office desk, he is even taken up one flight of stairs in an elevator. He sits at his desk and presses buttons and the work is done. What has all this done? It has taken away all of his physical activity and multiplied the work of the brain.... All these changes have been at the sacrifice of the demand for physical activity."[8] Officials within Manitoba's educational system also expressed concerns over the lack of physical activity undertaken by some students, particularly those living in urban environments. Edward Ernest Best, a Manitoba school inspector from 1888 to 1932, contrasted the rural student, whose long walks to school produced "a healthy vigour necessary to offset the ills of the school room," with the urban resident, who had to walk only a few blocks. The situation, in his view, was exacerbated by the development of automobiles. Best colourfully lamented that "one might sometimes wonder how many generations will pass before humanity becomes as legless as a tadpole."[9]

By the end of the nineteenth century, the "modern," degenerate male body was being contrasted with a physical ideal that emphasized a high degree of muscular development and symmetry.[10] Although the health benefits of sport and exercise had long been espoused, from the 1890s on authorities on health and physical development, termed "physical culturalists," drew heightened inspiration from the classical world.[11] Bernarr MacFadden, a former wrestler turned publishing entrepreneur and one of North America's best-known physical culture acolytes during the period, noted (and simultaneously promoted) the shift in popular perceptions concerning the ideal male physique: "Muscular power is beginning to assume its proper importance in the minds of every sensible man and woman. A few years ago, so-called refined persons were inclined to belittle its value. They affected to associate large, well-developed muscles with various undesirable mental and bodily characteristics."[12] Emphasizing the merits of classical Greek and Roman culture, MacFadden stressed that "we of to-day are becoming re-born in the wisdom of the ancients in that we no longer see anything but the pitiful or contemptible in the physique that is not strong, undefiled and wholesome."[13] MacFadden, as well as many of his contemporaries, drew their inspiration from both the physiques recorded for posterity in sculpted marble and the mythological legends of figures such as Apollo and Hercules.[14] However, they simultaneously recognized that ancient ideals of physical perfection, when combined with modern, "scientific" innovations, could produce a level of physical development that surpassed the accomplishments seen in previous millennia.[15] By applying rational, systematic principles, the same ideas that had shaped modern industrial-capitalist society, the problems associated with growing "degeneracy" could be overcome.[16]

The best-known exemplar of classical physical perfection made better through modern, "scientific" training was Eugen Sandow, a Prussian physical culturalist, strongman, stage performer, author, and wrestler who, at least according to his own publicity, transformed himself from a frail and sickly child into a man whose abilities "rank[ed] him with the heroes who are credited with doing heroic deeds in the Homeric age."[17] Although certainly not the first performer to earn a living through publicly exhibiting his strength and physique, Sandow, an excellent self-promoter and businessman, did much to further popularize the classically inspired image of muscular strength and development.[18] Manitoba's residents were well aware of his exploits during the 1890s and early 1900s and part of the larger movement toward embracing the new, highly muscular model of idealized masculinity that harkened back to the pre-Christian era. Newspapers throughout Manitoba often reported on his impressive physical development, and the Winnipeg Public Library added *Sandow's System of Physical Training* to its bookshelves shortly after the book's publication in 1894. Recognizing that the name Sandow was synonymous with strength and health, advertisers commonly invoked it in promoting various gadgets and pills aimed at customers wishing to enhance their physical capacities.[19] Winnipeggers were clearly fascinated by the subject of muscular development, and they attended stage performances such as those given by Santell, "The Modern Hercules," who appeared at the Bijou Theatre in March 1906.[20] Other physical culture experts, such as Professor J.B. Roche, who visited Winnipeg in 1903 and advertised himself in newspapers with a full-length engraving displaying his muscular physique, toured the continent offering training in "converting the human body from weakness into strength, curing by systematic, intelligent physical instruction."[21]

Part of professional wrestling's appeal during the same period derived from the notion that many of its practitioners represented the pinnacle of male physical development. They were heralded as experts in a sport that served as "an unfailing aid to health and longevity and a developer of every muscle," and both the press and the public frequently praised professional wrestlers for their aesthetic virtues. Like their strongman counterparts, matmen were described in terms that invoked classical heroic imagery.[22] Toronto's Artie Edmunds, a featherweight who made several appearances in Winnipeg as both a boxer and a wrestler between 1906 and 1910, performed under the moniker of "The Pocket Hercules."[23] Although he was only 122 pounds, the *Free Press* remarked that "he is such a bunch of symmetrical muscles. At chest expansion he even has the great Sandow skinned.... Every ounce of him is muscle and the shoulders resemble those of middleweights."[24] Remarkably similar language described other wrestlers. "Yankee" Rogers, an American heavyweight wrestler who expressed interest in wrestling in Winnipeg, was variously touted as a "young Hercules" with a "magnificent physique" as well as a "modern Samson" and a "close student of physical culture."[25]

Even if not drawing direct comparisons with mythological heroes, commentary testified to the notion that the grapplers appearing on Manitoba mats represented the ideal male form, and the phrase "magnificent specimens of manhood" frequently accompanied their descriptions.[26] The public clearly demonstrated its eagerness to show appreciation for such "specimens." When, for instance, Iowa's Frank Gotch, the heavyweight catch-as-catch-can wrestling champion of the world, appeared in the city in March 1911, both he and his opponent, George Eberg, received praise for the "remarkable development" displayed after removing their ring robes, and when they came to grips "a shout of admiration went up [in the audience] over their magnificent appearance."[27]

The public understood that attaining a wrestler's physique necessitated systematic training and self-discipline, and newspapers regularly reported on the training protocols followed by professional wrestlers prior to their matches.[28] Conscious self-denial for the purpose of improvement had a long-standing resonance within Protestant culture, and wrestlers were often touted for their adherence to this principle.[29] The well-developed physique represented an outward manifestation of conscious self-mastery: a process that involved adherence to a lifestyle that often necessitated a rejection of the very habits allegedly leading to widespread degeneracy. Professional wrestlers often reinforced the idea that rigorous self-discipline went hand in hand with success by publicly touting an abstemious lifestyle. "Yankee" Rogers, the Manitoba *Free Press* reported, "[did] not use tobacco or liquor in any form." Even more stringent in this respect was Martin "Farmer" Burns, trainer of future world champion Frank Gotch and claimant to the American catch-as-catch-can wrestling title during the mid-1890s. Burns remarked at fifty that "I do not indulge in any vice that weakens a man physically. I am regular in my daily life. I exercise judiciously, constantly, and observe all sensible rules of health and hygiene."[30]

Technological advances in the newspaper industry further reinforced the importance of muscular development as an attractive element of professional wrestling matches. Throughout the latter half of the nineteenth century, photographs were replicated in newspapers as engravings, an extremely time-consuming process that required skilled artisans. After 1897, however, it became possible to reproduce half-tone photographs on printing presses.[31] Newspapers, including those in Manitoba, quickly adopted the new technology. After 1900, many wrestlers, realizing that their bodies were marketable commodities, began to use their well-developed physiques to good advantage by appearing in photographs showcasing their muscular development.[32] Few athletes in any era took better advantage of their physiques to generate widespread publicity than the "Russian Lion," George Hackenschmidt, an excellent, all-round athlete who began his professional career as a Greco-Roman wrestler in 1899 and later earned recognition as the world's catch-as-catch-can champion after beating the American title claimant, Tom Jenkins, at Madison Square Garden in May 1905.[33] Hackenschmidt, in addition to appearing in wrestling matches throughout Europe, North America, and Australia, gave posing exhibitions, lectured to the public, and published extensively on the subjects of wrestling, physical culture, and philosophy.[34] His enormously muscled frame captivated audiences wherever he performed, and, with the introduction of photojournalism, members of the general public who lived outside the cities where he appeared were able to share in that appreciation. Although Hackenschmidt never visited Manitoba during his wrestling career, newspaper reports often carried photographs of the Russian Lion in muscular repose.[35] Naturally, wrestlers who appeared locally before the public also readily used photography to promote themselves for upcoming bouts, and by 1914 pictures depicting a grappler with his hands behind his back, showcasing his neck and torso development, or with his arms folded across his bare chest were well-established conventions in newspapers.[36]

During the two decades preceding the Great War, members of the public did not confine their fascination with a wrestler's physical development to qualitative descriptions, mythic images, and photographic representations. Interest also centred on a wrestler's precise bodily measurements. By the late nineteenth century, part of the public's curiosity with the male form included a near obsession with the tape measure. Popular physical culture texts from the era, including those written by wrestlers George Hackenschmidt and Arthur Saxon, as well as others outside the English-speaking world, such as Edmond Desbonnet in *Les rois de la lutte*, capitalized on this trend by devoting considerable space to either the author's physical proportions or those of other prominent wrestlers.[37]

The study of human physical proportions, termed "anthropometry," was centuries old by the time wrestlers began including measurements in their publications. Originating among European artists during the early modern era, it was popularized by members of the scientific community beginning in the 1830s. Within medical circles, it was hoped that careful study of the human form could establish links between physique and illness. Exercises could then be prescribed to remedy problems. There were also, however, distinctly dark social implications with the burgeoning field of study. In particular, associated disciplines such as craniology and phrenology sought to apply morality to measurement by determining the relations between physical morphology and personal character.[38]

Its more problematic applications aside, in the sporting realm anthropometry was also applied to bring a sense of predictability to human athletic endeavours. Driving this interest was the belief that, like the "scientific" industrial processes made more efficient through careful application of statistics and probability theory, similar data analysis could help to determine the "perfect" human form and predict athletic achievement.[39] Physical measurements were examined as a means of determining how proficient athletes could accomplish various physical feats. For example, in analyzing the unusual endurance of Stanislaus Zbyszko, a heavyweight wrestler whose "physique [was] almost beyond comprehension" and "looked upon by physical culturalists as a marvel," doctors speculated that his massive chest, measuring fifty-five inches on a five-foot-seven-inch frame, gave him the collective lung capacity of three average 200-pound men.[40] It was likewise common for newspapers to print charts comparing two combatants' physical measurements prior to a match with the goal of ascertaining, in an empirical sense, the probable outcome of the bout. The heavyweight catch-as-catch-can wrestling champions, Frank Gotch and George Hackenschmidt, met one another in title bouts on two occasions, the first encounter on 3 April 1908 and the second on 4 September 1911. Throughout North America, there was enormous public interest in both matches. Winnipeg, as part of the larger world of sport, shared in the enthusiasm, granting both encounters unprecedented media coverage. Part of the speculation preceding the matches centred on both men's physical proportions. Local wrestler Dan Simpson, in an interview with the *Free Press*, picked Hackenschmidt as the probable winner: "Hack, I think, is too strong and quick for the American."[41] Listing the Russian Lion's measurements, the *Free Press* reporter seemed to agree, commenting that, though technically more proficient at the catch-as-catch-can style, "[Gotch] will give away from ten to fifteen pounds in weight and physically will be inferior to his rival in all points of important comparison."[42] However, when official measurements were released a week later, the *Free Press* did not seem so disposed to offer strong support for the Russian grappler: "A comparison of measurements of Gotch and Hackenschmidt shows that the men are more evenly matched as to size and weight than most people imagine. Hackenschmidt has the bigger upper body, which is very essential to a successful wrestler, but in other respects there is little to choose between them."[43] Ultimately, anatomical quantification helped little in forecasting the match's outcome, since Gotch defeated his more muscular counterpart in just over two hours. Nevertheless, the results of a single match, no matter how high profile, did little to stem the larger social inclination toward such "scientific" analysis. Prior to their second title match, won in even more convincing fashion by the Iowa native, detailed measurements again formed part of the pre-match speculation.[44]

Although, on the surface, a wrestler's physical form represented a celebration of qualities such as physical strength, proper physical development, and self-discipline, for some individuals there were also undeniably erotic elements to both the images associated with wrestling and the matches themselves. The lack of attire in wrestling matches and promotional photographs could be contrasted with the much greater amount of clothing deemed acceptable in everyday social interaction. Even in public spaces that tolerated less clothing, such as beaches and swimming pools, an uncovered male torso breached the limits of respectability. Male visitors to Lake Winnipeg, for example, commonly wore full-length trousers and collared shirts when on the beach, and even those who went swimming were clothed, at a minimum, in shorts and sleeveless shirts. The selection of bathing suits offered to men by large-scale department stores such as Eaton's was likewise wholly in keeping with prevailing social mores.[45] For some segments of Manitoba's population, wrestling likely represented one of the few public environments in which they could witness the alluring spectacle of a male body in a combined state of action and undress. Notably, however, no concern was raised in Manitoba related to the sport's potentially homoerotic undertones, indicating that heterosexual interpretations of the sport's purpose remained distinctly privileged over the interests of those who, through wrestling, sought to explore alternative erotic desires.[46] The possibility of legal censure, common in the region, coupled with the ongoing efforts of civic officials to thwart challenges to heteronormative conduct, further silenced interpretations that openly deviated from the established norm.[47] Public wrestling matches were not safe spaces for the vocal expression of same-sex inclinations.

WRESTLING AS "SCIENCE"

The public appreciated wrestling as a form of training that helped to perfect the male form, and wrestlers were often heralded, on the basis of their impressive physical development, as exemplars of ideal manhood and self-mastery. However, wrestling was not merely popular because of the aesthetic qualities exhibited by its practitioners. It was described as a scientific undertaking by many of its advocates. Since, by the end of the nineteenth century, many members of Western industrialized society viewed science with a near-religious reverence for its capacity to further human progress, characterizing any undertaking as scientific lent it a degree of legitimacy. As was the case with prize fighting during this period, appropriating the language of science represented an attempt by the sport's advocates to create a broader public support base and dampen criticism that had long been levelled against wrestling.[48] However, using the term "science" in reference to wrestling was not purely a rhetorical device that veiled otherwise disreputable behaviour. Scientific wrestling referred to a specific style that emphasized an extensive technical knowledge base. In particular, wrestlers who could apply effective offensive manoeuvres and efficiently counter or escape from dangerous positions and holds were regarded as scientific.[49] Speed accompanied science, and wrestlers or matches branded as scientific were usually also described in terms that alluded to their brisk character.[50] Strength and science were not mutually exclusive, and both traits were considered important.[51] Yet a wrestler who accomplished by brute force what might have been otherwise accomplished by technique was not scientific.[52] Additionally, scientific wrestling implied a close adherence to the rules and was therefore also denoted as "clean" wrestling.[53] Thus, just as knowledge, efficiency, and speed were regarded as hallmarks of scientific progress in the larger social context, so too were they seen as the most desirable traits in a wrestler. Early-twentieth-century Manitobans clearly showed their enthusiastic support for scientific wrestling exhibitions. Jack Downs, for instance, "fairly electrified" Brandon wrestling fans with the "superior science" that he demonstrated during a January 1906 appearance in the Wheat City, and two years later "time after time the crowd jumped to their feet shouting their applause at some more than usually clever piece of attack or defensive work" during a "fast" bout of "scientific wrestling" between local

Winnipeg wrestlers Dan Simpson and Herman Mace.[54] Indeed, technical, fast, and clean bouts of this nature led the sports editor of the *Free Press* to label wrestling as "the world's most scientific indoor pastime."[55]

WRESTLING'S LOCAL APPEAL

Professional wrestling drew support from members of the Manitoba public because they found in it many of the values that they, as a society, held in high esteem.[56] However, wrestling also engendered a significant public following for more immediate reasons, the most significant being that a number of highly skilled athletes chose to take up residence in the province. In many sports, strong hometown talent proved to be critical to their long-term viability. Athletes with legitimate ties to a town or city became sources of civic pride, and their achievements were often seen to represent the community as a whole.[57] In professional wrestling, establishing oneself in a particular area was referred to as homesteading.[58] As the largest urban centre in the province, Winnipeg attracted wrestlers who called the city home for various lengths of time. Certainly, the three most prominent in this respect prior to the First World War, however, were Charles Gustafson, Ernest Sundberg, and Alex Stewart.

Born on 5 April 1886 in Halmstad, Sweden, Charles Gustafson arrived in Winnipeg in 1907 from the United States, where he had lived for the previous four years.[59] During his early years in the city, Gustafson worked for the local Nelson Sash and Door Manufacturing Company but later went into business for himself as a hotel proprietor.[60] Wrestling as a middleweight (158 pounds), he made his first appearance on Winnipeg mats on 4 October 1907.[61] As a member of the local Swedish community, Gustafson received considerable support from his fellow countrymen even during his earliest forays onto local mats.[62] Over the next several years, he secured numerous victories over both local and visiting wrestlers, and among Winnipeg's Swedish population, the *Free Press* noted in 1909, "[Gustafson] is their idol, and they believe him invincible."[63] However popular he was among his countrymen, it is also clear that, as he garnered further accolades, including claims to both the Manitoba and the Canadian middleweight titles in November 1907 and November 1909, respectively, his popularity became more widespread.[64] By 1910–11, he was hailed as "Winnipeg's pride" and "the pride of Winnipeg wrestling fans."[65]

MEETS WORTHY OPPONENT

CHAS. GUSTAFSON,
Winnipeg's Favorite Wrestler, Who Meets Charlie Conkle, of Hamilton, for the Middleweight Championship of Canada at Walker Theatre Monday Night.

2. Swedish-born middleweight Charles Gustafson was Winnipeg's most prominent professional mat artist in the decade before World War I and claimed the Canadian Middleweight Title. Source: Manitoba *Free Press*, 26 February 1910.

Ernest (Ernie) Sundberg, like Charles Gustafson, was a native of Sweden. Born in Lulea on 2 March 1884, he made his Winnipeg debut less than three weeks after his fellow countryman, appearing as a preliminary attraction prior to the main event between Gustafson and another well-known local wrestler, Herman Mace.[66] When not engaged in wrestling matches, Sundberg worked as a carpenter and carpentry foreman for the Nelson Sash and Door Manufacturing Company.[67] As a featherweight (124 pounds) wrestler, he did not garner the same degree of public attention as his larger counterpart. Between late 1907 and early 1910, he appeared exclusively on undercards, winning all but one of his matches.[68] Finally, on 8 February 1910, having defeated numerous local and visiting wrestlers, Sundberg bested Toronto's "Pocket Hercules," Artie Edmunds, in a main event for the American featherweight championship. It was described as a match "that [had] never been equalled in Winnipeg, and for speed, maybe never in America," and Sundberg had clearly gained a considerable local following by this point, for the theatre "reverberated with cheers" after his victory.[69]

As Ernie Sundberg reached his athletic zenith, a second featherweight wrestler, Alex Stewart, arrived in Winnipeg. Stewart had accrued numerous wrestling titles in both England and Scotland before moving to Manitoba in 1910 and taking employment as a clerk with the Timothy Eaton's Company.[70] Initially, he had difficulty securing an opponent in the city, but public interest soon dictated that he face Sundberg, who, as Winnipeg's featherweight standout, was his most logical opponent. Sundberg and Stewart, extremely well matched, wrestled each other three times, and it was only on their third encounter that the Scot managed to gain a victory over the Swede and, in doing so, secure a claim to the Canadian featherweight title.[71] Thereafter, Sundberg retired from professional mats, and Stewart took his place as Winnipeg's featherweight par excellence. Like Sundberg, Stewart proved to be a popular wrestler among local fans, and he went on to defend his title locally in main events against visiting wrestlers such as Moose Jaw's Bert Simmons and Boston's Jack Forbes.[72]

During the period before the Great War, various theatres, arenas, and halls throughout Winnipeg hosted professional wrestling, often before large and crowded houses. Between late 1906 and late 1909, however, one facility absent from that list was the city's largest and most prestigious venue for live entertainment, the Walker Theatre. Cornelius Powers (C.P.) Walker opened his namesake facility in December 1906, with the purpose of offering the public large-scale, "high-class" productions impossible to stage in Winnipeg's existing facilities.[73] By

ERNIE SUNBERG.

Clever Little Wrestler Who Meets Art Edmunds, the "Pocket Hercules," at Walker Theatre Tuesday Night.

St. Paul. Only one man on the five was not at his best, four working like Trojans.

There was nothing worth mention at the Royal. The ' caught napping and went u scores'.

AT THE ROYAL.

Venice—

Rocco	125
Brady	159
Caito ... ...'	153
Reeves	186
Cancilla	159
	782

Royals—

Crealock	161
Harkness	158
Daly	142
Adair	156
Grandage	196
	813

Royals 2, Venice 1.

AT THE SARATOG

Saratogas—

Roos	216
Gibson	167
Riley	159
McBeth	177
McKean	180
	899

Wanderers—

Ruggles	188
Scrase	160
Roblin	159
McLean	182
Cuthbert	136
	825

RAILROADERS' LEA

In the C. N. R. league at alleys last night the Freight three straight games from t vice. The score:

Car Service—

Nicol..	.129
Wiggins..	.161
McIntosh..	.79
MacKinley	.170
Totals	.539

Freight Tariff—

Buchanan	*161
Snell	.200
Grant..	.169
Brotman	.172
Blain	.174
Totals	.717

CARSON IN TEX

"Kit" Carson, formerly w

---

3. Ernest (Ernie) Sundberg stands at attention. Like his counterpart Charles Gustafson, Sundberg hailed from Sweden and had a large local following in Winnipeg. Source: Manitoba *Free Press*, 5 February 1910.

that time, Walker was already familiar with professional wrestling, having staged several bouts during the previous five years as owner of the smaller Winnipeg Theatre. His desire to ensure that his enterprise retained its status as legitimate theatre might have prevented him from staging wrestling on the premises. By November 1909, however, recognizing that the sport had considerable commercial appeal, he re-entered the wrestling business. In keeping with his existing approach to staging entertainment, Walker chose to feature only well-known talent in the main events. As established local wrestling stars, Gustafson and Sundberg headlined the first five wrestling programs staged at the Walker Theatre.

By early 1910, wrestling was a popular attraction for the theatre, and thereafter it began to host internationally known professional wrestlers, including Quebec's Eugene Tremblay, recognized as the holder of the *Police Gazette* lightweight (135 pounds) wrestling belt, and Minnesota's Walter Miller, claimant to the world's welterweight wrestling title.[74] Since 1896, Winnipeg had periodically staged heavyweight wrestling, but the vast majority of local matches, and local talent, were in the lighter weight divisions. In 1910, Walker began to book some of the world's most recognized heavyweights, beginning with Seattle's Benjamin Franklin (B.F.) Roller, who appeared against Ireland's Pat Connelly in June that year. Other elite heavyweight talent, including Stanislaus Zbyszko, contender for the world's heavyweight title, subsequently appeared before Winnipeg audiences in 1912. Certainly eclipsing all of them in fame, however, was the undisputed world's heavyweight champion, Frank Gotch.

When Gotch appeared at the Walker Theatre in March 1911, he was the most expensive athlete ever brought to the city.[75] Although the exact sum paid to retain his services was never disclosed, he generally commanded a minimum guarantee of $1,000 for an appearance.[76] Close to 3,000 people attended his match against George Eberg, with ticket prices ranging from seventy-five cents to three dollars, so it is probable that Walker received a substantial return on his investment.[77] Gustafson, Sundberg, and Stewart continued to wrestle in Winnipeg, but by the time Walker began to book internationally renowned athletes, beginning with B.F. Roller in March 1910, they generally did so either as preliminary attractions at the Walker Theatre or as headliners in the city's smaller venues.

As in virtually all other areas of economic and cultural life, Winnipeg remained Manitoba's dominant centre for professional wrestling. However, wrestling also proved to be an attraction in some of the province's smaller communities. Here again successful local talent provided much of the impetus for public interest. In Souris during 1908, for example, Herb Lee emerged as a popular attraction by defeating several prominent Winnipeg wrestlers, among them Charles Dalager, Herman Mace, and Dan Simpson. Particularly remarkable was the fact that Lee never trained for the sport and only stepped onto a mat to engage in matches.[78] As the Souris *Plaindealer* noted in October, "Lee has activity and strength, but has never been in a position to acquire the science."[79] Despite his technical shortcomings, his position as a Souris resident evidently granted him a vociferous local backing, and fans were "greatly elated over [his] success," and "the [Sowden Hall] roof was well raised high by the wild and appreciative cheering" when he proved to be the superior of out-of-town opponents.[80] In other Manitoba towns, including Minnedosa, professional wrestlers also made periodic appearances.[81] Even in the absence of local matches, however, the public, as in earlier years, was kept abreast of important contests staged both in Winnipeg and abroad.[82]

WRESTLING AND AGGRESSIVE MANHOOD

Professional wrestling's popularity in Manitoba before the First World War was certainly linked to prevailing notions of the male body and the sport as a "scientific" enterprise. Additionally, strong local talent helped to engender in local fans a deep sense of community pride. However, interwoven with these ideas were other interpretations of the sport often connected to less "progressive," and frequently more controversial, social aims and desires. Much like boxing, wrestling was what Kevin Wamsley and David Whitson termed a "confrontative sport."[83] As such, it had, as its central goal, the deliberate physical domination of another human being. As in the 1880s, many members of the public continued to value wrestling not only as a scientific exhibition of skill but also as an expression of masculinity that embraced physical toughness, aggressiveness, and overtly rough behaviour. Indeed, by the end of the nineteenth century and the beginning of the twentieth century, aggressive expressions of masculinity gained even more widespread acceptance than in previous decades and were contrasted with qualities such as gentleness and passivity, commonly derided for being effeminate and therefore unmanly.[84] Domination became increasingly regarded as a worthy, manly value.[85]

A degree of roughness was widely accepted, and even celebrated, in professional wrestling. To be certain, wrestling was not some form of free fighting, as had existed in the voyageur era. In Manitoba, professional wrestling was commonly conducted according to the *Police Gazette* rules, considered after the turn of the century as "the recognized authority on wrestling on this continent."[86] As early as 1904, the Manitoba *Free Press* retained a copy of *Police Gazette* publisher Richard K. Fox's *Book of Rules for All Sports*, which included the rules for wrestling, and it is clear that, even in smaller communities such as Souris, *Police Gazette* methods were followed.[87] However, in professional wrestling contests, it was expected that the referee governing the matches would "display a certain amount of discretion apart from the rules."[88] As such, "if Police Gazette rules [were] observed [in professional wrestling bouts] considerable roughing [was] to be expected."[89] In commenting on Frank Gotch's 1911 performance at the Walker Theatre against George Eberg, for instance, the *Free Press* noted that the challenger "roughed it about in the most approved style before they went to the mat after ten minutes."[90] In a corresponding, albeit more poetic, fashion, the *Tribune* stated that "in slapping one another for a hold they resembled two bulls about to engage in a death conflict."[91] Once on the mat, Gotch asserted his superior ground-wrestling skills, and Eberg "took a bit of roughing from a punishing arm-lock."[92] The *Tribune* likewise noted the many "punishing holds" employed by the world's champion and how, while he had his adversary splayed on the mat, "his knee was always pressing some portion of Eberg's body."[93] None of the three daily newspapers, however, evidenced any negative reaction to either Eberg's or Gotch's methods during the match, nor did the public object to the style of wrestling.[94] Indeed, the *Telegram* opined that "[Gotch] did not, however, show any trace of rough tactics ... but on the other hand there is nothing ladylike in the manner in which he goes after his opponent," further suggesting that his methods, though somewhat aggressive, were common in professional wrestling at the time and within the realm of public acceptability.[95] Such statements also implicitly emphasized the contrast between the explicitly masculine endeavour of aggressively striving for physical dominance and more feminine traits such as gentleness and passive civility. To highlight the point, it was often stated in celebratory terms that wrestling was "no pink tea affair."[96]

As might be expected, because of the sport's aggressive nature, wrestlers frequently ran the risk of physical harm in matches. Many matches did end as the direct result of an injury, or purported injury, sustained by one of the participants. Wrestlers found themselves subject to ear contusions, shoulder dislocations, various sprains, and even fractured bones.[97] Some of these injuries might have occurred because of the circumstances of the matches. By the early twentieth century, sporting equipment had improved considerably, with professionally manufactured products replacing many homemade items. Commercial sporting goods were widely available in Manitoba through a variety of manufacturers and distributors by the late nineteenth century.[98] Despite developments in sporting equipment technology, some professional wrestling matches were nevertheless contested under very adverse conditions. The most important piece of equipment in a wrestling match, the mat, was generally made of canvas, laid over some form of improvised padding, which could include straw, hay, or sawdust. Wrestling mats, depending on their construction, sometimes provided wholly inadequate protection for the participants. In a few instances, wrestlers refused to continue with a match after the mat proved to be unacceptable, but this was generally not the case.[99] Abrasions were extremely common during the period and one of the primary factors that dissuaded many would-be grapplers from participating in the sport.[100]

Since many in the public accepted a degree of roughness in a match, they also respected a wrestler who could endure the punishment meted out against him. In a match between Charles "Kid" Cutler and Henry Ordemann, from Minneapolis, both of whom later wrestled in Winnipeg, the former suffered a kneecap broken in two places during a match in the latter's home city in October 1910. Cutler eventually had to capitulate because of his injury, but, under the headline "Remarkable Pluck in Wrestling Bout," his performance was described in the Manitoba *Free Press* as "the most remarkable case of endurance under pain that has been seen on a Minneapolis mat for a long time."[101] Similarly, when Duluth's Walter Miller fractured his ankle in a bout with Charles Gustafson but continued to wrestle, he was hailed as a man with "pluck," and his "grit and gameness made him many friends."[102]

Although such qualities in a wrestler were respected, supporters of the sport in Manitoba were by no means unsympathetic to the physical and financial hardships caused by severe injuries. During Frank Gotch's appearance at the Walker Theatre in March 1911, Ernie Sundberg wrestled in a preliminary bout against another local professional grappler, Charles Dalager. Sundberg, by then well known among Winnipeg's sporting public, according to the Winnipeg *Tribune*, had "no men of his weight in this section of the country who seem[ed to be] able to give him a good argument, with the possible exception of Alex Stewart."[103] As a result, Sundberg expressed his keen desire to have Gotch watch him wrestle and, if advised to do so by the world's heavyweight champion, begin taking matches in major centres throughout North America.[104] Sundberg's enthusiasm to impress Gotch was soon halted when his opponent, in attempting to escape from one of the Swede's holds, banged his leg against the floorboards outside the mat. The bone in his leg fractured so forcibly that the crack could be heard throughout the hall. Three doctors immediately attended to Dalager's injury, applying chloroform for the pain before removing the wrestler to St. Boniface Hospital. The 3,000 fans occupying every seat in the theatre and crowding the aisles began to toss coins onto the mat until "it resembled a hail storm." Eventually, Walter Deering, who assisted C.P. Walker in promoting wrestling matches at the Walker Theatre, began to pass around a collection hat, and $251.62, which included two ten-dollar bills, was collected on Dalager's behalf.[105] In a letter to the *Free Press* the next day, Dalager extended his appreciation to the public for such generosity, stating that "when my leg is all right again I will challenge my friend Ernie Sundberg to a finished match and will thank them all personally."[106] The *Free Press* reporter who visited him in the hospital noted that, though in great pain, "he bore it well." To further emphasize his pluck and gameness, the reporter stated that, when being chloroformed, the injured wrestler said to the doctors "give me ten more minutes and I will beat him."[107] Unfortunately, despite his well-appreciated toughness, Dalager never wrestled again on Winnipeg mats.

THE PROBLEM OF EXCESSIVE VIOLENCE

Wrestlers were granted a certain amount of latitude with the rules and expected to show physical aggressiveness and determination in matches, but there was a limit to how much roughing the public would tolerate. By the end of the nineteenth century, professional wrestling still had a dubious reputation among many members of the public, and despite its rapid growth in popularity, largely because of the positive characteristics ascribed to the sport and its practitioners, it remained regularly embroiled in controversy. Professional sport, in general, still retained the stigma of dishonesty in the period before the First World War, and many wrestlers who appeared in Manitoba did little to dissuade the critical public from that perception.[108] Much of this had to do with athletes who regularly exceeded what was considered acceptable sportsmanship. Examples of such behaviour abound. However, one case, involving Winnipeg's most prominent wrestler, Charles Gustafson, will serve to illustrate the persistent problem.

On 8 June 1909, Charles Gustafson and Hume Duval (also known by the surname Macdonald) wrestled as the main attraction in an event staged at the Grand Opera House. Duval was already well known to the public as a result of many appearances two years earlier at the Happyland Amusement Park, where he gave numerous wrestling and weightlifting exhibitions on the grandstand stage.[109] He and Gustafson had also wrestled on two previous occasions in Winnipeg, and in both instances neither had secured a definitive win.[110] Their third bout was universally decried by the press and most of the attendant public as a "fiasco."[111] Upon commencement, Duval immediately resorted to slapping Gustafson "more in the nature of a prizefight," using "blows that echoed through the half empty house."[112] Gustafson, supported by the vast majority of the audience, appealed to the referee, a boxer named Caspar Franklin, who disregarded his protest. Duval then began to "rough-house" even more, striking his opponent in the nose and mouth with his palm heel and gouging his face. When further pleas to the official were disregarded, Gustafson refused to continue with the match, and Duval was immediately awarded the win. The majority of the people present were incensed over what was seen as incompetent officiating and grossly unfair tactics. Matters were made worse when one of Duval's seconds, Fred C. McLaglen, who had disappointed the audience earlier in the evening by refusing to engage in a boxing exhibition with his brother Victor on account of a sprained ankle, antagonized his detractors by inviting them backstage to settle their differences. According to *Tribune* reports, "only by the introduction of a little diplomacy was a small riot narrowly averted."[113] Commenting both on the match and on the general state of professional wrestling in the city, the *Tribune* warned that "the wrestling game in Winnipeg, apparently, is going from bad to worse, and it will only need a few more prods like those that have developed recently in the 'high class' bouts to disgust the local enthusiasts of the game so thoroughly that they will pass up the sport for all time to come."[114] In the days following, various parties spoke out in the *Free Press* concerning the incident. The first to do so was Gustafson, who stated that he would "never have anything more to do with the McLaglen or Duval clans" and that Duval "violated every rule of [the catch-as-catch-can] method" because "he ha[d] a yellow streak in him" and feared facing Gustafson in an honest match. Asserting his own propriety, he stated that "I am well known to the Winnipeg public as always having acted on the square, and I know they will believe me when I say I quit because of the foul methods used by my antagonist."[115]

A response, from an anonymous "Spectator," most likely Duval, one of the McLaglen brothers, or a close associate, followed the next day. In it, he asserted, to the contrary of all newspaper reports, that "I was an eye witness of the bout of which he speaks and did not see any of the foul play of which he complains." In a direct attack on Gustafson's masculinity, "Spectator" asserted that "if Gustafson is a wrestler at all he must be of a very effeminate type, but I have a very strong conviction that he knows very little of the game, but might put up a good exhibition at an afternoon tea." He likewise stressed both wrestling's value as a sport and Duval's and the McLaglen brothers' honesty: "Wrestling and boxing provide capital and manly entertainment, but the sport has been killed in Winnipeg by the cheapest kind of tin horns, and I for one earnestly hope that by the coming of such good sports as Duval and the McLaglen boys the day of the tin horn has passed." An offer was also made on behalf of Charles Herbert, owner of the Savoy Hotel, to back Duval in another match against Gustafson.[116]

Winnipeg resident J.W. Gibson, under the headline "An Injustice to Clean Sport," provided the final word on the subject. Gibson utterly dismissed "Spectator's" allegations, reinforcing the contemporary newspaper interpretations of the evening's events: "I have never seen a more brutal or unsportsmanlike exhibition than that of Duval. The treatment accorded to Gustafson by the former, by the former's seconds, the two McLaglens, and by the referee, was disgraceful throughout." He also opined that "Duval was no match for the Swede in the matter of science, and could only hope to beat him through superior weight and strength, so there can be little doubt as to his motive in roughing matters."[117]

Gibson's letter to the *Free Press* brings several issues to light. First, both his assertion, reinforced by public reaction the night of the bout, demonstrates that wrestling fans were far from passive consumers of public entertainment. Just as they were willing to applaud actions and attributes that they saw as meritorious, so too they were willing to condemn those that were viewed to be unacceptable. Additionally, there appeared to be a broad understanding among the public on what constituted "fair play" in wrestling matches by that period, and breaching the commonly held standard of etiquette would not be tolerated. Indeed, as an affirmation of their general disapproval, Duval was never again booked to wrestle before the Winnipeg public. Gibson's letter also indicates the conflicting sentiments felt by the public throughout the period toward professional wrestling, simultaneously attractive as an exhibition of numerous highly regarded attributes and a sport that seemed to foster unsportsmanlike behaviour.

FIXING MATCHES

Excessive roughness was not the only problem plaguing professional wrestling in Manitoba during this period. Outright fakery also proved to be an ongoing concern. Gibson's letter echoed the public's general frustration over, and ambivalence toward, the issue. Gibson declared that, "as a lover of the game, I have attended every wrestling match that has been pulled off in the city, paying the exorbitant prices demanded for what, in nearly every instance, have proved to be fakes."[118] In examining the period leading up to the Gustafson-Duval match, it is evident that Gibson's assertions were not wholly unfounded.

In January and February 1906, three wrestlers, Jack Root, Jack Downs, and "The Human Derrick" Ole Oleson, had a series of engagements in Winnipeg and Brandon in which various side bets were said to have been placed on the outcomes.[119] It is clear that the public was actively engaged in the betting process as well. In one instance, Oleson, by far the largest of the three, proposed to defeat two local wrestlers, James Theran and James Ramsay, as well as Downs, in one hour. Oleson disposed of the local wrestlers in thirty-four minutes, and, during the interval prior to the start of the match with Downs, Root, acting as "The Human Derrick's" manager, offered to bet ten dollars that his man would defeat his final opponent in the allotted time. According to the *Free Press*, "pandemonium then ensued, the audience falling over each other in the mad rush to place their money on the big fellow."[120] Oleson, however, was unable to accomplish the task.

One week later a letter appeared in the *Free Press* written by North Dakota professional wrestler Charles Moth, who attested to "the methods of the gang of confidence men and fake wrestlers" appearing in Winnipeg. Moth alleged that Downs and Root were in fact two brothers named Al and Frank Hallett who had appeared in wrestling matches under numerous assumed names. Moth also implicated Oleson in the fixing scheme, stating that he had "a reputation everywhere he appeared as a fakir." Appealing to public decency, Moth exhorted that "this gang operated through parts of Minnesota and as I am not in sympathy with anything that tends to degenerate athletic sports, I advertised them and now they are practically tarred out of most of the towns in that section."[121] A reply appeared in the paper two weeks later from Sidney A. Slocum, a local resident who occasionally refereed boxing and wrestling matches, defending Downs and Root while claiming to have testimonials from well-known wrestlers such as Frank Gotch, his trainer, Martin "Farmer" Burns, and Tom Jenkins that "condemn[ed] the methods and tactics of that famous hippodromer, Chas Moth, of Berthold, N.D."[122] Moth's testimonial proved to be enough to confirm public suspicion, for none of the three men appeared again on Manitoba mats.

Although a series of frauds was apparently perpetrated against the Manitoba public, professional wrestling matches continued to be staged regularly for the next year and a half, with little overt suspicion regarding them. In October 1907, amid considerable press fanfare, Duncan C. Ross, the well-known wrestler and all-round athlete, arrived in Winnipeg to face Donald Gaunt, "wrestling champion of Grey, Huron and Bruce counties," for an apparent side bet of $500.[123] By 1907, Ross had been well known to the Winnipeg public for more than twenty years, and the local press was not hesitant in detailing his many accomplishments. The *Tribune*, in outlining his various accolades, affirmed that "sceptics will say that such is impossible, as no athlete of these attainments lives or has ever lived, but records will show that the above assertions are true in every respect." Ross also received praise for his "excellently proportioned" physique, of which "every ounce of his 218 pounds [was] nothing but bone and muscle—pure muscle."[124] Advanced billing did not meet the Winnipeg public's expectations. Neither man appeared to extend much effort, and within a minute Ross "laid down" for his opponent. During the second period, the crowd arose from their seats and left the hall in disgust. The bout, scheduled for three out of five falls, was thereafter called off.[125] The Manitoba *Free Press* described the match as "a huge fake" and declared that "Winnipeg sportsmen have been 'up against' some fakes in the way of boxing and wrestling matches during the last few years but it is questionable if they have ever been stung so hard as the three hundred or more who journeyed to the German hall last night with the intention of seeing a really first class wrestling match."[126] Trouble evidently continued to follow Ross across the Prairies. Approximately three weeks later, he was once again involved in controversy, this time in Regina when he failed to appear in a match against a local police officer. The spectators chased him back to his hotel and demanded their admission fee back. Ross contended, however, that his manager had absconded with the gate receipts. The following day Ross was arrested by the police officer with whom he was scheduled to wrestle for failing to pay the appropriate licensing fee for staging the match.[127]

Despite the obvious "fake" carried out against them in Winnipeg, members of the public once again were not dissuaded from attending professional matches. Two weeks later a bout between Dan Simpson and Herman Mace at the German hall attracted "a very fair attendance."[128] On 26 October, in an attempt to further assuage public suspicion of the sport, Simpson announced that a new organization, the National Athletic Club, had been formed "for the purpose of pulling off legitimate boxing and wrestling matches" on a weekly basis.[129] Over the winter, the National Athletic Club staged more than twenty professional wrestling cards, featuring numerous local wrestlers, including Charles Gustafson, Ernie Sundberg, and Herman Mace. North Dakota's Charles Moth, who had previously exposed Root, Downs, and Oleson as co-conspirators, was also among the out-of-town talent to appear under the auspices of the new club.

Despite claiming to stage only legitimate matches, the National Athletic Club also found itself embroiled in controversy. In mid-December, Charles Dalager was immediately disqualified in a match with Herman Mace after his skin was discovered to be coated in Vaseline. Dan Simpson, refereeing the bout, was "almost furious with indignation" and declared that Dalager's action was "no manly thing to do."[130] The fans, though disappointed, nevertheless concurred with his decision. Dalager countered a few days later by asserting in a letter to the *Free Press* that Simpson had approached him to prearrange the match.[131] Public suspicion was evidently on Dalager's side, since a "big crowd of sympathisers" turned out to support Dalager in a rematch three months later. Mace quickly disposed of his adversary in two straight falls, which might have silenced public controversy surrounding the issue.[132] Nevertheless, the Dalager incident was not the last indictment to be levelled against Simpson, Mace, and the National Athletic Club. In April 1909, Dauphin's Charles Willis gave testimony to the Manitoba Amateur Athletic Association that, during the previous year, he had sought out Mace as a practice partner. Before he could locate him, however, he first encountered Simpson, who advised him not to meet Mace. Instead, Simpson arranged for a match between the two men, billing Willis from Brainerd, Minnesota.[133] Willis stated that "it was only a make believe show and I believe he advertised it for $100 a side."[134] By the time the allegations were made, neither Simpson nor Mace appears to have been actively involved in wrestling in Manitoba, yet the implications against them nevertheless contributed to the public lament articulated by J.W. Gibson two months later.

CONTROVERSIAL CHARACTERS
Professional wrestling attracted considerable adverse publicity for various transgressions in the ring. As in decades past, certain well-known individuals widely associated with the sport also continued to engage in dubious behaviour outside

the ring. One was Fred C. McLaglen, earlier noted as an associate of Hume Du-val and the older brother of Academy Award-winning actor Victor McLaglen.[135] Born in Kent, England, Fred moved to Manitoba and served as a member of the Winnipeg City Police between July 1907 and April 1908.[136] Following his resignation, "Big Mac," as he was colloquially known, became a bartender at the Savoy Hotel in Winnipeg's North End. He initially competed as an amateur wrestler, appearing in the inaugural Manitoba Amateur Wrestling Champion-ships in 1908. Afterward, he embarked on a marginally successful career as both a professional wrestler and a boxer.[137]

McLaglen frequently attracted public attention because of his proclivity for disrupting political rallies involving non-Conservative Party candidates. On 21 October 1908, he drew Manitoba *Free Press* editor John W. Dafoe's ire for causing a disturbance during a Liberal Party meeting at the Walker Theatre. "Big Mac," accompanied by a cadre of supporters, repeatedly interrupted former Minister of the Interior and *Free Press* owner Clifford Sifton during his address, appearing in various parts of the theatre and shouting questions at the prominent politician. The following morning Dafoe published a scathing front-page indict-ment of the affair. The report accused McLaglen as being "intimately bound up with the Conservative machine" and the leader of a "Band of Thugs and Toughs" constituted of "the scourings and riff-raff of the lowest dives and bar-rooms in the city." In addition to disrupting the rally with "unintelligible questions," McLa-glen allegedly demonstrated his "much-vaunted brute strength" by knocking a fifteen-year-old boy to the floor.[138] "Big Mac" sued Dafoe for defamatory libel because of the article but, in a decision heralded by the editor as an affirmation of freedom of the press, ultimately lost the case.[139]

This setback in the Sifton-Dafoe incident did not dampen McLaglen's political proclivities. In July 1910, he interrupted an open-air address by Labour candidate F.J. Dixon. Later in the year, he was ejected from the Grand Opera House by police for disruptive behaviour during a meeting staged by mayoral candidate E.D. Mar-tin.[140] During the 1910 municipal election campaign, McLaglen was also allegedly involved in a plan to manipulate voters lists in the Centre Winnipeg ward.[141]

"Big Mac" did not limit himself to public outbursts of a strictly political nature. He appeared in Winnipeg Police Court at least five times for assault, though the charges were dismissed on four of the occasions.[142] In February 1911, after what was described as "one of the most keenly contested legal fights in the history of the Winnipeg Police [C]ourt," McLaglen was sentenced to one month in prison for theft after assaulting Vassal resident Jilos Carpenter during a visit to the city's red-light district and subsequently relieving him of eighty dollars.[143] Because of his local fame, or perhaps infamy, the courtroom was crowded, and many in attendance refused to leave during the lunch intermission for fear of losing their seats when the session resumed.[144]

Other professional wrestlers, including McLaglen's one-time opponent, Knute Hoel, also encountered frequent legal difficulties. Hoel, brought before the Winnipeg Police Court on several occasions, faced conviction for theft on 30 July 1909 and was sentenced to one year of imprisonment with hard labour. Thirteen months later he was again convicted of the same crime after taking twenty dollars from a sick man's hotel room. Hoel had promised to use the funds to summon a doctor but instead kept the money. As a result, he received another year of imprisonment.[145]

Professional wrestlers who drifted into Winnipeg looking for matches also sometimes faced charges if authorities thought that they had overstayed their welcome or if legal troubles incurred for dubious wrestling-related activities in other jurisdictions came to police attention. In August 1912, for instance, Herman Mondi, who wrestled under the name "Young" Mondi, was arrested by the Winnipeg City Police for having obtained money under false pretenses while in North Bay, Ontario. The charges stemmed from his involvement in "fixed" wrestling matches. Mondi and his alleged manager, John Frazin, were ordered to leave the city within twenty-four hours or face three months in provincial jail for vagrancy.[146] With wrestlers embroiled in controversy not only on the mat but also off it, many of the assertions made by critics that "professional" was synonymous with "disreputable" seemed to be affirmed. Even among members of the public less sweeping in their judgments, such controversy could have done little to boost the sport's esteem in their eyes.

ATTEMPTS TO REGULATE PROFESSIONAL WRESTLING

Many professional wrestlers engaged in behaviour, both on and off the mat, widely considered disreputable, yet little evidence suggests that authorities at either the provincial or the municipal level took any action to regulate the sport or counteract the more egregious offences committed by its practitioners. The only attempt at regulation occurred in 1908 when Winnipeg City Council enacted an amendment to Bylaw 5069, pertaining to licensing, which stipulated that a fee of five dollars be paid to stage public wrestling exhibitions.[147] Evidently, city officials were primarily interested in capitalizing on the potential revenue generated by the National Athletic Club's then-weekly wrestling cards, not in directly controlling the conditions of the matches themselves.

It is apparent that, during this period, boxing faced considerably more public reproach than wrestling. Although the two sports were often staged together, wrestling escaped the legal censure that sporadically befell its fistic counterpart. During the spring of 1908, Winnipeg officials saw fit to implement a prohibition, but the sport's supporters believed that St. Boniface could serve as a "safe haven" for contests. However, on 31 March 1908, the local constabulary also intervened to halt boxing bouts in the predominantly francophone community. Importantly, wrestling matches, scheduled for the same evening on the same card, were allowed to continue.[148] Other Manitoba communities, such as Portage la Prairie, also occasionally took steps to prohibit boxing.[149] Boxers also continued to face periodic arrests for prize fighting, which, nebulously distinct from "boxing matches," remained prohibited under the Criminal Code of Canada.[150]

In 1913, boxing received one of its worst blows when heavyweight title contender Luther McCarty was killed in the first round of a fight with Arthur Pelkey in Calgary on 24 May. Backlash was seen across the country. In the months that followed, bouts were allowed to continue in Winnipeg—but not without reservation. On 3 July 1913, six boxers were taken into police court and required to put up bonds before their entry into the ring. The police seemed to be sufficiently satisfied that their encounters were "comparatively clean" sparring matches.[151] By the end of the year, however, professional boxing of any kind was temporarily banned in Winnipeg, partly because of the belief among city police that boxing matches were attracting too many "undesirable citizens" to the city.[152]

Even if government officials in Manitoba seemed to be far more concerned with preventing prize fighting than with limiting professional wrestling, some commentators nonetheless expressed the desire to regulate grappling matches as well. After a match in Winnipeg in January 1913 that resulted in Alex Stewart receiving two black eyes, the Winnipeg *Tribune* stated that "boxing is not the only sport that requires commission rule. There are numerous forms of athletics which would be all the better if the same taut rules as feature boxing in New York were adopted. As a follow up on the foregoing, the writer only has to cite the case of Alex Stewart as convincing proof of the disregard for sporting ethics."[153]

Although no regulation was forthcoming, promoters did make some efforts to allay various grievances against wrestling. As evidenced, certain athletes deemed to be guilty of unacceptable conduct were never again invited to appear before the public. Promoters also attempted to implement proactive measures to prevent potential problems, albeit with limited success. After a particularly disappointing performance by wrestler Ferdinand Cook, who appeared to give up in his match against Charles Gustafson, the Walker Theatre decided against booking any "unknown" wrestlers to appear on its stage.[154] As Manitoba's most prestigious theatre, it certainly had the ability to attract well-known talent, as it proved in subsequent years. However, this did not necessarily guarantee a satisfactory outcome. In one instance, the Walker Theatre attempted a different strategy. To ensure that his bouts remained "high class," manager Walter Deering ordered Eugene Tremblay and Walter Miller to arrive in Winnipeg several days before their 1 December 1913 match "so that there [would] be no chance for a hitch and that everything [would] be above board and on the level."[155] Miller, as ordered, arrived in the city four days ahead of time and completed his training with several local wrestlers at the Boys' Club.[156] Tremblay disregarded the stipulation and, citing prior bookings, did not appear in Winnipeg until two days before the match.[157] Deering's effort to implement his proviso was likely impotent because considerable advertising had already been purchased in local newspapers and advance ticket sales were already under way several days before the card.[158] Additionally, as the recognized world's lightweight champion because he held the *Police Gazette* belt, Tremblay was a high-class drawing card, and this gave him the leverage to ignore such requests if they were not in accord with his interests.

Another strategy employed by promoters was to modify the sport's conventions in an attempt to ensure more satisfactory outcomes for spectators. In professional wrestling, inappropriate conduct was not the sole source of public controversy. Another contentious issue was the occasional tendency for matches to devolve into marathon-like endurance contests in which neither athlete emerged victorious.[159] Under *Police Gazette* rules, professional wrestling matches could be lengthy affairs. If, at the end of a stipulated time limit (commonly about two hours), both men had secured a single fall, or neither had secured a fall, then the match was determined to be a draw. In some cases, despite the generous time limit, the question of the "better man" remained unsettled at the end of the match, an outcome generally unpopular with the public, who preferred to see a definitive victory in sporting contests. Obtaining a victory proved to be difficult, however, if one of the wrestlers chose to adopt defensive tactics.

In Winnipeg, debate over possible rule changes was particularly keen in 1912, when two main event matches ended with neither man scoring a fall. The first, between Charles Gustafson and Cleveland's Otto Suter at the Walker Theatre, ended after approximately two hours when the referee terminated the match.[160] The second, between local featherweight standouts Ernie Sundberg and Alex Stewart, was finally called off at 3 a.m.[161] Following the Stewart-Sundberg match, several ideas were proposed. One suggestion, brought forward by Tom Cannon, a contemporary of Duncan C. Ross, who visited Winnipeg in early 1912, was to award the victory to the man who wrestled most aggressively, even if both men had the same number of falls or if no falls occurred.[162] Another proposed method, utilized by promoter Harry W. Heagren in Salt Lake City, Utah, was to abolish time limits altogether and have the men wrestle until two falls were secured. If one wrestler left the mat, then his purse was withheld. Similarly, if both contestants tried to agree to a draw, then they received no pay.[163] When Stewart and Sundberg met for their final contest at the Empress Theatre, a third rule variation was implemented whereby both wrestlers agreed to go unpaid if no falls were secured. Furthermore, if no falls were recorded in one hour, then the wrestler to take the first fall would win the match. To quell possible public discontent, and to reassure Empress Theatre owner John M. Cook with respect to his facility's good reputation, the match's promoter, Tom Russell, also agreed to refund all gate money if either man failed to appear or refused to step on the mat.[164] That Stewart finally secured a victory suggests that the new rule structure might have assisted in overcoming the problem with stalemates. However, they were never again implemented in the province, and Manitoba remained adherent to the internationally recognized *Police Gazette* standards. Despite complaints about long, tiresome, and inconclusive wrestling, most matches did not end in such an unsatisfactory fashion. In subsequent months, debate over the issue appears to have abated, and wrestling matches continued to attract good audiences.

SURVIVAL AMID CONTROVERSY

In general, the question arises about why professional wrestling, so frequently embroiled in controversy, remained a viable form of public entertainment. In one instance, after wrestler George LePage refused to participate in a match with Charles Gustafson because of a sparse turnout, both the *Free Press* and the *Tribune* predicted that the sport had finally reached the point where public support was going to disappear. The *Free Press* described the incident as wrestling's "death blow," and the *Tribune* opined that "wrestling in Winnipeg, which for some time past has been tottering, had its last pin kicked out from under it."[165] The *Telegram*, though not as fatalistic in its pronouncement, called the match a "fizzle" and stated that "another black eye was given to the wrestling and boxing game in the city."[166] Still, shortly more than a month later, C.P. Walker and Walter Deering staged their first heavyweight contest at the Walker Theatre, and various venues throughout the city continued to host the sport, in many instances drawing large crowds.

Several factors appear to explain why wrestling, despite the numerous grievances against it, retained public favour. First, wrestling was not alone among professional sports in Manitoba that received public criticism. Beyond the aforementioned issues concerning boxing, charges of excessive violence and fixing bedevilled many other athletic undertakings, including both team games such as hockey and baseball and other individual sports such as running. Even newer sports, such as motorcycle racing, did not escape suspicion.[167] The stigma surrounding money and sport remained well ingrained in many people's minds in the years prior to the First World War, and professional wrestling was just one of numerous professional sports that attracted (and often warranted) adverse press. Although professionalism came under frequent attack, there was also a growing understanding that the most skilled athletes could demand and receive remuneration for their services. As a direct corollary, additional practice time, made possible by receiving money for athletic performances, allowed the practitioner's skills to be further honed.[168] Wrestling fans were cognizant that, when Charles Gustafson, Ernie Sundberg, Frank Gotch, Eugene Tremblay, and Walter Miller appeared before them, they were witnessing the best wrestlers that their province, and the world, had to offer.

Another critical element of professional wrestling's survival was the fact that, though many grapplers displayed poor sportsmanship, were exposed as "fakers," or exhibited otherwise controversial behaviour, this was not true of all practitioners. In Winnipeg, the three most prominent professional wrestlers, Gustafson, Sundberg, and Stewart, were involved in numerous bouts that elicited negative reactions from both the public and the press. However, it was consistently the actions of their opponents, not their own, that caused public complaints. To the contrary, all three men were seen to exemplify the many positive attributes accorded to professional wrestling, to the exclusion of its more nefarious elements. Gustafson's claim after the incident with Hume Duval at the Grand Opera House of "always having acted on the square" appears to have been a widely held perception. The *Free Press* noted in at least two instances that Gustafson was "always out to win" in his matches and described him as "the cleanest middleweight that has ever appeared in Winnipeg."[169] After George LePage's refusal to wrestle because of poor attendance in 1910, the *Tribune*, in foretelling the sport's doom, lamented that

> the popular local middleweight [Gustafson], together with Ernie
> Sundberg, has built up wrestling in this city, and it is unfortunate
> in the extreme that the end should come in a bout in which he was
> one of the principals. The writer does not hesitate to express the
> opinion that Gustafson is honest to the core. He has won his bouts
> on merit, and it is doubtful if a more straight-forward wrestler ever
> drew on pads. Gus has been a credit to the game and those who have
> followed his career since making Winnipeg his home will certainly
> not hold him responsible for the death blow dealt last night.[170]

During a retrospective look at wrestling matches staged during 1910, the *Tribune* again affirmed its position on the two men: "They may never arise beyond the local horizon, but when time has forced them from the arena they can look back on an honourable career.... Were all wrestlers as honest as Charlie Gustafson and Ernie Sunberg [sic] the game would never be under a shadow."[171] In a similar vein, after the wrestling match in which Alex Stewart received two black eyes, the *Tribune* contended that he was "as clean a little wrestler as ever stepped into a pair of wrestling trunks."[172] The newspaper reinforced the idea that dishonesty was not a universal axiom among paid athletes in its call for regulation, stating that "professional sport has suffered extensively as a result of a few renegades."[173]

Wrestling fans certainly expected matches to be legitimate encounters, and as in previous decades, when athletes were discovered to be "faking," the public no longer supported them. However, since the general perception of many athletes remained favourable, the public was not inclined to disavow interest in the sport. When the latest perpetrator had left the vicinity, wrestling aficionados were soon willing to forget past transgressions and reinvest their faith in local talent and well-known visiting grapplers with strong reputations. Newspaper sportswriters were likewise fickle in their condemnation; just two days after the *Free Press* sounded wrestling's "death blow" in Winnipeg, for example, they announced Stewart's arrival in the city, unabashedly singing his praises as an athlete who "plays the game fair every time."[174]

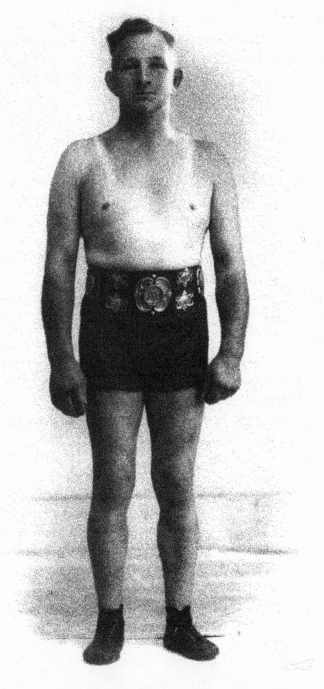

4. Alex Stewart, a professional featherweight, took on many different roles in wrestling during the 1910s and 1920s, serving as an athlete, coach, and referee. Source: Manitoba Sports Hall of Fame and Museum, MS2011.25.261.

CONCLUSION

By the First World War, professional wrestling, despite the controversies surrounding it, had emerged as an indisputably popular pastime, far eclipsing the immediate post-Confederation decades in terms of both the number of athletes involved and the frequency with which events were staged. Wrestling's popularity stemmed, in part, from the overall growth in interest in sport during the period. However, public affinity for wrestling can also be attributed in large measure to its growing capacity to represent, through ritualized physical combat, numerous values that Manitobans held to be important during the late nineteenth century and early twentieth century. Yet, as its popularity grew, wrestling was also beset by ever more frequent controversies that threatened to alienate its many supporters. Despite the many problems surrounding it, wrestling was able to thrive because of public faith that many athletes represented the better qualities intrinsic to the sport, not its abhorrent excesses.

Professional wrestling prospered in the years before the Great War not solely because its practitioners exemplified qualities such as ideal male physical development, scientific progressivism, and aggressive masculinity but also because, as Manitoba's population expanded rapidly after 1896, its ethnic composition likewise altered dramatically. Changing demographic characteristics had profound effects on wrestling, and various ideas related to nativism, ethnic pride, cultural survival, and ethnic nationalism found expression on the mat.

Chapter 3

WRESTLING WITH ETHNICITY, 1896–1914

As the summer of 1901 began, Winnipeg's residents were greeted by the sight of an immense, dark-skinned man on the city's downtown streets. At a height of six feet four and a half inches and a weight of 246 pounds, the new arrival certainly dwarfed most of the individuals around him. What made him stand out even more than his size was his adornment in "the costume of his country," a form of "picturesque oriental attire," that caused many Manitobans to pause and look as they went about their business. Soon accompanied by a cadre of admiring young boys, he made his way to the various newspaper offices, where it was officially announced that he would wrestle and defeat any ten men who would go against him in one hour or forfeit $200. He further expressed his willingness to deposit $500 "at a moment's notice" with the Winnipeg *Tribune* sports editor for a match in Winnipeg against "any man in the world, bar nobody." As both the summer and the century dawned, Mouradoulah, the "Terrible Turk," had arrived in town.[1]

The Terrible Turk's appearance in Winnipeg occurred during a period of dramatic demographic change in western Canada. At the turn of the twentieth century, both the region and, more particularly, its dominant metropolitan centre were undergoing a remarkable metamorphosis as large numbers of immigrant settlers arrived in Canada's "last best west." Although previous decades saw British Canadians establish both numerical and cultural dominance, after 1896 settlers were drawn from a variety of nations. Over the next two decades, Winnipeg was transformed from a city whose population was mainly of British heritage into Canada's most diverse multicultural urban centre. At the same time, professional wrestling grew remarkably in popularity. As a sport, it echoed western Canada's growing diversity, drawing athletes from a variety of nationalities. Because of its multicultural character, wrestling never carried a single, transcendent meaning that all Manitobans could agree on. Depending on the context in which it took place, wrestling could represent different things to different ethnic groups. For members of the Anglo-Canadian majority, wrestling often highlighted the apprehension that many residents felt about the region's growing diversity. Even among people of British ancestry, however, wrestling occasionally helped to illustrate old-country rivalries. For European immigrants in general, wrestling represented a culturally relevant and accessible form of public entertainment that served to reinforce their own nationalist sentiments. Although wrestling frequently fuelled intergroup enmity, it also served more constructive purposes. For non-Anglo-Protestant minority communities with long settlement histories in the west, traditional folk wrestling could be an expression of a desire to preserve their own customs. Representative of this point, for example, were the Icelanders, who saw in their ancient glima wrestling a way of retaining important links to their past in the face of assimilationist pressures. For other ethnic groups of more recent arrival, particularly those from regions of continental Europe, where statehood was tenuous or embryonic, the sport could serve more expressly political ends. As an examination of the Winnipeg Polish community suggests, wrestling provided a medium through which to express and publicize a blossoming sense of national consciousness.

THE IMMIGRATION BOOM

By the late 1890s, western Canada's ethnic composition began to alter dramatically because of a combination of international and domestic factors. The last few years of the decade marked the end of a global economic depression that had begun in 1873. Increased economic prosperity in Europe resulted in greater demand for prairie grain. Simultaneously, agricultural expansion ceased on the American frontier. The American west had long been the preferred destination for immigrants seeking homestead grants, but with land increasingly becoming unavailable settlers turned to the Canadian Prairies.[2] Although the majority of new settlers continued to be drawn from the United States, Great Britain, and eastern Canada, changes to immigration policy following the election of Wilfrid Laurier's Liberal Party in 1896 resulted in thousands of new arrivals from non-English-speaking countries. Clifford Sifton, member of Parliament for Brandon, was appointed minister of the interior by the new prime minister and made considerable effort to settle the west, since in 1892 immigration had fallen under that department's mandate.[3] Under his direction, the department undertook an aggressive campaign to lure immigrants from northern, eastern, and central Europe. His overarching objective was to populate the west with agrarian settlers, and Sifton believed it necessary to look beyond Britain and other English-speaking dominions to find a sufficient number of people suitable for the task of farming in the challenging prairie environment.[4] In contrast to many Canadians of his era, he later contended that he was "indifferent as to whether or not [the immigrant] is British born." Instead, he famously maintained that "a stalwart peasant in a sheep-skin coat, born on the soil, whose forefathers have been farmers for ten generations, with a stout wife and a half-dozen children," was of greater value to the expanding nation than, for example, an urban British trade unionist who would not engage in farm labour.[5]

The immigration boom that began during the late 1890s did not result in an equal distribution of population between Manitoba and the regions of the northwest that, after 1905, constituted Saskatchewan and Alberta. Although rural Manitoba received approximately 94,000 immigrants between 1896 and 1914, that number paled in comparison to the 244,000 and 215,000 that settled in Saskatchewan and Alberta, respectively.[6] Nevertheless, Manitoba's growth was impressive, and a comparison of the 1901 and 1911 censuses reveals an 80.8 percent increase in the province's population, compared with an overall national increase of 34.2 percent during the same period.[7] Winnipeg's growth was far more dramatic. In 1895, the city's population was approximately 38,500.[8] Over the next five years, growth continued at a modest pace, reaching 42,300 by 1901. In the decade thereafter, the city's population exploded, totalling over 136,000 by 1911.[9] As the "Gateway to the West," Winnipeg became the railway hub through which virtually all immigrants in western Canada passed. In many cases, the new arrivals took up residence in the city, either as itinerant labourers or as permanent residents.[10] After 1896, the city's ethnic character began to change considerably as the percentage of the population drawn from British ancestry steadily diminished.[11] Although Winnipeg society had never constituted a homogeneous mass in terms of either ethnicity or worldview, English-speaking Canadians were well established as the cultural majority by the mid-1890s, and the overwhelming consensus, at least among Anglo-Canadians, was that both Winnipeg and the rest of the province should retain their British Canadian character. As Alan Artibise notes, "the concept of cultural pluralism (or a cultural mosaic), used so often to describe Canadian society in later years, was not even contemplated in Winnipeg during this period."[12] However, Winnipeg's growing non-English-speaking "foreign" population was seen by many to hinder the ongoing mission, articulated decades earlier, of extending the British Empire onto prairie soil.[13]

As disturbing as the spectre of "foreign" immigration was for many members of Manitoba society during the period, attracting people of non-British origin to the Prairies proved to be necessary for further growth. Officially, the Immigration Branch of the Department of the Interior sought people who would assist in expanding the west's agricultural economy, either as homesteaders or as farm labourers.[14] Agricultural development did not occur in economic isolation, and rapid expansion of the existing railway infrastructure was required to ensure that farmers had efficient access to national and international grain markets. Winnipeg's growth during the years after 1896 was linked to its ongoing role as the central hub for the region's railway industry and grain trade. Additionally, as the prairie population continued to expand, Winnipeg became the region's major manufacturing centre, providing a variety of finished goods to the new settlers.[15] Officially, the federal government viewed homesteading and settlement as the objectives of its immigration policy, yet many immigrants, lacking the capital required to establish themselves on farms, instead provided the cheap labour required by prairie industry to support continued economic growth.[16]

Winnipeg became home to a large number of the new immigrant industrial proletariat. Although economic conditions during the first decade of the twentieth century were generally favourable and jobs relatively plentiful, immigrant wages, particularly among non-English-speaking segments of the population, frequently failed to reflect the region's overall prosperity. Prior to the beginning of the Great War, many immigrant workers earned less than half of the wage required to maintain an adequate standard of living in the city. Accordingly, many families were required to live in cramped, unsafe, and unsanitary conditions.[17] Civic authorities generally ignored the appeals made by charitable institutions on behalf of the poor and provided negligible funds for relief efforts.[18] During the last few years of the nineteenth century and the first decade of the twentieth century, Winnipeg's ethnic character took on a distinct spatial form, as poor immigrants came increasingly to settle in North End ethnic "ghettoes," isolated from the rest of the population by the massive railway marshalling yards north of Logan Street.[19] Their generally poor living conditions, and the resultant filth and disease, exacerbated existing ethnic tensions in the city, feeding Anglo-Canadian perceptions of many immigrant peoples as "dirty foreigners."[20] Additionally, many English-speaking labourers and their representatives in the union movement quickly became resentful of immigrant peoples who, through their willingness to work for wages "below the Canadian standard," drove the cost of labour down.[21]

Anglo-Canadians retained their pre-eminent position as the economic, political, and social leaders in Manitoba society, despite frequent cries by the press and public that immigrants posed a threat to the "proper" social order.[22] Tempering hostility toward immigrant peoples in the prewar period was the general belief that, over time, non-English-speaking Europeans could be assimilated into the dominant society's cultural norms and practices.[23] However, during the early twentieth century, assimilation remained largely a hopeful prognostication, not a description of contemporary reality. The shrill call for cultural uniformity according to the Anglo-Canadian model, in fact, did little to assuage the concerns of many immigrants that they were, and would remain, unwelcome second-class citizens with little opportunity for advancement in their new home.[24]

WRESTLING AND ETHNIC TENSIONS

In the first decade of the twentieth century, wrestling experienced remarkable growth in popularity in large part because its one-on-one character allowed ethnic diversity to be accentuated in a fashion not always possible with team sports. Although popular games such as hockey and baseball might have capitalized on specific players' nationalities to draw in spectators, it was difficult, though not impossible, to stock an entire roster with athletes from a single ethnic group. Thus, at least with respect to ethnicity, there typically existed ambiguity concerning a team's "representative" nature.[25] With wrestling, it was much more straightforward to create the conditions in which ethnic pride and interethnic tensions could play the central role in generating interest among spectators because only two individuals were directly involved in the contest.

During the 1880s and 1890s, Manitoba's wrestlers, much like the majority of the province's residents, were drawn from British Canadian backgrounds. John Blackey, John McKeown, John Allen, E.W. Johnston, F.H. Joslin, Elwood Rourke, and J.W. Moffitt, Manitoba's most prominent wrestlers during the period, all had British surnames. Matsuda Sorakichi's appearances in Winnipeg during 1886 do not appear to have generated any overt racism either from spectators or from the press, though both certainly noted his ethnicity. British Canadians at the time likely saw no concrete threat to their dominance from peoples of other ethnic backgrounds. A Japanese wrestler in Manitoba, while certainly a novelty, was not a cultural threat. Therefore, though commentary concerning wrestling's "respectability" as a sporting pastime appeared in public discourse, and would continue to do so, the cultural homogeneity of its partici-pants ensured that race and ethnicity were not yet significant concerns. However, by the turn of the century, with immigrant numbers rising, local wrestling bouts were becoming outlets for expressing nativist sentiments. A striking example of this emergent trend can be seen as early as 1901 and 1902 in the series of bouts featuring Mouradoulah, the Terrible Turk.

When Mouradoulah (also spelled Mourad Alah) arrived in Winnipeg on 18 June 1901, local wrestling devotees were already familiar with Turkish wrestlers. Three years earlier the original "Terrible Turk," Youssouf Ishmaelo, appeared on North American mats. During 1898, Winnipeg dailies reported regularly on his wrestling tour throughout the United States and central Canada.[26] Although Youssouf perished aboard the SS *La Bourgogne* when it sank off the coast of Newfoundland in July that year, a number of Turkish wrestlers (many of whom were actually Bulgarian by ethnicity) followed his example by emigrating to American shores.[27] Within a few days of Mouradoulah's arrival, a match was ar-ranged with American Tom Jenkins, "a wrestler of well known ability," in which the Turk agreed to pin him three times in an hour.[28]

The bout between "Terrible Turk" Mouradoulah and Tom Jenkins, held on 27 June at the Winnipeg Theatre, attracted a large audience. The Turk suc-ceeded in defeating his American opponent within the prescribed time limit, pinning him twice with a half-nelson and then forcing him to submit, or suffer a broken arm, with a hammerlock. One of the event's most striking features was the crowd's vocally partisan nature. Jenkins was the overwhelming favourite, and the people in attendance "cheered themselves hoarse" when he was able to extri-cate himself from Mouradoulah's grip.[29] Conversely, when the Turkish grappler scored his victories, "the gallery gods expressed their extreme disapprobation."[30] The crowd's reactions during the match do not appear to have been the result of direct antagonism by the Turk. The Winnipeg *Telegram* opined that he was "a born wrestler, and fully demonstrated his right to claim championship honours," and even in securing the painful hammerlock used "a skillful piece of strategy" as opposed to violence or brute force.[31] The *Free Press* corroborated these views, stating that "when the Turk was awarded his falls ... he was perfectly entitled to them."[32] Additionally, no reports appeared in the papers before the match testify-ing to Mouradoulah's poor behaviour while in the city, and even advertisements prior to his performance did nothing to accentuate a "terrible" reputation. To the contrary, the Turk himself expressed apprehension before the match about meeting Jenkins, stating that "He would not hesitate to put his fingers in my eyes if he got the chance, or commit other fouls. I have been warned by other people he has met and go prepared."[33]

Despite his adversary's concerns, the audience was firmly behind the American. Sympathy for a smaller man might have been a factor. The Turkish wrestler (six feet four inches and 246 pounds) was much larger than the American wrestler (six feet and 200 pounds).[34] However, when Mouradoulah wrestled Mont the "U.S. Giant" (six feet eight inches and 345 pounds) on 7 May the following year in a similarly well-attended and "scientific" match, crowd reaction was much the same.[35] It is therefore probable that audience belligerence was a direct result of his "foreign" nature. The apparently spontaneous character of the public's reaction is testimony to the already widespread nativist sentiment in the city at the turn of the century. Even J.S. Woodsworth, director of Winnipeg's All-Peoples Mission and one of Canada's greatest humanitarians, was a product of his time and context, writing under a decade later that peoples of Turkish descent, along with other so-called Levantine races, "constitute[d] one of the least desirable classes of immigrants."[36] Dr. Allan McLaughlin was more specific in his criticism, claiming that they had an "Oriental subtlety" and that years of oppression had bred in them the necessity to lie, deceive, and "only tell the truth when it will serve their purpose best."[37] Other sources on Turkey available to turn-of-the-century Manitobans, such as Reverend Edwin M. Bliss's *Turkey and the Armenian Atrocities*, were not as wholly condemnatory but nevertheless reinforced negative views: "With some noble qualities [the Turk] unites some that are brutal and contemptible in the extreme."[38] Although few Turks could be counted among Winnipeg's population at the turn of the twentieth century, Mouradoulah's strikingly "swarthy" appearance, and his keen ability to dispose of more domestic-looking foes, would have been a reminder of the perceived threat posed by "Mr. Sifton's Grand 'Round Up' of European Freaks and Hoboes" to British Canadian ascendancy.[39]

In the years after Mouradoulah's turn on local mats, ethnicity took on heightened importance in promoting wrestling matches. Beginning in 1905, another "Turk," James Theran, popularly billed as "The Young Turk," made Winnipeg his home and captured a great deal of attention in a number of matches with explicitly ethnic overtones. His first bout on local mats following his arrival from eastern Canada, staged as an additional attraction to an amateur boxing tournament, was against Tom Dixon (Dickinson), a native of London, England, a former member of the Finchley Harriers athletic club, and later the wrestling instructor at the Winnipeg YMCA.[40] Their bout, won by Theran after a single fall in eleven minutes, was described as "the prettiest exhibition of wrestling ever seen in the city."[41] Thereafter, Theran both issued and received numerous challenges for matches and posted cash forfeits with the *Free Press*. Several of his opponents and would-be challengers were clearly of British heritage, including Charles Beards and Duncan Johnston.[42] However, matches did not always simply adhere to the convention of pitting an Anglo-Canadian against a "foreigner" and thus reinforcing nativist sentiments toward "undesirable" immigrants.[43] To the contrary, turn-of-the-century wrestling reflected a far more dynamic interplay among various ethnic groups than simply placing members of Manitoba's economically and socially dominant British population against peoples of other ethnicities.

James Theran wrestled extensively in Manitoba during 1905 and 1906, in both Winnipeg and other centres, with his moniker of "The Young Turk" ever present in the press surrounding his matches. He made his first appearance in Brandon little more than a month after his initial match in Winnipeg. Performing before a "fairly good" crowd of spectators, Theran agreed to defeat Peter Larsen, "a Dane" from Brandon, three times in thirty minutes or forfeit twenty-five dollars to the local hospital. The crowd appeared to be strongly behind the local Danish grappler and became so excited that the referee threatened to stop the match. When Theran ultimately failed in his attempt, those in attendance took up a collection on Larsen's behalf in appreciation of his efforts. Although four boxing bouts were scheduled to take place after the wrestling match, they were called off because, "having spent all its enthusiasm," the crowd left.[44] Theran's matches continued to generate considerable interest in the ensuing months. In one instance, the sheer number and fervour of the spectators were too much for Winnipeg's Arcade Theatre, and the small facility's top balcony partially collapsed during a best three-of-five-falls match between "The Young Turk" and Minnesota grappler Jack Root.[45]

No evidence exists to suggest that Theran received the same degree of negative public reaction as his (alleged) countryman Mouradoulah three years earlier. Nevertheless, it was clear, by the attention surrounding his matches, that "The Young Turk" moniker was standing him in good stead as a box office attraction. Many other "ethnic" wrestlers subsequently appeared on mats in the province, including "Italian Champion" W. Vic, who faced "German Grappler" T. Cook, Pat Connelly, "The Irish Giant," who likewise faced "The German" Max Schultz, and many others.[46] Even a number of British-born wrestlers adopted explicitly ethnic monikers, including "Scotch Giant" Charles Taylor and Alex Munro, the "Scottish Lion."[47] In some cases, statements made by wrestlers clearly reflected, or capitalized on, feelings of interethnic rivalry. Although statements commonly exploited Anglo-Canadian concerns about "foreigners," sometimes the reverse was true. For instance, prior to Max Schultz's match with Pat Connelly, the *Free Press* commented that "the German says that he is going to insist on having either a German or Polish referee in this match ... and is asking for his kind of referee so as to have a fair shake, as he knows that Connelly is very popular here and thinks that unless he has one of his own countrymen for a referee they will show partiality to Connelly."[48] Schultz's statement, even if nothing more than promotional hyperbole, nevertheless illustrates that ethnic rivalry and mistrust were recognized by wrestlers from various backgrounds as viable means for attracting their fellow countrymen to wrestling contests.

Interethnic competition proved to be a strong drawing card in Manitoba during the early twentieth century, but it is also clear that, within British Canadian society itself, long-held rivalries among different regions in the ancestral homeland could engender similarly passionate feelings. Although the ratio of non-British settlers relative to British settlers in the Prairies increased in the years after 1896, Manitoba nevertheless continued to receive large numbers of English-speaking immigrants. Compared with the other prairie provinces, in fact, the percentage of British-born arrivals in the province remained higher than in both Alberta and Saskatchewan during the years prior to the Great War.[49] In general, as John Herd Thompson argues, a broad sense of British identity emerged in the Prairies that, through membership in common civic and religious institutions, dulled the intensity of differences among the English, Scottish, Welsh, and (Protestant) Irish. Perceived economic threats from continental European immigrants in particular served as the catalyst for uniting British peoples.[50] Nevertheless, old-country rivalries could be brought to the fore, particularly in events that did not generally include members from outside the English-speaking community, such as the inaugural Scottish Athletic Association's Highland Games.

Scottish athletics had a history in Manitoba dating back more than a generation by the time the Scottish Athletic Association of Winnipeg began staging annual Highland Games programs, beginning on Labour Day 1906. During the inaugural event, attended by over 3,000 people from across Manitoba, athletes competed in various events for cash prizes of up to twenty dollars. In subsequent years, the renamed Scottish Amateur Athletic Association of Winnipeg, eschewing the principle of monetary compensation for athletes, instead offered prizes to event winners such as gold cups, tobacco, cigars, medallions, and gold and silver watches.[51] The association officially invited "Men of All Nationalities" to compete in the Highland Games competitions, but an examination of prizewinner lists from the first year of competition suggests that nobody of non-British descent participated.[52] In the absence of "foreign" participants, parochialism instead came to the fore, especially in public commentary surrounding the wrestling events, in which debate following the Highland Games centred on the respective merits of highland and border Scot athletes.

Writing to the *Free Press* under the pseudonym "Icthart," a border county spectator jabbed the "kilted clans" for their failure to secure victory in the wrestling events. In open mockery of the clansmen's athletic prowess, Icthart noted that "a little elderly man called Robert Miller" from Denholm, Roxfordshire, and weighing 133 pounds, was able to "send to the grass the Highland champion Charles McLean, a man of 220 lbs."[53] Likewise, the wrestling tournament's winner, George Hume, "a raw plowman ... who came in on the morning train to share in the fun ... [and was] not within 50 lbs of the weight of the defeated Highland champion [J. McDermid]," earned praise for winning the first prize of twenty dollars.[54] Icthart's inflammatory remarks immediately elicited a response. A slighted Highlander, under the name "Mac Inopa," claimed that many of Icthart's allegations regarding the wrestling events were inaccurate. He concluded his response to the border man by stating that, "if any Border wrestler in the city wishes a match, either in Cumberland, Graeco-Roman, or catch-as-catch-can, he will be immediately accommodated. This I insert to hold up the honour of the highlands and to keep the Borderer from thinking mighty things."[55] The debate continued in the newspaper, though an Englishman named A. Tyke himself questioned the necessity for such vitriol: "Why does [Icthart] not take an interest in his countrymen from Scotland instead of knocking them down, as he is doing with his very clever and sarcastic remarks."[56] Little appears to have come of the highland-border Scot debate, though its colourful and heated character indicates that sporting rivalries could, at times, accentuate cultural cleavages among even the narrowest substrata of the population. Following the second-annual

Highland Games, the old-country regional antagonism does not appear to have been renewed, perhaps partly because non-British athletes were beginning to make inroads into the competition. In 1907, wrestling titles were contested under catch-as-catch-can rules in two weight divisions, with the heavyweight title going to Stanley Sielski, a local Polish wrestler. Two Polish athletes, S. Bolek and L. Stafek, also competed in the lightweight class (145 pounds and under).[57]

WRESTLING'S BROAD ETHNIC APPEAL

The widespread presence of non-Anglo-Canadian athletes in Manitoba wrestling by the first decade of the twentieth century reflected more general trends in which members of many ethnic groups began to adopt greater interest in sports.[58] However, wrestling appears to have had particularly wide appeal outside the English-speaking community, as evidenced by both the large number of "foreign" grapplers headlining professional wrestling cards and the success of non-British athletes in traditionally British events such as Highland Games wrestling competitions. Wrestling's strong multicultural appeal can be traced to a number of interrelated factors. Wrestling was one of the few sports that many European immigrants, regardless of their countries of origin, had some level of familiarity with upon their arrival in Canada. By the time the Canadian west became a popular destination for non-British settlers, many ethnic groups, including Austrians, Estonians, Finns, Germans, Hungarians, Italians, and Poles, could already boast a network of athletic organizations that taught wrestling, as well as national champion wrestlers, in their homelands.[59] Many sports, such as ice hockey, baseball, and soccer, were first imported by British Canadians and then adopted by or, in the case of soccer, consciously taught to immigrant peoples as part of the larger mission to assimilate them into Anglo-Canadian norms.[60] Wrestling certainly accompanied early English-speaking settlers to the Canadian west but could not claim a similar position as a unique element of their cultural heritage. To the contrary, because of its widespread popularity in Europe, wrestling facilitated a level of cultural continuity between the New World and the Old World. Although the most prevalent wrestling style in continental Europe during the period was Greco-Roman wrestling, many prominent European wrestlers proved themselves capable of adapting quickly to catch-as-catch-can rules and competing on even terms with their English-speaking counterparts.

Continued association with theatres aided wrestling's position as an intelligible and culturally relevant sporting pastime for many continental European immigrants. Soon after the turn of the century, Manitoba's theatre owners realized that the influx of European immigrants represented a new market for commercial entertainment. Although linguistic barriers made certain theatrical entertainments, such as plays, inaccessible to many European Canadians, vaudeville theatre, which often featured non-speaking physical performances, did not present the same obstacles to universal understanding.[61] For profit-seeking theatre owners, wrestling represented a similar form of "universal" entertainment in which language posed no impediment to enjoyment. As a result, wrestling matches were regularly staged in the province's many theatrical venues. In addition to the Arcade and Winnipeg Theatres, Manitoba's capital hosted matches featuring wrestlers of various ethnicities at the Dominion Theatre and Grand Opera House, and in Brandon wrestlers performed at the Wheat City's Opera House.[62] In some instances, wrestling acts were included as part of the vaudeville entertainment, such as when Scandinavian wrestler Ollie (Ole) Samson and the German, Max Schultz, agreed to "close the show" in a series of engagements at Winnipeg's Dominion Theatre by offering "a scientific demonstration of the art of wrestling" with "nothing fixed up" during the end of May and beginning of June 1910.[63] In a direct effort to appeal to non-English-speaking peoples, wrestling promoters also took out advertisements for matches in non-English-language newspapers.[64]

Wrestlers were drawn from a diverse array of backgrounds in Manitoba at the turn of the century, but it is evident that the meaning attached to the sport was not universal to all ethnic groups. Communities that displayed a particularly strong propensity for wrestling attached to it their own distinctive sets of cultural values and practices. Notable in both respects were two peoples with highly disparate histories: Icelanders and Poles. Both made unique contributions to Manitoba's early wrestling heritage.

WRESTLING AND THE ICELANDIC CANADIAN COMMUNITY

Icelandic settlement in Manitoba dates to the fall of 1875, just three years after passage of the Dominion Lands Act. The sojourners who made their way to the region from the North Atlantic island were the second major non-British ethnic group to populate the west after Confederation, having been preceded a year earlier by Mennonites from Russia, who formed bloc settlements southeast of Winnipeg along the Rat River. Unlike their Anabaptist contemporaries, environmental catastrophe, as opposed to religious persecution, provided the impetus for Icelanders to emigrate. Repeated volcanic eruptions on their island, beginning in 1783 and continuing throughout the nineteenth century, rendered large tracts of pasture unsuitable for agriculture. At the behest of Canadian immigration officials, several hundred farmers made the journey to western Canada to establish themselves on the land. Eschewing the southern grasslands in favour of the more rugged pastoral terrain in the Interlake district, the settlers founded the colony of Gimli on the shores of Lake Winnipeg in 1875, just north of what was then the Manitoba border. Following the initial Icelandic cohort of 285 individuals in 1875, a group of approximately 1,200 arrived the next summer. Despite numerous setbacks, including poor weather, flooding, and a smallpox outbreak in 1876, the colonists persevered, and by 1890 they numbered approximately 7,000.[65]

Once settled in their new homeland, Icelandic Canadians resumed many of their Old World economic practices, including animal husbandry and fishing. Unlike many immigrant peoples who came later from central and eastern Europe, literacy was virtually universal in the Icelandic community, and early residents devoted free time to Bible study and reading. Efforts by settlers therefore also focused on establishing churches, schools, and libraries.[66] The intensive nature of farming in the Interlake district, in general, left little time for sport and recreation. However, physical prowess was held in high regard among the Icelandic people, so qualities such as strength and endurance were well respected within the community.[67] Although team sports were growing rapidly in popularity in the English-speaking world during the period when Icelanders were establishing themselves in Manitoba, they appear to have held little appeal among the first generation of settlers. There was a strong cultural emphasis on individualism, and the few sports taken up by the Icelanders were of an individual nature.[68] Wrestling naturally lent itself well to this worldview and literally formed part of the sojourning experience, for members of the 1876 colonial cohort who travelled to Canada aboard the steamship *Phoenician* entertained themselves with songs, dances, and bouts of traditional glima.[69]

Glima formed an important role in cultural maintenance for Icelanders following their arrival in Canada, helping to preserve a sense of continuity between the Old World and the New World. Although there is debate over its cultural and etymological origins, glima, which means "game of gladness," traces its origins to the Viking settlement period.[70] Early written references to glima date to circa 1220 and 1230, appearing in, respectively, the *Snorra Edda* and

Egil's Saga.[71] Another early reference to the term appears in the 1325 law book *Johnsbok*, in which it was stated that anyone who participates in the activity must assume responsibility for himself if injured.[72]

In Iceland, three forms of wrestling developed. The first, *hryggspenna*, superficially similar to the British Cumberland-Westmoreland style, involved contestants grasping their hands together behind their opponent's back and attempting to trip or throw the opponent to the ground. A second system of wrestling, *lausatök*, or "loose-hold," had no opening stance and allowed grips to be taken anywhere on the body in an attempt to execute a throw. The third system, *brókartök*, or "trouser grip," entailed wrestlers grasping one another at the hip and attempting to execute throws. By the period coinciding with immigration to Manitoba, *brókartök* glima was the most commonly practised style of wrestling and the one used by the Icelandic settlers. Accordingly, in both Manitoba and Iceland, despite a broader array of traditional folk styles, *brókartök* and glima are popularly synonymous and are considered as such here.

Glima matches bore little resemblance to the wrestling systems imported to the Prairies by Anglo-Canadian settlers. Assuming a vertical posture, both contestants would take hold of the trouser cloth at the hip, with the left hand on the outside and the right hand on the inside. After securing the grip, they would move in a circular fashion, attempting to unbalance their opponent and toss him to the ground. Many throws feature ample use of the legs. Glima practitioners placed particular emphasis on skill and technique over brute strength. By emphasizing tripping and off-balancing using the legs, glima negated the advantage that wrestlers with superior upper body strength often had over their weaker adversaries.[73]

Very few records exist pertaining specifically to matches during the first decade and a half of settlement in Manitoba, but it is reasonable to assume that, if people practised certain wrestling styles en route to North America, they continued to do so once established in their new home. Therefore, the Icelandic national wrestling style was likely being enjoyed in the Interlake district during the same period that the McKeown brothers were earning fame, and notoriety, in Winnipeg sporting circles. By the last decade of the nineteenth century, glima formed an integral part of the events associated with the Islendingadagurinn celebration, held annually on or around 2 August to commemorate adoption of the Icelandic constitution on that day in 1874.[74]

Manitoba's Islendingadagurinn festivities, staged in Winnipeg between 1890 and 1932, and thereafter in Gimli, represented a conscious attempt to preserve important Icelandic traditions from assimilation. Simultaneously, the festivals also stressed the important role that Icelanders played in Canadian society. From the beginning, programs contained elements that accentuated both ideas with varying intensity. Speeches by important Icelandic Canadian officials emphasized the importance of cultural traditions and survival. During the inaugural event in 1890, organizer John Olaffson noted that Icelanders, "while they should aim to be ... citizens of this country[,] they should not forget to have warm emotions to the old land."[75] Similarly, E. Johannsson, speaking on the same occasion, opined that, "while he was opposed to building a Chinese wall around his [community] to prevent assimilation, he was equally against too rapid assimilation, holding that strength of character and a proper degree of conservatism was a good thing for the individual and the nationality."[76] Many of the events associated with the first Islendingadagurinn festivals also emphasized Icelanders' prominent place in their adopted homeland. Public addresses by dignitaries invited from outside the community spoke of Icelanders' many positive cultural traits, including industry, temperance, and thrift, well in accord with "proper" Anglo-Canadian values. Additionally, the day's festivities were concluded with a rendition of "God Save the Queen." Editorial commentary regarding Icelandic Canadians and their annual festival also emphasized their positive characteristics as immigrants.[77] Although early Icelandic immigrants, like any non-English-speaking peoples, faced prejudice upon their arrival in Canada, by the end of the nineteenth century the Islendingadagurinn festival also offered opportunities for assimilation-minded newspaper editorialists to contrast older, "desirable" immigrant peoples such as Icelanders to the newer central and southern Europeans taking up residence in the west. The Conservative-oriented Winnipeg *Telegram*, for example, no doubt taking a jab at the immigration policies of the Liberal government and Clifford Sifton in the process, commented in 1899 that "those who were present [at the festival] could not but have been impressed with the superior character of that element of our population over the class now being imported in such large numbers into the country."[78]

Although the Islendingadagurinn festivals contained aspects that highlighted both the Icelandic and the Canadian elements of their culture, the athletic programs staged during the 1890s and just after the turn of the century were a conscious expression of the former. Early events, adhering to Icelandic traditions of individualism in sports, favoured activities such as foot races, pole vaulting, and swimming. In particular, however, the Islendingadagurinn wrestling competitions represented an attempt to preserve Old World customs. Although the various other individual sports were popular throughout Manitoba and practised by athletes of various nationalities, glima wrestling was unique to Icelandic culture. Within a short time after their arrival in Manitoba, New Iceland's residents were already in the process of constructing a migration myth that placed their latest relocation within the context of a long-standing tradition of heroic voyage and settlement.[79] As an event that harkened back to the Viking age, glima wrestling placed Icelandic residents in a state of communion not only with their immediate predecessors but also with migrant ancestors from a millennium before.

An examination of records pertaining to the first twenty-five Islendingada-gurinn festivals reveals that glima contests were not staged every year. This fact does not suggest, however, that the sport was peripheral to the festivities. Glima contests, like the other Islendingadagurinn athletic events, were always staged outdoors, so poor weather or lack of daylight occasionally prevented scheduled bouts from being held.[80] Matches occurred whenever the August weather permitted them, allowing Icelandic men to showcase their prowess in their age-old combative sport. In addition to preserving the art itself, by the first decade of the twentieth century, efforts were also being made to recognize individuals who adhered to glima's prized principle of emphasizing technique over brute strength, even if they did not win their matches. In 1903, for instance, wrestler Paul Magnusson won a prize for "most skilful wrestling" despite finishing outside the top three positions, and in 1906 Halldor Mathusalemsson, though suffering defeat, earned an award for "most scientific wrestler."[81] Wrestlers who demonstrated the highest level of technical prowess at the annual festival were awarded the Jonas Pallson Cup in recognition of their abilities. During the same period, however, the Islendingadagurinn sports program also began to reflect Icelanders' growing acceptance of certain Anglo-Canadian customs.

In 1901 and 1902, catch-as-catch-can wrestling bouts were staged alongside glima, and by 1909 baseball, a popular activity among Icelandic Canadian youth for many years and periodically included in Islendingadagurinn programs, was also added to the regular program.[82] Simultaneously, the Icelanders who frequented the festival were themselves displaying evidence that a quarter century of living in a predominantly English-speaking province had resulted in them adopting many attributes of the dominant culture.[83] Nevertheless, British Canadian sporting traditions never achieved complete hegemony. Catch-as-catch-can's inclusion in the festival, for example, was only a short-lived venture. The fact that glima retained a place in the Islendingadagurinn festivities throughout the pre-war period suggests that, despite their status as highly desirable and assimilable immigrants, Icelandic Canadians thought that their traditional wrestling style was of sufficient importance to their identity to warrant its preservation in the face of pressures for cultural conformity.[84]

WRESTLING AND THE POLISH CANADIAN COMMUNITY

While Icelandic Canadians were seeking to maintain their native style of wrestling as a symbol of their unique ethnic heritage, Polish Canadians were making their own important impact on the sport in Manitoba. Unlike their Icelandic contemporaries, whose geographic separation from the rest of Europe had facilitated the maintenance of an indigenous wrestling form, Poland's location in central Europe had encouraged the adoption of the highly popular Greco-Roman style. During the late nineteenth century, Greco-Roman wrestling, which had originated in France, became the dominant wrestling system, and one of the most popular sports, in continental Europe. Early Polish wrestling stars such as Laudislaus Pytlasinski were earning international recognition for their victories in important tournaments by the early 1890s.[85]

By 1910, it was evident that Winnipeg's Poles, like members of other ethnic groups, were providing a great deal of patronage to wrestling matches, and over the next four years the city hosted the three most prominent Polish wrestlers then active in the sport. World welterweight title claimant Walter Miller, despite his rather Anglo-sounding surname, described himself to the Winnipeg press as "a Pole from the fingertips" and appeared on Winnipeg mats on five occasions in 1910–14.[86] Of even greater fame, however, were the Zbyszko brothers, Stanislaus and Wladek, two of the most well-known heavyweight grapplers in the world, who appeared on Winnipeg mats in 1912 and 1914, respectively. In each instance, the press noted a strong Polish contingent in the audience. Following his bout with "German Oak" Paul Sigfried on 24 April 1912, Stanislaus received "applause, then some more applause," from his fans, after which "a Polish maiden tripped up to the ring and handed the victor a large bunch of roses."[87] Wladek's appearance a little more than two years later against Joe Collon, the latter described as "a Teuton from the strip of bare scalp he carried aloft, six feet or more in the air, to the socks and running shoes beneath which the stage creaked," was similarly well attended by his fellow countrymen. Zbyszko

WELTERWEIGHT WRESTLING CHAMPION READY FOR MONDAY'S BIG MATCH

WALTER MILLER, OF ST. PAUL.

After working out for three hours at St. Boniface yesterday afternoon, and

5. American wrestler Walter Miller, featured in this newspaper action shot, enjoyed a following within the province's Polish community as a result of his ethnic heritage. Source: Manitoba *Free Press*, 29 September 1913.

defeated his larger German opponent, a substitute for the well-known Dr. B.F. Roller, winning two falls in one hour, "much to the gratification of the Polish section of the spectators, with whom, it was easy to see, the youthful European, and coming World's champion, was a regular hero."[88] Among Manitoba's Polish residents, however, local interest in wrestling did not begin with the appearance of internationally known athletes such as Miller and the Zbyszko brothers. To the contrary, wrestling was first kindled in the province by early immigrants with an explicitly nationalistic agenda.

In Manitoba, extensive Polish immigration occurred after 1896. It is critical to note, however, that Poland did not exist as a country during this period, its territory instead partitioned among Austria, Germany, and Russia.[89] The majority of immigrants came from Galicia, in the southwestern region of present-day Poland. Economic hardship was the primary reason for their departure from Europe, and, as with many other immigrant movements before and after, males made up a disproportionately large segment of the early cohort.[90] Winnipeg, already the dominant metropolitan centre in western Canada by 1896, soon became the centre for Polish cultural life in Manitoba. In general, early Polish immigrants had difficulty integrating into Canadian society given that their language, customs, and Catholic religion made participation in existing institutions problematic. Additionally, Polish immigrants, as part of the larger central and eastern European exodus to Canada, were generally regarded with suspicion and derision by assimilation-minded Anglo-Canadians.[91] Given both their cultural dissimilarity to the host society and the hostile attitudes exhibited toward them, few Poles likely would have chosen to participate in most English-language institutions even had they the opportunity to do so. In the decade following 1896, the vast majority of Polish immigrants came from peasant backgrounds in which familial and clerical relationships formed the cornerstone of everyday life. Polish organizational life during the late nineteenth century therefore centred on establishing separate religious institutions for Polish-language worship.[92] In 1897, Winnipeg's Poles established a church-building committee to raise funds for a Polish-language Roman Catholic church in the city. By the next year, sufficient funds allowed for the construction of the Holy Ghost Church at 341 Selkirk Avenue in Winnipeg's North End. At the time, because of a worldview that prioritized spiritual and familial matters, few immigrants possessed any larger sense of a Polish national consciousness. Such would remain the case throughout the period before the First World War.[93] However, by 1906, Winnipeg was also home to a small group of Polish Canadian citizens who saw sport as a vital component of the larger struggle to establish a sovereign Poland free from external rule.

Winnipeg's Polish nationalist sporting movement began in December 1906 with the formation of Branch 377 of the Polish Gymnastic Association Sokol (Falcons).[94] The Sokol movement originated in 1867 and came to Manitoba by way of the United States. Thereafter, as was generally the case with organized sport in the province, Sokol chapters were founded in other centres, including Brandon, whose club was formed in 1908.[95] During its initial years of operation, Winnipeg's Sokol club focused primarily on physical training, though in later years many activities were carried out under its banner, including military re-cruiting, scouting, Polish-language classes, and choir. The motivation for Sokol's physical training programs went beyond a simple interest in promoting members' health and well-being. Guided by an explicitly nationalist agenda, exercise was used to develop both physical fitness and mental alertness required to establish an independent Polish homeland. Additionally, Sokol's programs were viewed as a way to draw young people living in the city to the nationalist cause.[96] In 1907, the organization opened up a gymnasium on the corner of Magnus Avenue and Powers Street in Winnipeg's North End, equipped with dumbbells and hori-zontal bars. Classes were conducted twice a week for "the mental elevation of the Polish people," and the *Free Press* reported that "a large number of intelligent patriots [were] devoting time and energy to this sublime object" by the beginning of January 1908.[97] Although bearing the emblem of a gymnastics club, during the years before the First World War, Sokol athletes were actively involved in competitive wrestling. In particular, two of the organization's founders, Stanley and Ben Sielski, at whose home the organization conducted its first meeting, were among Winnipeg's most prominent wrestlers prior to the Great War.[98]

Although their exploits largely went unrecorded in the literature pertain-ing to Polish Canadian history, the Sielski brothers, through their involvement in wrestling, were the public faces of the early Polish nationalist movement in Manitoba. Stanley, who wrestled at a weight of 160 pounds, was a Greco-Roman practitioner in Europe, where he had won twenty-three medals prior to his ar-rival in Winnipeg.[99] After moving to Manitoba's capital, he worked variously as a printer and a bartender in addition to serving as the Sokol club's first athletic director.[100] Ben, who worked as a cook in the city, was smaller in stature than his brother and wrestled regularly in matches on Winnipeg professional wrestling cards.[101] The eldest brother, Kazimierz, does not appear to have been involved directly in wrestling but nevertheless retained an active role in the Sokol club.[102] A detailed account of the Sielski brothers' wrestling exploits in Manitoba would be lengthy. However, a brief exposition concerning Stanley's early wrestling activities will highlight their place within Manitoba's Polish community.

The first significant foray into Manitoba wrestling by either of the brothers came in late June 1907, when a public challenge to Scottish-born wrestler Hume Duval appeared in the *Free Press* on behalf of Stanley. Duval, at the time, was appearing at Happyland Park giving strongman exhibitions and entertaining public challenges in which he agreed to throw any wrestler in fifteen minutes or forfeit twenty dollars. The newspaper defi stemmed from his inability to meet Sielski after the Polish grappler had already approached him for a match on the park grounds.[103] Although there was nothing novel about a newspaper challenge for a wrestling match, in this instance it was issued on behalf of the Polish Gymnastic Association Sokol and its secretary-treasurer, C.P. Hamisusk.[104] Challenges, even if ghost-written, were almost as a rule issued under an individual's own name, suggesting in this instance that Sielski's appearance on the mat carried a high degree of importance not merely to himself but also to the larger movement to which Sielski belonged.

When Sielski and Duval met three days later in a match under Greco-Roman rules, it was immediately apparent that the former was indeed backed by a contingent of ardent supporters. Wrestling on a "poorly improvised heap of sawdust under a sheet of canvas," Sielski adopted a largely defensive posture because he merely had to last the required fifteen minutes with Duval to claim victory. After nine and a half minutes, Duval slipped on the edge of the mat and fell backward, his shoulders touching the ground. The referee declared the fall invalid, and the Sokol athlete, exhausted by that point, protested the ruling and refused to go on. Although the fall occurred off the mat, supporters firmly behind the Polish grappler were adamant that their man had pinned the Scot.[105] Although unsuccessful on this occasion in claiming the twenty dollar prize offered by Duval, both Sielski brothers had numerous opportunities thereafter to demonstrate their skills before the public on behalf of the Sokol club.

Although the brothers had a strong base of local supporters and carried out their wrestling activities as representatives of the Polish nationalist Sokol movement, they were not without their detractors within the Polish community. At the same time that they were beginning their local wrestling careers, they found themselves at the centre of a dispute that fractured Winnipeg's Poles into two opposing camps. By the early summer of 1908, the schism was significant enough to gain the attention of the English-language press in Winnipeg. On 29 May, the *Free Press* reported that "the congregation of the Holy Ghost Catholic church ... is split into two warring factions with Father [Groetsschel], the priest, and his friends on one side and the Sielski brothers and their followers on the other" and that "the breach between the two factions of the church is one of long standing."[106] The church, around which organizational life had its genesis within the Manitoba Polish community, objected to Sokol because of its secular charac-ter and its unwillingness to remain subject to clerical control. Conversely, Sokol members wished for the church to adopt a more explicitly nationalist outlook.[107] Conflict between the two factions became so heated during 1908 that both sides found themselves drawn into court over their differences.[108] Ultimately, Sokol retained its autonomy from clerical control and remained at the forefront of the Polish nationalist movement.[109]

The Sielski brothers, described as the "moving spirits" in the club, continued to appear on Winnipeg mats for the next several years and retained a sizable local following. One match, staged between Ben and the local Swedish Cana-dian middleweight champion Charles Gustafson in February 1912 following the vaudeville show at the Emperess Theatre, for example, saw "every seat being taken" by the time the men came to grips.[110] Although the involvement of the Sielski brothers in wrestling remains unheralded in subsequent literature, their extensive participation in the sport made them the public faces of the early Pol-ish nationalist community in Winnipeg. They fostered ethnic pride and helped to draw attention to the Sokol club and its vision of an independent Poland. Just as significantly, the Sielski brothers, living and wrestling in Winnipeg in the early twentieth century, represented an economically disadvantaged and socially marginalized community of people. Through their performances, and frequent successes, on the mat, which included wins against their alleged social betters in the Scottish Athletic Association, they achieved symbolic victories in a society otherwise marked by systemic inequalities and rampant prejudice. In this regard, the Poles were by no means alone. Just as they had the Sielski brothers, so too the Finns had Ole Samson, the French Canadians had Pierre Menard, and the Ger-mans had Max Schultz. Some, such as Charles Gustafson and Ernie Sundberg, were able to gain widespread appreciation from the Anglo-Canadian majority, but the bedrock of their support remained the Swedish community. Wrestling was the ultimate sport in which, for a host of reasons, ethnicity mattered.

CONCLUSION

During the two decades prior to the Great War, Manitoba grew rapidly in ethnic diversity as Anglo-Canadians were joined by large numbers of immigrants from a variety of non-English-speaking nations. Wrestling's popularity expanded markedly during the same period as athletes representing numerous nationalities began to appear on mats in the province. The sport's one-on-one nature made it easy to appeal both to the acute sense of Anglo-Canadian nativism then prevalent in the west and to various immigrant groups' own sense of ethnic pride. Although the sport promoted tensions among ethnic groups, it also helped to bolster group cohesion, often in very different ways. Among the Icelanders, glima wrestling helped to preserve their national identity and reinforce their self-identity as a sojourning Viking people. Conversely, among the Poles, wrestling served as a means of nurturing a growing sense of nationalism within their community and promoting a nationalist agenda. In the multicultural environment of early-twentieth-century Manitoba, wrestling therefore served a wide array of social purposes for the various peoples who made the province their home.

Chapter 4

THE "SIMON PURES"
AMATEUR WRESTLING TO 1914

By the outbreak of war in 1914, Winnipeg had hosted some of the world's most prominent professional wrestlers, and both it and some smaller centres could boast the accomplishments on the mat by local athletes. Professional wrestling also earned widespread popularity because many of its practitioners were seen to possess a host of culturally desirable attributes worthy of accolades. The sport's appeal likewise transcended ethnic boundaries, for various immigrant peoples, already familiar with wrestling before their arrival in Canada, patronized contests that featured their fellow countrymen. For all its appeal, professional wrestling was nevertheless beset by continual controversy as various allegations of corruption and impropriety impeded its path to universal acceptance. Additionally, by explicitly playing upon ethnic and regional rivalries, promoters made profits at the expense of fostering greater cultural tolerance. Professionalism, however, was not the only model for sport that existed in Manitoba.

During the decade and a half before the First World War, amateur wrestling also attracted many participants, particularly in Winnipeg, where the vast majority of organized wrestling took place. Amateur wrestling in Manitoba evolved in a fashion very different from its professional variant, and its growth can be divided into two stages, the demarcation point occurring between 1906 and 1908. Evolving understandings of amateurism, new methods of conducting wrestling contests, and greater organization and integration of amateur sporting bodies at the provincial, national, and international levels helped to further delineate differences between the sport's two branches. Many of the distinctions (and alleged distinctions) between professional and amateur wrestling emerged because of a conscious attempt by the latter to distance itself from its often disreputable cousin. Despite its advocates' intentions, amateur wrestling was unable to separate itself completely from its professional counterpart before the

First World War, and ironically professional expertise proved to be critical in ensuring that Manitoba's grapplers could compete at a high level with athletes from across the country. Additionally, though the sport experienced remarkable growth, participation remained largely limited to members of middle-class Anglo-Canadian society.

AMATEUR WRESTLING AT THE TURN OF THE TWENTIETH CENTURY

As noted in Chapter 1, amateur wrestling matches were staged in Manitoba under the auspices of the Winnipeg Gymnasium beginning in 1891. Evidence suggests that amateur wrestling matches might have been organized in the city, in fact, as early as 1884, when Winnipeg's Harry Warren was presented with a trophy for the provincial amateur wrestling title by local variety theatre owner Dan Rogers, described by the Manitoba *Free Press* in 1898 as the "father of the business" in Winnipeg.[1] However, documentation concerning Warren's amateur wrestling exploits during the 1880s has not surfaced, so little analysis can be offered.[2] During the last half of the 1890s, the sport did not garner much attention in Manitoba, but by the beginning of the twentieth century amateur wrestling began to capture public interest. A series of matches staged between October 1901 and January 1902, as well as the events surrounding them, illustrate amateur wrestling's character in Manitoba during the period.

On 18 September 1901, wrestlers Dave Simon and Bert Phillips, accompanied by several supporters, met at Winnipeg's Leland Hotel to arrange details for a match to decide the "amateur lightweight championship of Canada, Graeco-Roman style."[3] The specific conditions for the match were outlined in a contract, signed by both men as well as two witnesses.[4] Ten days later the date for the match was finally set at 16 October. Although a referee had not yet been agreed on, the Winnipeg Theatre, which hosted the contest, assured the public that "a match devoid of all fakish characteristics [was] promised."[5] Over the next several weeks, the Winnipeg public remained informed of the progress of both men in their training, and careful comparisons were made between their physical attributes, including over a dozen measurements.[6] The event itself, which included a boxing match, attracted between 300 and 400 spectators.[7] The *Free Press*, far more critical in its commentary than the *Telegram*, noted that attendance was low because of "the series of fizzles which have been perpetrated upon the Winnipeg public in the past under the name of ring contests."[8] Although there was some criticism over the long waits between features and the announcer's poor elocution, the wrestling match itself was well received, and at the evening's conclusion Phillips, who lost the match, offered to meet his conqueror again. The *Free Press*, clearly disillusioned with boxing matches, opined that "they may get some spectators if no 'ring' contests are announced in connection with it."[9] Phillips and Simon agreed to a second match under Greco-Roman rules, to be held on 22 November. As before, articles were signed at the Leland Hotel, and subsequent newspaper coverage provided reports on their training and detailed both men's respective physical merits.[10] Commentary also focused on the match's legitimacy, with the *Telegram* stating that "this is the kind of sport that Winni-peggers want and for which they are prepared to give money to see. They will not stand for a fake or a second-class show, but when the men are on the square like the recent match between these two wrestlers, and are out to win[,] there is no crowd that will be more quickly appreciative."[11] Simon once more earned victory in a "fast scientific contest" and was immediately challenged by another wrestler, Leo Dezino.[12] Press reports in this instance also made several references to pub-lic wagering on the match.[13] As against Phillips, Simon was victorious.[14]

Having proved his athletic superiority over both Phillips and Dezino, Si-mon then contracted to meet both men on the same night in a handicap contest in which Phillips, better versed in catch-as-catch-can wrestling, agreed to throw Simon three times in an hour. In the second match, Simon agreed to defeat Dezino five times in an hour under Greco-Roman rules.[15] Perhaps because of his decisive victories over both men on previous occasions, the event was poorly patronized by the Winnipeg public. Once again Simon defeated both men ac-cording to the stipulated conditions.[16] With the available talent depleted and perhaps realizing that Winnipeg offered few future opportunities to display his abilities, Simon relocated to Fargo, North Dakota.[17]

The purpose in providing this rather extended narrative on amateur wrest-ling in Manitoba at the beginning of the twentieth century is to show how closely the sport's conventions paralleled those seen in the professional ranks during the same period. Each of the matches focused intensely on the individual contestants and their respective physical and athletic merits, and training updates helped to build and maintain community interest. Public challenges were issued for future matches, and handicap conditions were arranged to help ensure public support for future encounters between athletes who proved to be unequal in ability. Each of the wrestlers also appeared to have supporters within Winnipeg's sporting community willing to back their performances through wagering on the outcomes. Additionally, assurances that the matches were "on the level" were much in keeping with public perceptions of professional sport's often "dirty" nature. Indeed, if not for the absence of discussions on the wrestlers' purses or proposed side bets and explicit declarations that the matches were "amateur," there would be virtually nothing to distinguish this series of bouts from many of the professional contests staged in the province before the First World War.

Amateur wrestling's pseudo-professional characteristics were attributable, in part, to the absence of any regulatory body to oversee its conduct. In Manitoba, as elsewhere in Canada, numerous self-declared amateur organizations existed, but there was no overarching body that governed athletes according to an established amateur code. At this time, the only umbrella organization for amateur sport in the country was the Canadian Amateur Athletic Union (CAAU), which, despite its lofty name, had no representation outside Ontario and Quebec.[18] Nevertheless, it was well understood that the primary characteristic distinguishing amateurs from professionals was that they never received monetary compensation for athletic performances. The CAAU, which existed from 1884 to 1898 as the Amateur Athletic Association of Canada (AAAC), established during its founding year a definition of amateur sport, which included "one who has never competed for a money prize, or staked [a] bet with or against any professional for any prize, or assisted in the practice of athletic exercises as a means of obtaining a livelihood, or has never entered into any competition under a name other than his own."[19] Although the organization had no jurisdiction outside Ontario and Quebec, its influence extended to other parts of Canada. Most amateur sporting organizations in Manitoba followed the course set by the CAAU in determining what constituted an amateur athlete.[20] However, no central authority existed in the province to dictate whether a wrestler qualified as an amateur, nor did any athletic body oversee amateur wrestling. Matches such as those involving Simon, Phillips, and Dezino were promoted by commercial interests such as C.P. Walker's Winnipeg Theatre, which had direct financial stakes in ensuring profitable outcomes, and they adhered to already proven methods used in professional matches. Yet, since all three athletes involved ostensibly met the basic amateur criterion (i.e., they wrestled without pay), the public appeared to accept their amateur status.

For the next several years, as professional wrestling gained an increased foothold in the city, amateur wrestling developed at a more modest pace. By 1906, it was moving away from its pseudo-professional conventions and toward a format more in keeping with what would be seen in the sport during the subsequent quarter-century. The institution most responsible for the shift was the YMCA, which quickly emerged as one of the city's premier athletic institutions following two decades of inactivity in the sporting realm.

THE WINNIPEG "Y" AND THE GROWTH OF AMATEUR WRESTLING

As a continually operating organization, the Winnipeg YMCA dates to 16 May 1879.[21] Sir J.A.M. Aikins and R.D. Richardson, both immigrants to Manitoba from Ontario, provided the initial impetus for the YMCA's activities in the western province. Aikins, a devout Methodist and temperance crusader who, among his many other distinctions, served as the organization's first president and later acted as the Manitoba Conservative Party leader and the province's lieutenant-governor, initially operated the institution out of his law office on the corner of Main Street and McDermott Avenue.[22] As noted in earlier chapters, many of the diversions offered to young men in Winnipeg were regarded with disdain by reform-minded members of the community. According to J.F. McIntyre, who succeeded Aikins as association president, the Winnipeg YMCA carried out its activities "as a counter attraction to the tendency of young men to seek pleasure in things and pursuits not elevating to their nature."[23] During its first two decades, the Winnipeg YMCA offered numerous educational programs aimed at both instilling Christian values in young men and inculcating practical skills, including Bible study, shorthand writing, vocal training, and Christian-based life counselling. Recreational diversions were also provided, including literary recitations, hymn singing, dinners for single men, and piano music.[24] Prominently absent from the list were distinctly athletic activities.

Until the mid-1860s, athletic training was not a part of the YMCA's organizational mandate, and a proposal by a representative from Brooklyn to build a gymnasium had been rejected, in fact, at the association's national convention in 1856.[25] In the ensuing decades, however, as Muscular Christianity gained greater resonance throughout the Anglo-Protestant world, the YMCA began to adapt its policies, embracing physical as well as intellectual and spiritual pursuits in an effort to produce well-rounded Christian citizens. The YMCA leader most generally associated with the shift toward integrating physical activity into the organization's existing educational and religious mandate was Luther Gulick. He took charge of physical development for the YMCA International Committee in

1889, committed to the notion that manhood, in its ideal form, represented a combination of Hercules, Socrates, and Jesus.[26] However, by the time Gulick assumed his position, such ideas were already in wide circulation. Unquestionably, the importance of physical training was not lost on the Winnipeg YMCA's directorate. In an 1886 address to the association, Reverend D.M. Gordon of Winnipeg's Knox Presbyterian Church drew heavily on contemporary views concerning physical activity's importance in fostering appropriate Christian manliness. The *Free Press*, in reporting his speech, noted that "physical culture was necessary for the higher culture intellectually and spiritual[ly] and it was ours to see that our bodies were what they were meant to be—temples of the Holy Ghost."[27] Gordon further stated that "manliness is needed in any association fitted to do good service in the community. Manly vigour strengthens, and we are entitled to seek this element from the young of the community."[28] Having listened to the annual reports made by YMCA officials earlier in the evening, Gordon also noted the scant attention paid to physical activities. The *Free Press* noted his remarks, stating that, "while the report said little of that matter, [Gordon] assumed it was because the various clubs in the city ... filled that part and did or should do a good work."[29]

In reality, the absence of athletic programs had less to do with the confidence among YMCA leadership that other organizations were adequately meeting the existing need and more to do with financial limitations; the Winnipeg YMCA lacked sufficient funds to secure the required space for athletic facilities. By 1896, the association was acutely aware that the problem was hampering its efforts in the city. YMCA officials recognized that, without a new building, which included a gymnasium, "the association is like a farmer with a hoe, scythe and flail, in a land of steam plows, self-binders and steam threshing machines."[30] Finally, after an aggressive fundraising campaign, the Winnipeg "Y" secured its own facility on the corner of Portage Avenue and Smith Street, which opened on 17 January 1901.[31] Reflecting a heightened emphasis on athletics, the new building contained a fully equipped gymnasium, swimming pool, and running track.[32] Within the first year of its operation, it also maintained quarters suitable for wrestling.[33]

The scope of the YMCA's earliest wrestling-related activities is unclear. However, a wrestling demonstration was included in an extensive public exhibition staged in the association's gymnasium on 2 March 1905.[34] By the next year, efforts were being made to foster competitive wrestling among young boys as well as adults.[35] On 5 April 1906, a tournament was held in the headquarters gym to decide the association's champion. Six athletes entered the competition, described by the *Free Press* as of "a most gentlemanly character" and "run off in a very sportsmanlike manner."[36] J. Hack, the winner, was presented with a gold medal at the annual YMCA physical department banquet eleven days later.[37] The YMCA wrestling tournament represented a departure from previous amateur "championship" contests inasmuch as it lacked virtually all of the promotional garnishments formerly associated with the sport. The event was not preceded by any challenges, contracts, or handicap conditions, nor was any effort made to "build up" interest in the individual wrestlers involved in the tournament. Additionally, Dr. Fischer, the YMCA athletic branch international secretary (and successor to Luther Gulick), who attended the local athletic banquet, was explicit in underscoring the "higher purpose" of sporting activities undertaken by the association, including wrestling: "When athletics become an end in themselves, when we must win at any price, we have prostituted the end and aim of athletics."[38] Although the number of participants in the 1906 organization championship was modest, membership in the YMCA's wrestling program expanded rapidly in subsequent years partly because of its association with the province's first broad-reaching amateur sporting body, the Manitoba Amateur Athletic Association.

THE MANITOBA AMATEUR ATHLETIC ASSOCIATION
AND THE REGULATION OF AMATEUR WRESTLING

The Manitoba Amateur Athletic Association (MAAA) was formed specifically because of concerns among many sporting organizations over rampant professionalism in the province. Although its inception dated from 1904, the MAAA was inactive for the first three years of its existence.[39] In 1907, amateur sport in Quebec and Ontario was in the midst of an internal crisis, which initiated the MAAA's reformation. Generally known as Canada's "Athletic War," the conflict centred on the CAAU and the newly formed Amateur Athletic Federation of Canada (AAFC). The CAAU, in response to growing concerns over professionalism, especially among popular team sports such as hockey and lacrosse, became increasingly restrictive in its definition of "amateur," altering the term's meaning to deal with the various ways in which athletes were "getting around" restrictions on monetary compensation. Many CAAU members recognized that amateur clubs were continuing to employ professionals and therefore favoured a system that would allow both professionals and amateurs to play together, providing that the professionals on the team openly declared their status. The CAAU rejected the proposal, first brought forward in 1904. Three years later, as a result of persistent conflict over the issue, many sporting organizations and their supporters, primarily based in Quebec, broke away to form the Amateur Athletic Federation of Canada (AAFC).[40] In an attempt to consolidate its status, the CAAU encouraged the formation of affiliate provincial organizations. The Winnipeg YMCA proved to be central in the CAAU's efforts to preserve "pure" amateurism in Manitoba. On 15 March 1907, a meeting was held at the "Y" headquarters in the interests of forming a provincial affiliate with the Toronto-based CAAU. The delegates present at the meeting, concerned that "the professional element [was] gaining ground in Manitoba," affirmed their commitment to "amateurism of the purest and highest type."[41] One month later a second meeting was held at the YMCA, with delegates from nineteen different sporting organizations from across the province in attendance, the result of which was the reformation of the MAAA. The MAAA adopted the CAAU's definition of "amateur," which by 1907 read thus:

> An amateur is a person who has not competed in any competition
> for a staked bet, moneys, private, public or gate receipts, or com-
> peted with or against a professional for a prize, who has never at
> any period of his life taught or assisted in the pursuit of any athletic
> exercise or sport as a means of livelihood, who has never directly or
> indirectly received any bonus, or a payment in lieu of loss of time
> while playing as a member of any club, or any money consideration
> whatever for any services rendered as an athlete, except his actual
> travelling and hotel expenses or who has never entered into any
> competition under a name other than his own.[42]

Affirming the YMCA's close affiliation with the MAAA, the "Y's" athletic director D.M. Duncan was appointed as the association's chairman.[43] In early May 1908, the MAAA held its first annual meeting at the YMCA headquarters and adopted a new constitution, which reaffirmed its association with the CAAU.[44]

SUCCESSES AND CHALLENGES IN THE GROWTH
OF COMPETITIVE AMATEUR WRESTLING

The MAAA's creation proved to be a boon for amateur wrestling in the province. The YMCA, in particular, began to turn its attention toward the sport, which, up to that point, had largely been associated with professionalism. In October 1907, the "Y" athletic department decided to commit greater resources to its wrestling program. A coach was hired specifically to instruct wrestling, and intensive thirty-minute lessons were offered to members, who could work with another athlete directly under the instructor's guidance.[45] Efforts evidently paid off, for the following March nineteen athletes entered the annual YMCA championships, up from seven the year before.[46] In November 1908, amateur wrestling's status was placed on an even firmer footing when the inaugural Manitoba Amateur Wrestling Championships were staged at the YMCA under the MAAA's patronage. Participation far exceeded any wrestling competition staged in any prairie province up to that time. Thirty-three athletes registered for the event, including one out-of-province entry from Maryfield, Saskatchewan.[47] At least twenty-six athletes ultimately competed in six separate weight classes in a two-evening tournament.[48] The tournament proved to be successful from an attendance perspective as well, the YMCA gymnasium and gallery being filled with spectators.[49] Evidently, however, public interest was not entirely generated by "pure" athletics alone. Prompting some of the enthusiasm for the event was the participation of Fred McLaglen, then in the midst of his high-profile court proceedings against J.W. Dafoe for defamatory libel.[50] No doubt betraying at least a hint of press partisanship, the attendant *Free Press* reporter noted that, upon McLaglen's defeat by A.J. Mitchell, who weighed nearly sixty pounds less than him, "the crowd nearly pulled the roof down with continuous rounds of applause."[51] Although displaying considerably less hyperbole, the rival Winnipeg Tribune nevertheless concurred that Mitchell's victory "seemed to be a popular win."[52] More important in the long term, however, were predictions that the championships would become an annual event.[53]

The following year, in an evident attempt to broaden the sport's scope, the YMCA staged the Western Canadian Wrestling Championships in place of the Manitoba Championships.[54] Amateur wrestling was clearly expanding beyond the YMCA, and athletes from nine other organizations entered the event. However, association athletes secured first place in all of the six weight divisions.[55] By that time, several athletes had established themselves as pre-eminent amateur competitors, among them McLaglen's conqueror Mitchell, 125 pound competitor Jack Macdonald, and the Akins brothers, Christie and George. All four wrestlers trained at the YMCA, though Macdonald also competed on behalf of the Winnipeg Rowing Club during 1909. The *Free Press*, in an extensive report on 16 June, stated that the previous year had been the most successful in the YMCA physical department's history and that wrestling was the "noted activity" to which the association had devoted particular attention.[56] Juxtaposing the association's efforts against the "disreputable" behaviour seen in the professional ranks, as well as previous efforts at promoting amateur wrestling in the province, the report commented that "the association has stood for a clean, manly competition in the sport, and has done a great deal to elevate the tone in contrast to the wrestling that had been conducted during the past two or three years. They are steadily forging ahead and have made possible the present splendid program in wrestling."[57]

Although the YMCA had a growing list of champions to its credit, officials maintained that commitment to "higher" goals remained the central focus. During the annual meeting in 1909, the YMCA affirmed its obligation to religious education, which remained the national organization's primary concern.[58] However, the ambitious expansion of athletic programs came to be understood as part of a general mission that, even if it could not save souls, would nevertheless provide wholesome alternatives to urban vice.[59] Reflecting the growing importance of "rational" exercise as a means of social improvement, the YMCA's 1909 *Annual Report* noted that, concerning the physical department's efforts, "it is not the aim of this department to produce star athletes. This may happen, but the endeavour is to give an opportunity to men and boys to get healthy exercise and to guide them while taking it…. It is the object of this department that it should be conducted on a sane and sound scientific basis in the interest of efficient manhood, and the greatest good to the greatest number."[60] Although producing champion athletes was officially regarded as of secondary importance, the Winnipeg YMCA continued to add to its unsurpassed competitive record during 1910 and ambitiously pursued the right to host other high-profile amateur wrestling competitions. In March, after some "aggressive work," the organization earned the recently renamed Amateur Athletic Union of Canada's (AAUC) sanction to conduct the 1910 Dominion Amateur Wrestling Championships.[61]

The Dominion Championships represented a significant step forward in Manitoba's continuing integration into the larger Canadian amateur athletic

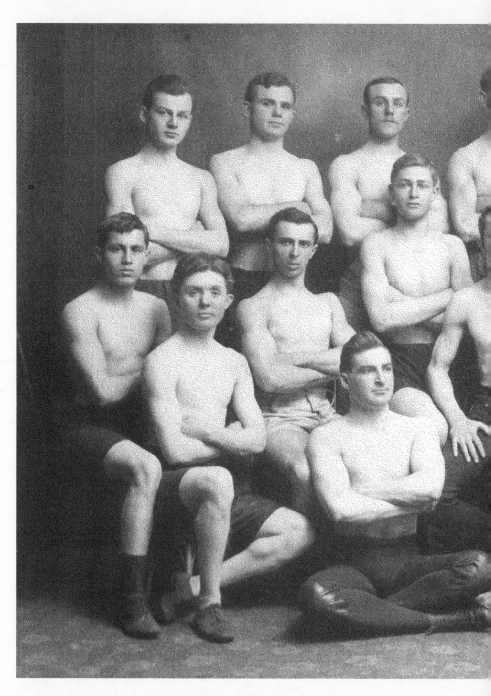

6. Winnipeg YMCA Wrestling Club, 1908–1909. Back row: H. Black, Jas. J. Bowskill, R.G. Bacon, R.J. Thompson, C.S. Judson, George Akins, H.R. Hadcock (Phys. Dir.) Middle row: P.F. Kennedy, Ray La Have, Christie Akins, Thomas Dickinson (Instructor), W. Bates, P.H. Dilts, A. Lockley. Front

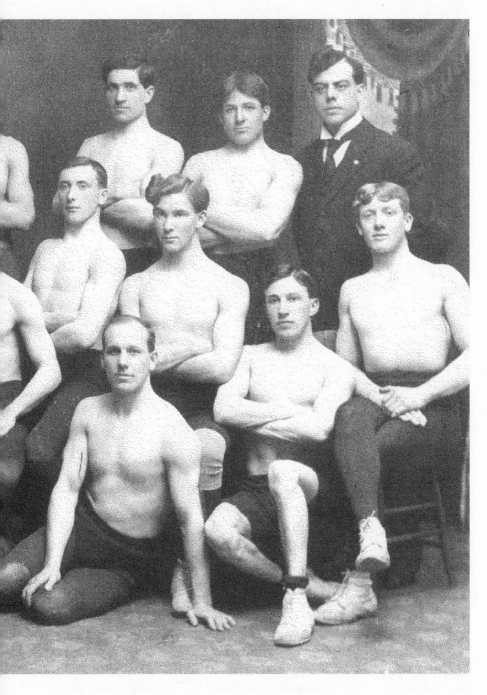

Row: John S. Honsberger, John A. MacDonald (Chairman), A.J. Mitchell, A.V. Ashley. Source: Manitoba Sports Hall of Fame and Museum, MS2013.21.1.

movement, being the first event of its kind ever held west of Ontario.[62] Simultaneously, the tournament also highlighted some of the ongoing problems facing amateur wrestling both in Manitoba and elsewhere in Canada. Because of the anticipated attendance, the championships were staged at the Winnipeg Theatre. The YMCA made efforts to advertise the event throughout Canada, and several prominent athletes, including Aubert Côté, bronze medallist at the 1908 Olympic Games in London, were reported to have expressed interest in attending the meet.[63] Thirty-one athletes ultimately entered the Dominion Championships, a respectable number, consistent with large-scale amateur wrestling events staged during the preceding two years in Manitoba. Yet, a closer examination of the competition roster reveals that wrestling, despite the growth of provincial governing bodies and their integration into the larger national amateur movement, was still not a truly "national" sport. Of the thirty-one, only three, Montreal's R.F. Eagan, Oshawa's J. Miller, and Toronto's Bruce Sutherland, were from out of province. Côté, the Olympic medallist, did not attend. The remaining twenty-eight competitors were from Winnipeg. The "local boys" swept the competition, earning titles in each of the seven contested weight divisions, and once again the YMCA proved itself to be the city's pre-eminent club, taking four of the seven first-place titles.[64] To the Winnipeg wrestlers' credit, however, each of the three visiting wrestlers was himself a former national champion. Similar to the situation in 1910, the next National Amateur Championships, held in Vancouver in 1912, saw members of the Vancouver Athletic Club take all titles.[65] Winnipeg, home to all reigning national champions, did not send any athletes to compete in the event.[66] Amateur wrestling therefore remained primarily, during its early years, a regional sport with national pretensions.

Part of the difficulty with engendering a truly national sport stemmed from the challenges associated with transportation. Although a national railway system was in place by the period, and Manitoba's railway infrastructure, because of ambitious branch line expansion under the Roblin government (1900–15), was largely complete by 1909, considerable time had to be invested in interprovincial travel.[67] Exacerbating the situation was the general disinclination for many amateur athletic organizations to cover their athletes' expenses. Although amateur regulations did not prohibit an athlete's travel expenses from being covered, organizations were sometimes hesitant, or lacked the funds, to pay for train fare and accommodations. Olympian Aubert Côté, for example, had to mortgage his farm in order to procure the necessary money to sail to England for the 1908

Olympic Games, and even after returning with a medal he had considerable difficulty in securing his expenses from the Canadian Olympic Committee.[68] Because of both cost and distance, wrestling, like many other sports, therefore continued to function primarily on a regional basis, despite the development of "national" championships.[69]

The 1910 National Amateur Championships also underscored the fact that, despite the desire of the AAUC, MAAA, and YMCA to foster pure amateur competition free from the corrupting influence of money, amateur wrestling was still driven by economic imperatives. In securing the Winnipeg Theatre for the event, the YMCA and MAAA did so in anticipation of a larger attendance than could be accommodated by the Portage Avenue YMCA, which by 1910 was already proving to be too small to meet the space demands imposed by its various athletic programs.[70] Ticket prices ranged from twenty-five cents to one dollar, generally comparable to the rates charged for professional cards.[71] Unfortunately for the organizers, the tournament's first night attracted "one of the slimmest crowds on record."[72] As a result of the poor attendance, the MAAA accrued a large deficit, unable to cover the costs of staging the event.[73] In discussing the MAAA's financial problems, the *Free Press* highlighted one of the great dilemmas endemic to wrestling: "Amateur competitions such as decided are clean and the competitors struggled to the best of their ability to win by fair and above-board methods.... It is strange, indeed, to chronicle that a professional contest, about which one always has one's doubts of honesty, should draw a crowded house and perhaps a hundred enthusiasts should witness genuine contests such as were the amateur championships."[74] The statement no doubt reflected, at least in part, the general bias that many Manitobans, particularly those in the middle class, had against professionalism in sport (a perspective that, as Morris Mott notes, occasionally led them to turn a blind eye to similar behaviour in the amateur ranks). Yet it was nevertheless true, as has been well established, that professional wrestling continued to attract spectators despite various offences to public decency.[75] Purveyors of the amateur ideal persisted in making every attempt to distance themselves from the "sullied" world of professional wrestling, praising the YMCA for having "done more to purify sport in America than any other organization."[76] The YMCA was later congratulated by the *Free Press* for its efforts in staging the Dominion Championships and trying to "clean up" the sport, declaring, in direct reference to wrestling, that, "when the association takes hold of a competition, no matter how questionable its past career or reputation is, to know that the association is at the back of it is a sufficient guarantee that it will not only be square and above board but it will be clean and void of any objectionable features."[77]

The 1910 Dominion Championships represented a financial setback for the MAAA and a failure as a spectator event. Still, amateur wrestling continued to prosper as a participant sport in Winnipeg, as evidenced by the 1911 provincial championships, once more hosted by the Winnipeg YMCA, which attracted twenty-two entries.[78] Additionally, despite an AAUC decision against holding a National Amateur Wrestling Championship in 1911, the city was the site for the most important series of matches staged in Canada during the year and certainly the most significant amateur wrestling event yet held in the province: an elimination tournament to determine who would represent Canada at the Festival of Empire sports championship.

The Festival of Empire, which opened on 12 May, was arranged in honour of George V's coronation. Held at London's Crystal Palace grounds, the festival celebrated the British Empire's historical development and various social and economic achievements. Exhibits included three-quarter-size replicas of the various colonial Parliament Buildings, a model railway, amusement park rides, and a feature called "London in the Year 2000," which offered a glimpse of the city's presumed future.[79] In addition to the various displays, the festival hosted numerous celebratory events, including the Inter-Empire Sports Championship, a precursor to the British Empire (later Commonwealth) Games. Athletes from Australia, Canada, New Zealand, South Africa, and Great Britain competed in running competitions (100 yards, 220 yards, 880 yards, one mile, and 120-yard hurdles), swimming (one mile and 100 yards), heavyweight boxing, and middleweight wrestling.

In early May, the AAUC began the selection process to determine Canada's representatives at the event. N.H. Crowe, AAUC secretary and member of the selection committee, proposed the idea that George Akins—the Manitoba, western Canadian, and dominion middleweight and heavyweight champion— face Vancouver's premier middleweight grappler, George Walker, in Winnipeg. The winner would then travel to Toronto to meet Kingston's J.A. MacDonald, Canada's reigning intercollegiate heavyweight wrestling champion.[80] As it happened, however, MacDonald, who had graduated from Queen's University in 1910, was already in the west, having accepted a teaching assignment at Coblenz, Saskatchewan. Although he was not aware that his name was even being considered, upon hearing of the event, MacDonald wrote to the *Free Press* expressing his intent to participate in it.[81] By a confluence of circumstances, Winnipeg

7. George Washington Akins, an early amateur wrestling standout in Manitoba. Source: Manitoba Sports Hall of Fame and Museum, MS2011.25.259.

therefore became the site for both matches. The YMCA gymnasium, with a seating capacity of 800, was "well filled" with a "large crowd" when Akins faced Walker on 31 May.[82] After forty-five minutes of wrestling, the visiting grappler defeated the local champion, and the following night he again proved to be victorious against the collegiate champion after forty-nine minutes on the mat.[83] On 10 June, Walker, along with eight other athletes, sailed for England.[84] He ultimately placed second in the competition, losing in the final to England's Stanley V. Bacon, 1908 Olympic gold medallist and brother to Winnipeg resident and 1910 dominion welterweight wrestling champion R.G. Bacon.[85]

The Festival of Empire wrestling elimination bouts generated more publicity than any amateur wrestling event staged in Manitoba before the Great War and, inasmuch as the middleweight title was concerned, can be considered Canada's first truly pan-national amateur wrestling championship. Additionally significant is that it directly connected Canadian amateur wrestling to the larger world of international amateur sport. Thus, amateur wrestling on regional, national, and international levels was finally linked together by the events that transpired in Winnipeg in May and June 1911. A similar situation would not occur for another thirteen years, when Canada sent its next wrestling team to the Paris Olympics in 1924. That the bouts transpired at all, however, was not without uncertainty. Once more underscoring amateur sport's precarious financial situation during the period, neither the MAAA nor the AAUC had available sufficient funds to cover all of the wrestlers' incidental costs in addition to travel fare.[86] Instead, J.D. Pratt, MAAA president, suggested that the proceeds from ticket sales could be directly handed over to the winner to cover his expenses.[87] The cost of renting one of the local theatres was considered by MAAA officials to be prohibitive and likely, given their experiences a year earlier, too risky a proposition.[88] Fortunately, the YMCA offered its gymnasium free of charge, and attendance, as noted, was very high, averting a difficult financial situation such as that faced by Côté three years earlier.[89]

Naturally, the high-profile event also provided an opportunity to contrast professional wrestling's various antics to the more "respectable" behaviour of amateur athletes. The *Free Press* cited Akins, Walker, and MacDonald as exemplars of "true" sportsmanship:

> [During their time in Winnipeg, a] friendship was cemented, for
> the trio are the best of palls [sic], chums in fact. While in the city

they went about together, took in the theatres and anything else
that was going on. They are out and out amateurs, being in the
sport for sport sake and are made of the right stuff. How different
to those other fellows who enter the roped arena as a means of
livelihood: they come here with tales of hatred for their opponents,
and while it is sometimes put on they often mean it. Then when the
decision is not given in their favour they vow vengeance against the
sporting editor: they would see the editor-in-chief and what not.
It is all in the game for them, for a licking will mean that they will
find difficulty in having other matches made for them.[90]

The MAAA devoted considerable energy to ensuring that young men, such as
Akins, Walker, and MacDonald, would continue to exhibit "the right stuff" by
endeavouring to police the sports under its stewardship and keep them free of
professionalism. Accordingly, tremendous energy was devoted to seeking out
veiled professionals in the amateur ranks and applying punitive actions against
the offenders.[91] Policing amateur sport often proved to be an onerous task, and
debates over mixing professionals and amateurs continued to find fertile ground
both in Manitoba and elsewhere in Canada.[92] However, both the AAUC and by
extension its provincial affiliate remained steadfastly opposed to the notion, fear-
ing, as J.D. Pratt worried, that mixing professional and amateur athletes would
be "the thin end of the wedge working in ... [to] lower the standard of athletics."[93]

Team sports such as hockey unquestionably drew the majority of the
MAAA's regulatory efforts, but wrestling was not exempt from scrutiny. In early
January 1910, for example, the MAAA issued a warning to its athletes on account of reports that amateur wrestlers had recently appeared on a number of
professional cards in the city.[94] It is unclear from examining the results of known
professional wrestling cards from the period which athletes had contravened the
policies of the AAUC/MAAA. Competing under an assumed name was not
uncommon (hence its inclusion in the definition of "amateur" adopted by the
MAAA in 1907), and it is probable that perpetrators did so to avoid detection
and rescission of their amateur status.[95]

THE PROFESSIONAL'S ROLE
As vociferously as amateur sporting organizations sought to free themselves
from professional "contamination," a constant irony was that many of them
nevertheless owed much of their success to professional skill and expertise. The

seven years between the MAAA's founding and the First World War represent organized amateur wrestling's infancy in the province. To develop their amateur wrestling programs, many clubs sought out the best coaches whom they could find, and, in a province with an already sizable cohort of professional wrestlers, the requisite skill was to be found in the professional ranks. Of course, the YMCA was dominant among amateur wrestling clubs in Manitoba before 1914. Upon deciding to concentrate attention and resources on its wrestling program in the fall of 1907, it enlisted the services of Thomas Dickinson, who had appeared both as a competitor and as an official on several professional wrestling cards in Winnipeg during the previous two years. Dickinson was hired with a salary by the YMCA, and he coached the club to its early championships.[96] Although employed by an explicitly amateur organization, Dickinson did not quit his professional activities while in the employ of the YMCA. Most prominently, he wrestled world lightweight champion Eugene Tremblay in a handicap match on 2 May 1910.[97] At the same time, other professional wrestlers acted in similar capacities. In 1910, professional middleweight champion Charles Gustafson served as the wrestling instructor for the newly formed Winnipeg Athletic Club, which fielded athletes to the Manitoba Amateur Wrestling Championships, and George LePage, later decried for dealing professional wrestling its "death blow" in refusing to meet Gustafson at the Winnipeg Auditorium because of poor attendance, taught wrestling at the Agricultural College.[98] In a related capacity, professional wrestlers also served as workout partners for amateur competitors. For instance, in preparation for the Festival of Empire competition, Charles Gustafson helped to train George Akins, the Swedish grappler pronouncing the local amateur "one of the best men in the middleweight division."[99]

The MAAA's definition of "amateur" did not allow an individual who "at any period of his life taught or assisted in the pursuit of any athletic exercise or sport as a means of livelihood" or received remuneration to hold amateur status. Yet amateur organizations were eager to hire professionals or professionalize individuals by hiring them to improve the calibre of athletics in the province. Such was the case in 1892, when E.W. Johnston was hired by the Winnipeg Athletic Association to oversee training, and the practice remained unchanged in the years after formal amateur athletic governance came to Manitoba. Although organizations such as the YMCA might have claimed character building as amateur sport's central purpose, there is little doubt that achievement in competitive athletics was becoming increasingly important before the First World War. Dedication to the threefold vision of human improvement continued, but it was clear that physical development was slowly emerging as "first among equals" in priority. Underscoring the increasing centrality of athletics in the organization's mandate, J.H. Ashdown, head of the YMCA building committee, iterated in 1912 that "association workers strive now to make a well-developed body the tenement of good mental capacity and moral nature."[100] The YMCA might have indicated that its intention was not to produce "star athletes," but it was nevertheless conscious of promoting its various championship laurels in indoor baseball, basketball, tennis, track and field, and wrestling.[101]

With a membership base rapidly expanding because of athletic programs, the Winnipeg YMCA opened a second facility on Selkirk Avenue in the city's North End in April 1912. Thomas Dickinson's services were in even greater demand than before, and during the fall of the year Dickinson was dividing his time equally between the two branches.[102] In 1913, a new, six-storey facility on Vaughan Street replaced the YMCA's Portage Avenue headquarters, for several years too small to meet the demands imposed by a growing membership, and by late 1913 Dickinson was once more active in his coaching capacity at both the Vaughan and the North End facilities.[103] In 1914, Winnipeg again hosted the Dominion Amateur Wrestling Championships, which, held in conjunction with the Provincial Amateur Boxing Championships, proved to be a better public drawing card than those staged four years earlier.[104] Once again local competitors made up the majority of the entrants and claimed first place in each weight division. However, unlike during previous provincial and national championships, the YMCA no longer monopolized the podium, winning championship honours in only two of the six contested categories. Three of the remaining titles went to the Winnipeg Boys' Club, coached by Canadian featherweight professional wrestling champion Alex Stewart.[105]

Amateur sporting organizations' willingness to hire active professional wrestlers to bolster their athletic programs, while simultaneously imposing strict prohibitions on their athletes against remuneration for fear of money's corrupting influence, was clearly a contradiction. If money was the poison that amateur sport's leaders maintained it to be, then how could young athletes' guidance and development be placed under the direct supervision of individuals who earned a portion of their living by the very means most despised in amateur sporting circles? How could amateur clubs consciously contrast the wholesome nature of their programs and the character of their wrestlers against the activities witnessed in the professional ranks? Winnipeg's most prominent wrestling coaches, after all, were not just men paid by their respective organizations for their services but also individuals with well-documented records on professional mats. The policy was clearly one that served the interests of competitive sports at the expense of the character-building nature allegedly endemic to "simon pure" amateurism. Many in the public recognized that the existing amateur code was problematic and primarily served the interests and values of those directing sport in the province: a small cadre of individuals, the vast majority of whom were of urban (Winnipeg), middle- and upper-middle-class, Anglo-Canadian extraction. Regulations were carefully crafted and in many cases selectively enforced to meet the desires of sport's ruling oligarchy, and sanctions were primarily imposed on those from poorer socio-economic backgrounds.[106]

PARTICIPATORY BASE

In wrestling's case, direct censure of amateur athletes did occur on occasion during the prewar era, as when 1908 provincial middleweight champion Les Moir, after winning a tournament the following spring, was subsequently disqualified for falsely claiming that he had never competed against a professional.[107] Although not altogether unknown, punitive measures were nonetheless more common in many other sports. However, competitive amateur wrestling also did not extend, on the whole, far beyond the urban Anglo-Canadian middle class in terms of participation. The surnames of Manitoba's amateur wrestlers from the period were mostly British, and it was not until 1914 that two individuals, Patsy Picciano and E. Abrahamson, broke the Anglo-Saxon monopoly on championships in all weight divisions. Picciano turned professional shortly after winning the dominion title, wrestling under the name Patsy Bachant.[108] The distinctly white and Anglo-Saxon character of amateur wrestling during this period extended to Canada's involvement in the fledgling international amateur sports movement. When George Walker competed for the right to represent Canada at the Festival of Empire in 1911, he did so against fellow Anglo-Canadians. Once in Britain, he likewise faced opponents, as did other athletes, from the Anglo-Saxon domains. Notably absent, for example, were participants from India, western and northeastern Africa, Southeast Asia, and other regions of the British Empire that had not been heavily settled by a white, English-speaking population. Indeed, the event was originally conceived of two decades earlier by J. Astley Cooper as an "Anglo-Saxon Olympiad."[109] The Festival of Empire sports competition was therefore less an attempt to bring peoples of all backgrounds together to celebrate their common membership in a pan-global political, cultural, and economic enterprise than an attempt to privilege the common sporting practices and achievements of the Anglo-Protestant settlers.

There were also strong class dimensions to amateur wrestling in Manitoba during this period. The YMCA, which produced the majority of high-calibre amateur wrestlers in the province, remained a predominantly middle-class institution whose membership extended only marginally into the semi-skilled and unskilled manual labour force. Statistics produced by the Winnipeg association in 1910, for example, provide a detailed breakdown of the local membership's occupational composition. Out of 1,693 registered adult members, office workers (consisting of clerks, bookkeepers, and stenographers) made up the single largest category (364), followed by college and business college students (174), merchants, managers, and real estate men (162). Unspecified or general labourers were wholly absent from the list.[110] Although a complete occupation-based analysis of all wrestlers in the province is not available, a careful examination likewise indicates that competitive amateurs were drawn largely from "white-collar" occupations and skilled trades.[111] Yet, as war loomed on the horizon, there was evidence, as seen through the success of the Winnipeg Boys' Club in 1914, that the sport was slowly reaching a broader cross-section of the population. Self-described as "The Street Boy's Y.M.C.A.," the Boys' Club drew many of its members from poorer segments of the young male population, many of whom had already run into legal difficulties.[112] However, by 1914, their success in competitive athletics was just beginning. Thus, while amateur wrestling experienced tremendous growth in the decade and a half before the Great War, being transformed from a sport with few competitors and no central administration into a well-organized athletic undertaking with connections to national and international sporting movements, it had yet to become a sport that, like its professional counterpart, was truly accessible and relevant to broad sections of Manitoba society.

CONCLUSION

Between 1900 and 1914, amateur wrestling underwent a remarkable transformation. Initially a sport whose conventions differed little from those seen in the professional ranks, by 1907 amateur wrestling was beginning to assume a very different form. Both the MAAA, the newly created provincial governing body for amateur sport, and like-minded sporting organizations, such as the YMCA, sought to reshape the "mat game" according to a shared set of amateur values that stood in conscious opposition to the perceived threat posed by professionalism. Under its new stewards' direction, amateur wrestling experienced tremendous growth in Manitoba, and the sport became increasingly connected (albeit often more in principle than in practice) to the larger national and international amateur wrestling movement. However, despite efforts to detach amateur and professional wrestling from one another, a growing desire to provide first-class coaching and achieve competitive victory ensured that they were never completely divorced during the prewar era. Additionally, though the sport could boast of remarkabe advances, its appeal as a competitive activity never extended far outside the province's middle-class, Anglo-Canadian population, whose members governed amateur sport. In the ensuing years, however, wartime conditions ensured that wrestling would once more undergo a remarkable, albeit brief, metamorphosis, as "simon pure" amateurism disappeared, to be replaced for a time by a military sporting movement that altogether blurred the barriers that had been deliberately constructed to separate amateurism from professionalism.

Chapter 5

GRAPPLING WITH THE GREAT WAR, 1914–18

Members of the 8th Battalion (90th Winnipeg Rifles), CEF, known affectionately as the "Little Black Devils," encircled the banks of a wide ditch that formed a makeshift earthen arena. Hundreds of infantrymen sat on the impromptu grass bleachers that were its sides, many with their tunics removed and their shirt sleeves rolled to the elbows in an effort to gain respite from the warm June sun. Others, wishing a better purchase to view the proceedings, stood on the ditch's topmost edge, eyes fixed, like the servicemen seated below, on the scene being played out before them. Two soldiers stripped to the waist and clad in shorts and shoes struggled "manfully" on the grass, their muscles straining from exertion, as the battalion looked on. Over them stood a higher-ranking official to give instructions or end the encounter when victory was achieved. One of the men secured the always-advantageous top position and endeavoured to press his opponent's shoulders firmly to the earth below them. Nearing the point of defeat, the man on the bottom fought back from his perilous situation. Securing a tight grip on his adversary's head, he intertwined their legs, seeking to throw the man up and to the side and in doing so regain a more favourable angle from which to continue his own attack.[1]

The soldiers serving with Winnipeg's Little Black Devils, much like those throughout the Canadian Expeditionary Force (CEF), enjoyed a hard-fought wrestling match. By the time the scene was captured for perpetuity by camera during the summer of 1918, wrestling, particularly contested according to catch-as-catch-can rules, was a well-established spectator and participatory sport in Manitoba at both the professional and the amateur levels. Following Canada's entry into the Great War in August 1914, the "mat game" played a notable, though largely unexamined, part in the Canadian war experience. As a popular sport, wrestling reinforced masculine militarist values and gender expectations widely held by Canadians between 1914 and 1918. Simultaneously, however, it also proved to be "contested territory" in which middle-class beliefs concerning the inherent dangers of mingling amateur and professional athletes were challenged. This occurred primarily because military-based sport came to replace civilian sport as an ideal site for demonstrating appropriate masculinity, and in this context professional athletes repeatedly demonstrated their value to the Canadian war cause. Over the course of the war, wrestling therefore assumed the dual role of bolstering widely held ideas related to masculinity while simultaneously confronting specific class-based prejudices concerning the "dirty" professional athlete.

During an era when manhood was increasingly conceptualized in aggressive and militaristic terms, wrestling served as an ideal "maker of men" that, in addition to inculcating desirable character traits, taught soldiers practical skills for warfare. On the home front, the long-standing popularity of wrestling immediately made the sport an excellent tool for publicizing the war effort and generating revenue for the Patriotic Fund, particularly in the first several months of the Great War, when public enthusiasm for the cause was high. Shortly after the declaration of hostilities, various civilian sporting organizations began to foster a close relationship with the Canadian military. As the conflict in Europe dragged on into its second year, competitive wrestling, previously conducted primarily under civilian auspices, took on added importance both as a means of ensuring the maintenance of what was considered by authorities to be appropriate conduct within the homosocial environment of military camps and as an aid to recruiting. However, with the proliferation of military athletics after late 1915, "khaki" athletic bodies came to threaten the long-held monopoly that the Amateur Athletic Union of Canada (AAUC) and its provincial affiliates held as the self-appointed moral guardians of sport. By 1916, military athletics became a site for challenging existing views concerning the relationship between amateurs and professionals, which represented at its core a philosophical divergence over sport's "proper" purpose in Canadian society.

HISTORICAL BACKGROUND

Within the ever-expanding body of literature concerning sport and society in Canada, there is a tendency among historians providing a longitudinal study of the subject to give cursory treatment to the period between 1914 and 1918.[2] Yet, despite their brief analyses, many works strongly affirm the war's importance in helping to reshape sport, much as it did other elements of Canadian society.[3] Conversely, academic works dedicated to Canada's role in the Great War, both on the home front and in the operational theatre, have tended to ignore sport altogether or give it only passing mention.[4] Fortunately, though, in recent years several Canadian historians have turned their attention to Canadian sport during the First World War.[5] The most significant work to date specifically dedicated to the subject is Andrew Horrall's examination of Canada's most popular summer game, baseball, in the CEF. His primary emphasis is on the sport's purpose, organization, and development overseas and on its eventual integration into official military practice.[6] Building on Horrall's seminal study, this chapter charts wrestling's evolution on the home front, especially in Manitoba, between 1914 and 1918. Bolstering an understanding of wartime wrestling in Manitoba are the numerous studies related to ideas on masculinity, militarism, and class, which provide vital contexts for its significance during the "war to end all wars."

MATMEN, MANLINESS, AND THE MILITIA

In Manitoba, wrestling had been practised in various forms since before the province entered Confederation. In the decade prior to 1914, however, the sport, as contested under catch-as-catch-can rules, grew considerably in popularity. Professional wrestling matches were regular features at various public venues, including theatres, clubs, halls, and sports arenas, particularly in Winnipeg, the province's capital. Amateur wrestling was slower to develop in the province, but by 1914 Provincial Championships had been held for six years, and in that period Dominion Championships had been staged in Winnipeg twice. Although wrestling appealed to members of the public for a variety of reasons, a key element of its widespread popularity, particularly within the middle-class amateur sports movement, was its perceived value in infusing an appropriate expression of manliness in young men.

Competitiveness and aggression were also closely equated with masculinity by the last decade of the nineteenth century, and sports promoting such behaviour were widely lauded as pathways to, and expressions of, proper manliness.[7] With a heightened emphasis on physicality, as Varda Burstyn asserts, "the aggressive male body [became] the site of provable masculinity for men."[8] Wrestling lent itself well to a worldview that celebrated male qualities such as strength, endurance, toughness, muscular development, and physical dominance. Victories on the mat were described in near-epic terms, adding weight to their significance as public spectacles and representations of male virtue.[9] Well-known public figures such as American president Theodore Roosevelt, whose popularity extended beyond his nation's borders, were staunch advocates for aggressive sport's worth as a man-maker, and they enthusiastically embraced wrestling for this reason, as did organizations such as the YMCA through its devotion to the physically vigorous doctrine of Muscular Christianity.[10] The growing sporting goods industry also published courses teaching men how to wrestle. Instructional texts by well-known manufacturers, including Spalding, offered more than mere techniques, exalting wrestling's physicality as a moral enterprise in its own right. The Spalding Athletic Library's *How to Wrestle* (1912) promoted wrestling as a natural, manly endeavour while juxtaposing it against less "respectable" versions of manhood that bred self-indulgence or a sedentary existence: "The fascination and rewards of wrestling are such that a man with virility and love of contest in his blood has but to taste of them in order to enlist among its votaries. The man or youth who wrestles feels his superiority over his associates who prefer to spend all of their spare moments in a billiard room, breathing tobacco laden air, or in kindred places.... He does twice as much business as the men, narrow chested and weak kneed, who toil at their desk until dinner time, and then go home at odds with the world."[11] Mail order courses in physical instruction also gained popularity after the turn of the century, promising to help young men fulfill widely held gender expectations.[12] Martin "Farmer" Burns, one of North America's pre-eminent wrestlers and physical trainers, offered his mail order course *Lessons in Wrestling and Physical Culture* "To REAL Men and Boys Everywhere," asserting, next to a photograph of two youths forcefully sparring for a takedown, that "Splendid Contests Like This Lay the Foundation for Future Health and Perfect Manhood."[13] His lessons also provided males with the means to gain masculine capital, equated explicitly with physical prowess, through their ability "to be able to handle, throw, baffle and mystify opponents far bigger and stronger than [they are]."[14] Such skills, Burns promised, would allow them "to be a man among men."[15] All of this, and more, could be achieved for an enrolment fee of thirty-five dollars.[16]

During the late nineteenth century and early twentieth century, aggressive expressions of manhood in sport were intimately tied to imperialism. Canadians, the majority of whom were of British birth or heritage, valued the dominion's connection to the British Empire. Nurtured by social Darwinist conceptions that placed Anglo-Protestant culture at the vanguard of human development, British customs and practices were necessarily held in the highest regard. Love of sport was her-alded as one reason for the British ascent as a world power, and by fostering sports in Canada the dominance of manly British values could, in part, be ensured.[17]

Militarist enthusiasm in Canada during the early twentieth century rein-forced bonds among empire, war, and sport. Connections between sport and the military had existed in some form since ancient Greece (whose culture was widely admired by the late Victorians), when athletes were known to compete in sporting events wearing their battle armour.[18] By the early 1900s, military and paramilitary organizations such as the Boy Scouts and boys' brigades flourished, their ranks swelled by boys' alleged "natural love for militarism."[19] Bolstering their purportedly innate enthusiasm, however, were financial endowments such as the Strathcona Trust, which provided funds for military drill training in Canadian schools. By 1911, all provinces in Canada had sanctioned the program and were implementing drill in public school physical education classes.[20] Sport, too, was directly equated with war, with conquest on the playing field analogous to military conflict.[21] Wrestling matches, as was the case with other sports, were commonly described as "battles," their back-and-forth nature akin to swaying fortunes in the theatre of war.[22] Conversely, however, as both Wanda Wakefield and Andrew Horrall illustrate, the military also used sports metaphors to con-vey its own messages to soldiers in a widely intelligible fashion, further reinforc-ing the intimate conceptual alliance forged between sport and militarism in the early twentieth century.[23]

Despite widespread militarism, not all of Manitoba's residents shared sentiments that made ready connections among male identity, sport, empire, and war. Most prominently, the province's Mennonites, who numbered approxi-mately 15,000 by the beginning of the First World War, were openly pacifist and therefore rejected notions of military manliness. Mennonites, on the basis of their religious views, were exempt from military service.[24] However, members of groups that held similar sentiments were not granted military exemption. Ca-nadians enlisted on a voluntary basis during the first three years of the war, but following the enactment of conscription in 1917 dissenters faced even greater pressures to "don the khaki."[25] Nevertheless, that such groups continued to exist and resist indicates that, even in a period marked by massive pressure to conform to prevailing Anglo-Canadian norms, alternative interpretations of masculinity persisted. Yet dissenting views did not gain broad currency, and in the decades before the First World War the link between militarism and sport became deeply entrenched.

In Canada, militia units participated in sports events of all kinds. Widespread interest in sport helped to forge solidarity within the militia's ranks between its working-class and middle-class members.[26] Official military training manuals from the period advocated sports, including wrestling, as complements to regular training in the belief that drill alone was insufficient to elevate a soldier's fitness.[27] Sport's inherent value as a character-building enterprise was additionally recognized, and unlike drill, athletic endeavours were considered an aid to addressing "bad habits too often acquired before enlistment."[28] Yet not all activities met with universal praise. For instance, competitive boxing conducted under military auspices came under public criticism in Ontario during 1901 for being unacceptably violent. Likely, however, as Mike O'Brien notes, prize fighting's long association with "disreputable" working-class elements in society contributed as much to competitive boxing's condemnation as its inherently violent nature.[29] In Manitoba, as elsewhere, wrestling never received the same level of censure accorded to boxing, and it proved to be a popular activity closely associated with the province's militia units. In particular, wrestling on horseback served as a common event at various military gymkhana staged in the province. In October 1892, a military sports program staged at Winnipeg's Fort Osborne barracks included a mounted wrestling tournament, in which Sergeant Young and Private Brown battled to a twenty-minute draw in the finals.[30] Similar events were staged throughout the period prior to the First World War.[31] As the results of the 1892 program betray, however, such spectacles served not only to test manly prowess within the peculiarly military context of mounted combat but also affirmed military hierarchy. Contests were reserved exclusively for the enlisted rank-and-file militia members and the non-commissioned officers corps. Officers were not generally active participants in the sport and certainly did not compete against their subordinates.[32] Evidently, however, even Canada's highest-ranking military officials took an interest in wrestling, among them Sam Hughes, minister of the militia. During the spring of 1914, he was rumoured to have engaged John Webster, the MP for Brockville, in an impromptu wrestling match in his office. When asked about the rumours during Question Period in the House of Commons, Hughes, clearly conversant with the conventions of catch-as-catch-can wrestling (and hyperbole), replied, "I didn't disable him completely. I just took two out of him and he took one out of me." Most of the MPs understood the joke as well, and his reply was greeted by roars of laughter.[33]

MOBILIZATION AND THE MAT GAME

By the time Canada entered the Great War on 3 August 1914, sport was already well integrated with ideas on militarism and formed an important part of militia life. However, the recruiting undertaken during the CEF's initial mobilization during 1914 did not lend itself to fostering military-based athletics in Manitoba. As noted by Robert Craig Brown and Donald Loveridge, CEF recruiting passed through three distinct periods: the Militia Phase, lasting from August to October 1914; the Patriotic Phase, which began shortly thereafter and continued until 1917; and finally the Conscription Phase, which began after 29 August 1917.[34] The changing character of recruiting, coupled with Canada's fortunes during the war, helped to shape wrestling's relationship with the military during the war years in Manitoba.

During the Militia Phase, Canada's volunteer army rapidly mobilized, with most of the 32,000 recruits converging haphazardly for training at Valcartier, Quebec.[35] Only two months after the declaration of war, Canada's first contingent sailed for Great Britain.[36] Because of the tight timetable under which all of this occurred, fostering military athletics was not a priority for the CEF in Manitoba, their central concern being to organize and prepare the nation's army for immediate deployment overseas.[37] However, simultaneously, ambitious civilian fundraising efforts were undertaken to assist with the war effort. In Winnipeg, the city's Industrial Bureau began drafting plans for organizing fundraising campaigns within one week of the call to arms, and on 17 August the bureau, along with representatives from all welfare societies in the city, endorsed the creation of a central committee "for funds to supply assistance to the families of soldiers and of others that may be unfortunately affected by the war."[38] By 14 September, a province-wide Patriotic Fund had been established, divided into various auxiliary committees.[39] The first action undertaken by the Patriotic Fund's subordinate Manitoba Athletic Patriotic Committee (MAPC), whose executive took office on 13 October, was to arrange an amateur boxing and wrestling benefit with the assistance of the Manitoba branch of the Amateur Athletic Union of Canada (MAAUC), known until February 1912 as the MAAA.[40] Joseph Fahey, president of the Winnipeg North End Amateur

Athletic Club, estimated that similar events could add $10,000 to the Patriotic Fund over the course of the season.[41]

The MAPC's first fundraiser, staged on 27 and 28 October at the Winnipeg Industrial Bureau, was a tournament to decide the city boxing and wrestling champions. Although not a military event, from the start there was an attempt to closely fuse civilian amateur sport with military patronage. Seven regiments lent their direct support to the program, and the event's prime sponsor was none other than Colonel Sam Steele, commander of Military District 10 (Manitoba).[42] Following the tournament, which ultimately netted $500 for the Patriotic Fund, the staunchly imperialist comments of former Winnipeg mayor Richard Waugh elicited a cheer from the large audience when, quoting King George, he testified to the noble cause for which the war in Europe was being waged.[43] Throughout the winter, events featuring wrestling, along with other entertainments, continued to draw strong public support and net revenue for the Patriotic Fund.[44]

From its genesis, the MAPC remained closely allied with the MAAUC, which governed all amateur sports in Manitoba, including wrestling. Yet, in the war's early months, professional wrestling continued to be staged in Winnipeg, completely independent of the Patriotic Fund. During the first half of 1915, matches were conducted by local theatre owners, as they had been prior to August 1914, as for-profit entertainments.[45] With enthusiasm for the war high and expectations for a quick victory in Europe still abundant, civilian sports did not attract widespread criticism in Manitoba during this period. As before the war, professional wrestlers' conduct continued to elicit substantial controversy, though not on explicitly patriotic grounds.[46] However, after mid-1915, as Canada's casualty toll rose following devastating battles such as the Second Battle of Ypres, public attitudes began to sour toward men who, still on the home front, continued to earn a living from their athletic skills.[47] After May 1915, professional wrestling virtually disappeared in the province, the only contest of any note before the war ended occurring when former Festival of Empire competitor George Walker faced Fort William's Ernie Arthur in Transcona in August 1917.[48] In his memoirs, Clarence Eklund, who wrestled in Winnipeg prior to the war, recalled the marked decrease in opportunities for professionals in the west: "I was booking some more towns figuring I would soon have a fortune, when Canada joined England in the First World War with Germany, in 1914. There was no more wrestling. Everyone went to fight the Kaiser." Eklund attempted to enlist but was rejected because of his poor eyesight.[49]

8. Wrestler Patsy Picciano was one of a small handful of non Anglo-Canadian wrestlers who achieved amateur championship laurels in Manitoba during the prewar era. During the early part of the Great War he wrestled professionally as Patsy Bachant, but as the conflict in Europe escalated, public demand for professional wrestling declined in the province. Source: Manitoba Sports Hall of Fame and Museum, MS2014.25.12.

By mid-1915, civilian organizations were also finding it increasingly difficult to organize amateur wrestling competitions, patriotic or otherwise, because of high enlistment rates among their members. Winnipeg's YMCA, for example, which had been the province's most ardent booster of amateur wrestling, found its membership numbers drop by over 70 percent as 3,000 men "rallied to the colours."[50] Among them was Thomas Dickinson, the club's long-standing wrestling coach, who enlisted with the No. 10 Field Ambulance Corps.[51] In June 1915, the Manitoba Provincial Championships, traditionally hosted by the YMCA, were discontinued because of the lack of entries, and other events, such as the Winnipeg City Championships, were likewise dropped from the annual sporting calendar.[52] Winnipeg's recently constructed Vaughan Street facility, purged of most members, became the unofficial headquarters for Military District 10.[53]

By mid-1915, the war had clearly impacted both amateur and professional wrestling. Yet, as noted by Horrall, public disdain for civilian sport in wartime was not as vociferous in Canada as it was in either Great Britain or Australia. Canadians, on the whole, maintained a somewhat more ambiguous stance on the matter, largely because of their proximity to the American sports market.[54] Until the American entry into the war in 1917, sports in the United States, including professional wrestling, continued on as they had before hostilities began in Europe.[55] Thus, while civilian-based wrestling declined in Manitoba and criticism of non-enlisted athletes grew, the public was kept abreast of the latest happenings in professional wrestling south of the border with reports devoid of similar moralizing.[56]

COMING TO GRIPS WITH LONG-TERM WAR

As civilian wrestling events became increasingly scarce in Manitoba, military authorities began to take a heightened interest in the sport. After the rapid enlistment and deployment of the CEF's first division in October 1914, recruitment and training began to unfold in a more organized and less hurried fashion. Instead of marshalling all troops at Valcartier, militia units in each military district took direct control of their own recruiting and training.[57] During the winter of 1914–15, with troops quartered in Winnipeg for the season, battalion commanders began to direct more attention to athletics. Within the Canadian 6th Infantry Brigade, which consisted of the 27th (Winnipeg), 28th (North-West), 29th (Vancouver), and 31st (Alberta) Battalions, time was spent conducting mock trench raids in the Happyland amusement park, target shooting at the

Main Street Armoury rifle range, and hiking along Portage Avenue.[58] However, the six months stationed in the city created idle time and a need for recreational diversions apart from training. The CEF, during this period, faced growing discipline problems among the troops still stationed on the home front.[59] Sport provided a means for maintaining interest among the troops and fostering esprit de corps.[60] Accordingly, the 27th and 28th Battalion commanders, Colonel J.R. Snider and Colonel J.F.L. Embury, respectively, encouraged wrestling and boxing training in the winter and sponsored a large interbattalion meet in January 1915 that provided "sport of the kind to delight the soldiers' hearts."[61] Here again, however, such competitions reaffirmed the importance of maintaining hierarchical distinctions between enlisted and officer classes. All entries were drawn exclusively from the non-commissioned ranks.[62] As formal sporting competitions continued to develop within the military, similar distinctions did not extend to the other athletic pursuits enjoyed by soldiers in the CEF. Competition between officers and men, in the context of other sports, was considered to help foster good relations between them and bolster, as opposed to overthrow, discipline.[63] However, in boxing as well as wrestling, the explicitly combative nature created concern that enlisted men might use the opportunity provided by competition to take revenge on an officer against whom they had a grudge. By the spring of 1916, the informal rule against matches between officers and non-commissioned members received formal sanction in at least one military district.[64] Yet to deny officers the opportunity to participate in wrestling was not only detrimental to the further cultivation of manly traits but also prevented them from learning skills that had direct battlefield application in hand-to-hand combat and self-defence. As a result, following a special request on their behalf, the Winnipeg YMCA began conducting classes twice a week for officers in training, teaching each student the requisite skills to "take care of himself in any form of encounter he may run up against."[65] Special officers' classes for horseback wrestling were also later included in sports programs.[66]

By mid-1915, growing casualty lists and the trench warfare stalemate that had developed on the Western Front dimmed patriotic enthusiasm for military service in Canada. Yet Prime Minister Borden's summer trip to England underscored the need for radically increased enlistment. Subsequently, the government announced its intent to put 250,000 Canadians into uniform, and by January 1916 the number rose to half a million.[67] In early 1916, the MAAUC's president, J. Coates Brown, reported that "the enlistment of such an overwhelming majority of our young men, interested in all branches of sport, has had the result of practically eliminating all hope of continuing senior activities during the duration of the war."[68] Accordingly, Brown advocated maintaining existing athletic clubs through "catering to the young lads who in the next few years will form the backbone of our senior athletics."[69] Conversely, with a massive increase in the number of men under arms, military sport expanded dramatically.

By the spring of 1916, competitions were being arranged on a grand scale at the Winnipeg Garrison. Wrestlers, boxers, and bayonet fighters competed first in interbattalion meets, with the winners earning the right to represent their battalions in a city-wide military competition.[70] By the beginning of April, the various meets seemed to occupy most of the attention of the soldiers stationed in Winnipeg.[71] Nearly a dozen battalions participated, and the finals, staged at Winnipeg's Amphitheatre Rink, were attended by over 3,000 people. The multiday inter- and intrabattalion meet was the largest wrestling tournament ever staged in Manitoba to that time, far eclipsing any event held prior to the war. Spectators were not confined to those in uniform, the Winnipeg *Telegram* noting that "the poor, the rich—all classes of society were drawn together by the love of contests, the daring and courage of the khaki boys who competed for athletic supremacy."[72] By 1916, then, military sport was providing an unprecedented opportunity for participation in wrestling and represented the primary venue for spectators from all walks of life wishing to indulge their interest in the manly sport.

Military-based wrestling was not confined to the battalions stationed at the Winnipeg Garrison. In 1915, the CEF abandoned its plans for training all troops centrally at Valcartier, and Camp Sewell (later renamed Camp Hughes), located west of Carberry, Manitoba, became the largest training grounds for soldiers in the Canadian west. A peak summer population of approximately 27,500 in 1916 temporarily made it the second largest population centre in Manitoba after Winnipeg.[73] The makeshift city, consisting primarily of tents, offered a variety of conveniences to the soldiers stationed there, including a number of movie theatres, one of which, the Strand, seated at least 1,000 people.[74] Most conspicuous to the visitor, however, were the ubiquitous symbols of sport at Camp Hughes. The Winnipeg *Tribune* noted that "what strikes a visitor very strongly on his first walk through the tented streets is the number of athletic grounds. Goal posts are much more numerous than trees. Tennis courts are here, there, and everywhere. Baseball diamonds are marked out. Cricket pitches are carefully prepared and practice nets erected. Lacrosse fields, quoiting grounds and sprint tracks are there. In fact every outdoor exercise has its devotees."[75] A ninety-minute film entitled *A Trip to Camp Sewell*, filmed in 1915, also testified to the importance of sport at the camp; in addition to depicting the work under way there, the film showed bayonet practice, wrestling, wrestling on horseback, and boxing.[76]

9. Wrestling matches on horseback, such as this one staged by members of the Canadian Expeditionary Forces during July 1916, were regular attractions at military sporting events. Source: Library and Archives Canada, PA-000221.

Early in the war, military sports were organized at the battalion level, with individual battalions likewise providing the patronage for large garrison-wide meets such as the one staged at Winnipeg in April 1916.[77] Yet, as the war continued, military authorities became "more firmly convinced that athletics should occupy a larger place than [had] previously been considered proper."[78] To coordinate such a large number of activities, the CEF relied heavily on non-military organizations. The YMCA, in particular, was involved not only with military sports at the local level but also wherever troops were stationed at home and overseas.[79] The YMCA Military Department operated separately from the local YMCAs but naturally drew on their manpower and expertise.[80] So heavily was the "Y" integrated into the Canadian military's sporting activities that "the net result ... was that the YMCA was given the opportunity of providing either directly or indirectly for the great part of the sports in the Canadian army."[81] Although the "Y" reported directly to the military authorities, its heavy involvement in athletics reflected the Department of the Militia's desire to have sport conducted according to the association's moral precepts.[82] Wrestling, therefore, was not only a tool to build manly physical and mental qualities (which the YMCA likewise espoused through its adherence to the doctrine of Muscular Christianity) but also a means by which young men could be diverted from various inappropriate activities.

By 1914, many within Canadian military circles viewed Canada's professional army in unflattering terms. Sam Hughes, minister of the militia and an ardent temperance advocate, categorized the permanent forces as no more than "bar room loafers" with a penchant for alcohol.[83] During the First World War, military camps prohibited the possession or distribution of alcohol, but soldiers at Camp Hughes were still left with considerable time to fill. The YMCA, a political advocate for temperance, promoted athletic programs "as a means to keep the men sober and clean [so as to] make them fit for Military service."[84] Sport also represented a bulwark against more carnal activities. During the early twentieth century, parents and moral leaders, concerned about young men's sexual purity, viewed athletic activity as a natural outlet for countering physical temptations. Wrestling instructors from the period, including "Farmer" Burns, in promoting his lessons specifically to parents, advised that, through his guidance, "many a student has thereby been saved from the vicious effects of a secret vice."[85] Military sport under the YMCA's guidance at the almost exclusively male Camp Hughes, therefore, was considered "the most wholesome way in which the repressions and monotonies of military life could be relieved."[86] Whether or not the sport actually achieved all of the moralistic goals ascribed to it is uncertain. Unquestionably, however, military officials increasingly came to believe that sport provided such benefits for the men in uniform, and it was on the basis of reports from both Canada and Great Britain that the American Commission on Training Camp Activities advocated the implementation of athletic training programs in their own armed forces.[87]

WRESTLING WITH RECRUITMENT

Although wrestling was perceived to provide multiple benefits for both the military establishment and the individual soldier, one of its most appreciated features, at least by senior authorities, was as an aid to recruiting. Such was particularly the case by late 1915 and early 1916 with Canada's expanded military commitment to the war effort. In the fall of 1915, the Department of the Militia granted patriotic citizens and communities the right to raise battalions and conduct their own recruiting. Although initially successful in its goal of attracting new enlistments, the scheme also created aggressive competition among battalions for men.[88] In this context, battalion-based sports became even more important. Opportunities for participation in sport naturally attracted athletes to military life, and battalions with successful competition records used their achievements to draw more recruits. The 196th Western Universities Battalion, formed in February 1916, drew members from students in all military districts west of Ontario. Its historical records, written during the war, note the importance that the battalion attached to its sporting acumen: "In the Realm of Sport, if [the 196th] does not lead it is at least the Battalion to beat."[89] Its official promotional literature emphasized the many "clean and manly" sporting competitions, including a camp-wide boxing and wrestling meet at Camp Hughes in which wrestler Private Ralph Lyons Corey and several boxers "showed class and gameness, and were easily the favourites with the large crowds."[90] In typically allegorical fashion linking sport to war, the 196th promotional material concluded that "it now remains for us to show our efficiency in probably the greatest game we will ever play, namely the '196th versus the Hun.'"[91]

Well-known sportsmen also aided in attracting men into khaki. Newspapers, enthusiastic in aiding the war cause, regularly reported on their enlistment and participation in military-sponsored meets. The Manitoba *Free Press*, commenting on the 184th Battalion's many skilled athletes, noted prior to the April

1916 tournament at the Winnipeg Garrison that "Joseph Lemieux, the strong man and champion wrestler of the Mariapolis district, is now with the battalion in the city and will make his first appearance on the mat in Winnipeg at this tournament."[92] Famous professional wrestlers were also held up as examples to their fellow citizens, serving simultaneously to inspire and pressure them into enlisting. Artie Edmunds, the "Pocket Hercules," who appeared prominently in Winnipeg as a professional wrestler prior to the war, enlisted with the 204th Beaver Battalion in Toronto after being rejected several times for his poor eyesight.[93] The 204th's Captain Joseph Lawson, certainly realizing the attention that could be garnered from having such a high-profile enlistee, took an active interest in his case and convened a special board of examiners to oversee his petition. Once more facing rejection, Edmunds stated to the board, "you know, I have been around here a good many times bothering you by trying to recruit. Now, you go out and pick out four men from any battalion you want to, put me in a room, tell your four men that I'm a nuisance around here and that you want me beat up. If they beat me up I'll stay away, but if I come out of the room and leave the four behind, then I want to be taken on."[94] This declaration of manly courage and aggression apparently convinced the examination board, and Edmunds was taken into the 204th on 3 May 1916.[95] Additionally, his testimonial served notice to the men not yet in uniform but physically capable of active service.

The showmanship characteristic of professional wrestling also provided unique opportunities to secure enlistments not possible with all other sports. The custom of challenging members of the audience to matches was common during the period, particularly with various travelling carnival athletic shows. Similar tactics were also employed by wrestlers Hume Duval and Victor McLaglen during appearances at Winnipeg's Happyland Amusement Park during 1907.[96] Three weeks after enrolling with the 204th, Edmunds, then promoted to the rank of sergeant, attended a wrestling performance at which a Greek matman named George Sparta had agreed to defeat any soldier who took the stage. The "Pocket Hercules" once more showed his flair for displays of manly virtue, and, as the Toronto *Evening Telegram* reported, though "ordered by his doctor to quit wrestling for a time, he felt the itch of battle ... when it grew too strong for him to resist."[97] Edmunds proposed that, if Sparta could not defeat him in ten minutes, he was to enlist with the 204th Battalion. Noting his opponent's diminutive stature, Sparta agreed that, if he did not win within the allotted period, his whole company would enlist with the Beavers. Edmunds first wrestled a smaller man in the troupe, Detoille, and after lasting the limit repeated the feat with Sparta. In addition to securing several new recruits, his matches earned him forty dollars, which Edmunds donated to the Red Cross.[98] Although it is impossible to ascertain whether the event was orchestrated beforehand, the showmanship emblematic to professional wrestling nevertheless generated positive publicity for the battalion during a period characterized by highly competitive recruiting.

The Canadian government's decision to allow patriotic civilians to raise battalions according to various affinities, including ethnicity, provided another opportunity for professional wrestling to prove its merit in wartime. Nativist sentiment, present among Anglo-Canadian citizens in western Canada since the influx of many non-English-speaking immigrants began in the late 1890s, became heightened following the declaration of war in 1914.[99] A common perception that "foreigners" were not contributing sufficiently to the war effort fed the distrust and resentment prevalent in the Prairies. Anglo-Canadian attitudes during the period were not uniformly opposed to all of the region's "foreign" residents. In particular, peoples originating from "enemy" nations such as the Austro-Hungarian Empire, Germany, and Bulgaria faced more intense discrimination.[100] Because of widely held racial theories, Scandinavians were typically considered close cultural cousins to the English-speaking majority and thus did not accrue the same hostility as either their central and eastern European counterparts or the once-favoured German immigrants.[101] Yet, even among "favoured" groups, pressures to assimilate to the norms of the Anglo-Canadian majority were strong.[102] During the First World War, the Scandinavian countries remained officially neutral, which created potential problems for immigrants living in a warring nation. In this context, the 197th Scandinavian Overseas Battalion (colloquially known as the Vikings of Canada), founded in February 1916, recruited among the Norwegian, Icelandic, Swedish, and Danish populations in the Prairies to demonstrate the Scandinavian population's "desire to help the British empire in its glorious fight for the freedom of all nations and the protection of small states."[103]

Professional wrestling had widespread appeal among many non-Anglo-Protestant immigrant groups in western Canada, and the presence of their best-known wrestlers in khaki served both to encourage men of similar ethnic descent to don uniforms and to provide a tangible public symbol of immigrant loyalty. In Charles Gustafson and Ernie Sundberg, Manitoba's Swedish population could boast the two most accomplished and well-known wrestlers in the province. The 197th's commanding officer, A.G. Fonesca, was acutely concerned with affirming Scandinavian Canadian loyalty, and company records, though brief, note enlistments drawn from his community's more prominent ranks. Both Gustafson and Sundberg receive special mention for their accomplishments on the mat, and both were quickly promoted in rank to lieutenant and sergeant, respectively, within the Vikings of Canada.[104] With Camp Hughes reopening in the summer of 1916, the Swedish grapplers were able to resume their wrestling careers, and their participation in a "monster athletic meet" in mid-August netted both them and the Vikings of Canada a disproportionate amount of the press surrounding the event. Gustafson and Sundberg, the best professionals in Manitoba, easily won first place in their respective divisions, generating publicity for their battalion while affirming Scandinavian Canadians' presence in the Canadian military and their commitment to the cause of dominion and empire.[105]

CONTESTING VISIONS

During the Great War, wrestling served as a means for affirming prevailing notions of militarist masculinity, ensuring military conformity, encouraging enlistment, and publicizing immigrant support for Canada's military commitments. Yet, despite its role in reinforcing values cherished by members of the Anglo-Canadian society, wrestling also proved to be a site for challenging specific beliefs held by many members of the middle class. Most notable in this respect were ideas concerning the inherent dangers associated with professional sports and professional athletes. By 1916, military sport had largely superseded civilian-based amateur sport in Manitoba, and competitions were becoming increasingly well organized. Civilian-based amateur sport withered during this period, but the MAAUC, as the self-appointed guardian of amateur sporting values, nevertheless sought to extend its previously uncontested authority into the military realm. Of primary concern were the intermingling of amateur and professional athletes and the presence of cash prizes in military sporting events. At the root of both issues, however, was the inherent assumption that money corrupted athletes and was anathema to sport's character-building purpose.

Among many members of the middle class during the late nineteenth century and early twentieth century was the widespread sentiment that professionalism in sport was synonymous with low moral standing, and amateur organizations maintained strict rules to ensure that those who chose to "play for pay" were excluded from sanctioned events.[106] By the spring of 1916, however, problems began to arise between the Amateur Athletic Union of Canada's provincial affiliates and military authorities over professional and amateur athletes mingling in battalion-sponsored competitions. The issue initially came to the public's attention in Toronto during mid-March 1916 when the Ontario branch of the Amateur Athletic Union of Canada (OAAUC) sought to stop a boxing card staged by the 170th Battalion because amateur fighters were competing with professionals.[107] Secretary W.J. Smith, on behalf of the union, declared that

> the impression apparently exists ... that an athlete, once he dons the King's uniform, is not subject to the laws of the union, and that he can compete against professionals for prizes, etc. at unsanctioned affairs. While the union has done and is doing all in their power to assist the work of recruiting and providing recreation for the soldiers, at the same time the stand taken by the delegates at the annual meeting of the branch was quite emphatic that no competitions would be permitted between amateurs and professionals for affairs run under the guise of "for patriotic purposes."[108]

The OAAUC immediately attracted criticism for its actions, deemed to be "ill timed" because of a strong drive for recruiting under way during that period.[109] Toronto *Evening Telegram* sports columnist and military sports booster Tom Flanagan chastised the union: "The action of the Athletic Union in putting spokes in the recruiting shows of the various battalions was a badly timed one. There is no profit of any kind to anybody except in that these events help materially in securing recruits. There has to date been no violation of the amateur laws either. The Athletic Union should be able to see beyond its own nose and let things alone as long as recruiting and patriotic purposes demand it."[110] Shortly thereafter, an athletic association was created to oversee all military sports in Ontario's Military District 2, with Flanagan as secretary.[111] Flanagan, who emphasized that khaki athletes received no financial compensation for their efforts, declared that "we will run our own show. There are no amateurs or professionals in the army, at least in war times, and we will make our own rules."[112]

In Manitoba, similar problems arose shortly thereafter in connection with the large interbattalion tournament staged at the Winnipeg Garrison in early

April. However, the MAAUC's concerns involved not only the mingling of professionals and amateurs but also the clear exchange of money. Athletes who were victorious in each weight class were offered cash prizes for their performances by military officials, a decision that alarmed the MAAUC. With mounting tensions between amateur and military authorities in the east, both sides sought to resolve the matter without a similar vitriolic escalation. On 2 April, representatives from the MAAUC and military met to discuss the matter. The latter declared the tournament to be a "closed event" over which the union had no jurisdiction to dictate whether professional and amateur athletes could participate together. As a concession, however, all cash prizes were withdrawn.[113] The Winnipeg *Telegram* reported that "the military officials were well pleased with the turn of affairs and so were the officials of the Manitoba branch of the Amateur Union."[114] As a goodwill gesture, the MAAUC's president, J. Coates Brown, and its secretary, Arthur R. Morrison, acted as timekeepers for the tournament.[115]

By the spring of 1916, amateur officials in Manitoba clearly realized that, with most amateur athletes in uniform, their once unassailable authority in the province had been broken. Both parties recognized, however, that ongoing cooperation was essential. During the annual meeting at the end of April, the MAAUC elected as president Lieutenant A.E.H. (Abby) Coo of the 184th Battalion, with J. Coates Brown retaining an advisory role as honorary president. Brown stated to his fellow board members that attempting to retain control over enlisted athletes in military-sponsored events would "not only antagonize those whose interest we wish to retain, but possibly defeat the primary object of this Union."[116] Six weeks later an athletic association was founded at Camp Hughes to coordinate the myriad events being staged at the tent city.[117] Although a military district-wide organization, as had been created in Ontario, did not follow until December, with most of the province's soldiers in camp during the summer of 1916, it certainly oversaw the majority of khaki athletic activities. Significantly, the MAAUC's Abby Coo was also named as the Camp Hughes Athletic Association president.[118]

The elimination of cash prizes in military sporting meets and continued affiliation between amateur and military sporting officials affirmed a middle-class definition that favoured "sport for sport's sake" and reinforced opposition to mixing money and sport. Yet, the challenge posed by military athletics to the AAUC's sovereignty also created an important distinction for athletes. Although taking money for performances was not acceptable, it did not necessarily follow that those who had done so in the past were of questionable character, nor did it mean that their presence would sully the values of those around them. To the contrary, professional wrestlers repeatedly demonstrated that they were an asset to recruiting and willing to compete, without pay, in sporting events to bolster esprit de corps. Thus, the evidence openly refuted arguments that professionals were in it purely for the money and of dubious moral standing.

Throughout the war, professional wrestlers also demonstrated their courage in the face of the enemy.[119] Additionally, in several instances, wrestlers who had appeared in Manitoba were injured or killed in battle, including Benjamin Sutton of the 79th Cameron Highlanders, who had wrestled before the public as Billy Marsh.[120] Most notable in this respect, however, was Fred C. McLaglen, one of Winnipeg's well-known grapplers prior to the war. Through his involvement in local politics and sporting events, McLaglen had earned considerable notoriety in Manitoba. Yet his death in battle as a member of the Lancashire Fusiliers underscored the fact that an inherent incongruity did not necessarily exist between controversy in professional sports and capacity for valour in battle.[121] In this context, public ideas about professionalism were reshaped, and negative views of professional wrestling were softened in the postwar period. Simultaneously, definitions of proper manliness underwent revision as sport within the military context was privileged as a maker of manhood over sport within a civilian context. The later war period saw strong public censure of athletes who had not yet enlisted. Tom Flanagan was vocal in his condemnation, stating that, save for military activities, "sport should be a dead letter, the sporting page go unread," during the conflict.[122] The virtual absence of professional wrestling events in Manitoba in the later years of the war, the inability to stage major amateur wrestling competitions, and a dramatic reduction of coverage for non-khaki events in the sports pages suggest that there was broad public support for, albeit never full complicity with, his position.[123] As Wanda Wakefield asserts, "the manliness of sport was clearly subordinate to the manliness of war."[124]

THE WAR'S LATER YEARS

After Canada's third contingent commenced disembarking in the late summer of 1916, competitive wrestling continued within military ranks in Manitoba.[125] The relationship forged early in the war between the YMCA Military Department and military officials continued after formation of the District Military Athletic Association in late 1916, with the association's secretary working out of the YMCA offices in Winnipeg to arrange competitions for soldiers on the home front.[126] However, by this time, the sport failed to generate significant public attention. The MAAUC and MAPC were again forced to cancel the Provincial Championships in December 1917, as they had during the previous two years, though a few wrestling matches were contested free of charge at the Industrial Bureau before a small audience.[127] Many of the province's well-known wrestlers were already in uniform, so a lack of local talent might have contributed to the situation. However, wrestling's decline in Manitoba during the latter part of the war must be directly contrasted with its growth in popularity overseas with the CEF, where athletic competitions took on additional significance as a respite from the immediate horrors of war and as a reminder of life back in Canada.[128] Sporting events were regularly organized for soldiers, and wrestling, including on horseback, formed an important element of the programs.[129] Although athletic meets were conducted at the battalion and interbattalion levels, the Canadian Forces did not grant official sanction to sport during the first three years of the conflict in Europe. In late December 1917, however, the Canadian General Staff proposed the formation of a Canadian Military Athletic Association (CMAA) to "encourage and facilitate military and athletic sports and competitions between the various Canadian Units in Great Britain."[130] In January, the Canadian General Staff authored *A Guide to Military Sports and Recreational Training*, which endorsed military-based sport and created an organizational structure consisting of battalion, regimental, area, and interarea competitions, culminating in a CEF championship.[131] The guide formally recognized sport's value as an aid to military training and provided official rules for conducting wrestling matches under military auspices.[132] The first CMAA Wrestling Championships were held on 24 April 1918 at Bramshott following a series of elimination events.[133] Nine weeks later, on Canada Day 1918, Canadian wrestlers competed at the Canadian Corps Championships in France before 30,000 spectators, including Prime Minister Robert Borden and Commander Arthur Currie.[134] Among the first-place winners were prominent Winnipeg professional wrestlers Alex Stewart (lightweight) and Tom Johnstone (heavyweight).[135] The event, as Horrall notes, symbolized "the four year evolution of sport within the Canadian forces and the final acknowledgement of its importance by military leaders."[136] The process by which this occurred was not straightforward, nor did wrestling survive the Great War in precisely the way that it had entered it.

CONCLUSION

The changing fortunes of the First World War heavily shaped wrestling's role in Manitoba society. By the time two Little Black Devils came to grips in the summer of 1918, wrestling, already widely valued for decades as an activity that helped to inculcate proper "manly" virtues, had become heavily integrated into the Canadian military structure because of the combined efforts of civilian athletic organizations, patriotic associations, religious movements, and Canadian Forces officers. Over four years, wrestling was transformed from a largely civilian-based enterprise that assisted with patriotic fundraising into a military-based sport that helped to maintain troop morale, ensure discipline, and prevent moral impropriety. As wrestling grew under military auspices, it subsequently faded within the civilian realm, for mounting casualties and pressures to enlist made senior sport outside the CEF increasingly unpalatable to the public. Within this context, a hierarchy was established and privileged athletes in uniform over those who did not "don the khaki." The same process, however, helped to reorient attitudes toward professional athletes. By permitting professionals to compete openly with amateurs, military sport challenged many of the negative stereotypes that had been attached to professionalism. Professional wrestlers who enlisted in the CEF proved to be valuable assets to the war effort. Because of their well-known status, their presence reinforced the connection between military service and masculine virtue and helped to bolster recruiting. Additionally, since professional wrestlers demonstrated heroism in battle, and in some instances were injured or even killed in the line of duty, negative public attitudes softened toward their vocation, and criticism subsequently diminished during the postwar period. Thus, the Great War served to further entrench the idea that wrestling was a valuable masculine enterprise while granting its professional athletes a level of legitimacy that they did not enjoy prior to 1914.

Chapter 6

PROFESSIONAL WRESTLING'S "GOLDEN AGE," 1919-29

Ten days after the armistice was signed, the Toronto *Globe*'s sporting editor acclaimed the pivotal role played by Canadian athletes during the Great War. Praising their efforts both in enhancing Canada's international reputation and in furthering the war effort, he declared that "[athletes] have caused the name of Canada and Canadian sport to ring around the world. They 'played the game' in war as in peace. Sport and the sporting spirit have been eloquently justified in the war which has resulted in the smashing of the unspeakable Hun." Not lost in the editorial was the tremendous toll on the nation's young athletes, who "numbered among the heroic dead, ... contributed their all to the end that the world might be safe, and [left] an example to be emulated by the generations of sportsmen to come." Echoing the collective sense of reprieve felt across the country after four years of catastrophic war, he concluded, in symbolic exhaltation, "having done their glorious bit for freedom, truth and justice, Canada's tens of thousands of valorous sportsmen overseas will shortly return to their play."[1] The Manitoba *Free Press*, in a similar fashion, declared on Victory Christmas that "Sportdom ha[d] done its bit nobly in the great struggle for liberty" by sending "the flower of the nation's manhood to the battlefields of Europe.... In the next few months, in which the period of reconstruction will get underway, a grand revival will be brought about in all branches of sport."[2]

The months following November 1918 were predicted to be a renaissance for sport in Manitoba after years of doing battle with "the bloody fist of Prussian militarism."[3] In the case of wrestling, however, resurgence was not immediately forthcoming. Professional wrestling remained dormant after the war, and it was not until 1920 that grapplers again began to grace Manitoba's mats. During the next two years, wrestling gained considerable popularity in several other centres, including Melita and Brandon, where, for a time, cards were staged with greater frequency than in the province's capital. Although wrestling made inroads into new markets, in many respects it replicated the practices in place before the First World War. However, subtle differences were already beginning to appear that differentiated the sport from its prewar counterpart in terms of how it was presented to, and received by, the public. Between August 1922 and June 1924, as North America entered into what was later termed the "golden age" of sports, Winnipeg experienced its own "golden age" of heavyweight wrestling, and the popularity was synonymous with a single name: Jack Taylor.[4] This age saw the establishment of regular heavyweight wrestling programs in the city whose success was predicated on pitting the Canadian "local boy" Taylor against various high-profile wrestlers on his march to a title match with the world's heavyweight champion, Ed "Strangler" Lewis. Professional wrestling had been stripped of most of the prewar sermonizing on its respectability, and much of the popularity of these matches stemmed from promoters' keen ability to present wrestling as a "rough" spectacle and capitalize on specific ethnic stereotypes, keen anti-foreigner sentiments, and the growing sense of regionalism prevalent in the west during the period.

By mid-1924, largely because of the sport's commercial success, Winnipeg became integrated into a North American heavyweight wrestling network controlled by a handful of eastern American promoters. Local talent became replaced by high-profile and infrequent appearances from well-known heavyweight American mat stars. Simultaneously, however, professional wrestling continued to thrive in other centres, such as Brandon, as it had in Winnipeg, on the basis of local talent. Although public attitudes toward the sport had altered remarkably by this period, even by the late 1920s, some of the long-standing concerns about professional wrestling's legitimacy were still evident.

A SLOW RETURN

After the end of the Great War, few of the professional wrestlers who had been active in Manitoba prior to the European conflict appeared to be either available or capable of resuming their mat careers. During late 1918 and throughout 1919, no matches were staged in Winnipeg or, evidently, anywhere else in the province. Professional wrestling's complete disappearance was a local phenomenon, since elsewhere the sport flourished during the immediate postwar period. At the Lakehead, for example, at least eleven cards were staged in either Fort William or Port Arthur during 1919 alone.[5] Winnipeg's "pride," Charles Gustafson, though certainly not beyond his wrestling years, had evidently let his physical condition lapse to such a degree following his victories at Camp Hughes that he found it difficult to obtain matches. On 24 January 1919, Gustafson was booked to appear in Saskatoon in a match against local wrestler Walter Anderson, but before the engagement could commence the police intervened on the ground that the once athletic middleweight champion would be no match for the Saskatchewan grappler in a competitive bout.[6] In early 1920, Gustafson issued a challenge in the Fort William *Daily Times-Journal* to meet either Ernie Arthur, the Lakehead middleweight, or George Walker, the former amateur standout and Festival of Empire competitor, who had turned professional in October 1912.[7] Arthur, weighing at or below the middleweight limit of 158 pounds, expressed his hesitancy after seeing a photo of Gustafson in which he appeared to "tip the beam at one hundred and eighty."[8] No match with either Arthur or Walker was arranged.

In March 1920, Gustafson decided to "revive the mat game" in Winnipeg, promoting a match for the Heavyweight Wrestling Championship of Manitoba against Winnipeg City Police constable Tom Johnstone, a native of Gilbert Plains. Born in 1888, Johnstone joined the city police in March 1909 and wrestled professionally in Manitoba prior to the First World War. His most prominent match before the war was against Clarence Eklund, Moose Jaw's "Mysterious Homesteader," in Winnipeg on 19 December 1910. Enlisting in the Canadian Expeditionary Forces in 1915, Johnstone served overseas with the 79th Battalion and continued to pursue his interest in wrestling, competing in numerous contests. While at Shorncliffe in England during August 1916, Johnstone, claiming to be the "champion heavyweight wrestler of Manitoba and Saskatchewan," issued a public challenge to all comers for wrestling bouts. In 1918, he won the Canadian Corps Championships in the heavyweight division.[9] In their bout at the Board of Trade Building, held on 25 March, the Winnipeg policeman proved to be the superior of his veteran Swedish opponent. Succumbing primarily because of his lack of conditioning, Gustafson yielded the second and final falls to Johnstone, whom some ringside spectators also viewed as his superior in "strength and science."[10] Although attended by a "somewhat small circle of mat enthusiasts," Winnipeg's first postwar professional wrestling bout brought Johnstone's talent to public attention and helped to stimulate a revival of the sport.[11]

READY TO MEET YANK GRAPPLER

TOM JOHNSTON

Well known local policeman, who tackles stiff opponent in Charles Peters at the Board of Trade building tomorrow night. Two boxing and one wrestling preliminary will precede the main attraction.

10. Winnipeg Police Officer and CEF veteran Tom Johnstone was instrumental in reviving professional wrestling in Manitoba after the Great War. Source: Manitoba *Free Press*, 5 October 1920.

Now Winnipeg's pre-eminent professional grappler, Johnstone continued to wrestle in the city periodically throughout 1920 and 1921. A match against John Albrecht of Minneapolis for the "police championship of America" during the summer of 1920 attracted approximately 2,000 spectators to Winnipeg's Riverside Park baseball grounds, a number that rivalled the attendance at some of the more prominent wrestling matches staged in the city between 1910 and 1914.[12] Additionally, Johnstone made significant forays into other Manitoba communities, including Dauphin, where, hailed as "practically a local man," he defeated Texan J. Sanders at the 1921 Northern Manitoba Fair before the largest crowd ever assembled in the community.[13]

Although Johnstone provided the impetus for reigniting the Winnipeg public's interest in professional wrestling, matches were held only sporadically compared with the prewar era. By late 1920, enthusiasm for the sport in other communities was surpassing, for the first time, that seen in Manitoba's capital. In Brandon, where matches had been staged intermittently for decades, local businessman Harry Willis began to hold regular cards during September 1920 at his eponymously named theatre. By that time, numerous professional middleweight and light-heavyweight wrestlers were appearing in towns throughout the Prairies and in northwestern Ontario, and Willis took advantage of the available talent.[14]

As professional wrestling made inroads in various communities across Manitoba, the sport held on to many of its old practices. Simultaneously, though, there were subtle differences that made it distinct from its prewar incarnation. Ethnicity continued to play an important role in promoting some of the matches, as when Harry McDonald, "holder of the middle-weight championship belt of Scotland" and deemed "The Pride of Scotland," faced "Swedish grappler" Charles Olson in February 1921.[15] Similar to before the war, the presence of side bets periodically featured in the publicity surrounding the bouts, and public wagers were still being placed on their outcomes.[16] However, discussion on the propriety of either the contestants or the matches themselves was far more muted both in Winnipeg and in Brandon than in previous decades. In general, the wrestling bouts staged before the Brandon public and covered with meticulous detail by the local press represented "clean" exhibitions, and the wrestlers only "rough[ed] it" according to "the perfectly proper fashion accorded under rules which test the stamina, speed, and strength of a man."[17] Injuries were still frequent and included torn neck ligaments, strained arms, and in one instance a broken collar bone that resulted in Harry McDonald cancelling

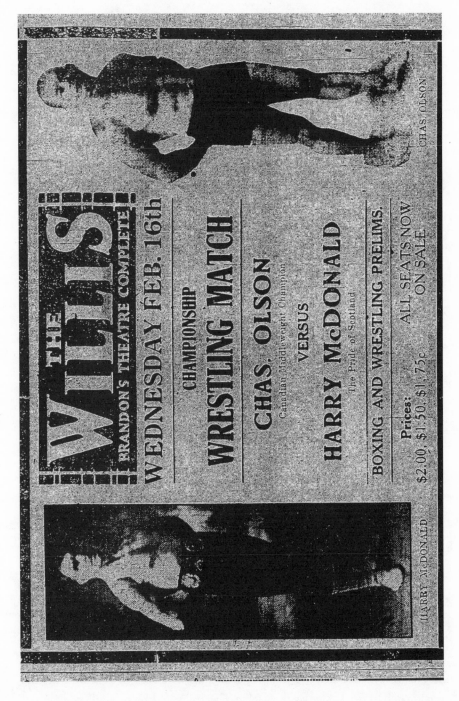

11. A playbill from Brandon's Willis Theatre, advertising a match between Harry McDonald and the "Terrible Swede" Charles Olson. Source: Brandon *Sun*, 12 February 1921.

subsequent engagements.[18] Although the majority of wrestling bouts constituted clean (albeit vigorous) athletic displays, during one bout between Charles Olson and Yorkton's Nels Moe, new methods were introduced to the Brandon public. The *Sun* noted that "both wrestlers mixed it up freely, and the match was about as tame as an Indian massacre. In all previous matches staged here, the wrestlers have kept strictly to wrestling. Moe commenced the tactics which later led to the introduction of many new phases of the game which local fans had not seen before. They consisted of short arm jabs, grinding each other's faces into the mat, head butting and in fact just about everything but biting in the clinches."[19]

Notably absent from the commentary was any condemnation of the methods used by the wrestlers. Tactics that, during the prewar period, elicited reproach from both the press and the attendant public drew no evident censure. To the contrary, the bout, which also included substantial technical wrestling, was heralded as "really the best match of the season."[20] Perhaps the lack of criticism was because the men were reciprocal in their aggression, so it was not a case of one man cheating while the other adhered to the rules. Nevertheless, such excessively rough wrestling had never been deemed altogether acceptable prior to the war, and the Olson-Moe contest foreshadowed changes that would soon occur in the sport.

As Harry Willis's regular wrestling cards were gaining popularity in the Wheat City, residents in other Manitoba communities were also developing a heightened interest in professional wrestling. In Melita, in particular, the sport was an attractive form of public entertainment when, during late 1920 and early 1921, Charles Gustafson "homesteaded" in the community, conducting his training out of the local Great War Veterans Association headquarters.[21] Touted as Melita's "local wonder" and "celebrated local mat artist," Gustafson, who had evidently regained some of his old conditioning, wrestled several matches at the Melita Theatre, adhering as always to "clean and gentlemanly" methods, even when confronted by an opponent such as fellow Swedish grappler Charles Olson, whose choice of techniques was "without any overflow of scruple."[22] Here again, however, strong indignation to his behaviour was not evident. Even though the roughing was one-sided, it drew only muted scorn. When their bout terminated in a draw, both men offered to put up side bets of $500 for a rematch.[23] Although no return contest transpired on local mats, fans were assured that the next and final match of the season at the Melita Theatre would be similarly competitive when Gustafson wrestled Lorne C. Curtis, billed as "Olson's best opponent in Brandon this season."[24]

Attendance numbers at bouts in Brandon and Melita during late 1920 and early 1921 did not approach those seen at high-profile matches in Winnipeg, yet both communities were staging cards with greater regularity than in the province's capital during the period. During the first half of 1922, the Winnipeg public demonstrated a lukewarm interest in professional wrestling, the only significant event in the city being a match on 5 May between Charles Gustafson and 1921 Manitoba amateur heavyweight champion Leo L'Heureux, making his professional debut. The bout, which attracted a "fair crowd, but ... deserved better attendance," lasted three hours without a single fall and was described as one that would "live in the memories of all those who witnessed it" and as "one of the hardest fought matches in Canada."[25] It also proved to be Gustafson's last appearance as a wrestler in the province after a fifteen-year career, though he remained a Winnipeg resident heavily involved with the local Swedish community until his death on 31 October 1956.[26] Two months after his retirement from local mats, professional wrestling entered a new phase in its local evolution, foreshadowed by earlier events in Brandon and Melita, but it was nevertheless distinct in many respects. Although new to Manitoba audiences, the changes witnessed in professional wrestling were symptomatic of a general shift in public attitudes toward sport during the period.

WRESTLING REAPPRAISED

By 1922, sport's purpose was being reimagined throughout North America, and as a popular public spectacle professional wrestling was a beneficiary. Continued improvements in transportation and communication technology, and the mass production of goods, aided in the shift from a production- to a consumer-oriented society in both Canada and the United States. Although the process was under way by the time Manitoba had entered Confederation in 1870 and had long played a vital role in facilitating public support for professional wrestling, it was largely complete by the 1920s.[27] Previously understood by reformers as a tool for imparting a host of values, sport increasingly came to be viewed by large segments of society as purely a form of entertainment.[28] The widespread reappraisal of long-held notions of sport's "proper" purpose also assisted in its transformation during the 1920s. Four years of horrific conflict had called into question the ability of reformers to positively reshape society, and many in the post–First World War period were disillusioned with the idealism that had permeated public discourse on sport prior to and during the war.[29] The scrutiny and criticism of professional sport also dissipated following the First World War because many professional athletes had served their country with distinction, making it difficult to credibly brand professional sports as inherently corrupting.[30] Additionally, many of the most influential figures associated with reform movements such as Muscular Christianity were dead by the 1920s, and few individuals emerged to replace them.[31] Although not everybody abandoned the prewar ideals (particularly those most actively associated with amateur sport), by the 1920s the reformers' fervour had largely been spent, and professional wrestling became less subject to moral condemnation.

In Manitoba, other developments aided in quelling public concerns about professional wrestling. Following the Great War, professional wrestling lost its association with the rowdy, masculine, sporting culture that often brought its practitioners into conflict with legal authorities. Wrestlers' names no longer appeared on dockets in police courts as they frequently had prior to 1914. Government regulation added to the sport's credibility and provided a bulwark against individuals who sought to unscrupulously benefit from public interest in mat contests. On 5 May 1921, the Manitoba legislature passed *An Act to Regulate and Control Boxing and Wrestling Exhibitions,* giving the provincial government strict control over the sport. Whereas the only stipulation previously placed on professional wrestling matches in the province had been the payment of licensing fees in certain municipal jurisdictions, promoters were now required to obtain a licence directly from a provincial government-appointed Board of Supervisors of Boxing and Wrestling.[32] Additionally, wrestlers themselves were required to undergo a medical exam by a board-appointed physician no more than twenty-four hours prior to a match and to submit the medical certificate to the local chief of police. Failure to comply with regulations could result in a fine of up to $250 or a maximum of three months in jail. Further, within Winnipeg, a minimum two-week interval was required between professional wrestling cards, and the act reserved for commission members the right to refund admission to the public if matches were not deemed to be fairly and openly contested.[33] The new legislation made it difficult for professional wrestlers and promoters to engage in some of the activities that had tarnished the sport's reputation, such as organized, gambling-driven, barnstorming tours, half-hearted performances, and refusal to participate in scheduled matches. On the rare occasions when professional wrestlers found themselves in contravention of the regulations, the commission exercised its power to bring punitive measures against the perpetrators.[34] Accordingly, a dimming of reformist fervour was accompanied by a decline in many of the activities against which it had been directed prior to the war.

Evolving public perceptions of professional wrestling were already apparent in Manitoba by 1922, as evidenced by the lack of public moralizing on overtly rough tactics in matches in both Brandon and Melita. Not until the summer of 1922, however, did promoters begin to capitalize heavily on Manitobans' changing tastes. Curiously, the first symbol of this change was vaguely familiar to many Manitobans from two decades earlier, when Mouradoulah, the "Terrible Turk," had strolled through Winnipeg. On 26 July 1922, adorned in "his Indian turban and many-coloured robes," Jatindra Gobar (born Jatindra Charan Guha), originally a practitioner of the traditional Indian *pehlwani* wrestling style, "caused no small amount of excitement around the streets" during a similar walkabout.[35] The "giant Hindu" was in Winnipeg, purportedly at a rajah's expense, as part of an extended campaign to gain a credible claim to the "championship of the British Empire."[36] His opponent on this occasion was the wrestler who would prove to be pivotal in elevating professional wrestling to unprecedented levels of popularity in Winnipeg: Jack Taylor.

JACK TAYLOR AND WRESTLING'S "GOLDEN AGE" IN WINNIPEG

Born on 6 January 1887, and raised on a farm near Chepstow, in Bruce County, Ontario, Jack Taylor spent his early adulthood in various jobs, including as a lumberjack for the Pigeon River Timber Company in northern Ontario and later as a policeman in Lethbridge.[37] Taylor began his mat career in Alberta in early 1912, training as a professional wrestler under the tutelage of Moose Jaw's "Mysterious Homesteader," Clarence Eklund, and later honing his skills under the supervision of Frank Gotch's trainer, Martin "Farmer" Burns.[38] Prior to arriving in Winnipeg in 1922, Taylor had spent most of the previous seven years in the United States, including several years ranching in Wyoming's Nine Mile country, where he had wrestled frequently in nearby Casper, in addition to making occasional forays to major centres on both coasts, such as San Francisco and New York.[39] Although he had spent many years in the United States, Taylor held the rather rare distinction of being a Canadian-born heavyweight wrestler, a point that received enthusiastic and repeated emphasis following his arrival in Winnipeg. Preceding his August 1922 match with Gobar, press reports frequently noted his domestic origins, describing him, in contrast to his "Hindu" opponent, as "a native born westerner and a real Canadian."[40] On 1 August, the two men met in a "lively" fifty-minute battle, made even more intense by the extreme summer heat.[41] Ultimately, the Canadian boy, through a combination of superior technical cunning and physical conditioning, was victorious over Gobar, first by forcing him into submission and then by pinning his shoulders to the mat.[42] This victory was the first in a long series of engagements that would see Taylor pitted against heavyweight wrestlers from around the globe. Invariably, the Canadian grappler emerged victorious in these bouts, both in the competitive sense and, perhaps more significantly, in terms of public sentiment.

Taylor's "inaugural" match in Winnipeg against Gobar proved to be an inauspicious beginning to what would ultimately be a "golden age" for wrestling in the city. Professional wrestling, as noted, had attracted little public interest in Winnipeg during the previous year. Consistent with prevailing uninterest in the sport, only 300 spectators attended the event, providing a gate that "hardly paid for the expense of the show."[43] However, under the management of Emil Klank, who had guided the career of Frank Gotch, world heavyweight wrestling champion, and local promoter D'Arcy McIlroy, various strategies were initiated to cultivate public interest in Taylor's wrestling career. Collectively, they represented the first intensive campaign to build up a wrestling star in the province and in doing so create a sports hero for western Canada.

Since the 1880s, several professional wrestlers had earned considerable fame in Manitoba for their athletic accomplishments and were well known to the public during their careers. However, in the 1920s, with a growing consumer culture, individual athletes became highly marketable commodities. In the United States, figures such as baseball player Herman "Babe" Ruth and pugilist Jack Dempsey achieved unprecedented fame as a result of careful management and increased coverage granted to sports in newspapers.[44] As Benjamin Rader notes, the growing appeal of the sports hero also owed much to a widespread feeling of powerlessness in an increasingly regulated and bureaucratized society. Sports heroes, with their natural talents, represented the ability to transcend the impersonal and seemingly impassable barriers to success and security that confronted most people.[45]

In promoting Taylor to the public, McIlroy and Klank, aided considerably by local sports reporters, created the image of an individual capable of overcoming virtually all of the daunting barriers placed in his path. Taylor was

12. Unrivalled as a talent in western Canada during the first half of the 1920s, Canadian-born Jack Taylor ushered in 'big time' heavyweight professional wrestling to Winnipeg in 1922 and appeared in communities of all sizes throughout the Prairies. Source: Glenbow Archives, NA-5602-59.

first presented as an up-and-coming contender for the world's heavyweight championship. In an October 1922 interview with the *Free Press*, Klank stated that "I have managed and trained the two greatest wrestling champions that ever lived—'Farmer' Burns and Frank Gotch—and [in] Jack [Taylor] I believe that I have a third world's champion in the making."[46] Part of the image cultivated for Taylor also portrayed him as a young talent on the ascent. Descriptions in newspaper reports during 1922 touted him as "Young Taylor," a wrestler with "youth and plenty of confidence on his side."[47] In actuality, at thirty-five, Taylor was well into his wrestling prime by 1922 and hardly a "young" athlete. Further, for many years he had been a prominent heavyweight wrestler, and for long-time fans of the sport in Winnipeg he was already a familiar face.[48] However, during his campaign in Winnipeg during the 1920s, reports were notably silent about his earlier forays onto local mats since they did little to affirm the image of a young star on the climb.

Taylor's portrayal as an up-and-coming heavyweight champion helped to generate public interest in his matches, but the most compelling element associated with his success in Winnipeg was the careful selection and depiction of his opponents. By frequently pitting Taylor against "foreign" wrestlers, promoters overtly juxtaposed the acceptably domestic, which he represented, against threatening alien adversaries who sought to derail his march to the championship. Clearly, by 1922, the appeal of ethnicity in professional wrestling was already well established. Wrestlers of various nationalities had been pitted against one another in Manitoba for decades. Although monikers such as the "Terrible Turk" effectively played on anti-foreigner sentiments in the prewar era, it was rare for ads and newspaper reports to ascribe specific (and typically unfavourable) attributes to wrestlers purely based on their places of birth. After 1922, however, promoters adopted a hard-sell approach that clearly delineated non-Anglo-Canadian wrestlers as the undesirable "other."

FOREIGN MENACES

Overt attempts to capitalize on Canadian nationalism became apparent prior to Jack Taylor's second match in Winnipeg, against Stanislaus Zbyszko, who had recently claimed the world's heavyweight title before losing to Ed "Strangler" Lewis.[49] It was announced on 18 September 1922 that, after two months of negotiating, D'Arcy McIlroy was close to securing former champion Zbyszko, "greatest of all wrestlers," for a match in Winnipeg.[50] Five days later McIlroy obtained Zbyszko's contract; although an opponent had apparently not been chosen, several well-known American wrestlers were suggested to fill the role.[51] The prospect of bringing in an American challenger elicited a "howl of protest" from Taylor's manager, Emil Klank, that was distinctly nationalistic in character. Klank queried, in an interview with the *Free Press*, "why send to New York or Chicago to get a man when they can get Taylor, a real Canadian and a real champion?"[52] He further asserted, "just put him on with Zbyszko and let me show the fans that a made-in-Canada product is just as good as any foreign importations."[53] On 6 October, Taylor signed a contract to meet the "Polish idol" at Winnipeg's Board of Trade Building two weeks hence.[54]

In the lead-up to their match, press reports on Zbyszko portrayed him in a very different fashion than those preceding his match against "German Oak" Paul Sigfried ten years earlier. Although still touted in one report for his "wonderful strength and perfect physique," the Polish grappler, then over forty and the veteran of over 1,000 wrestling matches, was also described as "one of the most brutal looking men in the game," with ears "twisted and out of shape" and a "huge neck, which measure[d] 22 inches, connect[ed] to a head that [was] perfectly hairless."[55] Matching his visage was a simian-like body, purportedly "covered with long black hairs, giving him more the appearance of a huge gorilla than a man."[56] The Polish grappler's tactics were alleged to mirror his frightening countenance, and it was reported that "in action Zbyszko is absolutely heartless and has never been known to spare an opponent." It was further surmised that "perhaps this is the reason he always wins."[57] Although wrestling had long been appreciated as a rough display of athletic manhood, for the first time promoters, aided enthusiastically by the press, were overtly using the promise of a rough spectacle to attract spectators, a tactic that would have been inimical during the prewar reformist era, when "science" was the sport's principal selling point. Once Zbyszko arrived in the city, reports softened somewhat, and the *Free Press*, still cognizant of his foreign origins, admitted that he was "a most genial chap and talks fairly good English with an accent to his voice."[58]

Enthusiastic efforts to promote the match between Zbyszko and Taylor were fruitful, and close to 3,000 spectators attended the event. The clearly nationalistic overtones that the contest evoked in pitting Canada's champion grappler against the Pole evidently played on many people's sentiments, and "by far the majority of the crowd was with Taylor."[59] Yet, despite his domestic origins, support in the audience for Taylor was not universal, suggesting that

Manitobans, not all of whom were of Anglo-Canadian stock, considered more than a wrestler's Canadian birth in deciding whom to cheer for. The Winnipeg *Tribune*, after observing the match, stated that "both grapplers had large followings."[60] Winnipeg's Poles undoubtedly turned out in large numbers, as they had done before the Great War, to support their national hero. Zbyszko's appearance in the city generated considerable coverage in the local Polish-language press. Expectedly, it also lacked the disparaging overtones of the English-language coverage of the event.[61]

In an attempt to ensure a fast-paced exhibition and to avoid the drawn-out endurance contests that had frequently characterized the sport prior to the First World War, wrestling was conducted in ten-minute rounds, an innovation that had already been introduced to New York audiences with positive results.[62] The changes were also evidently well received in Winnipeg, and the *Free Press*, generally accustomed to reporting on local matches staged among men in lighter weight divisions, conceded that, "though heavyweight wrestling is generally slow, last night['s] contest was full of action, and the crowd was on its toes on many occasions."[63] Although presented as an underdog against his more famous opponent, the Canadian performed better than expected, and when the master of ceremonies announced a draw "the crowd cheered him to the echo."[64] On the strength of public support, Taylor wired his wife, still living in the United States, to join him in Winnipeg.[65] Already in public favour for his status as a "real Canadian," he was thereafter able to garner additional support in Manitoba's capital through the well-established practice of homesteading.[66] From his new home base, the Canadian champion launched himself into an aggressive wrestling schedule, appearing in virtually all major prairie centres over the next three years, including Brandon, Saskatoon, Regina, Swift Current, Yorkton, Edmonton, and Lethbridge, as well as smaller communities such as Morris, Manitoba, and Radville, Saskatchewan.[67]

Taylor's match with Zbyszko ended professional wrestling's nadir in Winnipeg, and thereafter heavyweight professional wrestling cards staged at the Board of Trade Building under the auspices of D'Arcy McIlroy's Empire Athletic Club regularly attracted between 1,500 and 4,000 spectators. The events produced the largest attendance figures recorded for professional wrestling in the Prairies during the period, though interest in the sport was widespread. The success had much to do with the fact that McIlroy promoted his cards using messages that deeply resonated with large segments of the population during the period. Beginning with the Zbyszko match, press reports and advertisements for his matches in particular mirrored the growing anti-immigrant sentiment in western Canada during the post-First World War period. Although nativist attitudes, fed by notions of British exceptionalism and imperialism, had existed toward non-Anglo-Canadian peoples prior to the war, by the 1920s begrudging disdain was giving way to more overt hostility.[68] Part of the heightened antipathy toward non-Anglo-Canadians evident in the early interwar period stemmed from economic considerations.

Manitoba's economy experienced what W.L. Morton termed a "great boom" prior to 1912, spurred on largely by European demand for western Canadian grain, heightened British investment in the Canadian economy, and declining transportation costs for western products.[69] However, mounting political instability in Europe during 1912 and 1913 resulted in decreased investments in western Canadian markets.[70] Economic recovery, brought about by wartime demand for Manitoba wheat and livestock, was short-lived, and by 1920 the region entered a sustained economic depression.[71] Wheat prices fell to prewar levels while freight rates rose dramatically, precipitating a decline in many other western industries.[72] Although considerable animosity was directed toward central Canada, which many Manitobans perceived as the primary beneficiary of wartime industrial production and western Canadian war efforts, non-British immigrant groups living in the region also came to be viewed with heightened hostility. Prosperous economic conditions, which had helped to temper nativist resentment during the prewar years, evaporated in the wake of traumatic wartime experiences and Manitoba's subsequent economic downturn. During the Great War, many immigrant farmers thrived because of increased demand for agricultural staples. Generally speaking, European Canadian farmers solidified their economic base during wartime because they planted a variety of crops and were less inclined to engage in the price speculation that frequently gripped their English Canadian counterparts. Additionally, the sons of non-British immigrants were less likely to enlist, remaining on the family farms and precluding the need to hire farm hands. Western Anglo-Canadian resentment of immigrant farmers grew as a result of their prosperity, and many in the dominant group believed that the "foreigners" were reaping the war's benefits but not making correspondingly sufficient sacrifices. Public demand grew for the conscription of farm labourers. Such views were particularly directed at immigrants, by then termed "enemy aliens," who originated from the Austro-Hungarian Empire, even though many possessed a sense of nationality directly at odds with their former imperial overseer's aspirations.[73] Labour unrest, culminating in the Winnipeg General Strike during the spring of 1919, also exacerbated nativist hostility. Ironically, during a period marked by an acute schism between labour and capital, both factions agreed that "enemy aliens" were at the root of Winnipeg's problems.[74]

Changes to Canada's immigration policy in 1919 reflected growing public concern among the Anglo-Canadian majority over various immigrant groups' acceptability as prospective Canadian citizens. Prior to the war, economic imperatives, central among them expansion and development of the western agrarian economy, had dictated the adoption of a liberal approach to immigration. However, after the war, the federal government became primarily concerned with attracting immigrants deemed to be culturally suitable. Many peoples from northern and central Europe officially encouraged to immigrate to Canada prior to the war were faced with entrance restrictions or outright prohibitions after 1919.[75] Anglo-Saxon immigrants from either Britain or the United States were instead given priority.[76] Jack Taylor's arrival in Winnipeg thus occurred during a period when suspicion and outright derision characterized the sentiments among many within the Anglo-Canadian majority toward "foreigners," and the publicity surrounding his matches reflected this unguarded nativist sentiment.

Although there was a general sense of antipathy toward non-Anglo-Canadians during the period, it would be erroneous to suggest that all "foreigners" were viewed in precisely the same fashion by Manitoba's cultural majority. Prejudice, however, was undeniably widespread. A detailed examination of records on Taylor's matches suggests that the Empire Athletic Club used a layered but firmly racist combination of images to convey the importance of its events to Manitobans. None of the images employed was novel, drawing instead on long-standing stereotypes held by Anglo-Canadians. Racist views certainly were not universally held, but an analysis of Taylor's matches with Turkish wrestler Yussif Hussane, Japanese jiu-jitsu practitioner Taro Miyake, and Ethiopian wrestler Reginald Siki illustrates the complex perceptions, and often fears, of "foreigners" among Manitobans during the 1920s and how they were exploited for commercial success.

THE TERRIBLE TURK

During the first half of 1923, Jack Taylor twice faced Yussif Hussane, dubbed the "Terrible Turk" much like Youssouf Ishmaelo and Mouradoulah before him. As noted in Chapter 3, Turkish peoples were already widely regarded with suspicion in Manitoba prior to the First World War. Although the Ottoman Empire was in the process of dissolution when Taylor met Hussane on Winnipeg mats, the once-prominent world power's status as an adversary of the Allies during the Great War was still fresh in Manitobans' minds, intensifying distrust of a people who already, according to J.S. Woodsworth, "[did] not compare favourably even with the Chinese."[77] Between 1914 and 1918, frequent reports detailing the battlefield encounters between Turkish and Allied forces provided reminders of the former's belligerent status.[78] Particularly distressing, however, were the accounts circulated in newspapers pertaining to the systematic persecution of ethnic Armenians in the event now commonly termed the Armenian Genocide, deemed in one report "Horror Unequalled in [a] Thousand Years," and regular reports told of the numerous atrocities committed against noncombatants forced to yield to the "eternal ferocity of the Turk."[79] Turkey was condemned at the outset of the war as an empire "whose hands have dripped for centuries with the blood of her subjugated races," and the *Free Press* opined three years later that "German efficiency has simply organized the natural brutality of the Turk and made it many times more effective than before."[80] Criticism of Turkey was not confined to newspaper editorializing. The public attended lectures related to Turkey and Armenia and demonstrated a willingness to offer written commentary on the subject.[81] Such remarks often betrayed theistic, in addition to nationalistic, concerns. One Winnipeg resident, T.M. Thomas, cast "shame on Germany and the so-called Christian Kaiser who encourages the bloody Turk through his spies and mandates to massacre the helpless Armenian men, women, and children."[82] Harriet A. Walker, the wife of Winnipeg theatre impresario and wrestling promoter C.P. Walker, likewise alluded to theistic concerns through her wartime poetry. In "Behind the Throne—A Dream of the Kaisers," she wrote,

> Yes, Gott, your King supreme am I!
> I rule the earth, the sea the sky!
> I've beaten Satan out as well
> By making earth a living Hell!
>
> We are not partners any more.
> You are my prisoner of war.

I've planned for you a lot of work!
To beat the Christian with the Turk![83]

Images of unrestrained brutality resonated in the reports pertaining to Hussane's upcoming match with Taylor in January 1923, and the "Terrible Turk" was regularly described as a particularly rough wrestler.[84] Deemed in one instance a "man killer" and in another "the Bad Man of Wrestling," he was alleged to have "crippled more men than any three in the business."[85] As specific evidence of his tendencies, reports cited a previous match against well-known heavyweight wrestler Marin Plestina in Chicago in which Hussane's methods almost resulted in prohibition of the sport in the city.[86] Significantly, his tactics were deemed to stem not from his unique temperament and personality but from his cultural heritage. The *Tribune* informed the public that "Hussane is not an intentionally dirty wrestler, but simply ... the wrestling game in Turkey is different to what it is in America. In the land of the Sultan, wrestling is a test of strength and brutality and the man that can take and give the most punishment is hailed as a hero."[87] Therefore, "like all Turkish wrestlers, [Hussane] depends on his great strength and rough tactics to wear an opponent down before he throws him."[88] Upon his arrival in Winnipeg, his reportedly gruff disposition further reinforced his "terrible" image.[89] Although the wrestler from the land of the "star and crescent" was purported to present a menacing proposition for Taylor, fans were nevertheless assured that the manly Canadian was "no pink tea performer" and thus would not go down to defeat easily.[90]

Following weeks of publicity, the Winnipeg public responded keenly to the match, and approximately 3,000 spectators were in attendance.[91] Despite considerable efforts to create an image that corresponded to widely held stereotypes concerning peoples of Turkish descent, Hussane's performance against Taylor defied the ascriptive qualities that had been assigned to the "Terrible Turk." His methods, though occasionally described as "aggressive" and "punishing," were not viewed as particularly violent by either the crowd or newspaper reporters.[92] Overall, Hussane made a positive impression on Winnipeg spectators for his physical speed and wrestling knowledge and was disadvantaged in the match only because of his lighter weight.[93] During their second bout, staged three months later, Hussane actually gained the crowd's temporary sympathy when Taylor was awarded a controversial pinfall by referee Alex Stewart. Nevertheless, when Hussane righted the matter by winning the second fall in their best two-of-three fall contest, fans were once more on Taylor's side. The *Free Press* noted that "though the apparent injustice to the Turk in the first fall aroused the fans they veritably went wild when Taylor ultimately won."[94] Once more, aside from an accidental scratch that caused blood to "flow quite freely into Jack's eye," Hussane demonstrated none of his reputedly brutal tactics.

The obvious disparity between how "foreign" wrestlers such as Hussane were reported to behave and their actual conduct demonstrates that professional wrestlers were capable of challenging the ethnic stereotypes of them. Although wrestlers did not necessarily control the publicity surrounding their matches, they still exhibited a large measure of control over the matches themselves. Thus, during the early 1920s, wrestling itself had not yet descended into caricature and melodrama, even if the advertising and complicit newspaper reporting associated with it were moving in that direction. Crowd reactions during both matches likewise suggest that wrestlers were not only capable of defying ethnic stereotypes but also, at least marginally, able to sway public opinion in their favour. Wrestling fans, even if generally supportive of the Anglo-Canadian wrestler, were not so blinded by ethnic bias that they were entirely oblivious of sportsmanship. As a result, wrestlers such as Hussane were able to temporarily suspend negative perceptions, if only until an acute injustice committed against them had been deemed rectified by the public.

THE DEADLY AND MYSTERIOUS ART OF JAPANESE JIU-JITSU

A wrestler's ability to defy stereotypes did little to diminish them in professional wrestling. Taro Miyake, whom Jack Taylor wrestled in May and June 1923, posed a different threat to the ascendancy of the Anglo-Canadian. Unlike the Turk, whose cultural heritage had ostensibly bred in him unrestrained brutality, the danger of Miyake stemmed from the deadly efficiency and mystery of his knowledge of jiu-jitsu. A fascination with Japanese culture in general, and jiu-jitsu in particular, developed in the English-speaking world during the first decade of the twentieth century, spurred on in 1904 and 1905 by Japanese military success in the Russo-Japanese War.[95] Propaganda campaigns by Japanese authorities helped to disseminate the notion that their nation's seemingly improbable victory was attributable to jiu-jitsu, and by 1905 the art had become "the latest craze among the public" in North America.[96] Well-known publishers and sporting goods manufacturers such as Richard K. Fox and Spalding produced instructional books on jiu-jitsu, and educational institutions, including the United States Naval Academy and the University of Minnesota, hired instructors to offer classes to their students.[97] President Theodore Roosevelt, a firm believer in the value of "rough manly sports," displayed a keen interest in the subject, receiving personal instruction from Naval Academy instructor Yoshiaki Yamashita and entertaining exhibitions of the Japanese art at the White House.[98]

Fascination with jiu-jitsu stemmed, in part, from a belief that the art was both highly efficient and extremely dangerous.[99] The relatively diminutive size of Japanese compared with their European counterparts helped to popularize the idea that jiu-jitsu's mastery nullified the advantages normally garnered from superior size and strength. It was on precisely these grounds that Hume Duval, during his engagement at Happyland in 1907, offered jiu-jitsu lessons to women, "showing them how, by the tricks of the Japanese wrestlers, they might easily throw a man who molests them."[100] Duval was not Japanese, of course, nor was Leopold McLaglen, brother of Fred and Victor, who used his dubious credentials to capitalize on public interest in jiu-jitsu, staging public matches and publishing treatises on the art.[101] Winnipeg's theatregoing public, however, was also occasionally entertained by jiu-jitsu practitioners hailing from Japan, as when one Professor Tamita demonstrated the "science of the 'little brown men'" at the Dominion Theatre in late March and early April 1910.[102] In November 1914, shortly after Japanese forces gained victory over the German garrison at Tsing Tao, an appearance by Mikado's Own Jiu-Jitsu Troupe at Winnipeg's Pantages Theatre purported to "explain to the western mind why it is that the little brown people of Nippon are such valiant allies and such dreaded enemies."[103]

Amicable relations between Japan and the British Empire, strengthened by the 1902 Anglo-Japanese alliance and later by Japan's status as an ally during the Great War, helped to dampen general Canadian dislike of the Asian nation. However, Canadian perceptions of Japan were more ambiguous during the period than a long-standing alliance would suggest. Fierce anti-Japanese sentiment often accompanied periods of heightened immigration, particularly in British Columbia, where Japanese settlement was most frequent and numerically significant.[104] The federal government, primarily concerned with doing its part to maintain good British Empire-Japan relations, repeatedly thwarted attempts by members of the Anglo-Canadian majority to place restrictions on Japanese immigration through provincial legislation.[105] At no time were anti-Japanese sentiments as strong in Manitoba as they were in British Columbia, likely because of the tiny number of Japanese residents in the former province. Manitoba's first known settler of Japanese descent did not arrive until 1906, and as late as 1921 only fifty-three Japanese people were known to live in the province.[106] Nevertheless, alleged "racial" differences between Asians and Europeans also led editorialists and prominent social reformers in Manitoba to declare that Japanese people were incapable of assimilation.[107] Elements of Japanese culture were therefore held in high regard by Manitobans, but at the same time large-scale Japanese immigration was considered wholly undesirable among the Anglo-Canadian majority.

Press reports on Taro Miyake during 1923, unlike those on Yussif Hussane, did not suggest an intrinsic, culturally derived proclivity for brutality. Instead, it was mastery of the dangerous art of jiu-jitsu that made Miyake a particularly fearsome opponent. Unlike most wrestling bouts staged in the city during the previous two decades, the first Taylor-Miyake encounter, held on 18 May 1923, was a mixed-style contest. The men would compete first under jiu-jitsu rules wearing a *gi* (jacket), in which only a submission could earn a victory, and then under catch-as-catch-can rules. The third fall was to be decided by the athlete who won the preceding falls in the quickest fashion.[108] As had commonly been the case, Taylor was cast in the role of the underdog, and long-standing public perceptions of jiu-jitsu's efficacy were utilized to good effect. The *Tribune* warned, following announcement of the match, that "Taylor is going against the advice of his friends in meeting the man that [former world's heavyweight champion Joe] Stecher and [current champion Ed] Lewis have refused to have anything to do with.... It looks like very poor judgement on the part of the local boy to sign up for this match and take a chance of having a bone broken by the grappler from the land of the rising sun."[109]

Jiu-jitsu was likewise described as "wrestling in its most brutal form" and "the most brutal sport ever fostered on the Anglo Saxon sporting public."[110] Predictions of a particularly "rough" match were consistent throughout press reports leading up to the event.[111] Although Taylor was considerably larger and stronger than his Japanese opponent, jiu-jitsu's deadly efficiency nullified such advantages. Manitobans were reminded that "the Japanese can bring any opponent, no matter how strong he is, to his knees simply by twisting the wrist."[112] Additionally, a notion of Oriental mystery permeated discussions of the bout. The public was informed of the dangers posed by jiu-jitsu's "secret death blows" and that, despite the instructional materials and courses then available to the general populace, "there are some jiu-jitsu manoeuvres that have never been explained to Europeans and Americans and probably never will be."[113] The Taylor-Miyake match also represented a clash between cultural forms in which the domestic catch-as-catch-can system's combat efficacy would be measured against that of its Japanese counterpart.[114] The North American and western European public had long been fascinated with this subject, and dozens of mixed-style bouts had been held in Canada, the United States, and Great Britain since jiu-jitsu's introduction to Western society.[115] Nevertheless, this was a novel event for audiences in Manitoba. The Empire Athletic Club's wrestling programs generally offered an undercard made up of several boxing matches preceding the main event. Prior to the match between Taylor and Miyake, spectators were also offered the opportunity to witness another mixed match, pitting jiu-jitsu against the English-speaking world's other pre-eminent unarmed combat system, boxing.

Taylor's match with Miyake once again proved to be an intriguing and attractive event for the Empire Athletic Club. The spectacle, which drew a crowd of 3,000, was evidently far less brutal than anticipated by news reports but nevertheless "a thriller from start to finish" and "the best balanced card yet presented by the Empire Athletic Club since Jack Taylor started on his triumphant march."[116] The jiu-jitsu match, which lasted sixty minutes, did not result in a debilitating injury for the Canadian, who was effective at countering his Japanese opponent's attacks. Miyake was awarded the win under jiu-jitsu rules, dubiously, on "points" but was no match for Taylor at catch-as-catch-can.[117] One month later Taylor and Miyake met again in a jiu-jitsu-only match, the announcement of which prompted a *Free Press* report to conclude that "Taylor has proven to the fans that he is a game wrestler but trying to beat the Jap at his own brutal game is carrying gameness too far…. [He should] leave the jiu-jitsu to the Japanese and stick to the game he knows, catch-as-catch-can."[118] In this instance, however, his previous performance had diminished his underdog status, and *Free Press* reporter Billy Anderson predicted a win for the Canadian.[119] Indeed, "Taylor proved to be master of Taro Miyake at his own game," and after sixty-four minutes the Japanese grappler succumbed to exhaustion and the deleterious effects of being repeatedly thrown to the mat.[120]

Although widely held public perceptions cast jiu-jitsu as a deadly and mysterious art, by 1923 many wrestlers themselves believed that skilled catch-as-catch-can wrestlers, with their own knowledge of submission holds, were fully capable of competing against "foreign" opponents. New York Athletic Club wrestling instructor Hugh Leonard expressed such a view near the "jiu-jitsu craze's" out-set, stating in a May 1905 interview with *Cosmopolitan* that "I say with emphasis and without qualification that I have been unable to find anything in jujitsu which is not known to Western wrestling. So far as I can see, jujitsu is nothing more than an Oriental form of wrestling."[121] Other wrestling experts, including former American heavyweight catch-as-catch-can champion Tom Jenkins, were of the same mind. After investigating jiu-jitsu and meeting with a prominent instructor in the art, he commented in December 1904 that "there isn't a hold in the entire category they use and teach that hasn't been used in English schools by students for hundreds of years."[122] Martin "Farmer" Burns, trainer of both Frank Gotch and Jack Taylor, later offered similar pronouncements, stating in his instructional course *Lessons in Wrestling and Physical Culture* that "in my opinion there is very little in the so-called Jiu-Jitsu teaching that is not included in a full and complete knowledge of catch-as-catch-can wrestling.... I have per-sonally wrestled with the greatest Japanese experts, permitting them to use any and all holds that they wished, not even barring their so-called deadly throttle and strangle holds. In these contests I have invariably won."[123]

Not all catch-as-catch-can wrestlers, however, including "Pocket Hercules" Artie Edmunds, were so dismissive of the Japanese art. In a private letter, later printed in the Manitoba *Free Press*, Edmunds described a private no-holds-barred match against Japanese jiu-jitsu practitioner Katzi Karikucki in New York that lasted over four hours. Although the "Pocket Hercules" eventually managed to defeat his opponent, the trauma that he underwent in the process, vividly described in his correspondence, led him to concede that jiu-jitsu was "an awful game to go up against." Nevertheless, Edmunds was not universal in his praise for all jiu-jitsu practitioners: "This Jap says he is the only man in America who knows the real bone-breaking, strangling methods of Japan. I believe him now. These other jiu-jitsu wrestlers are all fakes. I have offered to wrestle any three in New York in one night, but none of them will take me."[124] All of the discussion, whether in favour of or against jiu-jitsu's merits, fuelled public speculation and sustained interest in potential East versus West wrestling matches.

An analysis of mixed-style contests pitting wrestlers against jiu-jitsu practi-tioners under various rules reveals that, out of sixty-five known matches staged before May 1923, wrestlers won on thirty-four occasions and jiu-jitsuka on twenty-seven, so neither *system* was intrinsically dominant, though certain *indi-viduals* certainly performed better than others.[125] Additionally, Taylor himself was by no means unfamiliar with jiu-jitsu prior to arriving in Winnipeg. In the preceding five years, he had participated in seven public matches against jiu-jitsu exponents, including five against Miyake. Although the *Tribune* conceded in one instance that "Taylor is not altogether a stranger to jiu-jitsu as the big fellow has made quite a study of the Japanese style of wrestling," mention of his past record was absent and would have done little to perpetuate jiu-jitsu's widely held public mystique or the danger posed by his "foreign" adversary.[126]

WINNIPEG'S FIRST BLACK WRESTLER

By the end of 1923, repeated victories for Jack Taylor made it difficult to depict him as an underdog prior to his matches. However, the appeal of seeing a Canadian-born heavyweight wrestler face off against an ethnic array of opponents had not yet diminished. Images of cultural superiority and, more specifically, racial hierarchy were starkly visible when Taylor met Reginald Siki on New Year's Day 1924. This bout marked the first time that a black wrestler appeared in Winnipeg. However, by 1924, ideas about black people's supposed evolutionary backwardness and "innate" physical prowess in combat were pervasive in Manitoba and became central to the profoundly racist commentary on Siki's match with Taylor.

Although no black wrestlers had appeared in Winnipeg prior to 1924, Manitoba had hosted many black boxers earlier in the century, particularly after Jack Johnson became the first non-white heavyweight boxing champion of the world in 1910. Press coverage was commonly racist or emphasized interracial rivalry. Two days after a local boxing card featuring African American boxer Albert "Kid" Ashe, a comic depicting him with a sloping brow and pronounced lips stated that "the Irish coon's whistling was better than his fighting."[127] Several months later an article on an upcoming boxing match between British-born Arthur McLaglen (brother to Fred, Victor, and Leopold) and African American fighter Charles Robertson described the contest as "Black and White in Ten Round Go."[128]

In addition to being depicted in explicitly derogatory terms by the popular media, black fighters were also occasionally enlisted to participate in demeaning spectacles for the gratification of all-white audiences. One such exhibition was the "battle royal," which involved several boxers simultaneously facing off against one another and fighting until one individual was left standing. Prior to the match between Eugene Tremblay and Walter Miller on 15 December 1913, Walker Theatre manager Walter Deering announced that he had "secured four husky darky boys" for such a purpose.[129] Noting that the battle royal had been popular in the United States, Deering likewise promised "barrels of fun" and "barrels of laughter" for Winnipeggers.[130] However, plans did not come to fruition when two of the fighters failed to appear.[131]

Black boxers were not a complete rarity to Manitoba audiences, but during the early twentieth century people of African descent made up a very small percentage of western Canada's population. Nevertheless, fear of their increased presence was widespread. Many newspapers in Canada took editorial stands against allowing black immigration in the west.[132] In the face of actual immigration, local authorities were willing to act to prevent settlement in the country. In March 1911, a group of 200 black settlers sought entry into Manitoba from North Dakota. Although all were in excellent health and good financial standing, the Winnipeg Board of Trade demanded a head tax.[133] In subsequent months, repeated efforts were undertaken by authorities in Winnipeg to ban black immigrants from entry into the country on the ground of their "undesirable" nature as settlers.[134] Federal government policy reinforced this position, and both Clifford Sifton and his successor as minister of the interior, Frank Oliver, actively discouraged black immigration.[135] The actions undertaken by the Laurier government, Winnipeg city officials, and other municipal authorities across the Prairies were representative of the widely held belief among the Anglo-Canadian majority that people of African descent were not merely a "foreign" people with undesirable customs but also innately uncivilized and thus unassimilable. This view placed them at the bottom of Canada's informal immigration hierarchy.[136]

The notion that black people were inherently unassimilable was based in part upon racist interpretations of evolution, which placed blacks at a less advanced stage on the evolutionary continuum than whites. However, their alleged "primitive" nature gave them certain "natural" physical advantages in combative sports. Following African American boxer Jack Johnston's victory in the prize ring over world heavyweight champion James Jeffries, the local *Free Press* reprinted an anthropologist's statement that "the civilized white man to-day is the result of evolution through countless centuries. The coloured man has not 'evoluted' to the same extent. With civilization has come a certain falling off in the battling propensities of the male. ... No matter how much we might like to see the white man win, the laws of evolution were against him."[137]

Similar ideas were still being exploited for commercial gain more than a decade later. Reginald Siki was not purported to possess the innate cunning and violent nature of the Turk, nor did he possess the dangerous and deadly skills accorded to him through mastery of the mysterious and (for Caucasians) unknowable jiu-jitsu. Instead, his natural, primitive capacities were what allegedly made him a formidable adversary.

Repeatedly dubbed "the gorilla man" in the press, Siki had supposedly been discovered by a reporter named Jack Stanley on a trip to Abyssinia.[138] His great strength allowed him to kill animals bare-handed, including a leopard, which he was said to have choked to death. Recognizing his strength, Stanley asked Siki to return to America, and after some cajoling the reporter "backed him into a suit of clothes and a pair of shoes."[139] Unlike Zbyszko, Hussane, and Miyake, Siki, according to reports, lacked the technical skill usually seen among wrestlers. Instead, "half savage, [and] unable to speak or understand English, the giant black depends on his wonderful strength and his native speed to tire out his opponents."[140] Harkening to the long-extant tradition within prize fighting of barring black fighters from challenging for the heavyweight title, both Joe Stecher and Ed Lewis were reported to have "drawn the colour line" on account of the "Abyssinian's" physical prowess.[141] Phrenology-inspired imagery was also used to good effect to build excitement for the match when fans were informed that Jack Taylor would, out of necessity, have to modify his approach to wrestling because "Siki's head is much smaller than his neck making it almost impossible to hold him with a head lock."[142]

Once more the wrestler's actual skill belied the stereotype; following the match, both the *Tribune* and the *Free Press* noted that Siki's abilities made a very favourable impression on the spectators.[143] The "Abyssinian" proved to be a technically competent wrestler, capable of applying and escaping from numerous holds. His much-heralded strength also played little role in the match, for the Canadian proved to be his superior in that quality. Likewise, despite predictions to the contrary, Taylor was able to defeat Siki with an arm and head hold during the first fall, much to the fans' delight.[144] However, with allusions to his "panther-like gilding" and "gorilla-like legs,"[145] his "subhuman" status retained a prominent place in newspaper reports the day after the match. A good wrestler, Siki was still not quite considered human in the Anglo-Canadian sense.

REGIONALISM AND THE TWO SOLITUDES

Jack Taylor's bouts against numerous "foreign" opponents between 1922 and 1924 proved to be the most popular drawing cards for Winnipeg audiences. During the same period, however, Taylor also cemented his claim to the Canadian and British Empire heavyweight titles. He disposed of the region's rather short roster of resident heavyweights or near heavyweights, including the former Manitoba amateur heavyweight champion, Leo L'Heureux, whom Taylor dominated in short exhibition bouts in Winnipeg and defeated in matches on several occasions in smaller prairie centres. After being challenged on numerous occasions, Taylor also met and easily defeated Tom Johnstone, the Winnipeg police officer whom he had supplanted as the city's top drawing card.[146] None of these matches was promoted by D'Arcy McIlroy's Empire Athletic Club, which instead preferred to place Taylor against opponents with more widely heralded reputations. McIlroy did seek, however, to bolster the "local boy's" standing as Canada's heavyweight wrestler par excellence, pitting him against Montreal's Emil Maupas, regarded earlier in the century as "King of Sohmer Park" and "*le lutteur idolatre du public montrealais.*"[147] Similar to Taylor's other matches under the Empire Athletic Club banner, widespread social tensions were manipulated to good effect. In this instance, western Canadian regionalism, coupled with anti-francophone sentiment, permeated discussions of the match.

Although western Canadian regionalism predated the First World War, the issue intensified after 1918 and into the 1920s. Many in the west were becoming increasingly dissatisfied with federal practices, including the long-standing National Policy, widely viewed as economically disadvantageous to the region. The belief among western Canadians that they had shouldered a disproportionately large proportion of the nation's war effort while reaping few of the economic benefits that had accrued in the east through wartime industrial production heightened dissatisfaction with the policy.[148] The deep economic recession experienced by Manitoba in the early 1920s stood in contrast to the growth seen in eastern Canada, reinforcing the conclusion among westerners that, in the words of John Herd Thompson and Allan Seager, "the cards of Confederation were stacked against them."[149]

Decades of settlement and mounting political discontent contributed to the notion that eastern Canada was no longer the wellspring for western Canadian settlement and cultural institutions but instead a colonial power.[150] By the early 1920s, westerners were seeking political alternatives to the existing two-party federal system, the most conscious expression of which was the emergence and remarkable (albeit short-lived) federal success of the Progressive movement.[151] Playbills describing the match between Maupas and Taylor as "Eastern Canada" versus "Western Canada" played on well-honed conceptions of regional self-identity.[152] The opportunity for western interests to get one up on eastern oppressors also proved to be a palatable proposition, and the *Free Press* noted that "Maupas' stock would take a big drop in the east if he loses."[153]

The Montrealer's francophone heritage was also frequently referenced; in one instance, it was ironically noted that Maupas had "plenty of supporters among his fellow countrymen."[154] Further accentuating his linguistic background, one report noted with a hint of derision that "Emile Maupas, the husky French-Canadian from Montreal ... talks very poor English and needs an interpreter in order to make headway with English-speaking people."[155] Tensions between French- and English-speaking Manitobans were long-standing in the province, dating back to Confederation and reaching their crescendo with debates over French-language schooling during the 1890s. The Taylor-Maupas contest once more brought the issue forward. The well-known eastern francophone Maupas lost to Taylor in two straight falls, solidly reinforcing the western grappler's claim to the Canadian heavyweight title while simultaneously bolstering western regional and anglophone pride.[156]

THE GOLD DUST TRIO AND AMERICAN EXPANSION

By the spring of 1924, Taylor had defeated nearly a dozen well-known heavyweight wrestlers in Winnipeg, several of them on more than one occasion and under handicap conditions, and had accomplished similar feats against scores of opponents in centres throughout the Prairies. Having buttressed his recognition as the Canadian heavyweight wrestling champion, Taylor sought to extend his titular laurels to include the British Empire.[157] Finally, in late April, the Empire Athletic Club announced that it had secured a contract with world heavyweight champion Ed "Strangler" Lewis for a match on Victoria Day in the Manitoba capital. Indicative of his commercial appeal during the period, Lewis demanded a $10,000 appearance fee and 35 percent of the gross gate, which constituted the largest guarantee ever offered to an athlete in Canada.[158] Significantly, however, the world's champion also stipulated that he would not agree to meet Taylor but instead wrestle the winner of a match between the Canadian and Washington state native Dick Daviscourt. Daviscourt (born Nicholas Dewiscourt) had already faced Lewis on several occasions prior to April 1924, losing in each instance.[159] However, Lewis's manager, Billy Sandow, declared that Daviscourt was the next closest contender for the champion's title.[160] Reports looked past the fact that yet another obstacle had been placed in their local pride's path. By the 1920s, supporters of sport in Winnipeg were already cognizant that their city, large as it was by standards in the Prairies, had difficulty competing with major American and eastern Canadian markets in attracting top athletic talent, a fact made apparent when skilled hockey players regularly defected from the capital.[161] Enlivened with civic boosterism at the prospect of such a high-profile event, the *Free Press* declared that "a world's heavyweight championship match should put Winnipeg on the sport map, as it will draw fans from all parts of Canada as well as from the neighbouring states across the border. Although for the past year there has been a great deal of talk about Lewis meeting Taylor for the title, very few of the local fans believed there was a chance of the world's championship being staged in this city."[162]

Local aspirations of seeing the Canadian champion in a match for the world's heavyweight title were dashed following his encounter with Daviscourt at the Pantages Theatre. Despite winning the first fall, Taylor was pinned to the mat by his American opponent during the following two stanzas before a crowd of approximately 2,000 spectators. Although described as a "Sensational Match," and "one of the best matches ever seen in the city," nearly two years of promotion by the Empire Athletic Club and Emil Klank nevertheless came to an anti-climactic end.[163] The public and attendant press, based upon what they witnessed, did not seriously doubt the legitimacy of the match; the *Free Press* stated, in a tone far more reminiscent of the period before the end of the Great War, that "the grapplers were 'shooting square' all the way. Even the cynics admit this."[164] Nevertheless, Lewis's condition for his appearance in the city, that Taylor face Daviscourt before being granted a title match, certainly reflects the reputation that the Canadian had developed in the United States prior to his arrival in Winnipeg.

By the end of the war, professional heavyweight wrestling in the United States was undergoing a radical organizational restructuring. Under the directorship of New York promoter Jack Curley (who had long been nicknamed the "tsar" of wrestling), a wrestling cartel, colloquially known as "the Trust," was formed among major promoters in the east and midwest to control the outcomes of professional wrestling matches and specifically the heavyweight championship. Accusations of cartel-like practices (often involving Curley) had long been levied at the sport in the United States, but the years before 1920 saw a further consolidation of power. Heavyweight wrestlers, who had exercised greater autonomy over their careers, were now placed under heightened pressure to acquiesce to promoters' demands to win or lose matches or face blacklisting as a consequence.[165] However, not all wrestlers submitted to the Trust's attempts to monopolize control over wrestling. A number of prominent wrestlers, colloquially termed "trustbusters," continued to operate independently, primarily in the west.[166] Jack Taylor was among the most well-known trustbusters wrestling in the western United States during this period.[167] By the time he arrived in Winnipeg, control over the heavyweight title had passed out of Curley's hands when then-champion Stanislaus Zbyszko agreed to lose the title to Ed "Strangler" Lewis without the New York promoter's consent. Lewis, his manager Sandow, and a third partner, Joseph "Toots" Mondt, informally dubbed "the Gold Dust Trio," thereafter became the dominant power in heavyweight wrestling through their control over the world's title, forming what *Fall Guy's* author, Marcus Griffin, termed in 1937 "the biggest sports combine ever controlled by three men."[168] In March 1924, following a trip to Chicago to negotiate a match with Lewis, manager Klank hinted to Winnipeg reporters that the Canadian was being deliberately denied a title match by the champion, who demanded instead that he again wrestle Zbyszko. However, Zbyszko, who had wrestled Lewis over a dozen times in the previous year, refused to meet Taylor again, making a title match nearly impossible.[169] Taylor's long-standing position as an outsider to eastern wrestling cartels suggests that Lewis might have been hesitant to face the potentially uncooperative Canadian grappler.[170] Indeed, though Taylor was one of the more well-known wrestlers on the continent, Lewis consented to wrestle him only years later.[171]

With Taylor removed as a challenger for the title, considerable efforts were invested in advertising and promoting the match between Lewis and Daviscourt. Anticipating a massive turnout, the Winnipeg Amphitheatre was outfitted to accommodate 12,000 spectators. The One Big Union *Bulletin* noted the event's widespread appeal: "There has never been a sporting event that has stirred up the interest of people of all classes the way the Lewis-Daviscourt bout is doing."[172] A film crew was contracted by the Empire Athletic Club to film the match from ringside, though the arrangement was later cancelled because of objections by Daviscourt that the intense lighting required could impair his performance.[173]

Taylor, for the first time in Winnipeg, served as a preliminary attraction to a wrestling main event, appearing against Harold "Hangman" Cantonwine, whom he had defeated earlier in the year in Saskatoon, Regina, and Medicine Hat.[174] Because of the appearance fee demanded by Lewis, ticket prices were considerably higher than at any previous wrestling event staged in the province. Despite predictions, however, the championship match, won by Lewis, failed to generate the anticipated public support. Only 3,000 spectators were in attendance, well under what had been expected. Although those in attendance were in overwhelming agreement that the Lewis-Daviscourt match was an excellent one, the *Free Press* noted that "the promoters were greatly disappointed at the apathy by local sportsmen."[175]

The appearance of Ed "Strangler" Lewis in Winnipeg proved to be the disappointing climax to an era that saw professional wrestling, and specifically its heavyweight variant, achieve unprecedented popularity in the city. Winnipeg's growth as a lucrative professional heavyweight wrestling market had ensured that powerful American interests, already firmly in control of the business in the United States, would inevitably turn their attention to the metropolitan centre of the Prairies. With the appearance of Lewis in the city, the Gold Dust Trio demonstrated its ability to dictate terms to local promoters, even at the cost of what would have potentially been the most heavily attended match in the province's history.

WRESTLING WANES IN WINNIPEG

After the summer of 1924, professional wrestling began a long decline in Winnipeg. In June, Jack Taylor once again faced Dick Daviscourt, losing to Lewis's challenger a second time before a relatively modest crowd of 1,500.[176] The Canadian champion left the city shortly thereafter. Following his departure, professional heavyweight wrestling matches became increasingly infrequent, with only one more card staged in 1924, two in 1925, and four in the remainder of the decade. The majority of main event matches featured grapplers imported from the United States, with local talent used in preliminary attractions. Only in April 1926, when Stanislaus Zbyszko returned to Winnipeg to face Ivan Poddubny, the Ukrainian Greco-Roman champion, did attendance numbers again rival those seen during Taylor's homesteading period. The two veterans had a long-standing rivalry that dated back two decades, and the Empire Athletic Club was once again able to capitalize on ethnicity's well-established appeal to local spectators by staging the final contest between the greatest wrestlers of Poland and Ukraine.[177]

Although heavyweight wrestling did not maintain its popularity, the One Big Union Athletic Association (OBUAA) continued to stage professional bouts featuring local talent in conjunction with its regular amateur boxing and wrestling cards at the Plebs Hall on Adelaide Street.[178] The OBUAA did not emulate the Empire Athletic Club's approach in promoting its cards, the talk concerning "rough" wrestling and an overt emphasis on ethnicity being absent from regular reports in the One Big Union's labour-oriented *Bulletin*. This was undoubtedly because the OBU relied heavily on support from a membership that was not only working class but also highly ethnically diverse. Among certain ethnic communities, including Ukrainians, the sport also retained some popularity, with matches being staged at the Ukrainian Labour Temple in Winnipeg's North End.[179] Although the OBUAA and specific ethnic groups kept the sport alive in Manitoba's capital, their modest facilities did not allow for the large-scale spectacles seen earlier in the decade.

WILLEY, WRESTLING, AND THE WHEAT CITY

The second half of the 1920s represented a low point for professional wrestling in Winnipeg, yet the sport experienced a resurgence in Brandon during 1928, following several years of strictly amateur cards. As a much smaller community a considerable distance from the province's capital, Brandon did not attract the attention of the large American-based wrestling trusts. With little financial incentive to take bookings in the Wheat City, the big-name heavyweight wrestlers who operated under the sway of the trusts never appeared there. Instead, while Manitoba's largest metropolis entertained the occasional cohort of visiting American wrestlers, Brandon continued to draw on talent both from the city and from the larger prairie region.

Foremost among Brandon's grapplers during the period was Bray Willey, a local middleweight amateur wrestler who, along with his brother Dave, had appeared in a number of contests in Brandon during 1926 and 1927 before turning professional in November 1928. Willey proved to be a popular local attraction for the remainder of the decade, appearing on joint boxing and wrestling cards staged by brothers Tom and Ollie Stark. When not appearing on the mat, Willey worked in the city's psychiatric hospital.[180]

In examining wrestling in Brandon at the close of the decade, it is clear that much had changed in the wrestling business from earlier decades. However, vestiges of the past still remained. As had been done in Winnipeg, matches were now regularly promoted on the basis of the "rough" entertainment that they offered to spectators.[181] However, despite the shift to a more sensationalistic approach to promoting matches, some of the older attractions and controversies of professional wrestling were not yet dead. In the Wheat City, gambling continued to be an important element of the sport as late as 1929. In October, the *Sun* noted of local favourite Bray Willey and his opponent, Mike Bilinsky, that "a side bet of considerable sum is being wagered between the two men, Bilinsky naming the sum and Willey taking it up without hesitation."[182] Following "one hour and a half of torturous work" on the mat, neither man secured a fall, so the stake money, fifty dollars, was returned to them.[183] In Brandon, too, reminders still existed that not everyone considered the sport primarily a form of entertainment. Brandon's wrestling promoters still sought to reassure some who remained deeply suspicious of professionalism. In an ad prior to their inaugural card, featuring a boxing and wrestling co-main event, the Stark brothers stated that "the promoters of these bouts hereby give the sporting public assurance that everything will be conducted above board, the bouts will not be prolonged for the 'benefit' of those attending, and in both events the winner gets the long end of the purse. This, the promoters feel, is what the fans wish, and confidently look forward to the best attendance at the best affair of this kind that has ever been billed for this city."[184]

Brandon sports reporters acknowledged public concern over professional wrestling's honesty but evidently were enthusiastic about boosting the sport's standing in the city. One report in January 1929, following a match between local favourite Bray Willey and visiting grappler Vic Jussack, contended that "few fans knew that Vic Jussack tried so hard to throw Bray Willey on Tuesday evening that he collapsed after the evening's entertainment. Medical men were in attendance on the wrestler for more than half an hour before he recovered sufficiently to leave for down town."[185] Despite testimonials confirming the honest efforts put forth by wrestlers, not all of the local population was wholly convinced on the issue. The *Sun*, ever cognizant of public opinion but still enthusiastic about championing the sport, asserted in November 1929 that "a lot of fans are sceptical about grappling matches. They need have no fear about the serious nature of the match on Tuesday night. Willey is serious about convincing a lot of people that Bilinsky can be rolled over on his back and pinned to the mat."[186] Discussion of professional wrestling's respectability as a public spectacle had subsided in Manitoba by the end of the 1920s, and no overt scandals threatened to extinguish public support. However, as the decade closed, professional wrestling was not, as it never had been, a sport wholly free from suspicion of its honesty as an athletic enterprise. Although public expectations of sport had changed considerably since before the Great War, long-established beliefs were not wholly abandoned in the ensuing years.

CONCLUSION

By the beginning of the Great Depression, Manitobans had witnessed remarkable changes in professional wrestling. The sport slowly re-emerged from oblivion after the First World War to become a viable form of public entertainment in several of the province's secondary centres. By 1922, Winnipeggers had once again vociferously embraced the sport as heavyweight standout Jack Taylor, aided by the promotional efforts of his manager Emil Klank, D'Arcy McIlroy's Empire Athletic Club, and an increasingly supportive sporting press, became the region's "star" grappler. Heavyweight wrestling's rise in popularity occurred during a period when ideas concerning sport's purpose were undergoing significant reappraisal. A decline in reformist sentiment and increased regulation meant that much of the criticism levelled at the sport subsided during the early interwar years. Viewed primarily as a form of entertainment, wrestling was presented by promoters as a "rough" spectacle, and they adopted aggressive strategies that played heavily on widespread public sentiments concerning race, ethnicity, and regionalism to draw spectators. The growing popularity of wrestling also made it further subject to American interests that sought to monopolize control over heavyweight wrestling. By the latter half of the 1920s, professional wrestling had lost much of its former popularity in Winnipeg, though to the west in Brandon, where local and regional wrestlers in the lighter weight divisions were used, it closed out the decade as a well-patronized athletic attraction. As the "lost decade" dawned, it was clear that public impressions of professional wrestling had altered considerably when measured against the prewar period. However, as the Brandon case illustrates, reform-era perspectives were not entirely cast aside by the public, despite a greater acceptance of professional wrestling as a form of entertainment.

Chapter 7

AMATEURISM EXPANDS
AMATEUR WRESTLING IN MANITOBA, 1919–29

By the time the Great War came to an end, amateur wrestling, like its professional counterpart, had been stripped of much of the momentum spurring its growth in the seven years prior to hostilities in Europe. Enlistment in military service depleted the sport's competitive and coaching ranks. At the YMCA, Winnipeg's initial stronghold of amateur wrestling, classes were offered during the fall and winter of 1918–19, once more under the supervision of Tom Dickinson, who, injured overseas, was reported six weeks before the armistice to be "completely recovered from his wounds" and ready to resume his coaching duties.[1] Although a large turnout was expected for classes, no amateur wrestling competition was staged during the season.[2] After early 1921, however, amateur wrestling experienced rapid growth that would continue for the remainder of the decade as the possibilities for competition at local, regional, national, and international levels became more frequent and as high-level competitive amateur athletics took on heightened importance. By the second half of the 1920s, amateur wrestling had superseded professional wrestling in both frequency of competition and volume of news coverage in the province.

As the possibilities for competition grew, so did the diversity of athletes. Unlike prior to the war, when the YMCA and its largely middle-class Anglo-Protestant membership dominated wrestling, the 1920s witnessed people of multiple class backgrounds and ethnicities embrace the mat game in Manitoba. Although the YMCA remained an important contributor to the sport, French Canadian athletes from St. Pierre and St. Boniface, the "company league" Winnipeg City Police Athletic Association, and the distinctly working-class One Big Union Athletic Association contributed tremendously to the growth of wrestling during the decade, spurred on not only by increased opportunities for competition but also by ethnic, employment, and class-based interests.

However, despite this apparent "democratization" of amateur wrestling during the 1920s, in which each organization embraced sport for varying purposes, the underlying tenets dictating what it meant to be an amateur athlete remained largely unchanged. Many of the principles guiding amateur sport before 1914 continued to hold sway in the early interwar period, and as a result important barriers to participation in amateur sport also remained in place. Thus, remarkable growth from and continuity with the prewar period simultaneously characterized amateur wrestling in Manitoba during the 1920s.

REBUILDING AFTER THE WAR

Competitive amateur wrestling took longer to reassert itself on the provincial sporting landscape than did professional wrestling, partly because of the convention of having multiple athletes participate in multiple weight divisions in a tournament format for championship honours. Unlike professional cards, generally built around single matchups, tournaments required a large number of entrants to make holding them worthwhile, and this number was not forthcoming in the immediate postwar period. Contrary to what was seen in professional wrestling, virtually none of the athletes active on Manitoba mats prior to the Great War resumed their careers in the postwar period, the one notable exception being 1914 dominion champion James H. (Jimmy) McKinnon.[3] During the fall and winter of 1920–21, the YMCA continued to offer wrestling instruction (but evidently no competition) under the direction of former professional wrestling standout Alex Stewart, while Thomas Dickinson concentrated on developing the boxing program at the "Y."[4]

The 1920s, on the whole, proved to be an exceedingly difficult period for the institution, which entered its fifth decade of operation in the city in dire financial straits. By 1922, the local association was forced to seek protection from creditors under the *Bankruptcy Act*, and in 1926 its Selkirk branch, located in Winnipeg's North End, had to be sold to forestall further financial catastrophe.[5] Official records later noted that the Selkirk branch "had not been operating long before it became apparent that it was doomed to failure," largely because the itinerant, multi-ethnic population in the district did not embrace the institution in the same way that the proportionally larger Anglo-Protestant population nearer to the city centre (and the Vaughan Street branch) had done.[6] The YMCA, on the whole, remained a predominantly middle-class Anglo-Protestant institution both in Winnipeg and elsewhere in Canada after the First World War.[7] Ultimately, however, other institutions more accessible to non-Anglo-Canadian segments of Manitoba's population arose to meet a growing interest in competitive amateur wrestling during the early 1920s. Notable in this respect were sports clubs based out of the Franco-Manitoban communities of St. Boniface and St. Pierre.

FRANCO-MANITOBANS

French Canadians had long maintained a strong interest in wrestling. In Montreal after 1900, professional wrestling cards were staged on a near-weekly basis at Sohmer Park during the non-summer months. Virtually every major heavyweight wrestler appeared before Montreal audiences, with some high-profile performers such as the Russian Lion, George Hackenschmidt, attracting in excess of 5,000 spectators, the majority of whom were French Canadian.[8] Even the legendary strongman Louis Cyr made occasional forays onto Montreal's wrestling mats, albeit with mixed success.[9] In addition to hosting visiting international talent, Montreal was home to numerous highly skilled grapplers of francophone extraction, including world's lightweight champion Eugene Tremblay, Canadian heavyweight champion Emil Maupas, and well-known heavyweight contender Aloise Gonthier (Carl Pons).[10] Tremblay appeared in Winnipeg on several occasions prior to 1915, and evidently he had a strong contingent of supporters among the local French Canadian population. Although he wrestled in the province's capital, he lodged and trained in the predominantly francophone St. Boniface, where he was reported to have "a number of friends" and to be "the idol of the many French sportsmen of [the community]."[11] The French-language newspaper *Le Manitoba* noted a similar appreciation for the Montreal star prior to his first match with Walter Miller in 1913: "Tremblay est Canadien-francais et nombreux seront les gens de Saint Boniface qui desireront assister a la recontre avec le champion de St. Paul."[12] St. Boniface also produced a number of well-known French wrestlers who appeared frequently on local mats, including Pierre (Pete) Menard and Rosario Duranleau. Yet all of the prominent French Canadian wrestlers prior to the First World War were in the province's professional, not amateur, ranks.

As a chiefly Anglo-Protestant institution, the YMCA, the early driving force behind amateur wrestling in the province, held little cultural appeal to members of the francophone community in St. Boniface, much as was the case with the various other non-British peoples in Winnipeg's North End. Indeed, an examination of both executive and active membership rosters from the prewar period testifies to the dearth of French Canadians enrolled in the "Y."[13] Nevertheless, by the early 1920s, officials with the Roman Catholic Church were sufficiently concerned with its growing popularity to warn parishioners against taking out a membership. *Les cloches de Saint-Boniface*, the community's local ecclesiastical and historical review, warned that, though the institution had the support of many influential citizens and offered a variety of attractive programs to its members, it nevertheless "propager l'indifference religieuse" and ultimately "corrompent l'integrite de la foi catholique en arrachment des enfants a l'Eglise leur mere."[14] Accordingly, papal authorities prohibited the distribution of any promotional materials related to the YMCA.[15]

Although the predominantly Roman Catholic francophone population in the province was discouraged from joining the YMCA because of both its ethnic composition and its unacceptable religious conduct, other organizations, such as the Union Canadienne, emerged to satisfy a growing interest in sport. Founded in 1915, the union served many functions within the French Canadian community. The organization maintained an informal but close association with the Roman Catholic Church, a link most evident through its St. Cecile choir, which performed "sacred concerts" at the St. Boniface Cathedral.[16] Additionally, it sponsored numerous faith-themed lectures delivered by prominent Roman Catholic officials.[17] Beginning in 1916, the Catholic-affiliated union formed an athletic committee and fielded baseball and hockey teams in the Winnipeg Amateur Baseball Association and Manitoba Amateur Hockey Association.[18] Wrestling does not appear to have been among its earliest athletic pursuits, but following the war the union opened a branch in St. Pierre (now St. Pierre-Jolys) south of Winnipeg that enthusiastically embraced the sport. The St. Pierre Union Canadienne boasted several highly talented amateur grapplers, including heavyweight Leo L'Heureux, lightweight Albert Choinard, and Armand Lavergne (weight unknown). By early 1921, the organization was staging amateur wrestling cards at the local municipal hall. The St. Pierre programs were unique inasmuch as they featured only French Canadian athletes, with St. Boniface's International Athletic Club providing the competition.[19] Manitoba's French Canadian population was appreciative, with spectators travelling from francophone communities such as St. Malo, St. Elisabeth, and Otterburne to witness the matches.[20]

The development of amateur wrestling programs that catered to Manitoba's French-speaking population coincided with the revitalization of the Manitoba

Amateur Wrestling Championships (staged for the remainder of the decade in conjunction with the Manitoba Amateur Boxing Championships) in April 1921. The near monopoly held by Anglo-Canadians during the prewar period was authoritatively broken when French Canadian wrestlers representing both the International Athletic Club and the Union Canadienne earned first-place finishes in three of the seven contested weight divisions.[21] Both 1922 and 1923 proved to be similarly propitious, with wrestlers from St. Boniface and St. Pierre earning titles in two of five and two of four weight divisions at the Manitoba Championships in both respective years.[22] In 1923, Manitoba hosted the Dominion Amateur Wrestling Championships (likewise staged in conjunction with the Dominion Amateur Boxing Championships) for the first time since 1914. Albert Choinard, the 1922 and 1923 Manitoba lightweight champion and the only Franco-Manitoban entrant, advanced to the finals before being defeated by Tauno Makela (Karl Maki) of the Port Arthur Finnish Canadian Nahjus club.[23]

As evidenced by the many successes experienced by Manitoba's French Canadian matmen, the early 1920s represented a period when amateur wrestling became increasingly accessible to non-anglophone and non-Protestant segments of the province's population. Nevertheless, amateur wrestling was by no means an enterprise in which ethnicity and religion ceased to be important factors. The maintenance of group identity remained important during the 1920s, and non-Anglo-Protestant athletes made remarkable progress in open competition through participation in clubs organized along distinctly ethnic lines and with clear religious affiliations.[24] The growing competitive opportunities in amateur wrestling for francophone athletes, as well as for athletes of other ethnicities, also formed a counterpoint to the situation developing in professional wrestling, in which anti-"foreigner" rhetoric, which cast athletes in roles based upon perceived racial or cultural traits, proved to be a critical element of promoting the sport to Winnipeg audiences.

WINNIPEG CITY POLICE

During the 1920s, groups that took a strong interest in wrestling also organized along occupational lines. Notable in this respect was the Winnipeg City Police Athletic Association (WCPAA), founded in September 1919. The WCPAA, which became the province's most frequent sponsor of high-profile amateur boxing and wrestling competitions during the 1920s, emerged as a direct result of the labour agitation surrounding the 1919 Winnipeg General Strike. In

1918, the Winnipeg police formed a union to negotiate on their behalf with the Winnipeg Police Commission and Winnipeg City Council.[25] Mounting labour discontent in the months following the First World War was driven, in part, by the failure of wages to keep pace with inflation and the inability of many veterans to secure employment following their return from Europe. Members of the Winnipeg police force, many of whom had also served overseas with the Canadian Expeditionary Force, were sympathetic to the plight of veterans.[26] On 15 May 1919, the police union, itself affiliated with the Winnipeg Trades and Labour Council, voted overwhelmingly in favour of general strike action. However, at the request of the Strike Committee, the police agreed to remain on duty to prevent the imposition of martial law.[27] As historian D.C. Masters notes, this decision placed the police in an "anomalous position," having declared their support for the general strike while remaining under the authority of a city council overwhelmingly against the strikers' cause.[28] Many members of Winnipeg City Council as well as other high-ranking government officials, such as Winnipeg's district military commander, Major General Herbert D.B. Ketchen, thought that the police, though still on duty, were firmly allied with the strikers.[29]

On 29 May, Winnipeg City Council requested that all members of the police force immediately sign a declaration recognizing the supreme authority of the Police Commission and agreeing not to participate in any type of sympathy strike. The police union responded the following day with a resolution stating that the ultimatum gave it insufficient time for due consideration and was in violation of the existing agreement between the union and the Police Commission. Its official statement also contained a vaguely worded pledge of allegiance, declaring that the union "[stood] behind constituted authority and [was] willing to do all in [its] power to preserve law and order as loyal British subjects." Only twenty-five officers signed the Winnipeg City Council pledge.[30] In an effort to forestall a complete impasse between the two sides, the Brotherhood of Locomotive Firemen and Enginemen agreed to act as a mediator. However, beginning on 5 June, city officials, still doubting the police force's loyalty, began recruiting special constables. On 9 June, having secured sufficient enlistment, the Police Commission fired 240 policemen. Only fifteen persons, most of whom were high-ranking officials, retained their jobs.[31] Reflecting the horrible blow to police morale sparked by the dismissal, the police union requested that the honour roll on display at the Central Police Station be covered and that the photographs of police officers who had died in the line of duty be removed from public display until the police force was reinstated.[32] Ultimately, most officers, save those most actively involved in the strike movement, were rehired.[33] Although Winnipeg's policemen regained their jobs, city officials no longer recognized the police union's bargaining rights. Officers were reinstated on the basis of agreeing to disavow union membership.[34] However, the events of May and June 1919 had adversely impacted the force's esprit de corps, so Winnipeg City Police Chief Constable Chris H. Newton, who assumed his position following the dismissal of Donald MacPherson on 11 June, permitted formation of the WCPAA.[35]

By the 1920s, company athletic associations had become relatively common throughout North America and western Europe. Since the 1890s, such organizations had been recognized as an effective means of ensuring amicable relations between workers and management and negating the potential for worker militancy.[36] In the case of the WCPAA, police officers themselves took a direct role in running the organization, which, from its outset, was devoted to "promoting Athletics, Social Entertainment and mutual welfare for the members of the Association, their wives and families."[37] Although not specifically an organ of the Police Commission, the WCPAA received its active endorsement through the provision of facilities for a reading room, billiard table, and gymnasium.[38] Additionally, the Police Commission provided occasional funds in support of WCPAA social functions, and a reading of the association's minutes from the 1920s suggests a favourable working relationship between the two organizations.[39]

Within six months of the WCPAA's formation, it became actively involved in promoting both boxing and wrestling in the city not only among its members but also within the larger community. Initially, the association was not specifically devoted to amateur sports. Its inaugural event, staged on 8 April 1920 at the Board of Trade Building, featured several boxing matches and a main event wrestling match between the well-known local professional wrestling champion Constable Tom Johnstone and Constable McSweeney.[40] Boxers were paid between $10 and $100 for their performances, though it does not appear that either wrestler received remuneration.[41] By October, however, the WCPAA had declared itself a strictly amateur organization, and it would remain so for the duration of its existence.[42] Beginning in April 1921, with its sponsorship of the Manitoba Amateur Boxing and Wrestling Championships, it assumed the YMCA's mantle as the province's main promoter of high-profile amateur wrestling tournaments. Excluding 1925 and 1926, the WCPAA hosted the event for the remainder of the decade. During the 1920s, the Dominion Boxing and

Saturday's results—M'ller 8, Russell

BOXING & WRESTLING
CHAMPIONSHIPS
TONIGHT
8.00 P.M.   Also TUESDAY NIGHT.
Old Alhambra Dance Gardens
225 FORT STREET.

TICKET SALE AT
CLUBB'S CIGAR STORES,
Portage and Fort St. and Portage
Avenue—$1.50 and $1.00.

OVER 30 CONTESTANTS
Dominion, Provincial and City
Champions participating. Tourna-
ment under auspices of Winnipeg
Rotary Club and sanctioned by the
C.A.A.U. Winnipeg Police Athletic
Association will handle all bouts.
2 NIGHTS OF THRILLING
BATTLES — COME.

HAVE YOUR

13. Playbill for a March 1928 Amateur Boxing and Wrestling card. The Winnipeg Police Athletic Association was an avid promoter of amateur wrestling during the 1920s. Source: Manitoba *Free Press*, 5 March 1928.

Wrestling Championships were staged in Manitoba three times, and on two of these occasions (1923 and 1927) the association was the sponsor. Additionally, regular tournaments were held at the Central Police Station gymnasium featuring athletes from both the WCPAA and various clubs across the city.[43] By January 1927, the WCPAA was staging monthly boxing and wrestling competitions at the gymnasium in the Central Police Station.[44]

During the 1920s, the WCPAA not only organized events but also produced a number of outstanding wrestlers, particularly within the upper (middleweight and over) weight classes, including Joseph Mulholland (1924 Manitoba middleweight champion), James Harvey Paddison (1925 Manitoba light-heavyweight champion), and Stewart Sinclair (1929 Manitoba middleweight champion).[45] However, certainly the most accomplished police wrestler during the period was William Lloyd McIntyre. Born in Prince Edward Island on 16 March 1900, McIntyre joined the police force in 1922.[46] He became actively involved in competitive amateur wrestling several years into his career, and by 1930 he claimed honours at multiple provincial (1927, 1928, and 1929) and dominion (1927, 1928, and 1930) championships in the heavyweight and light-heavyweight classes.[47] His many accomplishments made him, along with Jimmy McKinnon, the most decorated amateur wrestler in the sport's early history.[48] Many other police officers took an active interest in competitive wrestling throughout the 1920s, participating in various events arranged by the WCPAA or other clubs in the city.[49]

For the Winnipeg City Police, active involvement in boxing, and especially wrestling, made sense for members because they promoted skills that had direct application to their jobs. To this end, the association also took an interest in jiu-jitsu during the early 1920s. Although, as noted in Chapter 6, Manitoba's Japanese population was extremely low, at least three individuals of Japanese descent, Dr. Sumar Herota, C. Hanada, and Alex Takeuchea, were invited to showcase their skills on cards staged at the Central Police Station.[50] Their exhibitions were apparently well received by the local public, and the *Free Press* noted, following a match between Herota and W. Merritt, that "this style of wrestling certainly took with the gathering."[51] Although jiu-jitsu matches appear to have been a unique feature of WCPAA programs during the 1920s, the precise details of the Japanese athletes' affiliation with the Winnipeg City Police remains unknown.

The WCPAA's regular involvement in staging amateur wrestling competitions boosted the organization's visibility within Manitoba and gave its members an athletic outlet that had definite work-related benefits. However, it is also clear that the events provided a more immediate and tangible gain. Because the cards were generally well patronized by the public, they represented an extremely important source of revenue for the association. Considerable effort was made to promote the events, both in the newspapers and in other visible public venues. In March 1920, for example, 100 streetcar placards and fifteen large posters were purchased to publicize the inaugural show.[52] It is difficult to precisely determine the cost associated with staging the event, but calculations based upon known expenditures accrued between 27 March and 9 April reveal that approximately $832 were paid out to various parties.[53] The WCPAA secretary reported following the show that over $1,300 had been received at a cost per ticket ranging from one dollar to two dollars, "with a large number of ticket sellers still to be heard from."[54] By 1924, the association's annual financial report declared that boxing and wrestling events were "the chief source of revenue during the year" and that, save for the provincial Olympic trials, "the shows were a success from all points as the public press and our financial statement show."[55] Revenue-earning potential remained high throughout the decade, reports noting that, following the 1927 Dominion Championships, expenses totalled $2,100 and returns $3,500.[56] With such a profitable revenue stream, the WCPAA executive wanted to protect the organization's financial interests and reputation as an amateur sporting body by seeking prosecution against individuals who did not turn in money from ticket sales and by lobbying the province's amateur governing body, the MAAUC, to place athletes who failed to appear for a performance on suspension.[57] The decision to vigorously protect its interests was derived, in part, from the association's desire to fulfill the third element of its mandate: the provision of mutual welfare for association members and their families.

Although in title an athletic association, the organization took on additional duties over time to improve its members' personal welfare. In October 1923, the WCPAA's constitution was amended to grant benefits to officers forced to leave the police department on account of disability, and money was likewise allocated for the families of deceased members.[58] Donations were provided, if occasions warranted them, to the families of members removed from work because of extended illness.[59] The association also advocated on its members' behalf for pay increases and fielded a delegation to negotiate with Winnipeg City Council concerning pension benefits.[60] Clearly, the capacity to fulfill its expanding mandate required large amounts of revenue, the principal sources of which were the many amateur boxing and wrestling programs staged by the association. In the absence of an official police union, both sports provided the WCPAA with the principal means to improve the plight of all the city's constabulary and act as a strong advocate on their behalf.[61]

ONE BIG UNION

During the 1920s, the WCPAA sponsored the majority of tournaments staged to decide provincial and national honours. However, with respect to the sheer number of events held in the province during the decade, no institution rivalled the One Big Union Athletic Association (OBUAA), whose weekly boxing and wrestling cards attracted large numbers of spectators to its headquarters gymnasium at 54 Adelaide Street, colloquially known as Plebs Hall. Much like the history of its police counterpart, the history of the OBUAA is intimately connected to the 1919 Winnipeg General Strike. Although the OBU was formally founded in Calgary on 4 July 1919, several weeks after the strike ended, its central tenets—namely, the unification of all industrial workers under a single organization and advocacy of the general strike as a bargaining tool—were central to western Canadian labour militancy during the period.[62] By late 1919, the OBU had a membership of over 9,000 in Winnipeg alone, and by early 1920 approximately 75 percent of trade union members were affiliated with the union.[63] Despite its rapid growth, the organization went into an equally rapid decline the following year. Schisms developed between the OBU and a subsidiary organization, the Lumber Workers International Union (LWIU), during the second annual convention held in October 1920 in Port Arthur, Ontario. The disagreements between the OBU and LWIU ultimately led to the latter's withdrawal from the parent body.[64] Many other groups under the OBU banner followed suit. Beginning in mid-1920, economic recession adversely impacted the OBU's membership numbers and its ability to effectively pursue aggressive labour action.[65] By late 1921, further ideological disputes, this time with the Soviet Union's Comintern and its unofficial Canadian organ, the Worker's Party, whittled away at OBU membership.[66] In the ensuing years, the OBU had little representation outside Winnipeg and yielded little influence within the Canadian labour movement. However, the period associated with the union's precipitous decline, contrarily, saw its athletic organization ascend to prominence in the province.

Although by 1921 the One Big Union no longer carried the influence that it once did in labour politics, the organization was nevertheless able to forestall financial insolvency through an ingenious lottery system run through its weekly *Bulletin* newspaper. For twenty-five cents, a person could purchase a three-week subscription to the paper and, by joining a football lottery, have his or her name entered into a draw for a cash prize. Public reaction was overwhelming, and by April 1922 over 150,000 entries were pouring in per week. Although attempts were made by the provincial courts to shut down the betting scheme, the OBU was able to change the conditions of the contests (e.g., shifting from a football-guessing contest to a weather-guessing contest), and thus skirt the law, for many years.[67] Ample revenue from the OBU lottery allowed the organization to invest funds in a number of other enterprises.[68] Among the most well known was the OBUAA. On 20 February 1923, the OBU formed an Athletic Committee and thereafter constructed a gymnasium in its Adelaide Street headquarters.[69] Initially, the facility was open only to OBU members, and participation was disappointing. However, a month later the union's Central Committee, to which the Athletic Committee reported, extended membership to the general public.[70] By the following winter, "a crowd of boys" was training at the facility.[71] In February 1924, the OBUAA hosted its first amateur boxing competition at Plebs Hall and reported that "negotiations are now under way to hold semi-monthly amateur boxing and wrestling bouts between members of the various clubs and if successful it should prove a great stimulant to the amateurs and bring a lot more boys into this healthy and manly form of sport."[72] On the basis of initial strong public support, the club decided to "stage these invitation shows every week until further notice."[73] The programs operated between October and May for the remainder of the decade.

As might be expected for a union-based organization, the OBUAA catered specifically to Winnipeg's working-class population. Unlike the YMCA, whose leadership and membership were drawn primarily from the middle class, the OBU's athletic leadership, by its own admission, was "all working boys, who give their services free."[74] The club also attracted members who, because of financial strains, found the cost of enrolling in other clubs prohibitive and were permitted to pay "their way as they went along."[75] The organization's approach to securing funds from the public for its weekly programs also demonstrated the desire to make boxing and wrestling accessible to economically disadvantaged segments of the population. Unlike other amateur and professional cards staged throughout the province, the OBUAA typically did not charge admission. Instead, "voluntary collections" were taken at the door, allowing individuals to donate according to their financial circumstances.[76] When a set ticket price was announced for one of the weekly shows, it was far below that offered elsewhere.[77] The OBUAA was not above trumpeting its members' working-class connections, even noting in the spring of 1924 that Jack Taylor, training at its gym, "was a union boilermaker before he took up the wrestling game for a living."[78] One of the club's most prominent members was future Saskatchewan premier, federal New Democratic Party leader, and father of Canadian Medicare, Tommy Douglas. In later reminiscences, Douglas recalled his affiliation with the OBUAA as a boxer and had fond recollections of his association with the club's athletes, including Taylor, whom he described as "the man famous for his great toe hold, a very fine wrestler."[79]

Funds accrued through newspaper lotteries, weekly silver collections, and the modest membership fees charged to athletes allowed the OBU to equip its gymnasium with some of the best modern conveniences available. To attract members, new equipment was constantly being purchased by the club and advertised with pride through its weekly sports column in the OBU *Bulletin*.[80] By the fall of 1924, in addition to being "well lighted, heated, and ventilated," Plebs Hall boasted a padded boxing ring, wall weights that had six pulleys allowing both upright and ground exercise, six punching bags, ceiling rings, hurdles, boxing and bag-punching gloves, chest expander cables, and hot and cold showers.[81] Of particular pride for the club was its wrestling mat. Manufactured by the Ostermoor mattress manufacturing company and filled with "Ostermoor wool," it was covered by a double layer of smooth canvas, presumably to minimize the abrasions that kept so many athletes away from the sport.[82] The OBUAA testified that its mat was "claimed by both Canadian and American professional wrestlers who have used it to be the best that they have had the opportunity to wrestle on."[83] As an explicitly working-class venture, the association clearly took pride in the idea that its facilities and services were every bit the equal of more elite, middle-class institutions such as the YMCA. Workers could take heart in the fact that, though they did not possess equivalent economic power, the OBUAA provided the means for equality in athletic competition.

In keeping with long-standing practices in the province, in the fall of 1924 the club also secured the coaching services of a well-known professional, French Canadian heavyweight wrestler and former amateur champion Leo L'Heureux.[84] Middleweight professional Mike Bilinsky, though frequently absent from the city because of his wrestling schedule, also offered instruction to members.[85] Bilinsky's appointment was indicative of the club's desire to reach well beyond

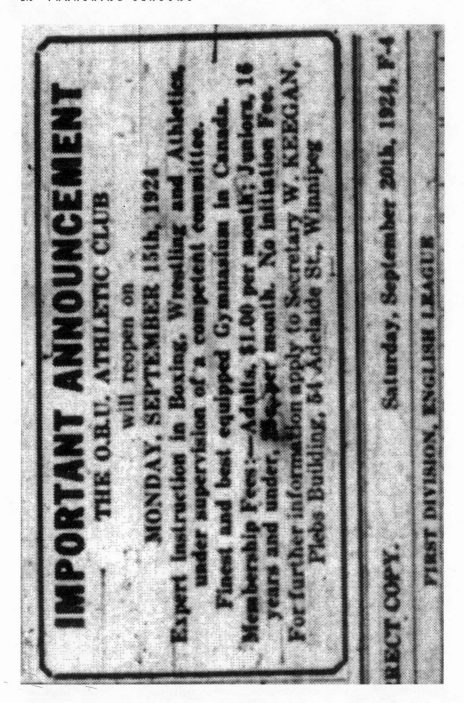

14. The working-class One Big Union enthusiastically promoted the quality of the facilities that they offered to their membership. Source: OBU *Bulletin*, 11 September 1924.

the Anglo-Protestant demographic who had, in years past, dominated amateur wrestling in Manitoba. Bilinsky demonstrated a particular interest in teaching young Ukrainian Canadians the sport, and at least one Ukrainian Canadian athlete, Vic Jussack, wrestled as an amateur under the auspices of the OBUAA before beginning his professional career.[86]

Unlike many other organizations, the OBUAA exhibited a willingness to mix amateurs and professionals on weekly cards.[87] Well-known international heavyweight professional wrestlers, who, admittedly, made increasingly infrequent trips to Winnipeg after the summer of 1924, appeared in the weekly shows, including Indian wrestler Jatindra Gobar and Holland native Tom Draak.[88] In some instances, the OBUAA even featured matches that pitted amateurs against professionals, as was the case when Mike Bilinsky wrestled against 1929 Manitoba amateur heavyweight champion William Crossley.[89] Boxing matches were occasionally contested under similar conditions.[90] The OBUAA's practice of accepting donations instead of gate receipts likely helped its amateur athletes to avoid punitive action from the MAAUC.

Although the OBUAA was an overtly working-class labour organization, as historian Bruce Kidd notes, its weekly reports in the *Bulletin*, unlike most of the newspaper's articles, did not espouse an explicitly socialist message.[91] This is not to say that the OBUAA did not attach a clear purpose to sport. To the contrary, well in keeping with the long-held tenets of amateurism, it is evident that the association considered itself a firm defender of "sport for sport's sake" and against commercialization.[92] Although boosters of amateurism had long criticized professionalism for its commercial nature, such a distinction posits a false dichotomy between both branches of sport. Since the 1870s and 1880s, amateur sporting clubs accepted that revenue, often accrued from gate receipts, was vital to ensuring their ongoing operations, a trend still evident half a century later with both the WCPAA and the OBUAA.[93] However, the OBU maintained that sport conducted primarily as a means to generate profits, like other explicitly capitalist enterprises, was an inherently degenerate practice. More specifically, commercialization, referring in the case of the OBUAA to sport that put money into the hands of specific entrepreneurs, was described as "a degrading process ... [that] has filled the majority of lovers of clean sports with disgust."[94] One anonymous writer to the *Bulletin*, in a letter evidently endorsed by the club, cited the proclivity for many promoters, described as "marauding nickel grabbers," to debase sport by offering unsatisfactory shows or outright "fakery" to the paying public.[95] In contrast, the efforts of the OBU were "a sterling tribute to what they have accomplished in fostering 'sport for sport's sake.'"[96]

The OBUAA's keen willingness to welcome professional wrestlers into its facility not only as trainers but also as competitors stands in apparent contradiction to its stance against the institution of commercialized sport to which the money-seeking professionals belonged. However, in line with a worldview that distinguished between capital and labour, the criticism against commercialism was directed more at the people running sporting enterprises than at the athletes themselves. The association asserted that its regular professional performers, such as Leo L'Heureux and Mike Bilinsky, approached their sporting careers with more admirable motives. L'Heureux was described by the *Bulletin* as "a strict believer in clean living and clean sport and looks at the game more from a sporting viewpoint."[97] Concerning Bilinsky, it maintained that, "although Mike is a professional wrestler, he is in the game more for the love of the sport than the money end. And this is well proven by the fact that he has never asked or received a cent from the club for his many wonderful exhibitions."[98] Bilinsky was also praised as "a great booster of amateur sport" and a "Jolly Good Sport."[99] Although amateur organizations in Manitoba rarely insisted on a complete disassociation between professionals and amateurs, the OBUAA was more willing than most to condone their interaction on both coaching and competitive levels if the athletes could be viewed to approach their craft with the proper motives.

During much of its existence, the OBU had strained relationships with other institutions in the province, particularly those that also possessed state-appointed authority and sought to restrict or curtail the union's activities. Ongoing battles with Manitoba's judiciary over newspaper-run betting programs brought the union into frequent contact with the police. The OBU *Bulletin* office, also located at Plebs Hall on Adelaide Street, was raided several times throughout the 1920s. In some instances, the police placed newspaper officials under arrest and brought them before the city police court.[100] Since OBU members were able to avoid conviction, the police later attempted to thwart their betting competitions by confiscating the papers from the OBU headquarters.[101] Despite this often antagonistic relationship between their parent organizations, the WCPAA and OBUAA maintained a very good working relationship. WCPAA wrestlers appeared on the weekly cards staged at the Adelaide Street gym, and OBU athletes participated in events staged at the Central Police Station gym.[102] The OBU *Bulletin* gave considerable publicity to the WCPAA in its weekly sports column, describing the association as being "capable and efficient" in its management of competitions.[103] When the police resumed their monthly cards during the fall of 1927, the OBU *Bulletin* editorialized them in glowing terms: "It is not necessary to say anything to those who have attended these bouts in the past, for they know just what kind of show this association puts on, but to those who have not witnessed these bouts before, we want to tell them that these shows are worth any man's money for they are the fastest, cleanest and peppiest bouts that can be seen anywhere."[104] This was a goodwill gesture, for earlier in the year OBUAA representatives had assisted with several WCPAA events. In response, the police association held a fundraiser on behalf of the OBUAA, contributing fifty dollars to the association and forty dollars to the individuals who had donated their time.[105] Shortly after the OBU built a gymnasium, the WCPAA also donated equipment to the facility.[106]

Although working relations with other amateur sporting organizations were generally amicable, the OBU still demonstrated its willingness, on rare occasions, to be critical of decisions taken by other associations if they were seen to impede amateur sport's development or violate working-class interests. On 16 February 1925, for instance, the WCPAA staged a dance on the same night as the City Amateur Boxing and Wrestling Championships, held under the auspices of the MAAUC Olympic Committee.[107] The OBUAA, which hosted the preliminary wrestling bouts for the championships at the OBU gymnasium a few days earlier, inquired, "if an amateur club had staged a counter attraction last year when the police association were running the bouts, would the said association have considered it an act of co-operation?"[108] The YMCA was also criticized on more ideological grounds in the *Bulletin* as "Help[ing] the Boss" by acting as an employment agent for the Alaskan fishery and requiring the workers whom it enlisted, most of whom were university and high school students, to pay a ten dollar membership fee in the association to be able to secure jobs. The *Bulletin* described the YMCA as "Another 'Employment Agency' that Needs Watching," but it never specifically criticized the traditionally middle-class institution's local activities or its involvement in sport.[109] Criticism of any nature levelled by one amateur wrestling club at another was extremely rare throughout the 1920s, for it was understood that the interests of amateur athletes were best served by ensuring that the doors to interclub competition remained open. Similarly, Manitoba's mainstream sports press demonstrated a commitment to boosterism by giving frequent free publicity to OBUAA boxing and wrestling cards, a courtesy gratefully acknowledged by the association itself.[110] The OBUAA reciprocated by assisting with newspaper-sponsored charity events such as the annual Winnipeg *Tribune* Readers Empty Stocking Fund boxing and wrestling tournament.[111]

AMATEUR WRESTLING'S GROWTH AND THE IMPORTANCE OF COMPETITIVE SPORT

The greater involvement in amateur wrestling of people from multiple ethnic and occupational backgrounds stood in contrast to the sport's more exclusive nature during the pre–First World War period. Throughout the 1920s, a large number of organizations contributed wrestlers to the various events staged in Winnipeg, including the ethnically oriented St. Jean Baptiste Society, the occupationally based Canadian National Railway Police Athletic Association, Winnipeg Light Infantry, Royal Canadian Horse Artillery, and Princess Patricia's Canadian Light Infantry, as well as private gyms such as the Pioneer Athletic Club, East Kildonan Athletic Club, and Beaver Boxing Club.[112] Amateur wrestling also began to expand beyond Winnipeg's metropolitan confines. In November 1926, Manitoba's second largest urban centre, Brandon, staged the inaugural City Amateur Boxing and Wrestling Championships, which featured one weight division and four competitors.[113] Prior to that point, professional contests had been the principal attraction in the Wheat City. On the strength of initial public support, a second amateur boxing and wrestling card was held one month later, with athletes performing before a "packed house" at Brandon City Hall.[114] By 1927, however, professional wrestling once again replaced amateur wrestling in the city when Brandon's best amateur grappler, Bray Willey, joined the ranks of the former. Once again Brandon suffered, as Winnipeg had shortly after the Great War, from an insufficient number of local participants to make viable the staging of unpaid amateur tournaments. During the latter half of the decade, amateur wrestling also expanded into smaller communities, including Carman, Minnedosa, and Pine Falls.[115] Without question, however, Winnipeg remained the province's main source of amateur wrestlers and the location of the vast majority of amateur wrestling competitions.

Amateur wrestling, which had suffered in the late First World War years and immediate postwar period from a "dearth of athletes," had grown to such an extent that by February 1924 the OBU *Bulletin* reported that "there never was a time in the city when so many amateurs were training [in boxing and wrestling], and despite the fact that there are many more clubs in existence than ever before, they all report that they are daily adding to their membership."[116] The newspaper declared in a later edition that "amateur boxing and wrestling bids fair to oust the professional game, and this is doubtless realized by the pros themselves for it is no uncommon thing to hear them say nowadays, 'Gee, I wish I could get my amateur card.'"[117] Although such a prediction might have been slightly premature, it was nonetheless prophetic. With hometown professional champion Jack Taylor's departure several months later and subsequently infrequent appearances in the city by well-known heavyweights because of the high fees that they commanded, amateur wrestling became predominant not only as a participant sport but also as a public attraction during the last half of the decade.[118] With weekly competitions at the OBU hall by 1924, monthly programs at the Central Police Station gym after 1926, and many other clubs (including the International Athletic Club, YMCA, Canoe Club, Rotary Boys' Club, and Pioneer Athletic Club) staging their own events throughout the decade, in addition to the yearly City and Provincial Championships, the sport's devotees had little time to wait between engagements from October to May.

Comparative analysis is beyond the scope of this study, but part of amateur wrestling's success during the 1920s certainly stemmed from its close association with boxing. The long-standing connection between boxing and wrestling became further entrenched during the decade, and it was rare to find amateur wrestling as a stand-alone sport in competitions. Typically, far more athletes registered for competition in boxing than in wrestling, both in high-profile tournaments such as the City, Provincial, and Dominion Championships and in regular attractions offered by organizations such as the OBUAA and WCPAA.[119] Interest in boxing rose to new heights in the 1920s, partly because of the enormous interest in the pugilistic exploits of Jack Dempsey, who ushered in "the golden age of boxing" with his well-publicized matches against Georges Carpentier, Luis Angel Firpo, and Gene Tunney. Each of Dempsey's matches against these men earned more than double the gate of any previous boxing match in history.[120] Simultaneously, aided by the sterling reputation that the sport had gained as an aid to military training during the First World War, professional boxing lost some of its long-standing stigma as it came under government regulation in many states, beginning with New York in 1920. Other jurisdictions in North America, including Manitoba, followed suit.[121] Although it is difficult to ascertain amateur wrestling's public popularity independent of boxing, reports testify to the favourable reception of the sport by the attendant public, and newspapers, including the *Free Press*, noted that "the mat sport has quite a large following in the city."[122] Yet amateur wrestling, though popular, was not equal in this regard to its fistic counterpart. Nevertheless, staging both sports together significantly bolstered the competitive opportunities for Manitoba's grapplers.

During the 1920s, a heightened emphasis on competitive athletics and nationalism also motivated interest in amateur wrestling. Although the trend was certainly under way during the pre-First World War period, between 1920 and 1930 Canada's amateur athletic movement put greater energy into promoting elite sport than in decades past. Part of the impetus for the change stemmed from the growing importance of international athletic competition, in particular the Olympic Games.[123] The modern Olympics began in 1896, but interest in the initial event was not particularly strong among Canadians, and no athlete from Canada competed. This was not the case a quarter century later.[124] Leading up to the first post-Great War Olympics, staged in Antwerp, Belgium, in 1920, Manitoba could boast few amateur wrestlers. However, in 1924 and 1928, with dozens of skilled athletes in the province, greater interest centred on earning a potential spot on Canada's Olympic team. The significance accorded to the Olympics resulted in unprecedented coordination between provincial and national amateur organizations. During 1924, provincial Olympic trials preceded national trials in Montreal.[125] In Manitoba, however, the trials were deemed a failure, both in terms of public support and in terms of talent displayed by many of the athletes.[126] On a larger scale, Canada's performance at the 1924 Olympics in Paris proved to be one of its worst, with medals awarded in only four events. No wrestlers achieved podium finishes.

Canadian wrestlers performed poorly in Paris, but many officials did not attribute the lacklustre showing entirely to athletic skill. The 1924 Canadian Olympic Committee's official report on the Paris Games contended that Canadian athletes would likely have performed much better had matches been conducted according to the rules commonly adhered to in North America and had officiating been more competent. Canadian team wrestling coach Sydney Chard opined that "the general organization and conduct of the Tournament was deplorable as an Olympic event." Of particular concern was the allowance of "rolling falls," whereby a competitor could inadvertently pin himself when executing an offensive technique that brought his shoulders into contact with the mat.[127] Regardless of such complaints, four years later, in an effort to prevent disgrace in a sporting spectacle increasingly viewed in nationalistic terms, greater efforts were made to select athletes who had the best chance to win medals.[128]

In Manitoba, instead of hosting a specific event devoted to determining potential Olympic team members, the MAAUC Board of Governors chose wrestlers on the basis of their long-standing and consistent track records at winning in high-level competitions.[129] Three wrestlers, Jimmy McKinnon, W.L. McIntyre, and Johnny Endelman (the 1925 and 1926 Winnipeg city champion as well as the 1926 and 1928 provincial champion), were chosen to represent the province at the Olympic trials in Montreal.[130] Both McKinnon and McIntyre advanced to the finals, with the Winnipeg police officer winning first place in the light-heavyweight division.[131] McIntyre, however, was not selected for the Canadian Olympic team. The exclusion of McIntyre and other athletes from the roster received criticism, but Toronto's C.E. Higginbottam, chair of the Olympic Boxing and Wrestling Selection Committee, defended their selections, given "the paramount idea of sending those that would be the best when pitted against the pick of other nations, even though such a course ran contrary to public favour and fancy."[132] Reflecting a growing sentiment for leaders of Canada's athletic movement to conceptualize their decisions in nationalistic terms, Higginbottam declared that "it was the duty of the committee to choose for the benefit of the country, and this it did to the best of its ability."[133] The committee's decisions were justified when three of the five wrestlers representing Canada in the Olympic Games earned medals, the best showing by a Canadian wrestling team in Olympic history.[134]

The emphasis on competitive success was clearly evident in many of Manitoba's sporting clubs during the 1920s. The OBUAA, despite advocating "sport for sport's sake," frequently boasted of its members' athletic accomplishments, with one report in the OBU *Bulletin* following the 1924 City Championships proclaiming that "the O.B.U. Athletic [C]lub again demonstrated its superiority over others by carrying off three [titles], and supplying the best all-around bunch of athletes of any club in town."[135] The YMCA, Manitoba's first institution to cultivate amateur wrestling and a long-standing advocate for sport's character-building qualities, also recognized the appeal that athletic success had with the sports-minded public. Following a successful showing at the 1929 Provincial Championships, the organization took out advertising in the *Free Press* declaring that "The Y.M.C.A. Trained and developed 11 Champions in Boxing and Wrestling, as shown in the Manitoba Championships last week! Use Your Y.M.C.A."[136] The "Y's" interest in maintaining high-level competitors

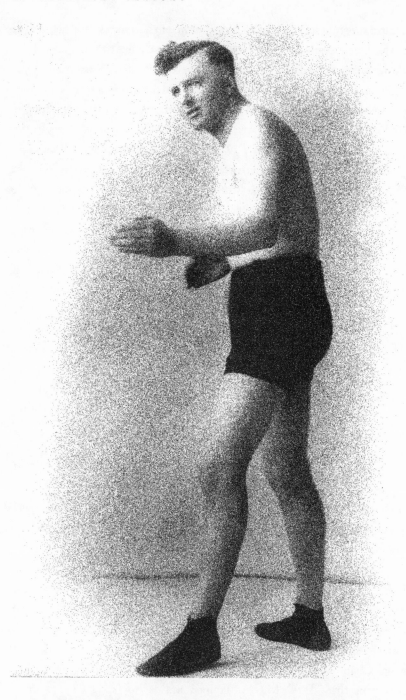

15. Winnipeg City Policeman William Loyd (W.L.) McIntyre, who won numerous local, provincial, national, and international amateur titles during the late 1920s and early 1930s. Source: Manitoba Sports Hall of Fame and Museum, MS2011.25.262.

also facilitated a liberal approach to granting memberships to athletes from non-Christian backgrounds. Two of the organization's most decorated wrestlers during the 1920s, multiple-time provincial and city champion Johnny Endelman and 1927 dominion champion silver medallist Lou Romalis, were both Jewish and competed under the YMCA banner for several years.[137] Despite their ethno-religious background, both men were drawn from middle-class clerical occupations, typical of the organization's membership during the period.[138] However, the YMCA's toleration of Jewish participation was certainly not without reservation, and in 1929 the organization, declaring that "the Y.M.C.A. were quite within their rights in keeping the Jews out of [their] membership," passed a motion aimed at reducing the group's membership to a maximum of 5 percent.[139] It was not until 1936 that the Young Men's Hebrew Association secured its own permanent facility and professional staff.[140]

NEW GROWTH, OLD PROBLEMS

Although the 1920s saw participation in amateur wrestling expand beyond its previously narrow class and ethnic boundaries, many of the difficulties facing athletes in Manitoba remained virtually identical to those in the pre-First World War period. Numerous clubs that promoted amateur wrestling did so according to their own unique interests and objectives, but the underlying principles guiding amateurism in the province remained virtually unchanged from their prewar incarnations. The AAUC and its provincial affiliate, the MAAUC, continued to adhere to the principle of "once a professional always a professional." In the months after the end of the war, it initially appeared that the AAUC's long-standing stance on professionalism might be softened when a schism developed between western and eastern Canada over the national directorate's refusal to grant reinstatement to soldier professionals who had served overseas.[141] Several directors from Saskatchewan and Alberta tendered their resignations to the parent body and declared their intention to form an independent western AAU. The fracture was averted when the AAUC agreed to a brief moratorium on professional soldier athletes deemed worthy of reintegration into amateur athletics by their provincial governing bodies. The AAUC's 26 September 1919 statement on the matter, however, made its continuing position on professionalism clear: "All such applications must be made before Jan. 1 1920 and [the] applicant must furnish an affidavit declaring that he will remain an amateur for the remainder of his life and that the reinstatement shall be recognized only in such provinces as it may be granted by."[142]

In May 1920, another schism, this time between the AAUC's parent body and its Thunder Bay branch, developed over granting amateur status to long-time Fort William professional wrestler Jack Belanger while denying it to two baseball players. Commentators attributed the AAUC's evolution toward embracing high-level amateur athletics as the reason for its decision, the *Free Press* opining that "Belanger is regarded as a fine Olympic prospect. The other two have no such pretensions."[143] His petition for amateur status was ultimately rejected by the AAUC because he could not supply an affidavit from his branch.[144] During the MAAUC's annual meeting the following spring, former president J.D. Pratt urged that "dramatic action" be taken against amateurs who engaged in professional sport, and later in the year the executive reaffirmed its commitment to the existing amateur definition.[145]

Throughout the decade, dissenting voices continued to challenge the stance of the AAUC as outdated. During a visit to Toronto, Judge Kenesaw Mountain Landis, a prominent figure in professional baseball, characterized the amateur code as an archaic representation of aristocratic values and noted the absurdity of the idea that a good college athlete could "sling hash in a cafeteria" to earn money in the summer to pay his way through college but would be scorned for deriving tuition funds from using the same athletic skills that brought his school glory.[146] Leaders in amateur sport, despite their own move toward emphasizing elite international competition, maintained that their rules ensured a level playing field for all athletes by preventing the participation of individuals whose ability to "play for pay" granted them the time to hone their skills.[147] Accordingly, despite various calls throughout the 1920s for reconsideration, their rigid stance toward professionalism remained largely unchanged.[148]

For several amateur wrestlers in Manitoba, the AAUC's policies on monetary compensation certainly had adverse impacts on their athletic careers. Throughout the 1920s, one of the greatest concerns among advocates for reform in amateur sport was the issue of "broken time payments." Extensive travel for competition was a far greater barrier to participation in Canada's expansive west than in its east, but the AAUC remained steadfast in its policy that no Canadian athlete would receive financial remuneration for time lost from work.[149] For athletes living outside Winnipeg, such as Brandon's Bray Willey, regular participation in amateur competition required travelling 200 kilometres to the provincial capital. Given such distances, competitive opportunities were slim, particularly if money for travel expenses was not forthcoming. Willey competed in the 1927 Manitoba Championships, losing to perennial champion Jimmy McKinnon in the welterweight division, but he was absent from other competitions staged in Winnipeg during the surrounding years. Ironically, the AAUC's stance against monetary compensation unwittingly drove athletes who wished to practise their craft out of the amateur ranks. Following his decision to turn pro in late 1928, financial inducements gave Willey opportunities to meet far more opponents on the mat in his hometown than had been the case during his amateur career.

Because of the sport's highly physical nature, wrestlers also continued to run the risk of sustaining injuries that could sideline them from work. During the 1920s, the MAAUC, much like the provincial commission governing professional contests, instituted mandatory medical exams for all participants prior to competitions.[150] The policy aided in preventing unfit athletes from participating but could do nothing to prevent acute injuries staged in training or competition. Compensation for injury was at the discretion of the organization sponsoring the event and was not always forthcoming. Following the 1922 Provincial Championships, for example, the WCPAA refused to pay the five dollar medical bill submitted by Dr. W. Harvey Smith for treatment of boxer H. Gregg of the International Athletic Club, stating that "the Executive Board would accept no responsibilities for injured athletes."[151] A similar resolution followed in April 1928 concerning injuries sustained by P.C. Roquette at a police-sponsored event.[152] However, the association was more amenable to its own members, later agreeing to pay Constable W.L. McIntyre's fifty dollar medical bill for injuries sustained while wrestling at the police station.[153]

The financial limitations facing amateur wrestlers during the 1920s did not result exclusively from the AAUC's and MAAUC's ideological aversion to compensating amateur athletes. Despite having far-reaching control over virtually all branches of amateur sport, neither body could boast a large supply of money in its treasury.[154] Winnipeg's Jack McLaughlin, the 158 pound dominion amateur champion in both 1923 and 1924, was denied a place on the Canadian Olympic team despite being victorious in his class at the 1924 Olympic trials, because of lack of available funds in the Olympic budget. J.H. Crocker, a member of the national selection committee, explained that, though McLaughlin was victorious, his performances were not deemed sufficiently impressive by the judges to warrant inclusion on the financially strapped team.[155] The Olympic Committee's decision contributed to the regionalist tension between the AAUC's western and eastern bodies, and in August 1924 the MAAUC passed a resolution declaring its intention to send a separate western Olympic team to the 1928 Olympics because of perceived discrimination against its athletes.[156] Although the plan was never realized, newspapers in the region continued to report bitterly on the McLaughlin incident, the *Free Press* noting in January 1925, for instance, in its annual recap of the previous year's sports, that "it was a great disappointment to his local admirers when he was deprived of his opportunity for world's honours."[157] Four years later W.L. McIntyre, as previously noted, was also denied a place on the Olympic team after earning a dominion title.

Despite attempts to couch the Canadian Olympic Committee's selections as stemming from regional prejudice, the MAAUC itself was forced to make similar decisions. In 1929, the MAAUC, then described as "far from wealthy," was only able to field a team to the Dominion Amateur Boxing and Wrestling Championships in Port Arthur after the Thunder Bay branch of the AAUC agreed to pay for the Manitoba contingent's lodging expenses while at the Lakehead. Even then only one wrestler, W.L. McIntyre, received sanction by the provincial governing body to attend, his expenses to be covered by the WCPAA.[158] Late financial contributions from outside sources finally allowed the MAAUC to expand its roster of three boxers and two wrestlers to include six boxers and two wrestlers, McIntyre and 1929 provincial welterweight champion Bjorn Johnson. McIntyre ultimately did not attend the 1929 Dominion Championships, and instead heavyweight William Crossley made the trip, apparently assisted by funds provided by the Winnipeg Electrical Company. Johnson, a Winnipeg railway fireman, earned a dominion title.[159]

Particularly during the second half of the 1920s, competition at the annual Dominion Championships was far more nationally representative than prior to the war. Events staged in the west nevertheless continued to produce a preponderance of western-based participants and champions, with a similar situation occurring when the event was held in the east.[160] In 1928, the MAAUC tried to deepen its coffers by demanding one-third of the profits generated from hosting the Manitoba Boxing and Wrestling Championships. However, the WCPAA, which had been chosen to host the event and relied on such cards for a sizable percentage of its annual revenue, simply refused. The MAAUC, despite its authority to grant or deny athletes amateur standing, proved to be impotent in dictating financial arrangements to its affiliate clubs, and the WCPAA was accordingly granted unconditional sanction to hold the event.[161] Regardless of its financial difficulties, the MAAUC clearly had more interest in ensuring continued participation in sport according to the doctrine of "once a professional always a professional," than it did in attempting to impose its own rigid monetary demands on its affiliates.

CONCLUSION

The 1920s proved to be a remarkable period for amateur wrestling in Manitoba. During the decade, participation in amateur wrestling expanded beyond its previously narrow class and ethnic boundaries as people from numerous cultural, religious, and occupational backgrounds embraced the sport. Various organizations that sponsored amateur wrestling did so, in part, according to their own particular desires and objectives. However, heightened enthusiasm for competitive athletics and a greater level of importance accorded to elite international amateur competition helped to fuel enthusiasm for the mat game among many segments of Manitoba's population. Yet, even as involvement in the sport increased and opportunities for regular competition grew, many of the factors shaping amateur athletics remained virtually unchanged from what had existed during the prewar period. Remarkable expansion therefore occurred within the context of both long-extant definitions of what it meant to be an amateur wrestler and ongoing struggles for financial stability on the part of the province's governing body for amateur sport.

CONCLUSION

In Jules Dassin's 1950 film noir adaptation of Gerald Kersh's novel *Night and the City*, grifter Harry Fabian, played by Richard Widmark, gains the confidence of retired professional wrestling champion Gregorius by promising to stage classical wrestling in London. Aged Polish wrestler Stanislaus Zbyszko, cast in the role of the Great Gregorius, laments his once-beloved sport's transformation into a clownish burlesque as well as his semi-estranged son Kristo's decision to promote its "modern" variant. Near the film's climax, the long-retired Gregorius is ultimately pitted in combat against Kristo's top wrestler, the Strangler, played by Mike Mazurki, in a bout that showcases the contrasting methods characteristic of both approaches. The submission holds and calculated application of technique by Gregorius stand in juxtaposition to the Strangler's frenetic brawling style, which includes eye gouging, choking, punching, and kicking. After weathering a barrage of such assaults, Gregorius finally subdues his younger adversary. Turning to his promoter son, who witnessed the battle's concluding moments, he admonishes him: "That's what I do to your clowns." Although his victory represents a brief symbolic vindication of his vision of wrestling, the strain caused by such intense exertion immediately overwhelms Gregorius, and he perishes in the gymnasium, a crumbled relic of a bygone era.

Dassin's dramatization highlights, both literally and symbolically, some of the transformations that occurred in professional wrestling during the quarter century preceding the film's release. By the late 1920s and early 1930s, the mat game was undergoing radical modifications that would revolutionize its presentation to the public and lay the foundations for what we currently recognize as professional wrestling. Although some critics, as represented by *Night and the City*'s Gregorius, bewailed the changes, their cause ultimately succumbed to consumers' evolving tastes. In Manitoba, as elsewhere, advances in communication technology and subsequent changes in public expectations of entertainment worked synergistically with acute economic hardship to drive demand for a faster and more dramatic form of wrestling than had existed in decades past.

The late 1920s saw the decline of heavyweight professional wrestling in Manitoba as high-profile American-based talent, which came to dominate the local market, made increasingly infrequent appearances in the province's capital. By 1928, widespread indifference to the once-popular sport was evident when a match between Winnipeg's one-time "local boy" Jack Taylor and former world's heavyweight champion Wayne "Big" Munn attracted a disappointingly small attendance for the Empire Athletic Club. For the remainder of the decade, no promoter was willing to risk paying the high appearance fees demanded by prominent American-based heavyweight professional grapplers in light of tenuous public support for their enterprise.

Professional wrestling's decline during the last few years of the 1920s was symptomatic of larger challenges facing live entertainment both in Manitoba and elsewhere in North America. Motion pictures had provided the public with relatively inexpensive amusement for more than two decades, and by the 1920s Hollywood-based studios were producing well-acted feature-length films with elaborate set and costume designs that rivalled those available in many of the better live theatre productions. "High-class" venues, including the Walker Theatre, which by 1920 relied largely on British-based theatre companies because of a collapsing American touring system, found it difficult to compete with the flourishing motion picture industry. In 1933, C.P. Walker was forced to close his once-nonpareil venue.[1] Vaudeville continued into the latter half of the 1920s, but further technological advances in the motion picture industry, most significantly the introduction of "talkies" after 1927, ultimately provided its death blow.[2] Aggressive attempts by the motion picture industry to solidify its control over the theatre market forced the already-tottering competition into ruin. Famous Players Canada Limited purchased most independently owned theatres and vaudeville houses in Canada during the late 1920s, and in 1930 the company banned live performances at its venues as the final effort to solidify motion picture market dominance.[3]

Growth of the motion picture industry, culminating in the introduction of "talkies," closed off many of the traditional theatrical venues available for staging professional wrestling in addition to reorienting much of the public's entertainment budget. Radio's heightened popularity by the late 1920s and early 1930s also altered existing recreational habits, taking previously public leisure forms and recasting them for home consumption. Sports programs, in addition to radio plays, became popular with the new medium, and as early as 1923 prairie residents were tuning in to broadcasts of professional wrestling matches from distant locales, such as Wichita, Kansas.[4] By the early 1930s, with radios more widely available, Manitobans regularly received their wrestling cards through the airwaves.[5] Significantly, the medium also helped to break down long-standing barriers between rural and urban environments by providing country residents with a comparable and simultaneous level of access to the same amusements as their city-dwelling contemporaries.[6] Typically, as with the "talkies," this came in the form of American-produced programs.[7]

Changing economic conditions after 1929 likewise assisted in reshaping public expectations concerning entertainment. By the end of the 1920s, Winnipeg was already beginning to lose its position as western Canada's dominant metropolitan centre, since grain shipments through the Panama Canal, which had opened in 1914, were redirecting prairie crops to Vancouver ports.[8] Declining wheat prices in 1929, coupled with the beginning of prairie drought, foretold the decade-long disaster that followed the stock market crash in October of that year.[9] By 1930, Manitoba was in full-scale economic depression as grain prices continued their plummet to unprecedented lows and crop output plunged. Large-scale civic infrastructure projects initiated in the 1920s, including the construction of a railway line to Churchill and the creation of associated harbour facilities, the development of hydroelectric power in the province's north, and in 1931 the construction of Winnipeg's Civic Auditorium, provided much-needed employment at the outset of the decade but were completed by 1932.[10] Many unemployed people migrated to Winnipeg, drawn either by the hope for jobs or by the city's relatively generous relief programs, exacerbating the widespread poverty there.[11]

Mass unemployment and generally difficult economic circumstances reduced the amount of disposable income for most individuals and families, but Depression conditions also increased available leisure time.[12] Trying economic times led to greater public interest in specific forms of entertainment, particularly those that offered a sharp counterpoint to the drudgery endemic to daily life. Manitobans explicitly sought escapist diversions as a tonic to adverse circumstances over which they had no direct control. Dance halls, such as Winnipeg's Paradise Gardens Dance Pavilion, were popular venues for socializing and listening to the latest music.[13] American influence on the western Canadian leisure market was long-standing by the 1930s, but the trend advanced at a rapid pace during the decade. W.L. Morton noted, with nostalgic derision, the influence of commercial entertainment originating from the United States, "which required nothing but the cash of the spectator."[14] He singled out motion pictures, musing that "with the movies came the imbecilities of American slang and popular music, and youthful Winnipeggers were impelled, like others of their generation, to mimic the banalities of the mechanized and commercialized entertainment purveyed by Hollywood."[15]

American-based motion pictures did not achieve universal acceptance, but their popularity was certainly undeniable among Depression-era Winnipeggers, an appeal driven not only by engaging storylines but also by their cost relative to live entertainment. For prices ranging from twenty-five to fifty-five cents, moviegoers could see the latest Hollywood offerings featuring well-known stars, such as Marlene Dietrich, Joan Bennett, Claudette Colbert, Maurice Chevalier, and former Winnipeg police officer and wrestler Victor McLaglen, at the many neighbourhood theatres throughout the city.[16] Radios, though considerably more expensive, could be purchased with a cash deposit and monthly payments, and prices dropped steadily as the decade progressed, making them more generally accessible.[17] To retain its relevance as a spectator activity, professional wrestling was forced to adapt to the public's interests by offering a spectacle that could compete for the consumer's limited discretionary funds with these popular new forms of entertainment.

During the 1920s, a growing appreciation for sport as an amusing diversion as opposed to a predominantly moral enterprise, coupled with professional athletes' contributions to the war effort, increased regulation, a flagging reform movement, and influence from American "trusts" (at least within the lucrative heavyweight ranks) inducing wrestlers to cooperate, allowed professional wrestling to escape many of the problems that bedevilled it prior to the Great War. Already touted to the public as an explicitly rough endeavour, wrestling was reintroduced to Manitobans in 1931 in a decidedly different, and altogether more spectacular, form than had previously existed in the province. Thanks to newsreel footage that preceded feature films, however, in addition to regular radio broadcasts, Manitobans were prepared, at least in part, for the new spectacle that they were about to witness in person.[18]

On 12 June, a consortium of prominent Winnipeg businessmen, led by Jack McVicar and collectively named the Amphitheatre Boxing and Wrestling Club, announced their intention to stage professional wrestling matches at the Amphi-theatre Rink.[19] Distinguishing it from what had been offered to the public in the past, the press explicitly billed the club's upcoming card, scheduled for 24 June, as the "new style" of professional wrestling. The Manitoba *Free Press* noted that "during the last few years wrestling has been enjoying the greatest popularity in its history and this is particularly due to the new style introduced since so many leading college athletes have entered the mat game."[20] The style had its genesis during the mid-1920s in the American midwest, where Joseph "Toots" Mondt, business partner with Ed "Strangler" Lewis and Billy Sandow, devised the idea to begin introducing elements from boxing, brawling, and theatrical stunt work into professional wrestling. Mondt's innovations, titled "Slam Bang Western Style Wrestling," proved to be popular and were soon adopted in venues through-out the United States.[21] During the ensuing years, more dramatic elements were added to the professional repertoire, and well-known athletes from other sports, in particular college football, entered into wrestling's ranks and used their spec-tacular gridiron manoeuvres to arouse excitement and generate revenue. Careful management by promoters, who sidestepped uncooperative grapplers, allowed college football recruits such as Dartmouth's "Dynamite" Gus Sonnenberg, who had no previous wrestling experience, to become top box office attractions.[22] The *Free Press*, in differentiating old from new, stated that, "instead of the old style of punishing and laying down and grinding with nothing in stock but strength, there is Sonnenberg's flying tackle ... [along with] the airplane spin, raising the opponent above the head, whirling him around and dashing him to the mat ... and many other ... holds and breaks too numerous to mention."[23] Tasked with presenting the sport's novel methods to Manitobans, however, was the already familiar Canadian champion, Jack Taylor. Two years earlier in Toronto, Taylor and promoter Ivan Michailoff introduced central Canadian audiences to "Slam Bang" wrestling.[24] After its establishment in southern Ontario, the former Win-nipeg resident, who "ha[d] taken to the new form of wrestling like the proverbial duck to water," returned to the Prairies.[25]

Reports following the 24 June card at Winnipeg's Amphitheatre colour-fully illustrate some of the mayhem witnessed by the audience as well as their reaction to it:

[A]ccording to all the accepted signs of success the fans have had their appetite for thrills and spills considerably whetted.... As far as the wrestling was concerned everything bar biting and eye gouging was passed off as O.K., and the crowd went into ecstasies as the bout proceeded blow by blow. Unprecedented scenes were witnessed as the matmen were in turn hurled out of the ring. On one occasion Jack Taylor manouevered [opponent Joe] Komar up against the ropes, feinted a la Dempsey with his right hand and caught the Lithuanian with a terrific kick in his "Johnny Risko" and sent him spinning through the ropes into the crowd. Komar showed intense dislike for such hard boiled methods and retaliated by picking up a chair and hurling it at Taylor's head as he stood in the centre of the ring.[26]

In addition to histrionic displays of anger, overt attempts to sensationalize pain and suffering were among the new innovations, and whenever Taylor secured a toe hold "the 'Wild Bull of Lithuania' tore his hair in pain and made desperate efforts to grab the ropes and drag himself out of the ring."[27] The *Free Press* commented after the "show" that "anyone who knows when people enjoy themselves will have to admit that Wednesday night['s] performance tickled the fans."[28]

The "new" version of professional wrestling, though favourably received by many, did not earn universal praise. The *Free Press* acknowledged that "it may be that it will take some time for the old-time wrestling enthusiasts who were willing to go and watch the old style tug and pull and grunt game, to get used to the action which is the stock and trade of the new crop of wrestlers."[29] More scathing was Winnipeg *Tribune* sports columnist Paul E. Warburg's review: "How anyone could have believed that the show was indicative of what wrestling really is, is far beyond comprehension. The exhibition was something that would have been a good gesture on the part of the wrestling commission to have intervened and prevented from continuing."[30] Yet Warburg was simultaneously forced to acknowledge that "there were actually some who witnessed the 'show' and enjoyed it. They were satisfied for the money they spent."[31] Following the Amphitheatre Boxing and Wrestling Club's second program three weeks later, a more acquiescent *Tribune* reporter acknowledged that, though there was "comparatively little wrestling," the grapplers nevertheless put on a good show for the appreciative crowd.[32] As had been the case throughout the United States, after the spring-summer of 1931, the "new" style permanently superseded the older, mat-oriented style of catch-as-catch-can wrestling in western Canada. In a 1936 visit to Winnipeg, Ed "Strangler" Lewis, who had begun his career in 1910, reflected pragmatically on the changes: "The public has shown they like it. Gate receipts have demonstrated it beyond our wildest prediction.... You may not 'go' for this modern wrestling. Neither do I, but the public wants it and I'm only merchandising my wares."[33]

The professional wrestling that emerged in Manitoba during the 1930s appealed to the public on several fronts. For a society increasingly accustomed to seeing its entertainment delivered through the heavily edited medium of film, the dramatics presented in (and frequently often outside) the ring provided a similarly fast-paced spectacle. Although skilled wrestlers were long heralded for their speed and science, an understanding of the sport's technical intricacies required greater study than the more readily discernible purpose of a flying tackle, toss from the ring, or well-placed kick to the "Johnny Risko."[34] Such tactics would, and certainly did, earn professional wrestlers censure in the decades prior to the Great War, but the growing appreciation for professional sport as a form of entertainment dulled, if never wholly eliminated, the moralistic, reform-era baggage attached to the mat game in the following decade. The sport's roughness, so heavily emphasized in the 1920s, gave way to orchestrated mayhem in the 1930s. Morton's observation that the emerging forms of entertainment seen during the Great Depression did not require, as a prerequisite, concerted intellectual effort from the spectator applied in considerable measure to professional wrestling. By adding dramatic displays of anger, pain, and suffering in addition to exciting new technical innovations, the action became more emotionally, as well as more technically, intelligible.[35] Coupled with substantially reduced ticket prices relative to earlier years, professional wrestling supplied an affordable form of escapist entertainment to the public during an emotionally trying period marked by economic hardship.[36]

Although "new" in several respects, the wrestling seen in Manitoba during 1931 cannot be wholly divorced from the sport that preceded it in the previous five decades. Professional wrestling remained an enterprise that drew heavily on ethnicity, and in the ensuing weeks and months Jack Witchon, the "local Frenchman," and the distinctly eastern European-surnamed Paul Danelko and Johnny Yurkovich followed the "Lithuanian champion" Komar in making appearances before Winnipeg audiences.[37] Local talent, too, continued to figure prominently in professional wrestling programs, capitalizing on civic pride and a long-standing booster spirit. Amateur wrestlers still transitioned into the professional ranks to earn incomes, though as competitive wrestling skill became less important fewer professional wrestlers were retained as coaches by local sporting organizations.[38] Divorced from much of the moralizing that surrounded all sports during the late nineteenth century and early twentieth century, professional wrestling nevertheless failed to achieve universal acceptance, in particular because certain elements within the province's public, echoing Warburg's sentiments, continued to expect pure sporting competition. Even though the "new" professional wrestling presented to the public was more spectacle than sport, such criticisms were already decades old by the Great Depression. Those wishing to patronize a "simon pure" sporting enterprise could still do so during the winter months at MAAUC-affiliated venues.

Amateur wrestling prospered on the national level during the early 1930s, the emphasis on high-level national and international competition persisting following onset of the Depression, despite harsh economic conditions. In August 1930, Canada hosted the inaugural British Empire Games in Hamilton, and the country's grapplers, including the WCPAA's W.L. McIntyre, won gold medals in all seven weight divisions. In 1931, the WCPAA again staged the Dominion Championships in Winnipeg. Contrasted with the competitions staged two decades earlier, the tournament had become far more "national" in character. Seventeen athletes from outside Manitoba participated in the championships, drawn from centres such as Victoria, Toronto, Montreal, and Regina.[39] Additionally, in 1931 the AAUC adopted the newly formulated Olympic rules for amateur wrestling, ensuring that Canada's submission to the global standardization process would not result in a repeat of the problems that had bedevilled North American wrestlers in Paris in 1924.[40] However, in Manitoba itself, the sport was clearly in decline. During the 1931 Dominion Championships, no Manitoba wrestler earned first prize in any weight division.[41] An examination of entry rosters for the Provincial Championships staged two weeks earlier also reveals that far fewer clubs were fielding entrants than in the past.[42] With professional wrestling's reintroduction to the province in 1931, fans proved, as they had frequently before the mid-1920s, that they were willing to turn out in greater numbers for professional cards than amateur tournaments: amateur wrestling's central strength therefore remained as a participatory, as opposed to spectator-driven, venture. Nevertheless, by the beginning of the Great Depression, the sport's foundation had been cemented in the province.

Wrestling in Manitoba underwent significant changes from its earliest documented inceptions in the pre-Confederation period to the genesis of what is largely recognizable today as professional wrestling. The sport was never hermetic from the values, beliefs, prejudices, entertainment expectations, and prevailing economic conditions of the people fostering its practice. Long before widespread European settlement, it served as a form of ritualized combat among the region's Aboriginal peoples, acting as a safety valve to stave off more serious violence. Strict social mores ensured that the combat did not extend beyond the parties directly involved. Among Chipewyan males, it was vital in arbitrating contested marriage relationships, and for Inuit, ritualized individual combat helped to preserve community cohesion. Wrestling, particularly among the Netsilik, also helped to forge communal bonds among married couples vital to their survival, and it served as a means by which individuals could demonstrate the strength requisite for effective hunting. Within the voyageur and tripmen subcultures that developed in the fur-trading industry, strength, endurance, and bravery were highly valued. Violent displays of fighting competence, wherein wrestling was a necessary element, earned participants considerable social capital among their peers, put them in a place of prominence in their communities, and conditioned them to the harsh realities of a vocation characterized by constant danger.

After Confederation, the province's new settlers, most of them from English Ontario, brought with them their own wrestling traditions. During this period, the sport reflected the competing values held among Anglo-Canadians. For some urban residents, in particular the large population of males who frequented the city's less prestigious liquor establishments and variety theatres, professional wrestling matches were a popular form of entertainment often connected to recreational alcohol and tobacco consumption, gambling, and various blood sports. Many of the sport's most well-known figures during the era did not live their lives in accord with the values held by other residents in the province, particularly middle-class social reformers who saw in wrestling an opportunity to promote their own visions of proper Christian manhood, which stressed, among other things, temperance, moral virtue, and healthy competition. Reformers saw money as the root cause of many of the woes afflicting sport in the province and, through their doctrine of amateurism, sought to prevent athletes from receiving financial compensation for their sporting performances. However, sport was not so easily compartmentalized into amateur and professional domains in Manitoba's early years. Reflecting a far more layered social existence, nascent amateur programs depended heavily on professional wrestlers for their coaching expertise, and these wrestlers, despite efforts to cultivate an image that adhered to middle-class tenets of respectability, often found themselves cajoled into returning to professional competition because of financial inducements and public demand.

During the first decade and a half of the twentieth century, growing interest in all sports, including wrestling, occurred with a rapid rise in population in Manitoba. Professional wrestling garnered popularity because of widespread cultural appreciation for physical expressions of masculinity that placed considerable value on muscular development. Many also valued it as a "scientific" undertaking that gave physical expression to the principles likewise revolutionizing economic, financial, and technological development in the Western world. In this context, the male body, developed through disciplined, systematic, "scientific" training, became an increasingly marketable commodity for display in professional wrestling matches. Wrestling was also valued by some as a "rough" activity that celebrated aggression and strength, and athletes were respected for their ability to give, and endure, physical hardship. Despite the many positive characteristics attributed to professional wrestling, however, it remained a site for considerable public controversy as excessive violence, fixing in matches, and poor public conduct of prominent athletes continued to embroil it in controversy.

Although sports promoters sought to adopt strategies to ensure that professional wrestling retained respectability, many among the public continued to reject it altogether as an appropriate venue of athletic expression. In particular, middle-class men of Anglo-Protestant extraction, aided by institutions such as the YMCA, devoted increased vigour to advancing amateur sport. Monetary compensation remained the central concern for the acolytes of amateurism. In the six years before the Great War, officials succeeded in creating a central governing body for all amateur sport in the province, created programs to instruct young men in wrestling, and successfully hosted competitions that not only brought Manitoba's grapplers together but also connected them to amateur sport on national and international levels. Despite considerable advances, however, amateur wrestling did not extend far beyond the Anglo-Protestant urban middle class, unlike professional wrestling, which catered to people from diverse ethnic and socio-economic backgrounds throughout the province.

During the immigration boom at the beginning of the twentieth century, people of non-British ancestry who arrived in Manitoba patronized professional wrestling matches, in part, because the linguistic barriers of many other commercial entertainments were not impediments to enjoying the show. Europeans also came to Canada with their own wrestling traditions, and entrepreneurial promoters capitalized on intercultural rivalry by staging matches between athletes representing various ethnic communities. With growing Anglo-Canadian nativism during the period because of perceived threats from continental European immigration, many matches also pitted members of the ethnic and linguistic majority against "foreign" adversaries. However popular such contests were, the merit of wrestling extended beyond its ability to capitalize on the intercultural enmity in Manitoba during the early twentieth century. For some groups, such as the Icelanders, wrestling represented a deliberate attempt to continue Old World traditions in the New World and preserve their culture from assimilation. Glima, the Icelandic wrestling style, celebrated individualism and rewarded speed and skill over brute strength. Additionally, the art, whose history dated back to the early Icelandic settlement period, linked the more recent North American sojourners to their Viking past, providing a thread of continuity among a people whose history was marked by a series of major upheavals and mass migrations. For others, including members of Manitoba's Polish community, wrestling had quite a different purpose. Their interest in professional wrestling was partially attributable to its popularity back in their homeland but also developed in Manitoba within the context of a fledgling nationalist movement. Wrestling programs represented a way of attracting people to the cause while providing them with the physical wherewithal that the movement's leaders saw as necessary for aiding the nationalist endeavour. Before the First World War, Polish wrestlers were the public face of the nationalist movement in the province. On a wider scale, professional wrestlers were often the public face of many immigrant communities in the region, and through them, economically and socially marginalized peoples found symbolic representation.

During the Great War, both amateur and professional wrestling were curtailed as the sport took on new significance as a military-related activity. The years preceding the European conflict were marked by a heightened emphasis on militarism in Canada, and wrestling lent itself well to aggressive expressions of masculinity, a view bolstered by popular literature and newspapers, in which the language used to describe wrestling was often analogous to that used to describe war. After the declaration of war, civilian amateur sports organizations forged a close relationship with Canadian military authorities, and wrestling became valued as one of many "patriotic" activities that helped to generate revenue for the families of overseas soldiers. Military authorities also considered wrestling to be a valuable tool for character building, fostering esprit de corps, reinforcing military hierarchy, and assuring proper conduct in the homosocial environment of military camps. Wrestling was also viewed as an aid to recruiting, and the availability of sporting competitions helped to attract men into uniform, especially as the war dragged on and casualty numbers rose.

Although professional wrestling fell into decline during this time, enlisted professional wrestlers, because of their prominence as public figures, were held up as examples to those who had not yet joined the services' ranks, a process that reinforced a vision of masculinity that privileged the soldier-athlete over those not yet in the military. For immigrant communities outside the Anglo-Protestant majority, their well-known professional wrestlers in uniform also served to publicize that they too were committed to the national and imperial cause. Although the period was marked by remarkable pressures to conform, wrestling also remained a site of power struggles, particularly as amateur organizations shrank and military-based sporting bodies grew because of high enlistment. In this context, ideas about the dangers of intermingling amateurs and professionals were challenged as the latter repeatedly demonstrated their value to the war effort both in and out of the theatre of conflict.

In the post-First World War decade, declining public concern over professional sport's moral propriety, coupled with increased regulation, allowed professional wrestling to avoid much of the controversy that had dogged it in previous decades. Changing public attitudes, chiefly an increased appreciation for sport as entertainment, allowed professional wrestling to be promoted as an explicitly "rough" enterprise throughout the decade. Capitalizing on heightened Anglo-Canadian nationalism and nativist sentiments, professional wrestling in Winnipeg achieved unprecedented popularity by pitting Canadian wrestler Jack Taylor against "foreigners" who, according to various widely entrenched racist stereotypes held during the period, posed peculiar threats to Anglo-Canadian dominance. Yet, despite extremely aggressive attempts to control their public personas during the decade, wrestlers, through their performances in the ring, were still capable of defying the images created for them by promoters. This period also witnessed growing American influence over the sport in Manitoba as trusts from south of the border sought to control matches staged in the province's capital.

Concerns over professional wrestling's respectability declined (but by no means disappeared) during the 1920s, but increased emphasis on national and international competition also allowed amateur wrestling to expand to include a greater cross-section of Manitoba society. Previously confined largely to the Anglo-Protestant middle class, the sport was adopted by various other ethnicities and occupational groups who also attached their own purposes to it. Within the francophone community, which had long taken an interest in wrestling, amateur programs were organized by the Union Canadienne as alternatives to those offered by Protestant organizations such as the YMCA, considered a threat to Roman Catholic authority. For occupationally based groups such as the Winnipeg City Police Athletic Association, the central concern, more material in nature, was to provide for the direct welfare of its members. With the inability to collectively organize on their own behalf, the WCPAA afforded recreational opportunities for the city's police force and served as a mutual aid society whose funds were procured, in large part, from sponsoring boxing and wrestling programs.

The working-class-based One Big Union Athletic Association offered the sport to individuals whose occupational backgrounds made memberships in other middle-class sports organizations prohibitive. The OBUAA, similar to middle-class amateur clubs, valued "sport for sport's sake" but nevertheless permitted considerable interaction between amateurs and professionals because of a class view that saw unscrupulous entrepreneurs, more than athletes themselves, as the main culprits in fostering "degenerate" sporting practices within professional ranks. Additionally, though wrestling frequently represented "contested territory" among different groups in Canadian society, the 1920s were marked by a considerable degree of cooperation, even among associations whose agendas frequently ran into conflict with one another. The relationship between the WCPAA and OBUAA, for example, indicated a rather more layered reality, in which common cause could bring about considerable collaboration, even in the midst of larger ideological conflict. Yet, despite amateur wrestling's growth beyond its narrow ethnic and class confines during the 1920s as well as repeated calls for reform, the rules governing amateurism remained largely unchanged throughout the decade, so many of the limitations to competition previously facing athletes likewise remained unchanged in the post–First World War years.

Overall, wrestling represented far more than just the physical act of two men coming to grips with one another on a padded mat. Throughout its long existence, wrestling was inseparably connected to widespread and shifting debates over acceptable public conduct, the social values that should be attached to sport, and the place of minority peoples in western Canadian society, both according to their own self-conceptions and according to how members of the Anglo-Protestant majority viewed them. Wrestling matches were brief, transient, and deliberately orchestrated episodes of human interaction around which ideas related to class, respectability, masculinity, and ethnicity found acute expression. Additionally, the training associated with the sport was conducted by organizations whose goal was more than to merely facilitate physical contests between men; instead, it was to ensure that, by conducting wrestling programs, "higher" goals were achieved.

Detailing the history of wrestling in Manitoba during the roughly century and a half before the Great Depression fills a considerable void in the existing historical literature on Canadian sport. In *Ringside*, Beekman noted that professional wrestling, to that point, was a sport without a history since virtually nobody had sought to grant it concerted examination.[43] Until relatively recently, academic scholars virtually ignored the sport, despite (or perhaps because of) its rich and colourful past. Even the modest number of popular histories on the subject barely extended their narratives beyond chronicling, and frequently re-chronicling, the exploits of the most well-known professional wrestlers, typically in the heavyweight ranks. Hundreds of athletes, many of them internationally known during their careers, but still more of them of regional and local repute, have been almost completely ignored by the sport's chroniclers and subsequently forgotten. At a basic level, creating an overarching narrative devoted to wrestling in Manitoba exhumes from obscurity the major figures and events associated with the sport's past. By placing the development of wrestling within a regional context, it also invites future comparative analysis that will lead to a greater understanding of the factors shaping the sport's growth in other regions of Canada and North America.

Although regionally based, many of the themes addressed here have resonance beyond both the wrestling mat itself and the geographic confines of a prairie province. By connecting wrestling to larger trends seen throughout the Anglo-Protestant world, what occurred in Manitoba can be seen within the context of broad social reform movements that sought to mould society according to value systems frequently defined and articulated by the English-speaking middle class. Through wrestling, there was an attempt to extend Anglo-Protestant values and British culture into new frontiers. Wrestling was therefore intimately tied to larger notions of middle-class respectability, Christian manliness, rational recreation, scientific progressivism, militarism, and Canada's place in the British Empire. Simultaneously, an examination of wrestling provides insight into how other groups, differentiated by indicators such as class and ethnicity, attempted, through various means, to negotiate their own places in society by moulding alternative visions of sport or by working within the existing system to achieve their own particular goals. The argument presented here fundamentally rejects a rigid class-based analysis that compartmentalizes certain practices and behaviours as explicitly and exclusively working or middle class. Interest in wrestling transcended such narrow boundaries, and the evidence suggests a more layered reality in which peoples from multiple backgrounds interacted, frequently in competition, but sometimes in concert, to shape the social landscape. The study also contributes to the scant body of literature in Canadian history related to the sporting traditions of Canada's non-British immigrant peoples during the early decades of settlement in the country. Conversely, it also provides further insight into the highly racialized understanding of the world held by many early western Canadian residents, particularly those within the English-speaking majority.

Linking wrestling to larger developments in transportation and communication technology further contributes to our understanding of late nineteenth-century and early twentieth-century leisure culture, charting how repeated advances in both fields brought Manitoba, once physically isolated from other important population centres, into ever more frequent contact with the entertainment forms seen elsewhere on the continent. In this regard, the analysis furthers our appreciation for America's growing influence on Canadian leisure pursuits. Additionally, focusing on wrestling as a commercial undertaking enhances an understanding of how critical social constructs, among them masculinity, respectability, ethnicity, race, racism, and the male body itself, evolved as marketable commodities during the late nineteenth century and early twentieth century.

Today amateur wrestling is again entering a period of growth in Manitoba, with the University of Winnipeg wrestling program now operating but a short distance from the old Wesley Hall quarters where the sport sprang to life more than a century ago. In the eight decades since the introduction of "modern" professional wrestling, the art has evolved into a more theatrical and less sporting form of entertainment. The current spectacle is a long way from the style practised by Jack McKeown, Charles Gustafson, and a younger Jack Taylor, and local wrestlers are no longer household names. The doors have long closed on D'Arcy McIlroy's Empire Athletic Club cards, and the fans have dispersed. Yet, if we follow their spirits from downtown Winnipeg, we find them drifting north to the city's working-class North End and further still to the Icelandic enclaves of the Interlake region. They travel south through St. Boniface and to other francophone communities such as St. Pierre-Jolys. Across the vast prairie to the west, they travel to Brandon and Melita, nestled like islands in a vast sea of grain. To the east, they enter the boreal forest and Ontario, stopping at Kenora, which, on the banks of Lake of the Woods, retains close ties to its western neighbours. These are the communities that shaped the wrestlers, and in turn the wrestlers shaped the communities, giving hard-working immigrants and rugged pioneers of western Canada a sense of pride in their identities and purpose to sport. The wrestlers have passed to dust, but the mosaic that was Manitoba remains.

Acknowledgements

This project would not have been possible without the efforts of many organizations and people who worked with me and on my behalf over the course of the researching and writing process.

I would like to thank Sport Canada and the Ontario Graduate Scholarship program for their generous funding, which helped get this book off the ground.

Working with the University of Manitoba Press was a genuine pleasure. A big thanks to Glenn Bergen, David Larsen, Jill McConkey, and Ariel Gordon, as well as copy editor Dallas Harrison, for their professionalism and expertise.

Considerable debt is owed to Ronald N. Harpelle and Michel Beaulieu, as well as Kelly Saxberg, who provided me with copious sage advice before, during, and after manuscript preparation. Their guidance was instrumental in completing this project. I would also like to thank Bruce Muirhead, Morris Mott, Julia Roberts and Alan McDougall for their earlier contributions to my work, as well as Winnipeg historian Henry Trachtenberg. Likewise, a big thanks to my doctoral colleagues Tavis Harris, Katie McGowan, and Simon Palamar, as well as Pat and Joe Kaufert.

A large amount of my research was conducted at the Archives of Manitoba, and, in particular, I would like to recognize the efforts of Chris Kotecki who was incredibly helpful and knowledgeable when it came to the facility's holdings. A huge thanks also goes out to all of the staff at the Manitoba Legislative Library (which for many months was my home away from home), including Stuart Hay, Jason Woloski, Louise Ayotte-Zaretski, Meghan Hansen, Leesa Girouard, Tannis Gretzinger, and Janina Smithson. In particular, I wish to extend my thanks to Monica Ball for all of her assistance. Likewise, thank you to the staff at the St. Boniface Archives, Jewish Heritage Centre, St. Boniface Museum, Manitoba Sports Hall of Fame, University of Manitoba's Icelandic Collection, Winnipeg

City Archives, Winnipeg Police Museum, Library and Archives Canada and the Canadian War Museum.

A body of dedicated wrestling researchers, authors, and enthusiasts helped provide groundwork for this project, beginning with Mark Hewitt, Joe Svinth, and Don Luce, who have done a great deal to inform the public on early wrestling in North America. I would like to thank J. Michael Kenyon for his insight into the professional wrestling business during the 1920s as well as the relationship between various wrestlers and promoters. Specifically within the context of this project, I wish to express my appreciation to Vern May, whose pioneering, tireless, and selfless work on wrestling in western Canada helped provide a springboard for my own research into the subject. Similarly, I wish to mention both Wayne Wilson and Yasutoshi Ishikawa who were generous in sharing, respectively, their research on the Klondike and rare book collections devoted to wrestling.

Members of the wrestling community have added to both my technical and historical appreciation of the sport, particularly its catch-as-catch-can variety. A big thank you therefore goes out to Jake Shannon, Jon Strickland, Jasse Junkaari, Billy Wicks, Frankie Cain and the late Billy Robinson, all of whom assisted directly or indirectly in this project. Likewise, a big thank you to Lakehead University wrestling coach Francis Clayton, coaches Matt Richer and Keith MacGillivray, and my teammates at Leading Edge Gym.

Finally, I would like to thank my parents, Dan and Kathleen Hatton, my brother and sister Tim Hatton and Rebecca Hatton, and my aunt Kristine Robinson for all of their support throughout the years.

Appendix 1

MANITOBA AMATEUR WRESTLING CHAMPIONS 1908-30

1908

Date(s): 27, 28 November
Location: YMCA
Officials: Thomas Dickinson (referee); R.W. Bonnifield, J. Williams (judges); Ed W. DuVal, J.D. Pratt, Major Macdonell (timekeepers); J.D. Ormaby, F.S. Filmer (weight inspectors); H.R. Hadcock (announcer)

Bantamweight (105 pounds)	J. Franklin
Featherweight (115 pounds)	R. Turner
Special class (125 pounds)	Jack Macdonald
Lightweight (135 pounds)	Christie Akins (Winnipeg, YMCA)
Welterweight (145 pounds)	P.H. Dilts (Winnipeg, YMCA)
Middleweight (158 pounds)	Les Moir
Heavyweight (over 158 pounds)	A.J. Mitchell (Winnipeg, YMCA)

1909

Date(s): 22, 23 April

Location: YMCA

Officials: Thomas Dickinson (referee); Dr. Jones, Dr. Mullally (judges); J.D. Pratt, F.F. Carruthers, Thomas Boyd (timekeepers); F. Filmer (weight inspector)

Featherweight (115 pounds)	P. Kennedy (Winnipeg, YMCA)
Special class (125 pounds)	Jack Macdonald
	(Winnipeg, Rowing Club, YMCA)
Lightweight (135 pounds)	Christie Akins (Winnipeg, YMCA)
Welterweight (145 pounds)	A.J. Mitchell (Winnipeg, YMCA)
Middleweight (158 pounds)	George Akins (Winnipeg, YMCA)
Heavyweight (over 158 pounds)	George Akins (Winnipeg, YMCA)

NOTE: Manitoba Championships were not held in 1909. This tournament was the Western Canadian Championships.

1910

Date(s): 27, 28 January

Location: YMCA

Officials: Thomas Dickinson (referee); Major Macdonell, Thomas Boyd (timekeepers)

Bantamweight (105 pounds)	Jack Deves (Winnipeg, YMCA)
Featherweight (115 pounds)	Jack Macdonald (Winnipeg)
Special class (125 pounds)	C. Boulton (Winnipeg, YMCA)
Lightweight (135 pounds)	R.M. Hillis (Winnipeg)
Welterweight (145 pounds)	A.J. Mitchell (Winnipeg, YMCA)
Middleweight (158 pounds)	George Akins (Winnipeg, YMCA)
Heavyweight (over 158 pounds)	George Akins (Winnipeg, YMCA)

1911

Date(s): 17, 18 March
Location: YMCA
Officials: A.J. Mitchell (referee)

Bantamweight (115 pounds)	A. McIntosh (Winnipeg, YMCA)
Lightweight (125 pounds)	J. Macdonald (Winnipeg, YMCA)
Special class (135 pounds)	R.L. (Bert) McAdam (Winnipeg, YMCA)
Welterweight (145 pounds)	Christie Akins (Winnipeg, YMCA)
Middleweight (153 pounds)	George Akins (Winnipeg, YMCA)
Heavyweight (over 153 pounds)	L.G. Ore (Winnipeg, YMCA)

1912

Amateur wrestling tournaments were held throughout the year but no Manitoba Championships were officially contested

1913

Amateur wrestling tournaments were held throughout the year but no Manitoba Championships were officially contested

1914

Date(s): 26, 27 May
Location: Drill Hall
Officials: Unknown

Bantamweight (115 pounds)	Patsy Picciano (Winnipeg, Boys' Club)
Special class (125 pounds)	J. Cordy (Winnipeg, Boys' Club)
Lightweight (135 pounds)	J. Holmes (Winnipeg, YMCA)
Welterweight (145 pounds)	J. McKinnon (Winnipeg, Boys' Club)
Middleweight (158 pounds)	George Akins (Winnipeg, YMCA)
Heavyweight (over 158 pounds)	E. Abrahamson (Winnipeg, Viking Athletic Club)

NOTE: The 1914 National Championships were held in Winnipeg in lieu of the Provincial Championships.

1921

Date(s): 22, 25 April
Location: Board of Trade Building
Officials: Sam Kennedy (referee); J. Coates Brown (timekeeper); A.E.H. Coo, Tim Ching (judges); A.R. Morrison (weight inspector); Joe Fahey (announcer)

Featherweight (115 pounds)	F. Runge (Winnipeg, YMCA)
Special class (125 pounds)	A. Leveille
	(St. Boniface, International Athletic Club)
Lightweight (135 pounds)	I. Gislason (Winnipeg, YMCA)
Welterweight (145 pounds)	F. Carter (Winnipeg, YMCA)
Middleweight (158 pounds)	H. Dusessoye
	(St. Boniface, International Athletic Club)
Light-heavyweight (175 pounds)	J.C. Rogers (Winnipeg, YMCA)
Heavyweight (over 175 pounds)	Leo L'Heureux
	(St. Pierre, Union Canadienne)

1922

Date(s): 3, 6 March
Location: Board of Trade Building
Officials: Sam Kennedy (referee); J.W. Finlay, Tim Ching (judges); J. Coates Brown, Thomas Boyd (timekeepers); Dr. W. Black (medical examiner); A.R. Morrison (weight inspector); Joe Fahey (announcer)

Featherweight (115 pounds)	S.C. Acheson (Winnipeg, YMCA)
Special class (125 pounds)	A. Leveille
	(St. Boniface, International Athletic Club)
Lightweight (135 pounds)	Albert Choinard (St. Pierre, Union Canadienne)
Welterweight (145 pounds)	J. McKinnon (Winnipeg, YMCA)
Middleweight (158 pounds)	Jens Eliasson (Winnipeg, YMCA)
Heavyweight (over 175 pounds)	J.E. Johnson (Winnipeg, YMCA)

1923

Date(s): 2, 5 March
Location: Board of Trade Building
Officials: Sam Kennedy (referee); George Steffen, "Steppy" Fairman
(judges); J. Coates Brown, John F. Thorogood (timekeepers); Dr. W.
Black, Dr. A.J. Douglas (medical examiners); R. Ridd, W. Asbury
(weight inspectors); Mike O'Connor, Joe Fahey (announcers)

Featherweight (115 pounds)	W.E. Shane (Winnipeg, YMCA)
Lightweight (135 pounds)	Albert Choinard
	(St. Pierre, Union Canadianne)
Welterweight (145 pounds)	Jens Eliasson (Winnipeg, YMCA)
Middleweight (158 pounds)	J.A. Pelletier
	(St. Boniface, International Athletic Club)

1924

Date(s): 8, 9 April
Location: Central Police Station Gymnasium
Officials: Sam Kennedy (referee); Billy Bowman, Art Allen (judges);
Joe Fahey (announcer)

Bantamweight	Frank Garrod (Winnipeg, YMCA)
Featherweight	I. Gislason (Winnipeg, YMCA)
Lightweight	W. Fray (Winnipeg, Pioneer Athletic Club)
Welterweight	Bill Hanburg
	(Winnipeg, Pioneer Athletic Club)
Middleweight	Andrew Borg
	(Winnipeg, Pioneer Athletic Club)
Light-heavyweight	Joe Geoffrion (St. Jean)
Heavyweight	Joe Mulholland
	(Winnipeg, City Police Athletic Association)

1925

Date(s): 1, 8, 9 January
Location: One Big Union Hall
Officials: Sam Kennedy (referee); J. Coates Brown, John F. Thorogood (timekeepers); Danny McIlroy, Billy Bowman (judges); Joe Fahey (announcer)

Bantamweight	Mike Robinson (Winnipeg, YMCA)
Featherweight	R. Douglas Scott (Winnipeg, YMCA)
Lightweight	Harry Vernon (Winnipeg, YMCA)
Welterweight	Jack McLaughlin (Winnipeg, YMCA)
Middleweight	Andrew Borg (Winnipeg, One Big Union)
Light-heavyweight	James Harvey Paddison (Winnipeg, City Police Athletic Association)

1926

Date(s): 5, 6 April
Location: Alhambra Hall
Officials: Alex Stewart (referee); Sam Kennedy, Christie Akins (judges); Joe Fahey (announcer)

Featherweight	Johnny Endelman (Winnipeg, YMCA)
Lightweight	A.G. Gislason (Winnipeg, YMCA)
Middleweight	J. McKinnon (Winnipeg, unattached)
Light-heavyweight	B.B. Anderson (Winnipeg, One Big Union)
Heavyweight	Jack McLaughlin (Winnipeg, YMCA)

1927

Date(s): 21, 22 March
Location: Central Police Station Gymnasium
Officials: Sam Kennedy (referee); Christie Akins, J. Coates Brown
(judges); John F. Thorogood (timekeeper); John Eccles (ring manager)

Featherweight	G. Stapleton (Winnipeg, Rotary Boys' Club)
Lightweight	Mark McDermott
	(Winnipeg, Royal Canadian Horse Artillery)
Welterweight	J. McKinnon (Winnipeg)
Light-heavyweight	B. Anderson (Kenora)
Heavyweight	W.L. McIntyre
	(Winnipeg, City Police Athletic Association)

1928

Date(s): 4 May
Location: Amphitheatre Rink
Officials: Alex Stewart (referee); Joe Fahey (announcer)

Bantamweight	W.F. Ketcheson (Winnipeg, One Big Union)
Featherweight	Johnny Endelman (Winnipeg, YMCA)
Lightweight	Mark McDermott
	(Winnipeg, Royal Canadian Horse Artillery)
Welterweight	W. Pitman (Kenora)
Light-heavyweight	B.B. Anderson (Kenora)
Heavyweight	W.L. McIntyre
	(Winnipeg, City Police Athletic Association)

1929

Date(s): 11, 12 April
Location: Central Police Station Gymnasium
Officials: Alex Stewart (referee); Christie Akins, Graham
Currie (judges); John F. Thorogood (timekeeper); George
McBeth (weight inspector); Joe Fahey (announcer)

Bantamweight	V. Clancy (Winnipeg, YMCA)
Featherweight	Johnny Endelman (Winnipeg, YMCA)
Lightweight	Melvin Dawson (Winnipeg, YMCA)
Welterweight	B. Johnson (Winnipeg, YMCA)
Middleweight	Stewart Sinclair (Winnipeg, City Police Athletic Association)
Light-heavyweight	W.L. McIntyre (Winnipeg, City Police Athletic Association)
Heavyweight	W. Crossley (Winnipeg, YMCA)

1930

Date(s): 22, 23 April
Location: Playhouse Theatre
Officials: Tom Johnstone (referee); Sam Kennedy, Christie Akins
(judges); John F. Thorogood (timekeeper); Joe Fahey (announcer); Hal
Moulder (weight inspector); George McBeth (master of ceremonies)

Featherweight	W. Fletcher
Lightweight	Mark McDermott (Winnipeg, Royal Canadian Horse Artillery)
Welterweight	W. Miller
Light-heavyweight	W.L. McIntyre (Winnipeg, City Police Athletic Association)
Heavyweight	J.H. Paddison (Winnipeg, City Police Athletic Association)

Appendix 2

MANITOBA ISLENDINGADAGURINN GLIMA CHAMPIONS BEFORE 1930

1890

Glima cancelled on account of rain

1891

No record of wrestling

1892

No record of wrestling

1893

Wrestling cancelled because of the program running late

1894

S. Johannson

1895

No wrestling held

1896

No wrestling held

1897

John Erickson (first)
E. Gislason (second)

1898

No wrestling held
Rival festival held 17 June

1899

Wrestling postponed because of the
athletic program running late

1900

H. Martenson (first)
J. Peterson (second)
S. Stevenson (third)

1901

I. Isfield (first)
E. Davidson (second)
A. Isfield (third)

1902

Sigurd Baldwinson (first)
Paul S. Palsson (second)
Baldwin Jonsson (third)

1903

Kitill Sigurgeirson (first)
Helgi Marteinson (second)
S. Baldwinson (third)
Paul Magnusson (most skillful)

1904

E. Davidson (first)
T.O. Sigurdson (second)
John Davidson (third)
K.S. Eyford (best glima)

1905

E. Davidson (first)
Helgi Marteinson (second, most
scientific wrestler)
E. Abrahamson (third)

1906

S.D.B. Stephenson
Halldor Mathusalemsson (most
scientific wrestler)
E. Abrahamsson (overcame greatest
number of opponents)

1907

Halldor Mathusalemsson (first)
Ketill Eyford (second)
Sveinn Bjornsson (third)

1908

H. Mathusalemsson (first)
Einar Abrahamsson (second)
Sig Stefansson (third)

NOTE: Matches were said to have been decided
by wrestling skill rather than by falls.

1909

Jon Arnason (first)
J. Halfliddison (second)
A. Johnson (third)

1910

Jon Arnasson (first)
Einar Abrahamsson (second)
Gisli Bemson (third)
Sig Stefansson (fourth)

1911

V. Olason (first)
J. Gilles (second)
Agust Eyjolfsson (third)

1912

Sig Sigfusson (first)
Vilhjalmur Petursson (second)
Thorliefur Hansson (third)

1913

Gudmundur Stefansson (Belt of Honour)
Einar Abrahamsson (second)

1914

Gudmundur Stefansson (Belt of Honour)
Adalsteinn Johannsson (most graceful performance)
Chris Oliver (most agile performance)

1915

J. Kristijansson (first)
Gudmundur Sigurjonsson (second)
B. Olaffson (third, best style of wrestling)

1916

Gudmundur Sigurjonsson (first)
Ben Olafsson (second)

1917

E. Erlendsson (first)
A. Siddell (second)

1918

Steindor Jakobson (gold medal)
Adalsteinn Johannsson (silver medal)

1919

Benedikt Olafsson (first)
Jens Eliasson (second)
Unnsteinn Jakobson (third)
Gudmundur Sigurjonsson (best style
of wrestling)

1920

Glima cancelled on account of rain

1921

A.E. Thorgrimsson (first)
Jens Eliasson (second)

1922

Jens Eliasson (belt)
A.E. Thorgrimsson

1923

Karl Magunusson (Hanneson Belt)
G.B. Gudmundsson (second)
Jens Eliasson (third)

1924

Jens Eliasson (Hanneson Belt)
Mr. Fabnis (second)
B. Olafsson (third)
N. Ottenson (best wrestling)

1925

Jens Eliasson (Hanneson Belt)
O.J. Thorgilsson (second)
Benedikt Olafsson (Jonas Palsson
Cup)

1926

Chris Oliver (Hanneson Belt)
B. Olafsson (Jonas Palsson Cup)
K.J. Johnson

1927

Sigudur Thorsteinson (awarded the
Hanneson Belt for first place and
the Palsson Cup for most artistic
execution)

1928

Bjorn Olafsson (Hanneson Belt)
Benedikt Olafsson (Jonas Palsson
Cup)

1929

Wrestling cancelled because of the
program running late

Notes

INTRODUCTION

1   See Archives of Manitoba, L.B. Foote Collection 1232, Negative 2209; Archives of Manitoba, Winnipeg-Buildings-General-Industrial Bureau 8, Negative 5276; Alex Colter Bell Stewart, Attestation Paper, Library and Archives Canada, RG150, Accession 1992-93/166, Box 9300–66; Canadian Census 1901, Ontario, District 48 East Bruce, Sub-District 4, Polling Sub-Division 5, Greenock Township, 2; Manitoba *Free Press*, 2 August 1922, 3 April 1923, 4 April 1923; Winnipeg *Tribune*, 4 April 1923; and Edmonton *Journal*, 23 May 1956.

2   In examining wrestling's history in Manitoba, I admit to a decidedly "presentist" view with respect to geography. Manitoba's initial borders, established following its entry into Confederation in 1870, were subsequently expanded in 1877, 1881, and finally 1912. However, the discussion here focuses on wrestling within the current provincial borders, even if some activities prior to 1912 might have occurred outside those borders. For a visual representation of Manitoba's geographic expansion, see John Warkentin and Richard I. Ruggles, *Historical Atlas of Manitoba, 1612–1969* (Winnipeg: Manitoba Historical Society, 1970), 164–65. A more detailed discussion related to the province's border changes can be found in Manitoba Historic Resources Branch, *Manitoba's Boundaries* (Winnipeg: Queen's Printer, 1994).

3   Ellis Cashmore notes in *Making Sense of Sport* (London: Routledge, 1990), 45, that wrestling is certainly among the most archaic forms of human competition and, "as such, it seems to have held wide appeal both for participants seeking a means to express their strength and resilience and for audiences who to this day are enraptured by the sight of humans disputing each other's physical superiority."

4   Although numerous scholars have devoted attention to defining "sport," it has been difficult to arrive at a universal agreement. Sociologists Donald W. Ball and John W. Loy humorously note that "the meaning of sport, like time, is self-evident until one is asked to define it." Ball and Loy as well as others argue that attempts to define the term will be somewhat inexact and open to contestation. Academic work in various fields has nevertheless attempted to define sport along with related terms such as "play" and "game." Despite less than unanimous agreement, some commonalities can be discerned. Consistent in most discussions related to sport is the necessity for bodily exertion and competition between two or more parties according to institutionalized standards or rules that establish the conditions for one of the said parties to achieve victory and thus termination of the activity. By these criteria, certain activities, such as poker and chess, are therefore not within the parameters of sport because, though they satisfy the latter two conditions, physical ability is not intrinsic to achieving a desired outcome. Similarly, activities such as circus acrobatics, though physically demanding, do not constitute a sport because the performances are non-competitive. For further reading, see Donald W. Ball and John W. Loy, *Sport and the Social Order: Contributions to the Sociology of Sport* (Reading, MA: Addison-Wesley Publishing Company, 1975), 11–12; Ann Hall et al., *Sport in Canadian Society* (Toronto: McClelland and Stewart, 1991), 11, 13; John

Huizinga, *Homo Ludens: A Study of the Play Element in Culture* (Boston: Beacon Press, 1955), 196–98; Paul Wiess, *Sport: A Philosophic Inquiry* (Carbondale: Southern Illinois University Press, 1969), 132–51; Harry Edwards, *Sociology of Sport* (Homewood, IL: Dorsey Press, 1973), 43–58; Morris Mott, "Manly Sports and Manitobans: Settlement Days to World War One" (PhD diss., Queen's University, 1980), 7–12; and G. Luschen, "The Interdependence of Sport and Culture," *International Review of Sport Sociology* 2 (1967): 127–41.

5   Arnold W. Umbach and Warren R. Johnson, *Wrestling* (Dubuque, IA: William C. Brown Company, 1966), 1–2. Perhaps, in the future, historians and anthropologists, like linguists in their analysis of language, will find it fruitful to apply evolutionary theory in an effort to understand wrestling's development over time and its diffusion across cultures.

6   Edwards, *Sociology of Sport*, 51.

7   I acknowledge the difficulty with this definition of "contest" or "match," for some individual sports, namely racquet sports such as tennis, badminton, and squash, are referred to as "games."

8   See, for example Greg Oliver, *The Pro Wrestling Hall of Fame: The Canadians* (Toronto: ECW Press, 2003), 10, 219, 221.

9   See, for example, Umbach and Johnson, *Wrestling*, 3; Harold E. Kenney and Glenn C. Law, *Wrestling* (New York: McGraw-Hill Book Company, 1952), 1; Gordon T. Garvie, *Wrestling for Young Wrestlers and Instructors* (Don Mills, ON: Collier-Macmillan Canada, 1972), 11; Frank G. Menke, rev. Suzanne Treat, *The Encyclopedia of Sports* (South Brunswick, NJ: A.S. Barnes and Company, 1975), 1088; and Pekka Pirskanen, "Wrestling as Seen by a Veteran Amateur," in *Sports Pioneers: A History of the Finnish-Canadian Amateur Sports Federation 1906–1986*, ed. Jim Tester (Sudbury: Alerts AC Historical Committee, 1986), 199.

10   See, for example, Mike Chapman, *Encyclopedia of American Wrestling* (Champaign, IL: Leisure Press, 1990), 473; John Rickard, "'The Spectacle of Excess': The Emergence of Modern Professional Wrestling in the United States and Australia," *Journal of Popular Culture* 33 (1999): 130–33; and Jeff Archer, *Theatre in the Squared Circle: The Mystique of Professional Wrestling* (Lafayette, CO: White Boucke Publishing, 1999), 20.

11   For an excellent guide to "carny" or "kayfabe," the terminology used in professional wrestling, including etymological origins, see B. Brian Blair, *Smarten Up! Say It Right!* (Tampa: Kayfabe Publishing Company, 2001).

12   Martti Jukola, *Athletics in Finland* (Helsinki: Werner Soderstrom Osakeyhtio, 1932), 107; Chapman, *Encyclopedia of American Wrestling*, 3, 159, 473; Charles Nathan Hatton, "Finnish-Canadian Wrestlers," in *Martial Arts of the World: An Encyclopedia of History and Innovation Volume II*, ed. Thomas Green and Joseph R. Svinth (Santa Barbara: ABC-CLIO, 2010), 462.

13   Even in instances in which the style of wrestling typically called for some form of specialized equipment, early Manitobans were capable of adapting to the limitations imposed by their circumstances, as evidenced by photographic records from 1915, which show two Icelandic settlers, one of them absent the customary belt that had been invented a decade earlier, practising glima by grasping the pants at the hip. See Archives of Manitoba, New Icelandic Collection 350, Negative N11343.

14   Although deaths were extremely rare, injuries were somewhat more common in casual encounters. See the *Nor'Wester*, 24 April 1895, 23 August 1897; and Winnipeg *Telegram*, 29 June 1899, 16 May 1904.

15   Allen Guttman, *From Ritual to Record: The Nature of Modern Sports* (New York: Columbia University Press, 1978), 12.

16   John C. Meyers's *Wrestling from Antiquity to Date* (St. Louis: By the Author, 1931) was one of the first attempts to create a survey history devoted specifically to wrestling. A former wrestler himself, Meyers offered a brief global overview of wrestling history combined with his own reminiscences of major events and personalities in American catch-as-catch-can wrestling. He also offered

some commentary on various contemporary topics, such as the role of referees during matches, professional wrestling's appeal as a form of entertainment, and instruction on how to wrestle. His work was followed in 1936 by *Ring* magazine publisher Nathaniel (Nat) Fleischer's *From Milo to Londos: The Story of Wrestling through the Ages* (New York: Ring, 1936). Fleischer's compendious work provided a more extensive synopsis of wrestling across time and location than did Meyers's earlier effort but can primarily be considered a history of the professional heavyweight wrestling championship in the United States since the Civil War. Except for a short concluding memoir written by lightweight wrestling champion George Bothner, athletes in the lighter weight divisions are largely absent from Fleischer's narrative. Unlike the book of either Meyers or Fleischer, Charles Morrow Wilson's *Magnificent Scufflers: Revealing the Great Days When America Wrestled the World* (Brattleboro, VT: Stephen Greene Press, 1959) focused extensively on wrestling in the northeastern United States, and its lasting value is its examination of collar-and-elbow-style wrestling in the region prior to the 1890s. Also notable among older historical surveys is Graeme Kent's *A Pictorial History of Wrestling* (London: Spring Books, 1968).

17 Marcus Griffin, *Fall Guys: The Barnums of Bounce* (Chicago: Reilly and Lee Company, 1937).

18 Griffin's book, for example, is written in a casual narrative style that includes considerable dialogue to illustrate the recounted events, and it is therefore difficult at times to precisely ascertain the boundary between artistic licence and factual accounting. Additionally, it is heavily biased toward presenting certain individuals in a positive light, in particular Joseph "Toots" Mondt and Ed "Strangler" Lewis. A detailed overview of the historical inaccuracies concerning events before the mid-1920s would also require considerable effort.

19 Issues of the *WAWLI Papers* are available at http://www.wrestlingclassics.com/wawli.

20 Mark S. Hewitt, *Catch Wrestling: A Wild and Wooly Look at the Early Days of Professional Wrestling in America* (Boulder, CO: Paladin Press, 2005); Mark S. Hewitt, *Catch Wrestling Round Two: More Wild and Wooly Tales from the Early Days of Pro Wrestling* (Boulder, CO: Paladin Press, 2009).

21 Tim Hornbaker, *National Wrestling Alliance: The Untold Story of the Monopoly that Strangled Pro Wrestling* (Toronto: ECW Press, 2007).

22 Jonathan Snowden, *Shooters: The Toughest Men in Professional Wrestling* (Toronto: ECW Press, 2012).

23 Vern May, *The Central Canadian Professional Wrestling Almanac* (Winnipeg: Canadian Wrestle-Media, 1999); Vance Nevada, *Wrestling in the Canadian West* (Gallatin, TN: Crowbar Press, 2009).

24 Other popular histories of note concerning regional professional wrestling promotions in Canada are Heath McCoy, *Pain and Passion: The History of Stampede Wrestling* (Toronto: ECW Press, 2007); Gary Howard, *The Rassler from Renfrew: Larry Kasaboski and Northland Wrestling Enterprises* (Renfrew, ON: General Store Publications, 2007); and Pat Laprade and Bertrand Hebert, *Mad Dogs, Midgets, and Screw Jobs: The Untold Story of How Montreal Shaped the World of Wrestling* (Toronto: ECW Press, 2012). All works focus on the post-Second World War period but nevertheless mention wrestling before the 1930s.

25 Royal Duncan and Gary Will's voluminous *Wrestling Title Histories* (Waterloo, ON: Archeus Communications, 2000) documents all known (to date of publication) professional wrestling title reigns, dating back to the 1860s, in dozens of countries around the world. Although considerably in need of revision in light of recent research, their manual is still essential for those interested in titular achievements in professional wrestling. Published biographies on wrestlers have a lengthy but scattered history. E.W. Halm's edited collection, *The Life Work of Farmer Burns* (Omaha: A.J. Kuhlman, 1911), was an early attempt to document both the life and the training philosophy of a well-known professional wrestler. Edward Van Every, *Muldoon: The Solid Man of Sport* (New York: Frederick A. Stokes, 1929), provided background (some of it apocryphal) on America's first nationally renowned professional grappler, accounts of his important matches, and comments on his efforts in later life as the commissioner for boxing in New York. Similar to Halm's earlier

collection on Burns, emphasis was placed on the "Solid Man's" approach to training. More recently, wrestling journalist Mike Chapman has chronicled the career of world heavyweight catch-as-catch-can champion and "Farmer" Burns student Frank Gotch, who appeared in Winnipeg in 1911 before a large audience. Chapman's *Frank Gotch: World's Greatest Wrestler* (Buffalo, NY: William S. Hein and Company, 1990) was followed seventeen years later by *The Life and Legacy of Frank Gotch King of the Catch-as-Catch-Can Wrestlers* (Boulder, CO: Paladin Press, 2007), both of which seek to affirm Gotch's place as the greatest wrestler ever. Also valuable, particularly for its chapters pertaining to early-twentieth-century French Canadian wrestler Emil Maupas, is Pierre Berthelet's *Yvon Robert, le Lion du Canada français: Le plus grand lutteur du Québec* (Montréal: Éditions Trustar, 2000). Greg Oliver's *The Pro Wrestling Hall of Fame: The Canadians* (Toronto: ECW Press, 2003), and Marsha Erb's *Stu Hart: Lord of the Ring* (Toronto: ECW Press, 2002), like the majority of biographical works on professional wrestlers, focus primarily on the period after the Depression, particularly after the Second World War. Both nonetheless offer some glimpses into early wrestling in the Canadian west. Also of interest pertaining to professional wrestling during the late 1920s is Kenneth Boness, *Pile Driver: The Life of Charles "Midget" Fischer* (Bloomington, IN: Xlibris Book Publishing, 2003).

26 Heavyweight wrestler George Hackenschmidt, colloquially known as the "Russian Lion," was an early and notable exception, with his part-autobiographical and part-training manual *The Way to Live* (1908; reprinted, Farmington, MI: William F. Hinbern, 1998). Swedish-born wrestler Hjalmir Lundin, whose *On the Mat and Off: Memoirs of a Wrestler* (New York: Albert Bonnier Publishing House, 1937) was released contemporaneously with *Fall Guys* (and criticizes the trend toward a more theatrical form of wrestling but does not make a similar effort to lay bare the underside of the business), also falls into the category of autobiography, but more in keeping with Meyers's 1931 effort it devotes considerable attention to profiling the prominent wrestlers whom Lundin met during his lengthy involvement in the sport.

27 Clarence Eklund, *Forty Years of Wrestling* (Buffalo, WY: By the Author, 1947); Hazel Eklund-Odegard, *Wyoming's Wrestling Rancher: Life and History of Clarence Eklund, Champion Wrestler* (Buffalo, WY: By the Author, 1993). Similar to Lundin, Eklund provides little hint of efforts (if there were any) to prearrange wrestling matches, maintaining a code of silence on the matter that remained characteristic of professional wrestling until the early 1990s. Yet his insights into the efforts associated with booking appearances, the physical conditions under which matches were contested, and the backgrounds of other wrestlers in the Prairies provide vital thematic contexts for this study.

28 Glynn A. Leyshon, *Of Mats and Men: The Story of Canadian Amateur and Olympic Wrestling from 1600 to 1984* (London, ON: Sports Dynamics, 1984).

29 J.J. Mondak, "The Politics of Professional Wrestling," *Journal of Popular Culture* 23, 2 (1989): 139–50.

30 Matthew Lindaman, "Wrestling's Hold on the Western World before the Great War," *Historian* 62, 2 (2000): 796.

31 Rickard, "'The Spectacle of Excess,'" 130.

32 Lindaman, "Wrestling's Hold," 795.

33 Scott M. Beekman, *Ringside: A History of Professional Wrestling in America* (Westport, CT: Praeger, 2006), 13, 16, 25.

34 Ibid., 14, 21, 22, 28, 29, 36.

35 Ibid., viii.

36 Mott, "Manly Sports." Alan Metcalfe's *Canada Learns to Play: The Emergence of Organized Sport, 1807–1914* (Toronto: McClelland and Stewart, 1987), likewise drawing inspiration from Donald Creighton's Laurentian thesis, stresses the role played by major urban centres in central Canada, notably Montreal and Toronto, in helping to shape sport's subsequent development throughout

the country. Other authors, notably Colin D. Howell in his study of Maritime baseball, *Northern Sandlots: A Social History of Maritime Baseball* (Toronto: University of Toronto Press, 1995), have provided alternatives to this model's universal application in Canada, highlighting the connections between the Atlantic provinces and New England (particularly Maine) in the development of the sport. In the present work, the role played by Anglo-Protestants from central Canada in shaping Manitoba's sporting values is an important theme, particularly during the early settlement period. However, also of vital importance to the analysis, particularly as it concerns professional wrestling, is the connection to the United States, which strengthened as time progressed.

37 See, for example, Metcalfe, *Canada Learns to Play*, particularly Chapters 1, 2, and 4; Jean Barman, "Sport and the Development of Character," in *Sports in Canada: Historical Readings*, ed. Morris Mott (Toronto: Copp Clark Pittman, 1989), 234; Gerald Redmond, "Some Aspects of Organized Sport and Leisure in Nineteenth-Century Canada," in Mott, *Sports in Canada*, 87; S.F. Wise, "Sport and Class Values in Old Ontario and Quebec," in Mott, *Sports in Canada*, 126; Hall et al., *Sport in Canadian Society*, 57; Nancy Bouchier, *For the Love of the Game: Amateur Sport in Small-Town Ontario, 1838–1895* (Montreal: McGill-Queen's University Press, 2003), particularly Chapters 3 and 7; and Don Morrow and Kevin Wamsley, *Sport in Canada: A History*, 3rd ed. (Toronto: Oxford University Press, 2005), 4, 70. Concerning the role of the middle class in shaping sport's moral imperatives, see Tony Collins, "Violence, Gamesmanship, and the Amateur Ideal in Middle Class Rugby," in *Disreputable Pleasures: Less Virtuous Victorians at Play*, ed. Mike Huggins and J.A. Mangan (New York: Frank Cass, 2004), 172. Frank Cosentino's doctoral dissertation, "A History of the Concept of Professionalism in Canadian Sport" (University of Alberta, 1973), though an older work, is also of great value in assessing Canadian society's changing understanding of professionalism in sport and, by way of contrast, key ideas guiding the amateur doctrine.

38 Elliott Gorn, "Gouge and Bite, Pull Hair, and Scratch: The Social Significance of Fighting in the Southern Backcountry," *American Historical Review* 90, 1 (1985): 18–43; Elliott Gorn, *The Manly Art: Bare-Knuckle Prize Fighting in America* (Ithaca, NY: Cornell University Press, 1986); Kevin B. Wamsley and David Whitson, "Celebrating Violent Masculinities: The Boxing Death of Luther McCarty," *Journal of Sport History* 25, 3 (1998): 419–31; Kevin B. Wamsley and Robert S. Kossuth, "Fighting It Out in Nineteenth-Century Upper Canada/Canada West: Masculinities and Physical Challenges in the Tavern," *Journal of Sport History* 27, 3 (2000): 405–30; Colin D. Howell, *Blood, Sweat, and Cheers: Sport and the Making of Modern Canada* (Toronto: University of Toronto Press, 2001). Although her analysis is not focused on the working class, Varda Burstyn's *The Rites of Men: Manhood, Politics, and the Culture of Sport* (Toronto: University of Toronto Press, 1999) is also vital in understanding the relationship between sport and male aggression.

39 See, for example Anthony Rotundo, *American Manhood: Transformations in Masculinity from the Revolution to the Modern Era* (New York: Basic Books, 1990), 7; Michael Kimmel, *Manhood in America: A Cultural History* (New York: Free Press, 1996), 2; Mike O'Brien, "Manhood and the Militia Myth: Masculinity, Class, and Militarism in Ontario, 1902–1914," *Labour/Le travail* 42 (1998): 116; Philip White and Kevin Young, eds., *Sport and Gender in Canada* (Don Mills, ON: Oxford University Press, 1999), xvii; and Gertrud Pfister, "Cold War Diplomats in Tracksuits: The Frauleinwunder of East German Sport," in *Militarism, Sport, Europe: War without Weapons*, ed. J.A. Mangan (New York: Frank Cass, 2004), 225.

40 O'Brien, "Manhood and the Militia Myth," 116.

41 For use of the term "contested territory," see Howell, *Northern Sandlots*, 4, 5. To date, scholarly work dedicated specifically to race, ethnicity, and sport in Canada is sparse. Howell's examination of black baseball players in *Northern Sandlots*, Chapter 9, is particularly insightful for its analysis of race and sport in Canada. Concerning racial prejudice, in particular exclusion from amateur sport on the basis of race, see also Frank Cosentino's *Afros, Aboriginals, and Amateur Sport in Pre World War One Canada* (Ottawa: Canadian Historical Society, 2000). Bruce Kidd's examination of organized sport among Canada's Finnish population in *The Struggle for Canadian Sport* (Toronto: University of Toronto Press, 1996) provides important context for understanding not only its role within non-

Anglo-Canadian communities during the 1920s but also its place in the country's organized labour movement.

42   Concerning Manitoba's ethnic composition relative to that of Ontario, see Plate 4 in Donald Kerr and Deryck W. Holdsworth, eds., *Historical Atlas of Canada Volume III: Addressing the Twentieth Century, 1891–1961* (Toronto: University of Toronto Press, 1990).

43   A number of survey works, beginning with W.L. Morton's seminal opus, *Manitoba: A History* (Toronto: University of Toronto Press, 1957), provide context for understanding the central events and themes shaping Manitoba's history. An essential resource for outlining the province's economic and political development, Morton's work, nearly sixty years after its publication, also contains valuable information on a number of immigrant groups who settled in Manitoba. However, literature on that subject has expanded considerably and tended to be more critical of the treatment accorded to many settlers who did not originate from the British Isles. John Herd Thompson's *Harvests of War* (Toronto: McClelland and Stewart, 1978) and *Forging the Prairie West* (Toronto: Oxford University Press, 1998), for example, provide further depth on topics related to immigration, assimilation, and western Canadian nativism than does Morton's earlier work. Since Morton's time, historians have also devoted greater effort to providing an inclusive narrative on prairie settlement and growth that integrates the experiences and achievements of the region's immigrant communities. Of particular value in this regard, as well as for its overall analysis of prairie life before and after Confederation, is Gerald Friesen's *The Canadian Prairies* (Toronto: University of Toronto Press, 1984). Also useful in understanding changing patterns of western immigration and the forces behind it is D.J. Hall's two-part biography of Clifford Sifton, *Clifford Sifton, Volume One: The Young Napoleon, 1861–1900* (Vancouver: UBC Press, 1981), and *Clifford Sifton, Volume Two: A Lonely Eminence, 1901–1929* (Vancouver: UBC Press, 1985). Additional insight into each of these topics is provided by Ken Coates and Fred McGuinness, *Manitoba: The Province and the People* (Edmonton: Hurtig, 1987).

44   Because of Winnipeg's towering influence over the region, analysis draws heavily on studies devoted specifically to Manitoba's capital. Background on Winnipeg's economic development and social impact is provided by Alan Artibise, *Winnipeg: A Social History of Urban Growth 1874–1914* (Montreal: McGill-Queen's University Press, 1975). Ruban Bellan, *Winnipeg First Century: An Economic History* (Winnipeg: Queenston House Publishing, 1978), is additionally useful for understanding, on practically a year-to-year basis, the city's cycles of economic growth and decline.

45   Research on wrestling's history in Manitoba commenced with reading the sports section in the Manitoba *Free Press*. Because virtually nothing was known about its history, I examined each issue of the *Free Press* between 1900 and 1930 to gain a foundational understanding of the major individuals, institutions, and events that shaped wrestling's past. Previous research on the Thunder Bay district prior to 1900, disseminated in my master's thesis, "Headlocks at the Lakehead: Wrestling in Fort William and Port Arthur, 1913–1933" (Lakehead University, 2007), 30–31, provided a starting point for investigating wrestling's earlier days in Manitoba before the popularization of dedicated sports pages. Building on my findings in the *Free Press*, I undertook further research in the long-standing Winnipeg *Tribune* and Winnipeg *Telegram* dailies, as well as various shorter-lived newspapers that had existed since the early Confederation period, to glean further information on events significant to this study. I likewise examined periodicals published in Manitoba's smaller communities, such as Brandon, Portage la Prairie, Melita, and Dauphin, for their records on local wrestling. I analyzed, and catalogued accordingly, all reports related to the various themes and questions guiding this work.

46   Jerry W. Knudson, "Late to the Feast: Newspapers as Historical Sources," American Historical Association *Perspectives* 31, 7 (October 1993), http://www.historians.org/perspectives/issues/1993/9310/9310ARC.cfm.

47   Joy Parr, *Gender of Breadwinners: Women, Men, and Change in Two Industrial Towns, 1880–1950* (Toronto: University of Toronto Press, 1990), 10, 11.

CHAPTER 1: BEFORE THE BOOM

1   Leyshon, *Of Mats and Men*, 3–4.

2   For a general overview of Samuel Hearne's exploration activities in the northwest interior, see C.S. Mackinnon's entry in the *Dictionary of Canadian Biography Online*, http://www.biographi. ca/009004-119.01-e.php?&id_nbr=1943&interval=25&&PHPSESSID=nc3qsetgi77rn9f69 41tmgnj05; and E.E. Rich, *The Fur Trade and the Northwest to 1857* (Toronto: McClelland and Stewart, 1967), 146–51.

3   Samuel Hearne, *A Journey from Prince of Wales's Fort, in Hudson's Bay, to the Northern Ocean in the Years 1769, 1770, 1771, 1772* (Toronto: Champlain Society, 1911), 141, 142.

4   For Clare Brant's comments on universal Aboriginal practices, see his 1982 lecture given at Liscombe Lodge, Nova Scotia, "Native Ethics and Principles," www.cbu.ca/indigenous-affairs/ unamaki-college/mikmaq-resource-centre/essays/native-ethics-principles/.

5   Ibid.; Kerry Abel, *Drum Songs: Glimpses of Dene History* (Montreal: McGill-Queen's University Press, 1995), 21, 41; Jean-Guy Goulet, *Ways of Knowing: Experience, Knowledge, and Power among the Dene Tha* (Lincoln: University of Nebraska Press, 1998), xxx, 28, 29.

6   Mott, "Manly Sports," 26, 28. See also Morris Mott, "Games and Contests of the First 'Manitobans,'" in Mott, *Sports in Canada*, 19, 21.

7   Henry S. Sharpe, "Asymmetrical Equals: Women and Men among the Chipewyans," in *Women and Power in Native North America*, ed. Laura F. Klein and Lillian A. Ackerman (Norman: University of Oklahoma Press, 1995), 57.

8   Donald Stewart McKay, "The Cultural Ecology of the Chipewyan" (MA thesis, University of British Columbia, 1965), 15.

9   Hearne, *A Journey*, 141.

10   Quoted in Sylvia Van Kirk, *Many Tender Ties: Women in Fur-Trade Society, 1670–1870* (Winnipeg: Watson and Dwyer Publishing, c.1980), 25.

11   Ibid., 24; Jennifer S.H. Brown, *Strangers in Blood: Fur Trade Company Families* (Vancouver: UBC Press, 1980), 63.

12   Hearne, *A Journey*, 141.

13   Ibid.

14   Ibid.

15   Ibid., 143.

16   Abel, *Drum Songs*, 39; Goulet, *Ways of Knowing*, xxvii.

17   Abel, *Drum Songs*, 40.

18   Ibid., 41.

19   Goulet, *Ways of Knowing*, 66.

20   Hearne, *A Journey*, 141.

21   John West, *The Substance of a Journal during Residence at the Red River Colony, British North America in the Years 1820–1823* (Vancouver: Alcuin Society, 1967), 170.

22   Hearne, *A Journey*, 142.

23   Ibid., 143.

24   Ibid.

25   Sharpe, "Asymmetrical Equals," 73.

26   Wendell H. Oswalt, *This Land Was Theirs: A Study of the North American Indian* (New York: John Wiley and Sons, 1966), 25.

27   Hearne, *A Journey*, 142.

28   Brown, *Strangers in Blood*, 63; Hearne, *A Journey*, 143.

29   Sharpe, "Asymmetrical Equals," 60.

30   Hearne, *A Journey*, 143.

31   Ibid., 144.

32   Ibid., 142, 143.

33   West, *The Substance of a Journal*, 170.

34   Van Kirk, *Many Tender Ties*, 25.

35   Ibid.

36   David T. Hanbury, who spent twenty months traversing Canada's north, observed in *Sport and Travel in the Northland of Canada* (London: Edward Arnold, 1904), 2, that the Inuit who worked at Churchill were particularly fond of wrestling. By the end of the nineteenth century, American sporting amusements were also being integrated into Inuit society, and Hanbury witnessed the children's affinity for baseball, which they had learned from American whalers (see 130).

37   Anthony D. Pellegrini and Peter K. Smith, *The Nature of Play: Great Apes and Humans* (New York: Guilford Press, 2005), 76; Michael Heine, *Inuit Style Wrestling: A Training and Resource Manual* (Yellowknife: Sport North Federation, 2002), I-12, I-60.

38   Leyshon, *Of Mats and Men*, 9.

39   Winnipeg *Voice*, 27 December 1901.

40   George Eisen, "Early European Attitudes toward Native American Sports and Pastimes," in *Ethnicity and Sport in North American History and Culture*, ed. George Eisen and David K. Wiggins (Westport, CT: Greenwood Press, 1994), 1.

41   Diamond Jenness, *A Report of the Canadian Arctic Expedition 1913–18 Volume XII: The Life of the Copper Eskimos* (Ottawa: F.A. Ackland, 1922), 221.

42   Heine, *Inuit Style Wrestling*, I-36, I-42.

43   Carolyn Podruchny, *Making the Voyageur World: Travellers and Traders in the North American Fur Trade* (Toronto: University of Toronto Press, 2006), 13, 186.

44   Daniel Williams Harmon, *Harmon's Journal 1800–1819* (Surrey, BC: TouchWood Editions, 2006), 43.

45   Both popular and academic historical accounts regularly mention the voyageurs' love of physically demonstrative revelry and fighting. See, for example, Greg Shilliday, ed., *Manitoba 125: A History Volume 1: Rupert's Land to Riel* (Winnipeg: Great Plains Publications, 1993), 89; Peter C. Newman, *Company of Adventurers* (Markham, ON: Penguin Books, 1985), 284; Podruchny, *Making the Voyageur World*, 159, 166, 175, 186; and Morrow and Wamsley, *Sport in Canada*, 20, 22.

46   Montreal *Gazette*, 29 September 1870.

47   Leyshon, *Of Mats and Men*, 23.

48   Victor Turner, "Liminal to Liminoid, in Play, Flow, and Ritual," *Rice University Studies: The Anthropological Study of Human Play* 60, 3 (1974): 83; Victor Turner, *Blazing the Trail* (Tucson: University of Arizona Press, 1992), 52; Podruchny, *Making the Voyageur World*, 166. Michael Payne's contention in *The Most Respectable Place in the Territory: Everyday Life in Hudson's Bay Company Service York Factory, 1788 to 1870* (Ottawa: Minister of Supply and Services Canada, 1989), 69, that fighting held greater appeal among voyageurs, tripmen, and sailors than among permanent York Factory residents supports this view.

49   Rhys Isaac, *The Transformation of Virginia, 1740–1790* (Chapel Hill: University of North Carolina Press, 1982), 120.

50   Ibid., 95, 99.

51   Gorn, "Gouge and Bite," 22.

52   Ibid., 21, 23, 34.

53   Grace Lee Nute, *The Voyageur* (St. Paul: Minnesota Historical Society, 1955), 4, 10.

54   Isaac, *The Transformation of Virginia*, 98; Gorn, *The Manly Art*, 27.

55   Arthur S. Morton, *A History of the Canadian West to 1870–71* (Toronto: University of Toronto Press, 1973), 454; Joseph James Hargrave, *Red River* (Montreal: J. Lovell, 1871), 163.

56   J.J. Gunn, *Echoes of the Red* (Toronto: Macmillan Company of Canada, 1930), 43, 54.

57   For a reprinting of the Broughton rules, as well as commentary on them, see John V. Grombach, *The Saga of the Fist: The 9,000 Year Story of Boxing in Text and Pictures* (Cranbury, NJ: A.S. Barnes and Company, 1977), 31–32.

58   Peter Arnold, *History of Boxing* (Secaucus, NJ: Chartwell Books, 1985), 34.

59   See, for example, Daniel Mendoza, *The Modern Art of Boxing* (England: By the Author, c. 1789); and Edmund E. Price, *Science of Self Defense* (New York: Dick and Fitzgerald, 1867).

60   Carl Berger, "William Morton: The Delicate Balance of Region and Nation," in *The West and the Nation: Essays in Honour of W.L. Morton*, ed. Carl Berger and Ramsay Cook (Toronto: McClelland and Stewart, 1976), 12, 17.

61   Quoted in John E. Foster, "Paulet Paul: Metis or 'House Indian' Folk-Hero?," *Manitoba History* 9 (1985), http://www.mhs.mb.ca/docs/mb_history/09/pauletpaul.shtml.

62   Gunn, *Echoes of the Red*, 57.

63   Hargrave, *Red River*, 167. See also Gunn, *Echoes of the Red*, 58. For biographical information on Hargrave and an analysis of his writings, see Lyle Dick, "Red River's Vernacular Historians," *Manitoba History* 71 (2013): 9–10.

64   Gunn, *Echoes of the Red*, 56.

65   Ibid., 56–57; Foster, "Paulet Paul," 2, 6.

66   Gunn, *Echoes of the Red*, 24.

67   Douglas Owram, *Promise of Eden: The Canadian Expansionist Movement and the Idea of the West, 1856–1900* (Toronto: University of Toronto Press, 1980), 4, 39–40, 57. See also Suzanne Zeller, *Inventing Canada: Early Victorian Science and the Idea of a Transcontinental Nation* (Toronto: University of Toronto Press, 1987), 162, 170–71.

68   See Owram, *Promise of Eden*, 43, 57.

69   The Red River resistance of 1869 to 1870, culminating in Manitoba's entry into Confederation, has been widely examined. For treatments of the subject, see Morton, *Manitoba*, 121–50; Fritz Pannekoek, *A Snug Little Flock: The Social Origins of the Riel Resistance of 1869–1870* (Winnipeg: Watson and Dwyer, 1991); and J.M. Bumsted, *The Red River Rebellion* (Winnipeg: Watson and Dwyer, 1996). For an overview of each of the seven prairie treaties negotiated during this period, see Friesen, *The Canadian Prairies*, 136–48; and Arthur J. Ray et al., *Bounty and Benevolence: A History of Saskatchewan Treaties* (Montreal: McGill-Queen's University Press, 2000).

70   Morton, *Manitoba*, 241; Artibise, *Winnipeg*, 194.

71   Jack Templeman, *From Force to Service: A Pictorial History of the Winnipeg Police Department* (Winnipeg: Winnipeg Police Museum, 1998), 9–10.

72   Ibid., 10; David H. Breen, "The Turner Thesis and the Canadian West: A Closer Look at the Ranching Frontier," in *Essays on Western History*, ed. Lewis H. Thomas (Edmonton: University of

Alberta, 1976), 150. Outside Manitoba, in the regions later known as Saskatchewan and Alberta, Breen argues that the NWMP represented "the determination of the central authority to reach out and integrate the new territory into the established institutional framework." For additional information on the NWMP's connection to British Canadian society and central Canada, see David H. Breen, *The Canadian Prairie West and the Ranching Frontier 1874–1924* (Toronto: University of Toronto Press, 1983), 30; and Friesen, *The Canadian Prairies*, 170–71.

73 Mott, "Manly Sports," 55, 67, 73–77.

74 Rotundo, *American Manhood*, 223.

75 Howell, *Northern Sandlots*, 98; Clifford Putney, *Muscular Christianity: Manhood and Sports in Protestant America, 1880–1920* (Cambridge, MA: Harvard University Press, 2001), 11; Rotundo, *American Manhood*, 223.

76 Anne Bloomfield, "Muscular Christian or Mystic? Charles Kingsley Reappraised," *International Journal of the History of Sport* 71, 1 (1994): 173, 174; Benjamin Rader, *American Sports from the Age of Folk Games to the Age of Televised Sports* (Englewood Cliffs, NJ: Prentice Hall, 1996), 24.

77 Steven A. Riess, "Sport and the Redefinition of Middle Class Masculinity," *International Journal of the History of Sport* 8 (1991): 11.

78 Ibid., 5.

79 Rader, *American Sports*, 124.

80 Mott, "Manly Sports," 60. For an excellent overview of the manly qualities that Tom Brown learns through sport, see 61–62.

81 Howell, *Blood, Sweat, and Cheers*, 32–34.

82 Janet Guildford, "Creating the Ideal Man: Middle-Class Women's Constructions of Masculinity in Nova Scotia, 1840–1880," *Acadiensis* 24, 2 (1995): 23.

83 Ibid., 10–12.

84 Michael Kimmel, *History of Men: Essays on the History of American and British Masculinities* (New York: SUNY Press, 2005), 82, 83, 108. See also Robert K. Nelson and Kenneth M. Price, "Debating Manliness: Thomas Wentworth Higginson, William Sloane Kennedy, and the Question of Walt Whitman," *American Literature* 73, 3 (2001): 497–524.

85 As Julia Roberts notes in "The Games People Played: Tavern Amusements and Colonial Relations," *Ontario History* 52, 2 (2010): 157–58, taverns themselves could take on a plethora of physical forms depending on time and location, ranging from simple rural log cabins with the barest of amenities to more palatial, multiroom, and multistorey hotels.

86 Ibid., 159, 164; Julia Roberts, *In Mixed Company: Taverns and Public Life in Upper Canada* (Vancouver: UBC Press, 2009), 84. For similar observations concerning the nearly unlimited variety of activities offered in public drinking establishments, albeit during a slightly later period, see Madelon Powers, *Faces along the Road: Lore and Order in the Workingman's Saloon, 1870–1920* (Chicago: University of Chicago Press, 1998), 138.

87 Roberts, "The Games People Played," 163.

88 Roberts, *In Mixed Company*, 94, 96, 97, 98.

89 One notable example in this regard concerned William Penner of Steinbach, who died on 8 February 1902 following a friendly wrestling match at Winnipeg's Tremont Hotel the prior afternoon. Penner, described as "a large muscular man," and quite proud of his strength, gave several impromptu exhibitions of his abilities to patrons in the Tremont Hotel barroom, including a challenge to pry a two dollar bill out of his clenched fist. Retiring to the sitting parlour, Penner engaged St. Boniface resident Alex Marion in a friendly wrestling match, which ended after Penner said that he did not feel well. He was later taken to St. Boniface Hospital, where he died as the result of an internal rupture. Penner, a father of five, had two pre-existing hernias for which he wore an abdominal

brace. Despite its ultimately tragic conclusion, this case demonstrates a concerted effort to ensure that the Tremont Hotel remained an orderly social space. The decision of Penner and Marion to relocate from the barroom to the sitting parlour to conduct their friendly match indicates a respect for their surroundings and an acute understanding that some activities, whether to prevent injury or property damage, were best confined to certain clearly defined areas within a public setting. See Manitoba *Free Press*, 10 February 1902.

90   Morrow and Wamsley, *Sport in Canada*, 155; Tony Joyce, "Sport and the Cash Nexus in Nineteenth Century Toronto," *Sport History Review* 30, 2 (1999): 142–44.

91   Dennis Brailsford, *Sport, Time, and Society* (London: Routledge, 1991), 77. See also *Trades Free Press*, 28 October 1827.

92   *Bell's Life in London and Sporting Chronicle*, 22 September 1839, 17 October 1841, 14 December 1845.

93   Metcalfe, *Canada Learns to Play*, 134, 159, 162; Joyce, "Sport and the Cash Nexus," 143.

94   Boston *Daily Globe*, 23 July 1873. Concerning McMahon's career, including commentary on this match, see Mark Hewitt, "John McMahon," *Journal of Manly Arts and Sciences* 2 (2002), http://ejmas.com/jmanly/jmanlyframe.htm.

95   Roberts, *In Mixed Company*, 81–82.

96   Gorn, *The Manly Art*, 137; Beekman, *Ringside*, 14; Steven A. Riess, *City Games: The Evolution of American Urban Society and the Rise of Sports* (Urbana: University of Illinois Press, 1989), 86.

97   Henry Roxborough, *One Hundred—Not Out: The Story of Nineteenth Century Canadian Sport* (Toronto: Ryerson Press, 1966), 222–24; Morrow and Wamsley, *Sport in Canada*, 28–29.

98   Suzanne Morton, *At Odds: Gambling and Canadians 1919–1969* (Toronto: University of Toronto Press, 2003), 8, 16; Gorn, *The Manly Art*, 140; Stephen Hardy, *How Boston Played: Sport, Recreation, and Community, 1865–1915* (Boston: Northeastern University Press, 1982), 48.

99   Payne, *The Most Respectable Place*, 73–74, 78. For a detailed retelling of the physical routes by which goods, as well as information, diffused throughout the region during the mid-nineteenth century, see Hargrave, *Red River*, 155–59.

100   John A. Eagle, "The Development of Transportation and Communications, 1870–1905," in *The Prairie West to 1905: A Canadian Sourcebook*, ed. Lewis G. Thomas (Toronto: Oxford University Press, 1975), 315.

101   Ibid., 354.

102   David R. Richeson, "Telegraph Construction and Community Formation in the North-West Territories," in *The Developing West*, ed. John E. Foster (Edmonton: University of Alberta Press, 1983), 141; Gerald Friesen, *Citizens and Nation: An Essay on History, Communication, and Canada* (Toronto: University of Toronto Press, 2000), 6.

103   Friesen, *Citizens and Nation*, 222; Richeson, "Telegraph Construction," 139.

104   Eagle, "Development," 315; Richeson, "Telegraphic Construction," 140, 147.

105   Stacy L. Lorenz, "'A Lively Interest on the Prairies': Western Canada, the Mass Media, and the 'World of Sport,' 1870–1939," *Journal of Sport History* 27, 2 (2000): 199.

106   Friesen, *The Canadian Prairies*, 201.

107   Other newspapers appearing in Manitoba during this period include Manitoba *Herald* (January 1877); Manitoba *Gazette* (October 1878); Portage la Prairie weekly *Tribune* (September 1881); and Winnipeg *Sun* (August 1881).

108   Lorenz, "'A Lively Interest,'" 196.

109 The only reference to local wrestling contained in the Manitoba *Free Press* during the decade is a report, dated 28 March 1876, in which a local resident named "Big Dan" fell and broke his arm while wrestling. No further details of the incident are given.

110 For two such reports, see Manitoba *Free Press*, 11 January 1876, 20 October 1879.

111 For examples of wrestling matches from each of these cities, see, respectively, Manitoba *Free Press*, 30 November 1882, 2 February 1883, 5 January 1884, 25 March 1884, 25 October 1884, 14 April 1883, 24 July 1884, 31 July 1884, 16 October 1884, 9 April 1884, 4 April 1884, 6 September 1884, 9 June 1883, and 31 December 1883.

112 Douglas Hill, *The Opening of the Canadian West: Where Strong Men Gathered* (New York: John Day Company, 1967), 146–47; P.B. Waite, *Canada 1874–1896: Arduous Destiny* (Toronto: McClelland and Stewart, 1971), 60–61; Eagle, "Development," 310; A.A. den Otter, "The Hudson Bay Company's Prairie Transportation Problem," in Foster, *The Developing West*, 36–37; Holly S. Seaman, *Manitoba Landmarks and Red Letter Days, 1610 to 1920* (Winnipeg: By the Author, 1920), 70.

113 Artibise, *Winnipeg*, 10, 130; Friesen, *The Canadian Prairies*, 202; Coates and McGuinness, *Manitoba*, 17.

114 Quoted in W.J. Healy, *Winnipeg's Early Days* (Winnipeg: Stovel Company, 1927), 27–28.

115 See Morton, *Manitoba*, 194; Artibise, *Winnipeg*, 69–74; Alan F.J. Artibise, ed., *Gateway City: Documents on the City of Winnipeg 1873–1913* (Winnipeg: University of Manitoba Press, 1979), 57–69; Bellan, *Winnipeg First Century*, 26–38; Randy Rostecki, "The Growth of Winnipeg, 1870–1886" (MA thesis, University of Manitoba, 1980), 29–48; and Friesen, *The Canadian Prairies*, 205–07.

116 Department of Agriculture, *Census of Canada 1880–81 Volume II* (Ottawa: Queen's Printer, 1884), 119–21, 162; Artibise, *Winnipeg*, 130.

117 Morton, *Manitoba*, 171; James H. Gray, *Red Lights on the Prairies* (Toronto: Macmillan of Canada, 1971), xi, 5, 7; Mott, "Manly Sports," 67.

118 Morton, *Manitoba*, 171; Robert Hutchison, *A Century of Service: A History of the Winnipeg Police Force 1874–1974* (Winnipeg: City of Winnipeg Police Force, 1974), 19.

119 Mott, "Manly Sports," 66.

120 Ibid., 73.

121 For a sample of their advertisement, see Manitoba *Free Press*, 15 April 1882.

122 Winnipeg *Daily Sun*, 26 March 1884; Manitoba *Free Press*, 27 March 1884. Nott and Robinson were frequent advertisers in the Manitoba *Free Press* during the early 1880s. See, for example, their advertisement printed on the paper's first page on 2 May 1883.

123 Manitoba *Free Press*, 4 December 1879; Minnedosa *Tribune*, 29 January 1891.

124 Manitoba *Free Press*, 18 May 1907.

125 Manitoba *Free Press*, 8 August 1903.

126 Quoted in Manitoba *Free Press*, 8 August 1903.

127 Rugby's casualty rate, far greater than wrestling's rate, did generate public concern, but the sport continued to grow in popularity. Over time, rule reform assisted in reducing injuries and fatalities. See William J. Baker, *Sports in the Western World* (Totowa, NJ: Rowman and Littlefield, 1982), 120, 191; Roberta J. Park, "'Mended or Ended?' Football Injuries and the British and American Medical Press, 1870–1910," *International Journal of the History of Sport* 18, 2 (2001): 110–33; and Winnipeg *Tribune*, 2 November 1907.

128 Manitoba *Free Press*, 22 March 1882.

129 Winnipeg *Sun*, 27 March 1882.

130 Winnipeg *Sun*, 17 April 1884. The Theatre Comique was one of eight theatres operating in Winnipeg between 1882 and 1884. It was opened in September 1883 by Richard Farrell, a local restaurant owner who had been a member of the city police force. Financial difficulties forced the theatre's closure just eight months later. See Carol Budnick, "Theatre on the Frontier: Winnipeg in the 1880s," *Theatre Research in Canada* 4, 1 (1983), http://journals.hil.unb.ca/index.php/tric/article/view/7475/8534.

131 Budnick, "Theatre on the Frontier."

132 Ibid.

133 Quoted in Manitoba *Free Press*, 16 June 1920.

134 Manitoba *Free Press*, 20 October 1887.

135 At the Dominion Day celebrations in 1883, for instance, Peter McKeown received third and first prizes, respectively, in both sports. He appears to have been particularly skilled with the caber; reports from the Catholic picnic sporting program held on 29 July 1885 note that he easily won the event. For information on his athletic exploits, see, for example, Manitoba *Free Press*, 3 July 1883, 30 July 1885, and 16 August 1892. See also Canada Census 1891, RG31, Manitoba, Winnipeg District 10, Ward 5, 62.

136 The McKeown brothers reflected wider trends in their multidisciplinary approach to sport. A number of internationally prominent wrestlers participated in various sports in addition to wrestling to earn a living. Most notable in this regard were Donald Dinnie and Duncan C. Ross. Dinnie wrestled, competed in field athletics, and engaged in strength contests. Ross, styled the world's champion "all around athlete," likewise competed in field athletics and sword fighting in addition to wrestling. For an overview of Dinnie's career, see David Webster, *Donald Dinnie: The First Sporting Superstar* (Aberdeenshire, UK: Ardo Publishing, 1999). Newspaper accounts on Ross's exploits in sports besides wrestling were numerous and widespread during the 1880s and 1890s. See, for example, Manitoba *Free Press*, 19 July 1882; New York *Times*, 5 August 1888; Lowell *Sun*, 7 November 1885; Logansport *Journal*, 24 April 1888; Logansport *Pharos*, 20 September 1889; and Chillicothe *Constitution*, 17 January 1890. For a general discussion of multidisciplinary athletes during the period, see Frank Zarnowski, *All-Around Men: Heroes of a Forgotten Sport* (Lanham, MD: Scarecrow Press, 2005).

137 For general commentary on pedestrianism, see Mott, "Manly Sports," 67; and Metcalfe, *Canada Learns to Play*, 160–61. For further information on John McKeown's exploits in this field, see, respectively, Winnipeg *Free Press*, 26 February 1999; and Manitoba *Free Press*, 7 August 1879, 22 October 1879, 23 October 1879.

138 For reports on McKeown's ring appearances against boxers Holmes, Ike Fullerton, and William Barry, see, respectively, Winnipeg *Sun*, 17 April 1884; and Manitoba *Free Press*, 26 January 1885, 28 October 1885.

139 Winnipeg *Henderson's Directory*, 1887 and 1889; Winnipeg *Siftings*,16 February 1889.

140 For accounts of Ed McKeown's involvement as a wrestling official, see, for example, Manitoba *Free Press*, 5 November 1890, 22 February 1894.

141 McKeown, for example, refereed in a shooting match in which J.C. Cockburn was to break thirty glass balls in one minute and ten seconds for a side bet, and he acted as a stakeholder for Caledonian Games athlete and wrestling aspirant John McPherson. See Manitoba *Free Press*, 12 March 1885, 10 May 1887.

142 See Archives of Manitoba, Police Court Winnipeg, ATG0030, GR 651, M1213, Roll 4, no. 2254, 19 March 1885; M1214, Roll 5, no. 4796, 8 October 1886; no. 5711, 22 August 1887; and M1215, Roll 6, no. 16142, 15 June 1896.

143 Archives of Manitoba, Police Court Winnipeg, ATG0030, GR 651, M1213, Roll 4, no. 1350, 19 September 1884.

144 Archives of Manitoba, Police Court Winnipeg, ATG0030, GR 651, M1214, Roll 5, no. 5710, 22 August 1887; no. 5717, 23 August 1887.

145 See Manitoba *Free Press*, 26 January 1885; and Archives of Manitoba, Police Court Winnipeg, ATG0030, GR 651, M1213, Roll 4, no. 2135, 18 February 1885; no. 2296, 31 March 1885.

146 For Ed McKeown's court appearances related to assault/assault and beating, see Archives of Manitoba, Police Court Winnipeg, ATG0030, GR 651, M1213, Roll 4, no. 2562, 19 May 1885; no. 2910, 31 July 1885; M1214, Roll 5, no. 4900, 6 November 1886; no. 5741, 1 September 1887; no. 5798, 21 September 1887; M1215, Roll 6, no. 11781, 8 December 1892; no. 16067, 15 June 1896; and M1218, Roll 9, no. 12866, 31 July 1907. For each of the other individual charges, see, respectively, M1213, Roll 4, no. 2905, 31 July 1885; M1214, Roll 5, no. 7363, 23 March 1889; no. 9795, 22 May 1891; and M1215, Roll 6, no. 11865, 10 January 1893.

147 Winnipeg *Sun*, 15 September 1886.

148 Greg Shilliday, ed., *Manitoba 125—A History Volume 3: Gateway to the West* (Winnipeg: Great Plains Publications, 1994), 78–79. See Manitoba *Free Press*, 23 January 1888.

149 On 9 July 1881, H. McAlpine and James Close were brought to Winnipeg City Police Court on dog-fighting charges but released with a reprimand. Ed Burluig and Henry Minto faced more serious censure in October 1884 when both men were arrested for encouraging two dogs to fight. The matter was sent to Provincial Police Court for trial. See Manitoba *Free Press*, 11 July 1881; and Archives of Manitoba, Police Court Winnipeg, ATG0030, GR 651, M1213, Roll 4, no. 1484, 13 October 1884.

150 For a related discussion of the idea of how sport-related values, originating among the lower social orders, could be internalized, and even co-opted, by the social elite, see Michael A. Robidoux, "Historical Interpretations of First Nations Masculinity and Its Influence on Canada's Sport Heritage," in *Native Americans and Sport in North America: Other People's Games*, ed. C. Richard King (New York: Routledge, 2008), 130–47.

151 Manitoba *Free Press*, 12 January 1889.

152 Manitoba *Free Press*, 14 February 1889, 5 March 1896; *Nor'Wester*, 14 December 1896.

153 Henry Trachtenberg, "Ethnic Politics on the Urban Frontier: 'Fighting Joe' Martin and the Jews of Winnipeg, 1893–1896," *Manitoba History* 35 (1998): 2, 11; Ottawa *Journal*, 28 March 1922.

154 Vincent Leah, *Alarm of Fire: 100 Years of Firefighting in Winnipeg 1882–1982* (Winnipeg: Fire Fighters Burn Fund, 1982), 71.

155 Beekman, *Ringside*, 16, 17; Michael T. Isenberg, *John L. Sullivan and His America* (Chicago: University of Illinois Press, 1988), 92–96.

156 Lorenz, "A Lively Interest,'" 196–97. Concerning the invention and development of newsprint, see, for example, Peter Burger, *Charles Fenerty and His Paper Invention* (Toronto: PB Publishing, 2007).

157 Sut Jhally, "The Spectacle of Accumulation: Material and Cultural Factors in the Evolution of the Sports/Media Complex," *Critical Sociology* 12 (1984): 43–44.

158 Ibid., 198.

159 For a general overview of Sorakichi's wrestling career, including major matches, see Joseph R. Svinth, "Japanese Professional Wrestling Pioneer: Sorakichi Matsuda," *In Yo: Journal of Alternative Perspectives on the Martial Arts and Sciences* 1 (2000), http://ejmas.com/jalt/jaltframe.htm.

160 Reports on Sorakichi's wrestling matches were numerous. See Manitoba *Free Press*, 9 April 1884, 5 July 1884, 22 May 1885, 29 January 1886, 16 February 1886; and Winnipeg *Sun*, 9 April 1884, 20 May 1884, 5 July 1884.

161 Manitoba *Free Press*, 18 August 1886.

162 For more on the trend toward statistics and quantification that developed in sports during the nineteenth century, see Guttman, *From Ritual to Record*, 47–51, 54.

163 Richard Gruneau and David Whitson, *Hockey Night in Canada: Sport, Identities, and Cultural Politics* (Toronto: Garamond Press, 1993), 61–62.

164 Maxwell L. Howell and Nancy Howell, *Sports and Games in Canadian Life, 1700 to the Present* (Toronto: Macmillan of Canada, 1969), 127.

165 Ashton's Edwin Bibby, who had begun his wrestling career by 1868, was the first of the great catch-as-catch-can exponents to sail to North America. His arrival in 1880 was followed in the spring of 1882 by Wigan's Joe Acton. Bibby and Acton had wrestled one another on eight occasions in England, the first match occurring on 27 December 1873 and the last on 3 May 1879. Following the latter's arrival, they renewed their Old World rivalry, wrestling a ninth match at New York's Madison Square Garden on 7 August 1882. Another prominent catch-as-catch-can stylist, Tom Cannon, a former miner who worked in the coal pits at Tyldesley, also arrived in 1882, followed by Manchester's Tom Connors in February 1883. All of them toured extensively, wrestling in their native Lancashire style. Subsequent generations of North American wrestlers would continue to refine the catch-as-catch-can method, building upon the technical base provided by its Lancastrian progenitors. See *Bell's Life in London and Sporting Chronicle*, 2 May 1868, 20 November 1875; Salt Lake City *Daily Tribune*, 1 February 1880; New York *Herald*, 7 May 1882; New York *Times*, 8 August 1882; Tom Connors, *The Modern Athlete* (Milwaukee: Ed Bulfin, 1890), xv; and J.W. McWhinnie, *Modern Wrestling: Graeco-Roman and Catch-as-Catch-Can Styles* (London: Health and Strength Magazine Company, c. 1901), 46.

166 For an early published compendium of catch-as-catch-can rules, see Connors, *Modern Athlete*, 33–36. See also Walter Armstrong, "Wrestling," in *The Badminton Library* (London: Longmans, Green and Company, 1889), 230–37; and Warren S. Boring, *Science and Skills of Wrestling* (St. Louis: C.V. Mosby Company, 1975), 7–8.

167 For a thorough history of Cornish wrestling and its conventions, including the role of "stickler," see Michael Tripp, "Persistence of Difference: A History of Cornish Wrestling" (PhD diss., University of Exeter, 2009).

168 See, for example, *Bell's Life in London and Sporting Chronicle*, 14 December 1845, 7 April 1850.

169 Connors, *Modern Athlete*, 36.

170 Manitoba *Free Press*, 19 August 1886.

171 Ibid.

172 Ibid.

173 McKeown ultimately emerged victorious in the match since Sorakichi, who had undertaken to pin the local man three times in one hour, gained only one fall in thirty-nine minutes. Manitoba *Free Press*, 21 August 1886.

174 Quoted in Manitoba *Free Press*, 16 June 1920.

175 Manitoba *Free Press*, 7 October 1887, 13 October 1887, 20 October 1887, 14 November 1887, 21 November 1887. Evidently, as noted on 20 October, the spectators attending the matches in Vancouver were of similar disposition to those commonly seen in Winnipeg, amusing themselves with "cat-calls and chaff" during the long wait before the main event.

176 Quoted in Manitoba *Free Press*, 13 August 1888.

177 Previous court records show that Jack had assisted his brother in training for boxing contests.

178 Manitoba *Free Press*, 3 November 1890, 5 November 1890.

179 Manitoba *Free Press*, 5 November 1890.

180 In 1892, Manitoba held a plebiscite on the provincial sale of liquor. The majority of voters cast their ballots in favour of prohibition, but the province did not act on the resolution because of uncertainties over constitutional jurisdiction. See Morton, *Manitoba*, 251.

181 Budnick, "Theatre on the Frontier."

182 Although regarded as a vast improvement over Winnipeg's many variety theatres, the Princess still had a number of structural problems. Its all-wood construction and inadequate exits, coupled with wood stoves for heating and outdated kerosene lamps for illumination, made it a fire trap. Indeed, on 1 May 1892, flames consumed the entire structure, burning it to the ground. See E. Ross Stuart, *The History of Prairie Theatre* (Toronto: Simon and Pierre, 1984), 25; and James B. Hartman, "On Stage: Theatre and Theatres in Early Winnipeg," *Manitoba History* 43 (2002), http://www.mhs. mb.ca/docs/mb_history/43/theatrehistory.shtml.

183 Plato, *The Republic*, trans. Benjamin Jowett (Mineola, NY: Dover Publications, 2000), 200.

184 Baker, *Sports in the Western World*, 25.

185 John R. Betts, "Mind and Body in Early American Thought," *Journal of American History* 54, 4 (1968): 793, 796.

186 Morrow and Wamsley, *Sport in Canada*, 181−82.

187 Mary Keyes and Don Morrow, *A Concise History of Sport in Canada* (Don Mills, ON: Oxford University Press, 1989), 76.

188 For a photograph of the Winnipeg Athletic Club training in Wesley Hall dated to 1883, see Manitoba *Free Press*, 16 July 1920.

189 The Winnipeg Gymnasium, originally named the Winnipeg Lacrosse Club Gymnasium, formed under the patronage of the Winnipeg Lacrosse Club in early November 1887. Classes began on 19 November, and reports five days later noted that the club was "booming." Its grand opening was held on 28 November under the patronage of Mayor Lyman Melvin Jones. In the fall of 1889, the Winnipeg Lacrosse Club decided to relinquish control of the gymnasium, and on 26 October the club became independently incorporated as the Winnipeg Gymnastic Association. Evidence suggests that no wrestling took place at the club between 1887 and 1890, for reports on its equipment, ads for its classes, and reports on its public programs make no mention of the sport. See Manitoba *Free Press*, 8 November 1887, 24 November 1887, 16 November 1888, 24 October 1889, 28 October 1889, 12 April 1890.

190 Manitoba *Free Press*, 12 March 1891.

191 Ibid.

192 See Manitoba *Free Press*, 28 March 1891, 30 March 1891.

193 Manitoba *Free Press*, 29 February 1892.

194 Mott, "Manly Sports," 110.

195 Betts, "Mind and Body," 803.

196 Manitoba *Free Press*, 28 March 1891.

197 Metcalfe, *Canada Learns to Play*, 100.

198 Hall et Al., *Sport in Canadian Society*, 103.

199 Mott, "Manly Sports," 242−44; Metcalfe, *Canada Learns to Play*, 104.

200 Mott, "Manly Sports," 244.

201 Manitoba *Free Press*, 29 February 1892.

202 For details on the Winnipeg Athletic Association, see Manitoba *Free Press*, 10 September 1892.

203 Manitoba *Free Press*, 31 August 1892.

204 Ibid.

205 Manitoba *Free Press*, 9 September 1892.

206 Gorn, *The Manly Art*, 99; Wamsley and Kossuth, "Fighting It Out," 418−19; Beekman, *Ringside*, 16.

207 Gorn, *The Manly Art*, 100.

208 Like Johnston, McPherson was a well-known athlete, excelling in particular at the shot put. Prior to 1892, both men competed against one another in Caledonian Games competitions. By the end of the 1880s, McPherson had also turned his attention to wrestling, sometimes with unfavourable results, as in January 1888, when he suffered a broken arm at the hands of Jack Carkeek, one of North America's most prominent wrestlers. For McPherson's letter, see Manitoba *Free Press*, 13 September 1892. Concerning his records in shot put, see Manitoba *Free Press*, 16 April 1887, 9 August 1890. On Johnston and McPherson participating in Caledonian Games competition, see, for example, Buffalo *Courier*, 25 July 1890.

209 Manitoba *Free Press*, 14 September 1892.

210 Manitoba *Free Press*, 23 September 1892.

211 Concerning the opening of Plaisted's gymnasium in Winnipeg, see Manitoba *Free Press*, 28 November 1893. For reports on public performances, see Manitoba *Free Press*, 9 February 1894, 10 February 1894; and Nor'*Wester*, 10 February 1894.

212 See Manitoba *Free Press*, 15 December 1893, 18 December 1893.

213 Brandon *Sun*, 29 June 1893.

214 Cumberland-Westmoreland wrestling has its origins in the northern districts of England for which it is named. Also widely practised in southern Scotland, it was frequently included in Caledonian Games competitions. Under Cumberland-Westmoreland rules, a wrestler would place his left arm over his opponent's right arm and clasp his hands together behind his opponent's back. A match was won when any part of the body except the feet touched the ground or if one of the contestants failed to maintain his grip. For a contemporary overview of the sport's techniques, see Armstrong, "Wrestling," 190–96.

215 Manitoba *Free Press*, 28 December 1893.

216 Winnipeg *Tribune*, 5 January 1894; Manitoba *Free Press*, 5 January 1894.

217 Winnipeg *Tribune*, 5 January 1894.

218 Ibid.

219 Manitoba *Free Press*, 5 January 1894; Winnipeg *Tribune*, 5 January 1894.

220 Manitoba *Free Press*, 5 January 1894.

221 Manitoba *Free Press*, 8 January 1894.

222 Nor'*Wester*, 19 February 1894; Manitoba *Free Press*, 21 January 1894.

223 Concerning Dunbar's achievements in track and field, especially running, see Manitoba *Free Press*, 28 October 1886, 21 July 1888. For information on his various cycling exploits, including provincial speed records, see Nor'*Wester*, 14 April 1896; Portage la Prairie *Weekly Review*, 10 June 1897; and Winnipeg *Telegram*, 18 July 1901. A synopsis of Dunbar's curling achievements is provided by Mott in "Manly Sports," 138–39. See also Morris Mott and John Allardyce, *Curling Capital: Winnipeg and the Roarin' Game, 1876–1988* (Winnipeg: University of Manitoba Press, 1989), especially 24–25.

224 Manitoba *Free Press*, 21 February 1894. In 1883, the precise location of Manitoba's eastern border remained undetermined. In 1884, however, the Judicial Committee of the Privy Council settled the matter, placing Rat Portage, which a year earlier had elected a member to the Manitoba legislature, within Ontario's borders. The political decision had little bearing on wrestling, since athletes from Rat Portage (later Kenora) continued to contest for Manitoba provincial titles as late as the 1920s. See Morton, *Manitoba*, 218–19.

225 Detailed reports concerning each of the matches are provided in Manitoba *Free Press*, 23 February 1894; Nor'*Wester*, 23 February 1894; and Winnipeg *Tribune*, 23 February 1894.

226 Manitoba *Free Press*, 23 February 1894. For reports of similar responses to drunken rowdiness at wrestling events in Winnipeg during the period, see Winnipeg *Tribune*, 17 May 1894.

227 Ibid.

228 On 21 March 1894, wrestler John Allen defeated E.W. Johnston at the Brandon Opera Hall before a crowd of 150. Signifying their continuing interest in wrestling matches, "a large gathering of the local sporting fraternity" assembled at a local hotel ten days later to arrange a benefit program for Johnston that included boxing, club swinging, swordsmanship, and music in addition to wrestling. See Brandon *Sun*, 22 March 1894; and Manitoba *Free Press*, 2 April 1894.

229 *Nor'Wester*, 5 July 1894.

230 *Nor'Wester*, 31 July 1894. For more on Johnston and Joslin's visit to Fort William, see Hatton, "Headlocks at the Lakehead," 32–36.

231 A wrestling and boxing card held at Winnipeg's Bijou Theatre on 17 May was poorly attended and considered a financial failure for the management. See Manitoba *Free Press*, 18 May 1894, 19 May 1894.

232 In the 1894 Winnipeg *Henderson's Directory*, Johnston is listed as the instructor at the Winnipeg Gymnasium, residing at 798 Main Street. However, he does not appear in subsequent city directories. Johnston did return to the city several years later and opened an "athletic room," along with pugilist and wrestler Arthur Stemyer, where lessons were taught in boxing and gymnastics. However, Johnston no longer played a significant role in wrestling and had apparently abandoned his business partnership with Stemyer by late 1901. See Manitoba *Free Press*, 13 January 1900, 13 February 1900, 6 December 1901.

233 For newspaper challenges following the summer of 1894, see, for example, Manitoba *Free Press*, 22 June 1895. Joslin wrestled three matches in association with the Winnipeg Industrial and Agricultural Exhibition between 19 and 23 July 1895. The first bout, against W.B. Faulkner of California, resulted in a draw. Four days later Joslin defeated Faulkner, who acted as a substitute when a grappler named McCurdy failed to appear, followed by Andrew Crystal, the self-professed "champion of America." Controversy arose over the incident when claims made by Joslin that McCurdy was ill and had retired in favour of Faulkner proved to be untrue. Opinion circulated that Joslin had taken advantage of McCurdy's absence to "steal a match on him." Joslin later professed his innocence. See Manitoba *Free Press*, 21 June 1895, 20 July 1895, 23 July 1895, 24 July 1895.

CHAPTER 2: MANITOBA'S PROS

1 In July 1896, for example, American wrestler Frank S. Lewis, who passed through Winnipeg after wrestling on the Pacific coast, expressed his desire to meet any wrestler in Manitoba in either a handicap match or on even terms. No wrestler appears to have taken up his offer. W.H. West announced his willingness to meet any wrestler in the province weighing 154 pounds in either a catch-as-catch-can or a Greco-Roman bout for a purse and side bet exceeding $100 on 22 August 1898. See Manitoba *Free Press*, 7 July 1896; *Nor-Wester*, 7 July 1896; and Manitoba *Free Press*, 22 August 1898, respectively.

2 By the summer of 1898, boxing and wrestling matches were staged roughly every two weeks in Dawson City at facilities such as the Monte Carlo saloon and Trivoli Theatre. By the beginning of 1899, boxing and wrestling bouts were weekly features in the city, and pugilists such as Kid Williams and Pat Rooney and grapplers such as Ben Trennaman were making regular public appearances. In 1901, future world heavyweight wrestling champion Frank Gotch, under the *nom de guerre* Frank Kennedy, wrestled a series of matches in Dawson City against Ole Marsh and Colonel J.H. McLaughlin in addition to an unsuccessful turn in the boxing ring against Frank "Paddy" Slavin. For accounts of boxing and wrestling matches in Dawson City, see, for example, Klondike *Nugget*, 4 July 1898, 30 July 1898, 3 August 1898, 13 August 1898, 26 August 1898, 15 September 1898, 20 January 1899, 27 January 1899, 29 January 1899; and Yukon *Sun*, 17 January 1899, 20

January 1899. Various sources provide accounts of Gotch's activities in the Yukon Territory. For the most accurate retelling, see Hewitt, *Catch Wrestling*, 13–34. See also Pierre Berton's account of wrestling and boxing matches in *Klondike: The Last Great Gold Rush, 1896–1899* (Toronto: McClelland and Stewart, 1986), 363–65.

3   For an account of McKeown's activities in the Yukon Territory, see Manitoba *Free Press*, 26 October 1900.

4   James A. Jackson, *The Centennial History of Manitoba* (Toronto: McClelland and Stewart, 1970), 158.

5   For use of the phrase "an explosion of activity" in connection with Manitoba sports after the turn of the century, see, for example, Mott, "Manly Sports," 173, 174, 226. For a list of new sports introduced during this period, see 175.

6   See, for example, James H. Smart, *Smart's Manual of Free Gymnastic and Dumb-Bell Exercises* (Cincinnati: Wilson, Hinkle and Company, 1863), 3; William Blaikie, *How to Get Strong and How to Stay So* (New York: Harper and Brothers Publishers, 1879), 5–6, 14–16; J.J. Miller, *Physical Culture* (London: John Leng and Company, c. 1908), 2; Luther Gulick, *Spalding's Athletic Library No. 1: Muscle Building* (London: Renwick of Otley, 1916), 5; and Hackenschmidt, *The Way to Live*, 10, 14. For a further discussion of ideas related to physical degeneracy prior to the First World War, see Howell, *Northern Sandlots*, 103–04.

7   Portage la Prairie *Weekly Review*, 7 August 1907.

8   Manitoba *Free Press*, 7 November 1908.

9   Archives of Manitoba, MG9 A95-1, Edward Ernest Best Collection, "Memoirs of a School Inspector, 1888–1932—Revised," 108.

10   Gail Bederman, *Manliness and Civilization: A Cultural History of Gender and Race in the United States, 1880–1917* (Chicago: University of Chicago Press, 1995), 15; Morrow and Wamsley, *Sport in Canada*, 166.

11   Mark Moss, *Manliness and Militarism: Educating Young Boys in Ontario for War* (Don Mills, ON: Oxford University Press, 2001), 57.

12   Bernarr MacFadden, *Muscular Power and Beauty* (New York: Physical Culture Publishing Company, 1902), 9.

13   Ibid., 13.

14   Ibid., 15, 16.

15   Ibid., 14; G. Mercer Adam, ed., *Sandow's System of Physical Training* (London: Gale and Polden, 1894), 2.

16   Howell, *Blood, Sweat, and Cheers*, 107.

17   David L. Chapman, *Sandow the Magnificent* (Urbana: University of Illinois Press, 1994), 4; Adam, *Sandow's System*, 12.

18   Lindaman, "Wrestling's Hold," 782. For more on Sandow's rise to international fame and his influence on ideas of the male form, see Chapman, *Sandow the Magnificent*, especially Chapters 3–6; and John F. Kasson, *Houdini, Tarzan, and the Perfect Man: The White Male Body and the Challenge of Modernity in America* (New York: Hill and Wang, 2001), Chapter 1.

19   See, for example, Winnipeg *Telegram*, 6 May 1903, 9 November 1901; *Daily Nor'Wester*, 16 May 1894; Minnedosa *Tribune*, 19 March 1903; and Manitoba *Free Press*, 30 August 1904.

20   For a photo of a sandal-clad Santell exhibiting his muscular development, see Manitoba *Free Press*, 29 March 1906.

21   Manitoba *Free Press*, 6 July 1903.

22   Manitoba *Free Press*, 14 November 1908.

23 For uses of the moniker, see, for example, Manitoba *Free Press*, 21 April 1906, 5 February 1910; and Winnipeg *Telegram*, 7 February 1910.

24 Manitoba *Free Press*, 21 April 1906.

25 Manitoba *Free Press*, 21 September 1906.

26 The phrase "magnificent specimen of manhood" was used in reference to wrestlers such as Hume Duval, Young Tom Sharkey (Victor McLaglen), Chris Person, Jack Taylor, and B.F. Roller. Similarly, "splendid specimen of manhood" accompanied descriptions of St. Boniface wrestler Pete Menard and Winnipeg's Knute Hoel. See, respectively, Manitoba *Free Press*, 20 July 1907; Winnipeg *Tribune*, 17 April 1913, 29 January 1909; and Manitoba *Free Press*, 30 November 1907, 18 February 1909.

27 Winnipeg *Telegram*, 10 March 1911.

28 Manitoba *Free Press*, 4 September 1911, 1 September 1911, 6 December 1913, 9 December 1913, 11 December 1913, 12 December 1913; Winnipeg *Telegram*, 29 November 1913; and Winnipeg *Tribune*, 12 December 1913.

29 On the value of self-denial in Protestant culture, see Steven J. Overman, *The Influence of the Protestant Ethic on Sport and Recreation* (Suffolk: Ipswich Book Company, 1997), 202–03.

30 Manitoba *Free Press*, 21 September 1906; Burns, quoted in Halm, *The Life Work of Farmer Burns*, 48.

31 W. Joseph Campbell, "1897 American Journalism's Exceptional Year," *Journalism History* 29, 4 (2004), http://academic2.american.edu/~wjc/exceptyear1.htm.

32 The first known newspaper photo of a wrestler in Manitoba, featuring Mont, "The U.S. Giant," appeared in Manitoba *Free Press* on 6 May 1902.

33 For details concerning Hackenschmidt's earliest forays into professional wrestling, see *The Way to Live*, 123. His victory over Jenkins was well covered by daily newspapers throughout North America, including those in Manitoba. See Manitoba *Free Press*, 5 May 1905; and Winnipeg *Telegram*, 5 May 1905.

34 Within the Canadian context, see Montreal *Gazette*, 11 May 1905, for a proposed lecture in Montreal by Hackenschmidt on "physical culture ... giving explanations on how to develop the different muscles and how to diet." For a detailed assessment of Hackenschmidt's philosophy on physical culture, see Terry Todd, "Muscles, Memory, and George Hackenschmidt," *Iron Game History* 2, 3 (1992): 10–15.

35 Photographs of Hackenschmidt appeared many times in Manitoba newspapers, the most impressive of which was a collage that appeared in the Manitoba *Free Press* on 17 December 1910. See also Manitoba *Free Press*, 21 January 1910, 2 September 1911.

36 For examples of photographs featuring professional wrestlers posed with their hands behind their backs, see *Le Manitoba*, 19 November 1913; Manitoba *Free Press*, 17 August 1910, 19 November 1910; Winnipeg *Telegram*, 16 December 1909; and Winnipeg *Tribune*, 4 June 1909, 5 May 1910, 7 February 1911. For photographs depicting wrestlers with their arms crossed on their chests, see Manitoba *Free Press*, 13 November 1911, 21 December 1911; Winnipeg *Telegram*, 13 December 1907; and Winnipeg *Tribune*, 18 December 1907, 20 April 1912, 22 June 1912, 26 June 1912.

37 See Hackenschmidt, *The Way to Live*, 108, 112, 118–19, 161; Arthur Saxon, *The Development of Physical Power* (reprinted, Farmington, MI: William F. Hinbern, 1997), 112, 115, 117; and Edmond Desbonnet, *Les rois de la lutte* (Paris: Berger-Levrault et Cie, 1910), 90, 91, 111, 117, 177, 181.

38 Roberta J. Park, "Muscles, Symmetry, and Action: 'Do You Measure Up?' Defining Masculinity in Britain and America from the 1860s to the Early 1900s," *International Journal of the History of Sport* 24, 12 (2007): 1616–18.

39 Howell, *Northern Sandlots*, 100; Howell, *Blood, Sweat, and Cheers*, 109.

40 Manitoba *Free Press*, 20 April 1912.

41 Quoted in Manitoba *Free Press*, 25 March 1908. Simpson was a well-known local wrestler and referee for wrestling bouts who appeared throughout Manitoba, as well as in Kenora, during 1907 and 1908.

42 Ibid.

43 Manitoba *Free Press*, 2 April 1908.

44 See, for example, Manitoba *Free Press*, 2 September 1911, 4 September 1911.

45 See Archives of Manitoba, L.B. Foote Collection 1217-1, Negative 2197, and Archives of Manitoba, L.B. Foote Collection 1201, Negative 20837, for photos taken on Lake Winnipeg and at Winnipeg Beach in 1912 and 1915, respectively. The illustrations for men's bathing suits available for purchase through the Eaton's catalogue during the first decade of the twentieth century suggest that modesty had greater commercial appeal than exhibitionism. In 1901, suits were available with tops that not only covered the upper portion of the arm but also had hems that extended down to the upper thigh. A decade later similar attire was still for sale, though one of the six suits listed in the catalogue was of the sleeveless variety. See the 1901 and 1911 editions of the *Timothy Eaton's Spring-Summer Catalogue*.

46 The absence of direct documentation related to men patronizing wrestling matches for erotic purposes does not necessarily indicate that such activities did not take place, since by necessity they would have been covert. As demonstrated by Maria Wyke's analysis of "beefcake" bodybuilding literature from the 1950s and 1960s, photographers were often prosecuted for producing what censors considered to be obscene material. One method of circumventing legal troubles was to ensure that pictures appearing in magazines were accompanied by pseudo-Greek and Roman imagery. Appealing to "higher" culture meant that, as Wyke notes, "a man's body could now be looked at, admired, and even desired safely, without appearing to exceed the constraints imposed by state censorship." It is probable, therefore, that wrestling matches in Manitoba provided a similar "cover" for some segments of the community. See Maria Wyke, "Herculean Muscle! The Classicizing Rhetoric of Bodybuilding," *Arion* 4, 3 (1997): 61.

47 For a more general discussion of the topic in the Canadian west, see Lyle Dick, "The Queer Frontier: Male Same-Sex Experience in Canada's Western Settlement Era," *Journal of Canadian Studies* 48, 1 (2014): 1548.

48 Wamsley and Whitson, "Celebrating Violent Masculinities," 421.

49 Manitoba *Free Press*, 26 October 1907, 30 November 1907, 11 March 1910, 2 December 1913; and Winnipeg *Telegram*, 27 January 1906.

50 Manitoba *Free Press*, 27 June 1908, 23 November 1907, 27 June 1910, 22 November 1910.

51 Manitoba *Free Press*, 20 October 1905, 27 November 1907.

52 Manitoba *Free Press*, 7 November 1907, 30 November 1907, 21 December 1907.

53 Manitoba *Free Press*, 25 September 1909.

54 Winnipeg *Telegram*, 1 February 1906; Manitoba *Free Press*, 27 February 1908. Mace appeared on professional mats many times in Manitoba and Kenora during 1907 and 1908 and claimed the Manitoba lightweight championship.

55 Manitoba *Free Press*, 2 December 1913.

56 For a discussion of the same feature in Manitoba hockey during the late nineteenth century and early twentieth century, see Morris Mott, "Flawed Games, Splendid Ceremonies: Hockey Matches of the Winnipeg Vics, 1890–1903," *Prairie Forum* 10, 1 (1985): 178–79.

57 Ibid., 180; Howell, *Northern Sandlots*, 157; Kidd, *The Struggle for Canadian Sport*, 189.

58 Lou Thesz, *Hooker: An Authentic Wrestler's Adventures inside the Bizarre World of Professional Wrestling* (Norfolk, VA: By the Author, 1995), 8.

59 Winnipeg *Free Press*, 2 November 1956. Gustafson's place of birth is provided on his 28 April 1915 Attestation Paper, Library and Archives Canada, RG 150, Accession 1992-93/166, Box 3893–35.

60 Gustafson is listed as an employee of N. Nelson in the 1910 Winnipeg *Henderson's Directory*. Nicholas Nelson owned the Nelson Sash and Door Manufacturing Company. There are difficulties in ascertaining exactly when Gustafson began his own business. However, in the 1911 Canadian Census, Manitoba, Winnipeg District, Winnipeg Sub-District, Enumeration District 46, 33, his occupation is listed as a "manager" and "employer," suggesting that he embarked on his career as a hotelier either during late 1910 or in 1911. According to the 1914 *Henderson's Directory*, Gustafson was manager of the Oberon Club, and his Attestation Paper from a year later lists him as a hotel proprietor.

61 Winnipeg *Telegram*, 5 October 1907; Manitoba *Free Press*, 5 October 1907.

62 Swedish Canadian fans were present at Gustafson's first wrestling match in Winnipeg, and the *Free Press* noted on 13 November 1907 that Gustafson had a "large following" among the local Swedish population.

63 For commentary on Gustafson's reputation among the Swedish population in Winnipeg, see, for example, Manitoba *Free Press*, 21 November 1909.

64 On the basis of his victory over Pete Menard on 29 November 1907, Gustafson claimed the middleweight title of Manitoba. Nearly two years later, billed as the "Champion of Western Canada," he defeated Montreal's George LePage, the "Champion of Eastern Canada," on 26 November 1909, in a match advertised as "For the Middleweight Championship of Canada." See Manitoba *Free Press*, 30 November 1907; Winnipeg *Telegram*, 26 November 1909; and Manitoba *Free Press*, 27 November 1909.

65 For terms referring to Gustafson, see, for example, Manitoba *Free Press*, 10 February 1910, 21 March 1910, 12 April 1910, 28 January 1911. A caption accompanying a photo of Gustafson in the 26 February 1910 Manitoba *Free Press* labelled him "Winnipeg's Favorite Wrestler."

66 For Sundberg's place and date of birth, see his Attestation Paper, Library and Archives Canada, RG 150, Accession 1992-93/166, Box 9425–24. Details concerning his first match in Winnipeg can be found in Manitoba *Free Press*, 16 November 1907.

67 Winnipeg *Henderson's Directory* 1908, 1910. See also his Attestation Paper concerning his occupation. Curiously, the 1911 Canadian Census, Manitoba, Winnipeg District, Winnipeg Sub-District, Enumeration District 46, 33, lists Sundberg's ethnicity as Icelandic. All other sources, however, give his ethnicity as Swedish.

68 A brief overview of Sundberg's wrestling record to date was also provided by Manitoba *Free Press*, 1 February 1910.

69 Winnipeg *Telegram*, 9 February 1910.

70 See Manitoba *Free Press*, 21 May 1910; and the 1911 Canadian Census, Manitoba, Winnipeg District, Winnipeg Sub-District, Enumeration District 37, 1.

71 For details of their matches, see Manitoba *Free Press*, 22 November 1910, 6 April 1912; and Winnipeg *Telegram*, 24 May 1912.

72 For details of Stewart's match with Simmons, see Manitoba *Free Press*, 15 January 1913; and Winnipeg *Tribune*, 15 January 1913. Concerning Stewart's match with Forbes, see Manitoba *Free Press*, 4 March 1914. See Manitoba *Free Press*, 21 February 1914, for commentary on Stewart's local popularity.

73 Reg Skene, "C.P. Walker and the Business of Theatre: Merchandizing Entertainment in a Continental Context," in *The Political Economy of Manitoba*, ed. James Silver and Jeremy Hull (Regina: Canadian Plains Research Center, 1990), 144; *Winnipeg Real Estate News*, 4 March 1994; Stuart, *The History of Prairie Theatre*, 32.

74 Tremblay won the world's lightweight professional wrestling title on the basis of victories over George Bothner in Montreal and Brooklyn, New York. On Tremblay's victories over Bothner and his claim to the *Police Gazette* title, see, respectively, Montreal *Gazette*, 6 April 1907, 10 October 1908, 28 November 1908; and Manitoba *Free Press*, 2 May 1910. According to one account, Miller began his wrestling career after coming to the attention of George A. Barton, sports editor for the Minneapolis *Daily News*, in 1906. Miller, then working at the coal docks in Duluth, began his training as a boxer, but soon after he switched to wrestling. Arthur A. Moeller, who acted as his manager, also claimed credit for discovering the welterweight grappler. Regardless of the veracity of either claim, by the time Miller first appeared in Winnipeg in 1910, he was billed as the world's welterweight champion. See George A. Barton, *My Lifetime in Sports* (Minneapolis: Lund Press, 1957), 10–11; Manitoba *Free Press*, 17 January 1914; and Winnipeg *Tribune*, 5 May 1910.

75 Manitoba *Free Press*, 8 March 1911; Winnipeg *Telegram*, 8 March 1911.

76 Manitoba *Free Press*, 8 March 1911.

77 Winnipeg *Telegram*, 10 March 1911.

78 Manitoba *Free Press*, 26 March 1908, 17 June 1908.

79 Souris *Plaindealer*, 30 October 1908.

80 Manitoba *Free Press*, 17 June 1908; Souris *Plaindealer*, 30 October 1908.

81 See, for example, Minnedosa *Tribune*, 3 March 1910, 4 August 1910.

82 In Portage la Prairie, for example, little professional wrestling appears to have occurred during this period. Nevertheless, the local newspaper carried reports of various matches staged in Winnipeg. See Portage la Prairie *Weekly Review*, 13 January 1909, 8 June 1910, 15 March 1911, 10 December 1913.

83 Wamsley and Whitson, "Celebrating Violent Masculinities," 420.

84 Burstyn, *Rites of Men*, 68, 72.

85 Rotundo, *American Manhood*, 234, 236; Howell, *Blood, Sweat, and Cheers*, 33; Moss, *Manliness and Militarism*, 127.

86 Manitoba *Free Press*, 22 March 1910. For professional *Police Gazette* catch-as-catch-can rules, see George Bothner, *Scientific Wrestling* (New York: Richard K. Fox Publishing Company, 1912), 11–13.

87 Manitoba *Free Press*, 22 November 1904; Souris *Plaindealer*, 9 October 1908.

88 Manitoba *Free Press*, 4 June 1910.

89 Manitoba *Free Press*, 16 March 1910. Overman similarly notes the "loose" interpretation of rules common in wrestling matches in *The Influence of the Protestant Ethic*, 141.

90 Manitoba *Free Press*, 10 March 1911.

91 Winnipeg *Telegram*, 10 March 1911.

92 Manitoba *Free Press*, 10 March 1911.

93 Winnipeg *Tribune*, 10 March 1911.

94 Despite a generally favourable reception, not all Winnipeg fans received Gotch warmly. Many of those present were supporters of Hackenschmidt and greeted the American grappler with "hisses and booing" when he made his appearance. Their reactions were undoubtedly the results of accusations made by the "Russian Lion" that the Iowan had employed unfair tactics in their first encounter. Concerning local reactions to Gotch, see Manitoba *Free Press*, 10 March 1911.

95 Winnipeg *Telegram*, 10 March 1911.

96 Manitoba *Free Press*, 16 March 1910, 14 May 1910; Winnipeg *Tribune*, 28 February 1910.

97   See, respectively, Manitoba *Free Press*, 18 March 1909; Winnipeg *Tribune*, 18 March 1909; Manitoba *Free Press*, 5 April 1909; Winnipeg *Telegram*, 5 April 1909; and Manitoba *Free Press*, 18 December 1907, 2 April 1908, 17 September 1910, 27 February 1908, 21 February 1907, 20 February 1908, 11 July 1911.

98   Mott, "Manly Sports," 133–34; Morrow and Wamsley, *Sport in Canada*, 48–50.

99   Winnipeg *Telegram*, 31 August 1906, 5 October 1907. In the latter instance, Gustafson's debut in Winnipeg, the Swedish grappler refused to continue after six minutes of wrestling, partly because of construction of the mat, which consisted of a rug spread over a bale of hay.

100 Leyshon, *Of Mats and Men*, 49.

101 Manitoba *Free Press*, 26 October 1910.

102 Manitoba *Free Press*, 11 July 1911. See also Peter Gay, *The Cultivation of Hatred: The Bourgeois Experience, Victoria to Freud Volume III* (New York: W.W. Norton and Company, 1993), 236.

103 Winnipeg *Tribune*, 7 March 1911.

104 Ibid.

105 Manitoba *Free Press*, 10 March 1911; Winnipeg *Telegram*, 10 March 1911; Winnipeg *Tribune*, 10 March 1911.

106 Quoted in Manitoba *Free Press*, 11 March 1911.

107 Ibid.

108 Cosentino, "A History of the Concept of Professionalism," 255.

109 Happyland Park, constructed by the American Park Company and managed by W.O. Edmunds, was built on thirty-two acres of land in Winnipeg's west end, south of Portage Avenue in the area between Aubrey and Dominion Streets. Opened in May 1906, it boasted various rides, including a circular swing eighty feet tall, ferris wheel, mirror gallery, miniature railway, merry-go-round, and roller coaster, in addition to a restaurant, Japanese tea garden, athletic grounds, and a grandstand capable of holding 3,000 people. For more on Happyland's rise and fall as a popular Winnipeg recreational attraction, see Edith Paterson's articles in Winnipeg *Free Press*, 1 June 1974 and 8 June 1974, as well as Bruce Cherney, "Happyland: Winnipeg's 'Mammoth Amusement Park' First Opened on 23 May 1906," http://www.winnipegrealtors.ca/editorials.aspx?id=43. For ads pertaining to Duval's various strongman acts and wrestling challenges at Happyland during the summer of 1907, see, for example, Manitoba *Free Press*, 29 May 1907; Winnipeg *Telegram*, 3 June 1907, 25 June 1907; and Winnipeg *Voice*, 7 June 1907.

110 In their first match, staged on 20 December 1907, Gustafson won as a result of a handicap, Duval being unable to secure three falls in one hour. Neither man secured any fall. Their second match, held on 17 March 1909, ended prematurely when an attending physician refused to allow Gustafson to continue as a result of an ear injury. Both men had secured one fall by that point. See Manitoba *Free Press*, 21 December 1907; and Winnipeg *Tribune*, 18 March 1909.

111 Both the Manitoba *Free Press* and the Winnipeg *Tribune* used the word *fiasco* to describe the match in their headlines. The Winnipeg *Telegram* did not explicitly use the term, but the article's general tenor suggests the same conclusion. Likewise, the Winnipeg *Voice*, on 11 June 1909, stated that the audience "got little or nothing for their money" and that "the entertainment was dependent upon a very poor class of sports."

112 Winnipeg *Tribune*, 9 June 1909; Winnipeg *Telegram*, 9 June 1909.

113 Winnipeg *Tribune*, 9 June 1909. Reports by all three Winnipeg dailies described the events surrounding the match in a similar fashion.

114 Ibid.

115 Quoted in Manitoba *Free Press*, 10 June 1909.

116 "Spectator," Manitoba *Free Press*, 11 June 1909.

117 Quoted in Manitoba *Free Press*, 12 June 1909.

118 Ibid.

119 Concerning side bets, see Manitoba *Free Press*, 1 February 1906, 3 February 1906, 8 February 1906.

120 Manitoba *Free Press*, 15 February 1908.

121 Quoted in Manitoba *Free Press*, 22 February 1906.

122 Quoted in Manitoba *Free Press*, 5 March 1906. Moth, despite his purported desire for clean athletic competition, did not escape similar controversy himself. On 25 April 1902, the Marshfield, Wisconsin, *Times* reported that Moth, having "worked Milwaukee so persistently that he found it advisable to seek other pastures," was now wrestling and boxing in other centres under assumed names such as Charles Wright and W.H. West. The paper condemned his practices and those of other professional wrestlers: "Wrestling has been irretrievably damaged by faking." See http://wrestlingperspective.com/working/1902/marti0425.html.

123 Manitoba *Free Press*, 1 October 1907; Winnipeg *Telegram*, 1 October 1907; Winnipeg *Tribune*, 1 October 1907.

124 Winnipeg *Tribune*, 3 October 1907.

125 Winnipeg *Telegram*, 5 October 1907; Manitoba *Free Press*, 5 October 1907.

126 Manitoba *Free Press*, 5 October 1907.

127 Manitoba *Free Press*, 24 October 1907.

128 Manitoba *Free Press*, 19 October 1907.

129 Manitoba *Free Press*, 26 October 1907.

130 Winnipeg *Telegram*, 14 December 1907. Similar accusations were made against Dalager during a match in Souris in October 1908. His opponent, Mack Moir, complained to the referee that Dalager "had drugs in his hair that were affecting him prejudicially." In this instance, the referee saw no evidence to substantiate the claim. See Souris *Plaindealer*, 9 October 1908.

131 Manitoba *Free Press*, 16 December 1907.

132 Manitoba *Free Press*, 26 March 1908.

133 Manitoba *Free Press*, 3 April 1909.

134 Quoted in Manitoba *Free Press*, 3 April 1909.

135 Victor McLaglen, like his brother Fred, lived in Winnipeg and was active in the local wrestling scene. See C. Nathan Hatton, "Winnipeg's 'Quiet' Man: The Early Public Life of Film Star Victor McLaglen," *Manitoba History* 67 (2012): 22–28.

136 Winnipeg Police Museum, Police Commission Books; Winnipeg *Henderson's Directory* 1908.

137 See Manitoba *Free Press*, 22 October 1908 and 6 August 1910, concerning the employment of Fred McLaglen at the Savoy Hotel. As a professional, his most well-publicized wrestling bout was against Knute Hoel. It was described as a "very tame" contest by the Winnipeg *Telegram* since Hoel was forced to withdraw because of an injury after losing the first fall. See Manitoba *Free Press*, 27 November 1908; and Winnipeg *Telegram*, 5 April 1909. Concerning McLaglen's boxing career in Manitoba, see, for example, the reports pertaining to his January 1910 fight in Dauphin against Walter Adams for the "Heavyweight Championship of Manitoba" in Dauphin *Herald*, 27 January 1910; and Dauphin *Press*, 27 January 1910. See also the reports related to his match against Tony Caponi in Winnipeg four months later, detailed in Manitoba *Free Press*, 17 May 1910; Winnipeg *Tribune*, 17 May 1910; and Winnipeg *Telegram*, 17 May 1910.

138 Manitoba *Free Press*, 22 October 1908.

139 Court proceedings on the case, which ran between 14 November and 2 December, were covered in copious detail by the Manitoba *Free Press*. Concerning the charges brought against John W.

Dafoe, see Archives of Manitoba, Police Court Winnipeg, ATG0030, GR 651, M1219, Roll 10, no. 22235, 4 November 1908. See also, for reports on the trial, Manitoba *Free Press*, 25 November 1908, 28 November 1908, 30 November 1908, 1 December 1908, 2 December 1908, 3 December 1908.

140 Manitoba *Free Press*, 7 July 1910, 9 December 1910.

141 Manitoba *Free Press*, 21 June 1910, 30 June 1910.

142 Concerning dismissed assault charges brought against McLaglen, see Archives of Manitoba, Police Court Winnipeg, ATG0030, GR 651, M1219, Roll 10, no. 2415, 6 July 1909; no. 31043, 9 December 1909; no. 32462, 17 February 1910; and Roll 11, no. 39911, 18 November 1910. On 15 December 1910, McLaglen was required to pay a fine of five dollars, plus court costs, after he struck a man named Alex M. Young twice in the face outside the Savoy Hotel. Several witnesses testified on McLaglen's behalf, stating that Young had called him foul names. See Archives of Manitoba, Police Court Winnipeg, ATG0030, GR 651, M1220, Roll 10, no. 40529, 15 December 1910; and Manitoba *Free Press*, 16 December 1910.

143 Winnipeg *Telegram*, 6 February 1911.

144 Ibid. Further details pertaining to the case can be found in Manitoba *Free Press*, 6 February 1911; and Winnipeg *Tribune*, 6 February 1911.

145 Archives of Manitoba, Police Court Winnipeg, ATG0030, GR 651, M1219, Roll 10, no. 27750, 30 July 1909; and M1220, Roll 11, no. 37496, 1 September 1910. For details on the latter case, see Manitoba *Free Press*, 2 September 1910.

146 See Archives of Manitoba, Police Court Winnipeg, ATG0030, GR 651, M1221, Roll 12, no. 61361; no. 61402, 3 August 1912; and Winnipeg *Tribune*, 5 August 1912.

147 See Winnipeg City Archives, City of Winnipeg Minutes of Council, 121, 181; Winnipeg City Archives, City of Winnipeg Bylaws 1908, 74; and Winnipeg City Archives, City of Winnipeg Municipal Manual 1909, 72.

148 Winnipeg *Telegram*, 1 April 1908. The *Free Press* incorrectly reported on 1 April that both boxing and wrestling matches had been stopped in the city, but action had been taken to prohibit only the former.

149 In early May 1909, the Town of Portage la Prairie Council voted to disallow a Victoria Day boxing contest featuring Hume Duval. See Manitoba *Free Press*, 6 May 1909.

150 Under the Criminal Code of Canada, a prize fight was defined as "an encounter or fight with fists or hands, between two persons who have met for such purpose by previous arrangement made by or for them." Such a broad definition seems to apply to any boxing encounter. In general, however, a prize fight was perceived to be distinct from a boxing match insofar as the former carried the intention to inflict sufficient harm on an opponent to incapacitate him from either fatigue or injury, whereas the latter was merely considered to be an exhibition of skill. In reality, it was difficult to discern the difference between them, and many professed boxing matches in Manitoba ended in knockouts or some other form of physical incapacitation. Periodically, fighters were arrested prior to their matches as a precaution against their encounters escalating into prize fights. On 14 January 1911, pugilists "Young" Peter Jackson and John Willie were taken into police custody for being "about to engage in a prize fight." Jackson was released on a $1,000 peace bond, and his opponent, having already posted a bond the year earlier, was not required to rebond. Their match went on as scheduled, and both men gave "a good exposition of the art." For the original act regulating prize fighting, which received royal assent on 21 March 1881, see "Chapter 30: An Act Respecting Prize Fighting," in *Orders in Council, Proclamations, and Regulations Having Force of Law in the Dominion of Canada Issued during the Years 1880 and 1881* (Ottawa: Queen's Printer, 1881), 174. Concerning the aforementioned arrests, see Archives of Manitoba, Police Court Winnipeg, ATG0030, GR 651, N1220, Roll 11, no. 41221, 14 January 1911; and Manitoba *Free Press*, 16 January 1911, 17 January 1911, 4 July 1913.

151 Manitoba *Free Press*, 4 July 1913. The Pelkey-McCarty incident received extensive newspaper coverage throughout North America. For detailed synopsis and analysis, see Murray Greig, *Goin' the Distance: Canada's Boxing Heritage* (Toronto: Macmillan Canada, 1996), 44–52; and Wamsley and Whitson, "Celebrating Violent Masculinities," 419–31.

152 Manitoba *Free Press*, 3 December 1913.

153 Winnipeg *Tribune*, 22 January 1913.

154 Winnipeg *Telegram*, 17 December 1909.

155 Manitoba *Free Press*, 18 November 1913.

156 Manitoba *Free Press*, 27 November 1913.

157 Winnipeg *Telegram*, 1 December 1913.

158 Manitoba *Free Press*, 27 November 1913, 28 November 1913.

159 Winnipeg *Tribune*, 23 April 1912.

160 With the time approaching midnight and both Suter and Gustafson visibly tiring, spectators began to call for a draw. After five minutes of virtual inactivity, referee R. Sutherland ended the match, and "there were few objections" expressed to his decision by those present. See Manitoba *Free Press*, 22 December 1911.

161 Manitoba *Free Press*, 6 April 1912.

162 Winnipeg *Tribune*, 17 April 1912.

163 Winnipeg *Tribune*, 23 April 1912.

164 Manitoba *Free Press*, 21 May 1912, 23 May 1912; Winnipeg *Telegram*, 23 May 1912.

165 Manitoba *Free Press*, 19 May 1910; Winnipeg *Tribune*, 19 May 1910.

166 Winnipeg *Telegram*, 19 May 1910.

167 Mott, "Manly Sports," 244–45; Manitoba *Free Press*, 20 May 1910, 25 March 1911, 24 August 1912, 22 July 1914.

168 Frank Cosentino, "A History of the Concept of Professionalism in Canadian Sport," in *Proceedings from the Third Canadian Symposium on the History of Sport and Physical Education, 18–21 August 1974* (Halifax: Dalhousie University, 1974), 9. Cosentino, "A History of the Concept of Professionalism," 177, 205.

169 Manitoba *Free Press*, 26 February 1910, 28 January 1911.

170 Winnipeg *Tribune*, 19 May 1910.

171 Winnipeg *Tribune*, 17 December 1910.

172 Winnipeg *Tribune*, 22 January 1913.

173 Ibid.

174 Manitoba *Free Press*, 20 May 1910.

CHAPTER 3: WRESTLING WITH ETHNICITY

1 Manitoba *Free Press*, 19 June 1901; Winnipeg *Tribune*, 19 June 1901.

2 Morton, *Manitoba*, 264; Bellan, *Winnipeg First Century*, 59, 62; Thompson, *Forging*, 72.

3 Hall, *Clifford Sifton Volume One*, 123.

4 Bellan, *Winnipeg First Century*, 63; Hall, *Clifford Sifton Volume One*, 261–65; Hall, *Clifford Sifton Volume Two*, 68.

5 Clifford Sifton, "The Immigrants Canada Wants," *Maclean's*, 1 April 1922.

6   Marvin McInnis, "Migration," in *Historical Atlas of Canada Volume III*, Plate 27.

7   W. Peter Ward, "Population Growth in Western Canada, 1901–1971," in *The Developing West*, 159.

8   Bellan, *Winnipeg First Century*, 56.

9   Artibise, *Winnipeg*, 142.

10   Coates and McGuinness, *Manitoba*, 62, 65.

11   Daniel J. Hiebert, "Winnipeg: A Divided City," in *Historical Atlas of Canada Volume III*, Plate 31.

12   Artibise, *Winnipeg*, 196.

13   Ibid., 197–98.

14   Donald Avery, *Reluctant Host: Canada's Response to Immigrant Workers, 1896–1994* (Toronto: McClelland and Stewart, 1995), 20.

15   Paul Phillips, "The Prairie Urban System, 1911–1961: Specialization and Change," in *Town and City: Aspects of Western Canadian Urban Development*, ed. Alan Artibise (Regina: Canadian Plains Research Center, 1981), 11–13. For a discussion of the manufacturing industries that appeared in Winnipeg during this time, see Bellan, *Winnipeg First Century*, 76–77.

16   Avery, *Reluctant Host*, 21; Friesen, *The Canadian Prairies*, 246–47; Thompson, *Forging*, 77.

17   Artibise, *Winnipeg*, 186; David Jay Bercuson, *Confrontation at Winnipeg: Labour, Industrial Relations, and General Strike* (Montreal: McGill-Queen's University Press, 1974), 4; Coates and McGuinness, *Manitoba*, 75.

18   Artibise, *Winnipeg*, 186.

19   For an excellent visual representation of Winnipeg's growing ethnic diversity and the spatial separation that accompanied it, see Hiebert, "Winnipeg."

20   Les Wawrow, "Nativism in English Canada: Attitudes of Anglo-Saxons to the Influx of 1896–1914 Immigration," in *From Prairies to Cities: Papers on the Poles in Canada*, ed. Benedykt Heydenkorn (Toronto: Canadian-Polish Research Institute, 1975), 73, 75.

21   Elisabeth B. Mitchell, *In Western Canada before the War: Impressions of Early Twentieth Century Prairie Communities* (Saskatoon: Western Producer Prairie Books, 1981), 184; Doug Smith, *Let Us Rise! A History of the Manitoba Labour Movement* (Winnipeg: Public Press, 1985), 21.

22   Thompson, *Forging*, 76, 77. See, for example, "The Menace of Anti-Canadian Nationalism," *Manitoba Free Press*, 29 July 1914.

23   Mitchell, *In Western Canada*, 177.

24   Artibise, *Winnipeg*, 196.

25   One notable exception in this regard, albeit from a later period, concerns the Manitoba Falcons hockey team, which won Canada's first gold medal at the 1920 Olympic Games in Antwerp. The Falcons' squad was composed almost entirely of Icelandic Canadian players.

26   See, for example, Manitoba *Free Press*, 2 May 1898, 6 June 1898, and 27 June 1898; and *Nor'Wester*, 21 March 1898, 5 May 1898, and 19 May 1898.

27   Graham Noble provides an excellent examination of the original "Terrible Turk's" North American tour and the racist legends that developed surrounding his demise in "The Life and Death of the Terrible Turk," *Journal of Manly Arts* 1 (2001), http://ejmas.com/jmanly/articles/2001/jmanlyart_noble_0501.htm. Hali Adali, variously termed "The Sultan's Lion" and the "Lion of Constantinople," was one of the Turkish wrestlers who arrived in North America shortly after Youssouf's demise. Press reports during his 1899 tour noted his easy handling of American and British wrestlers such as "Farmer" Burns, "Gripman" Rooney, and Tom Cannon, who "bowed to his strength and cunning." Adali was reputed to be even more dangerous than his predecessor, whom he was said to have defeated in the presence of the Sultan of Constantinople. See Winnipeg *Voice*, 3 March 1899.

28 Manitoba *Free Press*, 24 June 1901, 26 June 1901. The Tom Jenkins appearing in Winnipeg was not the more famous grappler of the same name who claimed the American heavyweight catch-as-catch-can title on several occasions. He did, however, claim to be his cousin. See Manitoba *Free Press*, 25 June 1901.

29 Winnipeg *Telegram*, 28 June 1901.

30 Manitoba *Free Press*, 28 June 1901.

31 Winnipeg *Telegram*, 28 June 1901.

32 Manitoba *Free Press*, 28 June 1901.

33 Winnipeg *Tribune*, 26 June 1901; Manitoba *Free Press*, 26 June 1901.

34 Both men's measurements are given in the Manitoba *Free Press*, 19 June 1901 and 25 June 1901, respectively.

35 Manitoba *Free Press*, 7 May 1902, 8 May 1902.

36 J.S. Woodsworth, *Strangers within Our Gates or Coming Canadians* (1909; reprinted, Toronto: University of Toronto Press, 1972), 167.

37 Quoted in ibid., 169.

38 Edwin M. Bliss, *Turkey and the Armenian Atrocities* (n.p.: J. Coghlan, 1896), 84.

39 Manitoba *Free Press*, 28 June 1901; Coates and McGuinness, *Manitoba*, 65.

40 Manitoba *Free Press*, 20 October 1905. Founded in 1879, the Finchley Harriers was a prominent athletic club in England's Middlesex County particularly well known for its many regional and national titles in cross-country running. See William Page, ed., *A History of the County of Middlesex Volume 2* (Suffolk: Boydell and Brewer, 2004), 302.

41 Manitoba *Free Press*, 30 June 1901.

42 See Manitoba *Free Press*, 3 November 1905, 6 November 1905, and 9 November 1905.

43 In mid-November, for example, Theran's manager was also approached by "two Russians" in the city who wished to face the Turk for a side bet match. Manitoba *Free Press*, 15 November 1905.

44 Manitoba *Free Press*, 27 November 1905.

45 Manitoba *Free Press*, 27 January 1906; Winnipeg *Telegram*, 27 January 1906.

46 See Winnipeg *Tribune*, 5 November 1910; and Manitoba *Free Press*, 18 July 1910.

47 Manitoba *Free Press*, 2 January 1908, 15 March 1912.

48 Manitoba *Free Press*, 20 July 1910.

49 McInnis, "Migration."

50 Thompson, *Forging*, 76–77.

51 Winnipeg *Telegram*, 4 September 1906; Manitoba *Free Press*, 4 September 1906; Archives of Manitoba, MG10 D3, Scottish Amateur Athletic Association of Manitoba Collection, Scottish Amateur Athletic Association of Winnipeg Highland Games Official Program, 1907, 1908, 1909, 1911.

52 See Manitoba *Free Press*, 4 September 1906.

53 Quoted in Manitoba *Free Press*, 5 September 1906.

54 Ibid.

55 Quoted in Manitoba *Free Press*, 6 September 1906.

56 Quoted in Manitoba *Free Press*, 6 September 1906.

57 Archives of Manitoba, MG10 D3, Scottish Amateur Athletic Association of Manitoba Collection, Scottish Amateur Athletic Association of Winnipeg Highland Games Official Program, 1907.

58   Morris Mott, "One Solution to the Urban Crisis: Manly Sports and Winnipeggers, 1900–1914," *Urban History Review* 12, 2 (1983): 64.

59   For a historical overview of wrestling in each respective country, see Heikki Lehmusto, *History of Wrestling* (Helsinki: By the Author, 1939), 58–85. In continental Europe prior to 1900, important wrestling tournaments were attracting participants from many nations. One tournament, held in Paris during November 1899, for instance, attracted athletes from France, Switzerland, Germany, Denmark, Italy, Belgium, Turkey, and Russia. One athlete from Africa also participated. See Hackenschmidt, *The Way to Live*, 123.

60   Mott, "One Solution," 64, 65–66.

61   Reg Skene, "C.P. Walker and the Business of Theatre: Merchandizing Entertainment in a Continental Context," in *The Political Economy of Manitoba*, ed. James Silver and Jeremy Hull (Regina: Canadian Plains Research Center, 1990), 137.

62   See, respectively, Winnipeg *Tribune*, 18 March 1909, 5 April 1909; and Brandon *Sun*, 15 May 1902.

63   Manitoba *Free Press*, 25 May 1910, 28 May 1910.

64   See, for example, *Le Manitoba*, 26 November 1913, for an advertisement concerning an upcoming match at Winnipeg's Walker Theatre between French Canadian Eugene Tremblay and Polish-born Walter Miller.

65   Morton, *Manitoba*, 160, 162; Waite, *Canada, 1874–1896*, 62; Jean R. Burnet and Howard Palmer, *"Coming Canadians": An Introduction to a History of Canada's Peoples* (Toronto: McClelland and Stewart, 1988), 26.

66   W. Kristjanon, *The Icelandic People in Manitoba* (Winnipeg: By the Author, 1965), 42, 44; Ingibjorg Sigurgeirsson McKillop, *Mikley the Magnificent Island: Treasure of Memories, Hecla Island 1876–1976* (Steinbach, MB: By the Author, 1979), 183.

67   Nelson S. Gerrard, *Icelandic River Saga* (Arborg, MB: Saga Publications, 1985), 147.

68   Ibid.

69   Kristjanon, *The Icelandic People*, 45.

70   As noted by M. Nicholas Bennett in *Glima: Icelandic Wrestling* (New Orleans: By the Author, n.d.), 7–8, historical debate surrounds wrestling's origins in Iceland. Some historians, notably Guy Jaouen and Henri Beon, argue for an exclusively Celtic origin to the activity, whereas Bennett himself rejects the theory as too simplistic, suggesting that a blending of traditional Celtic and Viking practices might have ultimately contributed to glima's development. Recent work by Lars Magnar Enoksen, however, highlights that glima, as practised in Iceland, was part of a larger pan-Scandinavian wrestling tradition with shared common practices. See, for example, Lars Magnar Enoksen, "What Does a Mythological Text in Snorra Edda Tell Us about the Ritual Ceremonies that Surrounded Glima Fights in Ancient Times?," Glima Viking Federation, http://www.viking-glima.com/history.html.

71   Enoksen, "What Does a Mythological Text"; Bennett, *Glima*, 13.

72   Pete Kautz, "The Gripping History of Glima," *Journal of Western Martial Art* 1 (2000), http://ejmas.com/jwma/articles/2000/jwmaart_kautz_0100.htm.

73   Kristjanon, *The Icelandic People*, 461; Manitoba *Free Press*, 4 August 1903.

74   Quill Lake Historical Society, *Reflection on the Quills* (Quill Lake, SK: Quill Lake Historical Society, 1981), 676. The decision to hold the festival annually on 2 August occurred only after considerable debate within the Icelandic community, which, during the late nineteenth century and early twentieth century, was prone to factional infighting. For details concerning both the decision-making and the planning processes surrounding the first Islendingadagurinn Festival, see Jonas Dor, *Islendingadagurinn 1890–1989: Saga Islendingadagsins: An Illustrated History* (Gimli, MB: Icelandic Festival of Manitoba, 1989), 21–23.

75   Manitoba *Free Press*, 4 August 1890.

76   Ibid.

77   Ibid. Editorial comments in the *Free Press* on the same day noted that "we in the Northwest have no better immigrants…. The Icelanders possess to a large degree the power of adaptation, as well as the valuable faculty of assimilation. They become of ourselves without the least apparent effort. They adopt the ways of the country and lose no time in mastering the language of the majority…. They are bound to succeed here and we can only wish that we had more of them."

78   Winnipeg *Telegram*, 3 August 1899.

79   Kirsten Wolf, "Emigration and Mythmaking: The Case of the Icelanders in Canada," *Canadian Ethnic Studies* 33, 2 (2001): 1.

80   Such was the case, for instance, in 1890 and 1899. See Manitoba *Free Press*, 4 August 1890 and 3 August 1899.

81   Manitoba *Free Press*, 4 August 1903, 3 August 1906. See also Appendix 2.

82   Winnipeg *Telegram*, 3 August 1901; Winnipeg *Voice*, 15 August 1902; Manitoba *Free Press*, 31 July 1909. See also Gerrard, *Icelandic River Saga*, 148; and Kristjanon, *The Icelandic People*, 459, concerning baseball's adoption as a popular sporting pastime among Icelanders by the 1890s. Manitoba school inspector Edward Ernest Best noted that Magnus Bjarnason, a schoolteacher in the rural Arnes school in the Interlake district, and "an ardent lover of clean sport," introduced baseball and other games to the Icelandic students there in 1889. See Archives of Manitoba, MG9 A95-1, Edward Ernest Best Collection, "Memoirs of a School Inspector, 1888–1932—Revised," 95.

83   The Manitoba *Free Press* noted on 3 August 1899, for example, that "it was doubtful whether a majority of those present had ever seen Iceland. The picturesque Icelandic costumes worn in former years by a few of the ladies were yesterday absent, and so far as dress was concerned, there was nothing to distinguish any of the people from other citizens. Had a stranger been told that they were Scotch, he would never have known."

84   See, for example, Manitoba *Free Press*, 3 August 1911 and 3 August 1914, respectively.

85   Bruce Sharp, "Short History of Wrestling from 3000 B.C. to the Present Day," in *The Science of Wrestling*, ed. Dick Cameron (Sydney: Scotow Press, n.d.), 4; Meyers, *Wrestling from Antiquity to Date*, 68–69; Beekman, *Ringside*, 19; Wojciech Liponski, "Still and Unknown European Tradition: Polish Sport in the European Cultural Heritage," *International Journal of the History of Sport* 13, 2 (1996): 18. Pytlasinski, recognized as one of Poland's earliest wrestling stars, learned Greco-Roman wrestling in Paris while visiting the city in 1888, and he won a world title in the sport in 1892. See Lehmusto, *History of Wrestling*, 68–69.

86   Manitoba *Free Press*, 10 July 1911; Winnipeg *Tribune*, 5 May 1910.

87   Winnipeg *Telegram*, 25 April 1912.

88   Manitoba *Free Press*, 12 May 1914.

89   Henry Radecki and Benedyky Heydenkorn, *A Member of a Distinguished Family: The Polish Group in Canada* (Toronto: McClelland and Stewart, 1976), 3.

90   Wiktor Turek, *Poles in Manitoba* (Toronto: Polish Alliance Press, 1967), 33; Radecki and Heydenkorn, *Distinguished Family*, 55; Fred Stambrook and Stella Hryniuk, "Who Were They Really? Reflections on East European Immigrants to Manitoba before 1914," *Prairie Forum* 25, 2 (2000): 216.

91   Radecki and Heydenkorn, *Distinguished Family*, 55; Avery, *Reluctant Host*, 42; Wawrow, "Nativism in English Canada," 75–79.

92   See Henry Radecki, *Ethnic Organizational Dynamics: The Polish Group in Canada* (Waterloo, ON: Wilfrid Laurier University Press, 1979), 48.

93 Ibid., 43, 45.

94 Manitoba *Free Press*, 2 June 1907. The precise date of the organization's founding was either 3 or 13 December 1906. See also Sokol Polish Folk Ensemble, *Historia Zespolu Piesne I Tanca Sokol: History of the Sokol Polish Folk Ensemble 1906–1990* (Winnipeg: Sokol Polish Folk Ensemble, 1990), 1.

95 Turek, *Poles in Manitoba*, 207; Radecki, *Ethnic Organizational Dynamics*, 51, 63; Liponski, "Still an Unknown," 12.

96 Turek, *Poles in Manitoba*, 234; "History of the Polish Gymnastic Association Sokol," http://www.poloniacanada.ca/winnipeg/images/historia_polskie_tow_gimn_sokol_en.pdf; Manitoba *Free Press*, 1 March 1913.

97 Manitoba *Free Press*, 5 January 1908.

98 Sokol Polish Folk Ensemble, *Historia Zespolu*, 1, notes that the inaugural Sokol meeting occurred at the Sielski home on Selkirk Avenue.

99 Manitoba *Free Press*, 24 October 1907.

100 Winnipeg *Henderson's Directory*, 1910, 1911; Manitoba *Free Press*, 5 January 1908.

101 Winnipeg *Henderson's Directory*, 1910.

102 Sokol Polish Folk Ensemble, *Historia Zespolu*, 1.

103 Manitoba *Free Press*, 25 June 1907.

104 Manitoba *Free Press*, 24 June 1907.

105 Manitoba *Free Press*, 27 June 1907.

106 Manitoba *Free Press*, 29 May 1908.

107 Turek, *Poles in Manitoba*, 197. For further discussion of the schism between the nationalistic Sokol members and the Polish Roman Catholic clergy in Winnipeg, see Wictor Turek, *Polish-Language Press in Canada* (Toronto: Polish Alliance Press, 1962), 66–67, 100.

108 On 28 May 1908, Stanley Sielski was brought up on charges of disorderly conduct stemming from an argument with Father Groetsschel following mass on 24 May. The plaintiff accused Sielski of causing a disturbance at the church and publicly ridiculing him. Sielski, who claimed that Groetsschel had started the dispute by calling him "a pig," likewise contemplated taking legal action against the priest. See Manitoba *Free Press*, 29 May 1908.

109 Sokol diversified its activities rapidly during and after the Great War, and by 1922 it could boast approximately ninety active members. By mid-century, Winnipeg's Sokol Gymnastic Club, which had expanded vastly beyond its athletic roots, had a local membership of 270, in addition to branches in Brandon and St. Boniface. More than a century after its founding, both the Sokol Gymnastic Club and the Sokol Polish Folk Ensemble, which it spawned in 1914, continue to promote Polish culture in Manitoba. See Manitoba *Free Press*, 2 January 1922; Turek, *Poles in Manitoba*, 208; and http://www.sokolensemble.ca/history/.

110 Manitoba *Free Press*, 29 May 1908, 16 February 1912, 17 February 1912.

CHAPTER 4: THE "SIMON PURES"

1 Variety theatre owner Dan Rogers moved to the province's capital in 1881. During his first few years in the city, he owned and operated the Hub Saloon and promoted various athletic contests, notably female pedestrian races. In February 1884, he opened the Royal Theatre on the premises of the old Winnipeg courthouse. Unable to obtain a liquor licence, he ceased operations in late May. In November, Rogers opened the Victoria Theatre, but four months later, after facing numerous fines for alcohol-related infractions, he was once again forced out of business. Thereafter, he returned to the United States, where he owned a saloon in Huron City and later managed a tobacco

plantation in Virginia. Concerning pedestrian races, see Manitoba *Free Press*, 9 October 1882, 12 October 1882, 17 October 1882, 18 October 1882, and 20 October 1882; and Winnipeg *Sun*, 10 October 1882. For an overview of Rogers's theatre ventures, see Budnick, "Theatre on the Frontier." On his later activities after leaving Winnipeg, see Manitoba *Free Press*, 29 July 1890 and 31 December 1898.

2   Warren claimed in the Manitoba *Free Press* on 13 March 1894 to have been given his title by Dan Rogers "ten years ago." Unfortunately, Rogers's advertisements in the local press concerning entertainment features at the Royal or Victoria Theatre did not typically describe the events in any detail, so it is difficult to ascertain when Warren was awarded the distinction.

3   Manitoba *Free Press*, 19 September 1901; Winnipeg *Telegram*, 19 September 1901.

4   Ibid.

5   Manitoba *Free Press*, 28 September 1901.

6   Manitoba *Free Press*, 1 October 1901, 10 October 1901; Winnipeg *Telegram*, 1 October 1901, 8 October 1901.

7   Winnipeg *Telegram*, 17 October 1901.

8   Manitoba *Free Press*, 17 October 1901.

9   Ibid.

10   Manitoba *Free Press*, 24 October 1901, 8 November 1901, 15 November 1901, 18 November 1901, 20 November 1901.

11   Winnipeg *Telegram*, 21 November 1901.

12   Manitoba *Free Press*, 23 November 1901; Winnipeg *Telegram*, 23 November 1901.

13   The Manitoba *Free Press* noted, on 20 December 1901 and 2 January 1902, respectively, that public odds were 10 to 7 in favour of Simon to win and that even odds were being taken for Simon to secure victory in straight falls.

14   The contest was decided on the basis of best three of five falls, Simon winning three straight falls. See Manitoba *Free Press*, 21 January 1902.

15   For a copy of the contract signed by all three men, see Manitoba *Free Press*, 7 January 1902.

16   Manitoba *Free Press*, 21 January 1902; Winnipeg *Telegram*, 21 January 1902.

17   Manitoba *Free Press*, 1 May 1902.

18   Metcalfe, *Canada Learns to Play*, 107.

19   Ibid., 123.

20   Mott, "Manly Sports," 250.

21   Winnipeg's first YMCA was formed on 17 October 1874 by Colonel W.N. Kennedy and A. Bowerman. The association maintained a reading room and operated as late as January 1878. Few other records pertaining to the original Winnipeg YMCA exist. See Manitoba *Free Press*, 21 December 1889.

22   Archives of Manitoba, P 3818, Young Men's Christian Association, 1939 YMCA of Winnipeg Scrapbook, "The Winnipeg Y.M.C.A. News." For further biographical information on J.A.M. Aikins, see *Dictionary of Canadian Biography Online*, http://www.biographi.ca/009004-119.01-e.php?&id_nbr=7886. In addition to his legal and political career, Aikins "held the somewhat unique position of being a millionaire lawyer" because of his successful involvement in land speculation during Winnipeg's boom period during the early 1880s. See also Artibise, *Gateway City*, 119; and Artibise, *Winnipeg*, 46.

23   J.F. McIntyre at the 1886 YMCA general meeting. For detailed reports on the meeting's proceedings, see Manitoba *Free Press*, 15 September 1886. McIntyre's pronouncement was directly in keeping with the institution's original goals. Concerning the circumstances surrounding the YMCA's

founding in London, England, in 1844, see Mayer N. Zald, *Organizational Change: The Political Economy of the YMCA* (Chicago: University of Chicago Press, 1970), 25–26.

24 Manitoba *Free Press*, 15 September 1886, 2 October 1886, 8 November 1889.

25 Owen E. Pence, *The YMCA and Social Need: A Study of Institutional Adaptation* (New York: Association Press, 1939), 17.

26 Murray G. Ross, *The Y.M.C.A. in Canada: The Chronicle of a Century* (Toronto: Ryerson Press, 1951), 168–69.

27 Manitoba *Free Press*, 15 September 1886.

28 Ibid. D.M. Gordon acted as the minister at Knox Presbyterian Church from 1882 to 1887. In addition to his pastoral duties in Winnipeg, he served as chaplain for the 90th Regiment during the 1885 North-West Rebellion. See Hugh John Robertson, comp., *The Story of Knox Church, Winnipeg: Seventy-Five Years, 1872–1947*, University of Alberta Libraries, Peel's Prairie Provinces Online Collection, Peel 6964, http://peel.library.ualberta.ca/bibliography/6964/21.html.

29 Manitoba *Free Press*, 15 September 1886.

30 Manitoba *Free Press*, 18 February 1896.

31 Manitoba *Free Press*, 18 January 1901.

32 Ibid.

33 Bert Phillips, in preparing for his handicap match with Dave Simon in January 1902, conducted his training out of the YMCA quarters. See Manitoba *Free Press*, 16 January 1902.

34 Manitoba *Free Press*, 3 March 1905.

35 The Winnipeg *Telegram* noted on 27 March 1906 that "the first wrestling club ever formed in Winnipeg for boys has been organized at the YMCA. The boys are very enthusiastic and purpose [sic] giving an exhibition on April 10, to which the public are invited."

36 Manitoba *Free Press*, 6 April 1906.

37 Ibid. and 17 April 1906; Winnipeg *Telegram*, 6 April 1906.

38 Quoted in Manitoba *Free Press*, 17 April 1906.

39 Mott, "Manly Sports," 251.

40 A number of historians have examined Canada's "Athletic War" in considerable detail. See, for example, Metcalfe, *Canada Learns to Play*, 111–17; Don Morrow, "A Case Study in Amateur Conflict: The Athletic War in Canada, 1906–1908," in *Sports in Canada*, 201–19; Morrow and Wamsley, *Sport in Canada*, 77–78; and Mott, "Manly Sports," 250–51.

41 Although all present affirmed their strong commitment to amateur sport, concerns were also expressed, particularly by representatives of the Western Canadian Lacrosse Association and Manitoba Football Association, that strict adherence to CAAU rules would result in several teams being "professionalized," because athletes who competed in one sport as professionals would be declared professionals in others, leading to entire teams being declared professional. See Manitoba *Free Press*, 16 March 1907.

42 Ibid. By 1909, the MAAA continued to use similar wording in its definition of "amateur" but added other restrictions, including being found guilty of "selling or pledging prizes" and "compet[ing] against a professional, professional team, club or individual, when there is a gate or entrance fee charged." See Archives of Manitoba, MG10 D17, Amateur Athletic Union of Canada Manitoba Section, Constitution and By-Laws Manitoba Amateur Athletic Association 1909, 2.

43 Ibid.

44 For a copy of the MAAA constitution, see Manitoba *Free Press*, 4 May 1908. See also Archives of Manitoba, MG10 D17, Amateur Athletic Union of Canada Manitoba Section, Minutes of the MAAA 1908–12.

45 Manitoba *Free Press*, 14 October 1907.

46 For reports of the participants and results of both tournaments, see Manitoba *Free Press*, 14 March 1907 and 28 March 1908.

47 Manitoba *Free Press*, 24 November 1908.

48 Manitoba *Free Press*, 27 November 1908, 30 November 1908.

49 Manitoba *Free Press*, 27 November 1908.

50 The Winnipeg *Telegram*, 28 November 1908, commenting on his notoriety at the time, mused that "[McLaglen's] name is perhaps more often seen in print these days than that of any municipal candidate."

51 Manitoba *Free Press*, 28 November 1908.

52 Winnipeg *Tribune*, 28 November 1908.

53 Manitoba *Free Press*, 26 November 1908.

54 Manitoba *Free Press*, 22 April 1909, 23 April 1909, 24 April 1909.

55 See Appendix 1.

56 Manitoba *Free Press*, 12 June 1909.

57 Ibid.

58 Ross, *Y.M.C.A. in Canada*, 171.

59 Ibid., 172.

60 Winnipeg YMCA 1909 *Annual Report*, quoted in Manitoba *Free Press*, 12 June 1909. Such comments echoed those made by Dr. Fischer at the annual YMCA banquet a year earlier, when he characterized the association as "scientific in its organization and social in its methods." See Manitoba *Free Press*, 7 April 1908.

61 Winnipeg *Telegram*, 11 March 1910. Formation of the AAUC, which resulted in the reintegration of the CAAU and AAFC, marked the end of Canada's Athletic War. The "new" organization, however, remained steadfastly committed to the CAAU's definition of amateur.

62 Leyshon, *Of Mats and Men*, 109.

63 Manitoba *Free Press*, 2 April 1910, 7 April 1910.

64 Manitoba *Free Press*, 11 April 1910.

65 Similarly, previous national championships, held in the east, produced champions hailing from the region. In 1908, Canada's first national championship, staged by the rival AAFC, produced a roster of medallists hailing solely from Quebec. The following year, when the competition was held in Ottawa, athletes from Canada's capital city and Toronto shared the honours in all weight divisions. See Leyshon, *Of Mats and Men*, 109; and Glynn A. Leyshon, "Wrestling in Canada II, 1860–1914," *Journal of Manly Arts* (2001), http://ejmas.com/jmanly/articles/2001/jmanlyart_leyshon2_0701.htm.

66 Of the twenty-one entries in the 1912 Dominion Championships, only one competitor, Toronto's J. Miller, hailed from outside the Pacific Northwest. For a complete list of all competitors, including results, see Vancouver *Sun*, 30 April 1912.

67 The final significant step in railway building in Manitoba prior to construction of the Hudson Bay Railway Line in the 1920s was the transcontinental Grand Trunk Railway across the province between 1905 and 1909. See Morton, *Manitoba*, 285.

68 Leyshon, *Of Mats and Men*, 86, 88. The Vancouver *Sun* noted on 29 April 1912 that the lack of outside entries in the 1912 Dominion Championships in Vancouver was "because the Eastern clubs could not see their way to spend a little coin."

69   Kidd, *The Struggle for Canadian Sport*, 64–65. Sport's regional nature in Canada prior to the First World War also extended to popular team games, including hockey and baseball. See John Chi-Kit Wong, *Lords of the Rinks: The Emergence of the National Hockey League, 1875–1936* (Toronto: University of Toronto Press, 1995), especially Chapter 5; and Howell, *Northern Sandlots*, 142–44.

70   Archives of Manitoba, P 3818, Young Men's Christian Association, 1939 YMCA of Winnipeg Scrapbook.

71   For a playbill advertising the Canadian Amateur Wrestling Championships, including ticket prices, see Manitoba *Free Press*, 7 April 1910.

72   Manitoba *Free Press*, 9 April 1910.

73   Manitoba *Free Press*, 12 April 1910.

74   Ibid.

75   Mott, "Manly Sports," 246–47.

76   This particular accolade is attributed to James E. Sullivan, founder and then president of the United States Amateur Athletic Union. See Manitoba *Free Press*, 25 September 1909.

77   Manitoba *Free Press*, 24 September 1910.

78   Manitoba *Free Press*, 18 March 1911, 20 March 1911.

79   Photographs from the 1911 Festival of Empire and a brief descriptive overview of the exhibits are available at "Festival of Empire Imperial Exhibition and Pageant of London Crystal Palace 1911," http://www.studygroup.org.uk/Exhibitions/Pages/1911%20Crystal.htm.

80   Pratt's telegram, outlining the proposed elimination contests, was printed in both the Winnipeg *Tribune*, 12 May 1911, and the Winnipeg *Telegram*, 13 May 1911. George Walker, at the time, had won two successive BC amateur wrestling titles in the middleweight and heavyweight divisions, in addition to the 1910 Pacific Northwest middleweight championship. See Manitoba *Free Press*, 17 May 1911 and 19 May 1911.

81   For MacDonald's letter, see Manitoba *Free Press*, 26 May 1911.

82   Manitoba *Free Press*, 1 June 1911.

83   Ibid. and 3 June 1911; Winnipeg *Telegram*, 1 June 1911, 3 June 1911; Winnipeg *Tribune*, 1 June 1911, 3 June 1911.

84   Manitoba *Free Press*, 10 June 1911.

85   Before losing to Bacon, Walker defeated Australian W. Smythe in the semifinal. See Manitoba *Free Press*, 6 July 1911, 13 July 1911, and 18 July 1911.

86   Manitoba *Free Press*, 13 May 1911.

87   Manitoba *Free Press*, 16 May 1911; Winnipeg *Tribune*, 12 May 1911.

88   Manitoba *Free Press*, 16 May 1911.

89   Winnipeg *Tribune*, 16 May 1911.

90   Manitoba *Free Press*, 6 June 1911.

91   See, for example, Manitoba *Free Press*, 7 January 1911 and 13 January 1911.

92   Manitoba *Free Press*, 22 February 1913, 22 October 1913, 13 December 1913.

93   Quoted in Manitoba *Free Press*, 22 February 1913.

94   Manitoba *Free Press*, 14 January 1910.

95   Several names featured in preliminary wrestling bouts clearly bore the markings of a nom de guerre, such as "Zbyszko" and "Americus," who appeared at the Queen's Theatre on 3 February 1913.

96 It is unknown if Dickinson served as the wrestling coach during 1907, but it is certain that, prior to the inaugural Manitoba Amateur Wrestling Championships in 1908, he was already employed in that capacity by the YMCA. During the September 1910 monthly meeting of the YMCA, it was noted that he was to be rehired for the months of October to May inclusive, at a rate of sixty-five dollars per month for the first three months and seventy dollars per month for the remaining five months. See Manitoba *Free Press*, 14 November 1908 and 12 September 1910; and Archives of Manitoba, P 3798, Young Men's Christian Association, Minutes: YMCA Board of Directors 1910–13.

97 Manitoba *Free Press*, 3 May 1910; Winnipeg *Tribune*, 3 May 1910.

98 Manitoba *Free Press*, 14 January 1910.

99 Manitoba *Free Press*, 27 May 1911.

100 Manitoba *Free Press*, 26 April 1912.

101 See, for example, Manitoba *Free Press*, 25 September 1909 and 24 September 1910.

102 Manitoba *Free Press*, 5 October 1912.

103 Because of delays in construction, the Portage Avenue YMCA had to be vacated before the Vaughan Street facility was opened in May 1913. As a result, Dickinson's wrestling classes were conducted solely out of the Selkirk Avenue YMCA from late January to May. Concerning delays in opening the Vaughan Street YMCA, see Archives of Manitoba, P 3812, Young Men's Christian Association, YMCA—History Sketch and Material 1883–1935, "Y—One Hundred: A Winnipeg Commemorative Publication," 16. On YMCA wrestling classes during 1913 and 1914, see Manitoba *Free Press*, 31 January 1913 and 27 September 1913.

104 The 1914 Dominion Wrestling and Manitoba Boxing Championships were staged at the Drill Hall on Broadway Avenue and drew "a large attendance of spectators." Manitoba *Free Press*, 28 May 1914.

105 Information related to the Winnipeg Boys' Club wrestling program is sparse. However, much like the YMCA, the Boys' Club sought to instil "appropriate" amateur sporting values in its members and as such explicitly offered "clean methods in wrestling" at the headquarters on the corner of Sherbrook Street and Pacific Avenue. On 28 April 1913, it staged its first club championships. Stewart was assisted in his coaching duties by James McKinnon, who claimed the dominion amateur title in the 145 pound class in 1914. Photographs previously on display at the Winnipeg Arena included Patsy Picciano, dominion champion in the 115 pound class. Picciano represented the Winnipeg Boys' Club in the championships, and the photograph notes that he was coached by Alex Stewart. See Manitoba *Free Press*, 26 April 1913; and Archives of Manitoba, Manitoba Sports Hall of Fame Collection Photos, no. 260.

106 Mott, "Manly Sports," 255–57, 260. Middle-class control of amateur sport was a feature that extended beyond Manitoba to all parts of the country. See Kidd, *The Struggle for Canadian Sport*, 25; and Metcalfe, *Canada Learns to Play*, 13.

107 Winnipeg *Telegram*, 11 March 1909.

108 On 15 December 1914, Picciano issued a challenge in the Manitoba *Free Press* to meet any wrestler weighing between 115 and 125 pounds.

109 Cleve Dheensaw, *The Commonwealth Games: The First 60 Years 1930–1990* (Victoria: Orca Book Publishers, 1994), 8.

110 Archives of Manitoba, P 3817, Young Men's Christian Association, YMCA of Winnipeg Scrapbook, "Analysis of Membership of the Young Men's Christian Association Winnipeg," compiled in November 1910. Reinforcing these statistics are those presented in the YMCA's annual yearbook, which indicate that labourers comprised only 20 percent of the institution's total North American membership. See Zald, *Organizational Change*, 40.

111   Given the custom of typically including only the first initial in reports pertaining to amateur wrestling, coupled with the commonality of some surnames, it is difficult to conclusively identify all amateur wrestlers in the city by occupation. However, in instances in which it is possible, the evidence suggests that the overwhelming majority of amateur wrestlers were drawn from the ranks of clerical workers and skilled tradesmen. They include, from the 1910 Winnipeg *Henderson's Directory*, H.C. Andrews (clerk), E. Barter (clerk), C. Boulton (clerk), R.M. Hillis (machinist), R.L. (Bert) McAdam (clerk), J. McEachern (machinist), A.J. Mitchell (clerk), and L.G. Ore (printer). In the 1911 Winnipeg *Henderson's Directory*, listed wrestlers include E. Abrahamson (carpenter), R.G. Bacon (Western Canada Military Institute steward), P. Breen (telephone cable man), J. Cordy (typewriter expert), and W.E. Shane (clerk). The 1914 Winnipeg *Henderson's Directory* includes G.W. Akins (carpentry foreman) and A.A. Broughton (bookkeeper).

112   Archives of Manitoba, MG10 B15, Winnipeg Boys' Club, Winnipeg Boys' Club Fifth Annual Report 1909, 7, 8.

CHAPTER 5: GRAPPLING WITH THE GREAT WAR

1   For a photograph of the scene, see "(Wrestling) Men of the Little Black Devils of Winnipeg Watching Two Men of Their Battalion Wrestling. June, 1918," Library and Archives Canada, Box 54, Negative PA-040159.

2   See, for example, Burstyn, *Rites of Men*. Also see Morrow and Wamsley, *Sport in Canada*, the most comprehensive general history of Canadian sport to date. They make five brief references to sport during the First World War (4, 81, 167, 228, and 229).

3   As Bruce Kidd notes in *The Struggle for Canadian Sport*, 10, studies of early Canadian sport typically conclude their analyses in 1914. For example, Alan Metcalfe's seminal monograph on amateur sport, *Canada Learns to Play: The Emergence of Organized Sport, 1807–1914*, as the title implies, concludes its analysis at the beginning of the First World War, a year that Barbara Schrodt, in "Problems of Periodization in Canadian Sports History," *Canadian Journal of History of Sport* 21, 1 (1990): 72, contends provides a better division point than the more arbitrary years used by early Canadian sport historians during the 1970s and early 1980s. In works covering a broader time frame, the importance of the war is clearly evident yet largely unexamined in its own right. In *Sport in Canadian Society*, for example, Ann Hall et al. demarcate their analysis into the period preceding 1914 and following 1918 (see 56, 62–66, and 71). Similarly, Colin D. Howell's *Blood, Sweat, and Cheers* compares and contrasts the values held by advocates of sport before and after the Great War but does not explore in any detail sport during the war period itself.

4   See, for example, Thompson, *Harvests of War*; Desmond Morton, *When Your Number's Up: The Canadian Soldiers during the First World War* (Toronto: Random House, 1993); Briton C. Busch, ed., *Canada and the Great War: Western Front Association Papers* (Montreal: McGill-Queen's University Press, 2003); J.L. Granatstein, *Hell's Corner: An Illustrated History of Canada's Great War, 1914–1918* (Vancouver: Douglas and McIntyre, 2004); Robert Rutherdale, *Hometown Horizons* (Vancouver: UBC Press, 2004); and David Mackenzie, ed., *Canada and the First World War: Essays in Honour of Robert Craig Brown* (Toronto: University of Toronto Press, 2005). More recently, Tim Cook's work on the first half of the war, *At the Sharp End: Canadians Fighting in the Great War 1914–1916* (Toronto: Viking Canada, 2007), 403, notes the role played by sport in helping to "humanize the war and rejuvenate men who had lived in squalor and experienced the unimaginable."

5   See J.J. Wilson, "Skating to Armageddon: Canada, Hockey, and the First World War," *International Journal of the History of Sport* 22, 3 (2005): 315–43; and C. Nathan Hatton, "A Little Diversion to Dispel the Gloom: Sport at the Lakehead during the Great War, 1914–1918," *Thunder Bay Historical Museum Society Papers and Records* 42 (2014): 45–66.

6   Andrew Horrall, "'Keep-a-Fighting! Play the Game!' Baseball and the Canadian Forces during the First World War," *Canadian Military History* 10, 2 (2001): 27–40.

7   Rotundo, *American Manhood*, 5; Rotundo, "Body and Soul: Changing Ideas of American Middle
     Class Manhood, 1770–1920," *Journal of Social History* 16 (1983): 30; Clyde Griffen, "Recon-
     structing Masculinity from the Evangelical Revival to the Waning of Progressivism: A Specula-
     tive Synthesis," in *Meanings for Manhood: Constructions of Masculinity in Victorian America*, ed.
     Mark C. Carnes and Clyde Griffen (Chicago: University of Chicago Press, 1990), 200; Wanda
     Ellen Wakefield, *Playing to Win: Sports and the American Military, 1898–1945* (Albany: SUNY
     Press, 1997), 8; Burstyn, *Rites of Men*, 72; Moss, *Manliness and Militarism*, 30; Putney, *Muscular
     Christianity*, 5. An important component of football's popularity during the late nineteenth century
     stemmed from the belief that aggressive displays of violence on the field were expressions of ideal
     masculinity. Injuries were rampant, and deaths were common, leading some to condemn its brutal-
     ity and rally for major reforms. Yet, these criticisms aside, the sport remained popular. See Riess,
     "Sport and the Redefinition of American Middle-Class Masculinity," 18–19; and Park, "Mended or
     Ended," 110–33.

8   Burstyn, *Rites of Men*, 68.

9   Reports following a match between Montreal's Eugene Tremblay and Walter Miller in Winnipeg
     were typical of the time, the 7 May 1910 Winnipeg *Tribune* describing the contest as "a master of
     defence, artful, modelled on Samsonian lines in strength and speed, versus a perfect little whirl-
     wind, an aggressive wrestler, tricky, clean and willing."

10   Rader, *American Sports*, 100, 125; Riess, "Sport and the Redefinition of American Middle-Class
     Masculinity," 16–17; Lindaman, "Wrestling's Hold," 782.

11   Frederick R. Toombs, *How to Wrestle* (New York: American Sports Publishing Company, 1912),
     1–2. His comments also reflected pervasive fears that the modern, sedentary life typical for middle-
     class males during the industrial era was leading to widespread physical degeneracy. Competitive
     sport offered a tonic to the growing problem. See Howell, *Northern Sandlots*, 103–04; and Putney,
     Muscular Christianity, 4.

12   Physical fitness entrepreneur Earle E. Liederman, for example, employed 150 secretaries in his
     mail order business during the 1920s. Many other successful mail order entrepreneurs, including
     Edmond Desbonnet, Eugen Sandow, and Bernarr MacFadden, preceded him. See Terry Todd,
     "Brief History of Resistance Exercise," in *Getting Stronger: Weight Training for Men and Women*, ed.
     Bill Pearl (Bolinas, CA: Shelter Publications, 1986), 401.

13   Martin "Farmer" Burns, *Physical Culture Wrestling* (Omaha: Farmer Burns School of Wrestling,
     1914?), 6, 18.

14   Ibid., 30.

15   Ibid.

16   Ibid., 31.

17   Morris Mott, "The Anglo-Protestant Pioneers and the Establishment of Manly Sports in
     Manitoba, 1870–1886," in *Proceedings, Fourth Canadian Symposium on the History of Sport and
     Physical Education* (Vancouver: University of British Columbia, 1979), 8–11; Brian Stoddart,
     "Sport, Cultural Imperialism, and Colonial Response in the British Empire," *Comparative Studies in
     Society and History* 30, 4 (1988): 651. Wrestling matches proved to be popular public spectacles in
     Great Britain during this time as well, and contests were staged at various public venues. A match
     between Alex Munro, who later wrestled in Winnipeg, and George Hackenschmidt at Glasgow's
     Ibrox Park, for example, attracted 20,000 spectators. See *Lloyd's Weekly News*, 29 October 1905.

18   Allan Guttman, *The Erotic in Sports* (New York: Columbia University Press, 1996), 17; Nancy B.
     Reed, *More than Just a Game: The Military Nature of Greek Athletic Contests* (Chicago Ridge, IL:
     Ares Publishers, 1998), 9–21.

19   Burstyn, *Rites of Men*, 68; Howell, *Blood, Sweat, and Cheers*, 33.

20   Frank Cosentino, *A History of Physical Education* (Toronto: Captus Press, 1988), 247–48; Des-
     mond Morton, *A Military History of Canada* (Toronto: McClelland and Stewart, 2007), 122–23.

Concerning the adoption of military drill in British schools, which before 1906 "remained an official component of the curriculum of physical education in elementary education and the criteria for receiving [a] government grant," see J.A. Mangan and Hamad S. Ndee, "Military Drill—Rather More than 'Brief and Basic': English Elementary Schools and English Militarism," in *Militarism, Sport, Europe*, 65–96.

21   Burstyn, *Rites of Men*, 72; Moss, *Manliness and Militarism*, 56, 145; Baker, *Sports in the Western World*, 130.

22   See, for example, Manitoba *Free Press*, 2 April 1908, 5 May 1910, 25 November 1911, and 17 April 1913; Winnipeg *Voice*, 28 November 1913; and Portage la Prairie *Weekly Review*, 10 December 1913.

23   Wakefield, *Playing to Win*, 16, 17; Horrall, "Keep-a-Fighting," 37.

24   Mennonite communities contributed heavily to war-related charities and Victory Bond drives, which helped to relieve some of the animosity felt by the Anglo-Canadian majority toward their pacifist beliefs. However, as the war's casualty toll mounted, they faced increased discrimination. See Thompson, *Harvests of War*, 80–81.

25   Although Mennonites were not required to engage in active military duty, other groups of conscientious objectors were not granted similar lenience. During the war's later stages, after the implementation of conscription in 1917, Russelites (now commonly known as Jehovah's Witnesses) faced legal difficulties in Manitoba for their unwillingness to acquiesce to enforced military service. At least three members of their community were allegedly assaulted by military police in Winnipeg. One individual, Robert Clegg, was sentenced to two years of hard labour in Stony Mountain Penitentiary. Although his sentence was suspended, Clegg was shipped overseas to the training grounds at Shorncliffe, England, under military guard. Other prominent religious leaders, among them Methodist minister and social activist J.S. Woodsworth, were relieved of their official duties because of dissenting views, including the advocacy of pacifism. After being denied reappointment as a missionary in Gibson's Landing by the British Columbia Methodist Conference, Woodsworth resigned as a Methodist minister. See Jim Blanchard, *Winnipeg's Great War: A City Comes of Age* (Winnipeg: University of Manitoba Press, 2010), 223–32; and Kenneth McNaught, *A Prophet in Politics: A Biography of J.S. Woodsworth* (Toronto: University of Toronto Press, 1959), 82–87.

26   O'Brien, "Manhood and the Militia Myth," 131.

27   War Office, *Manual of Physical Training* (London: King's Printer, 1908), 8.

28   Ibid.

29   O'Brien, "Manhood and the Militia Myth," 131.

30   Manitoba *Free Press*, 4 October 1892.

31   See, for example, Manitoba *Free Press*, 11 May 1898, 7 July 1903, 9 May 1905, 18 October 1909, and 6 March 1914.

32   In particular, see Manitoba *Free Press*, 11 May 1898.

33   Sam Hughes, in *The Official Report of the Debates of the House of Commons on the Dominion of Canada Vol. 115* (Ottawa: King's Printer, 1914), 2082. Concerning reaction to his comment, as well as the context in which it was made, see Manitoba *Free Press*, 27 March 1914.

34   Robert Craig Brown and Donald Loveridge, "Unrequited Faith: Recruiting in the CEF 1914–1918," *Revue internationale d'histoire militaire* 54 (1982): 53–79.

35   Concerning Canada's rapid mobilization for war and Valcartier's transformation into a training camp, see J.L. Granatstein, *Canada's Army: Waging War and Keeping the Peace* (Toronto: University of Toronto Press, 2002), 56–57; and Cook, *At the Sharp End*, 35–37.

36   Morton, *A Military History*, 130–31.

37 On the lack of organized military sports during the war's earliest stages, see Horrall, "Keep-a-Fighting," 30.

38 From the official resolution passed at the 17 August meeting of the Winnipeg Industrial Bureau, quoted by D.M. Solant, "Manitoba," in *The Canadian Patriotic Fund: A Record of Its Activities from 1914 to 1919*, ed. Phillip Morris (Ottawa: Canadian Patriotic Fund, 1919?), 107–08.

39 Ibid., 109.

40 Ibid.; Manitoba *Free Press*, 14 October 1914. On 6 November 1911, the MAAA Board of Governors passed a resolution concerning the name change, ratified at the annual meeting on 19 February 1912. See 6 November 1911, Archives of Manitoba, MG10 D17, Amateur Athletic Union of Canada Manitoba Section, Minutes of the MAAA 1908–12; and 19 February 1912, Archives of Manitoba, MG10 D17, Amateur Athletic Union of Canada Manitoba Section, Minutes of the MAAA 1908–12.

41 Manitoba *Free Press*, 14 October 1914. Typically, the amateur wrestling "season" lasted from fall until spring of the following year.

42 For a complete list of all regiments patronizing the Patriotic Athletic Committee's 27 and 28 October boxing and wrestling tournament, see Manitoba *Free Press*, 15 October 1914.

43 Manitoba *Free Press*, 19 October 1914.

44 Manitoba *Free Press*, 18 December 1914.

45 See, for instance, Manitoba *Free Press* and Winnipeg *Tribune*, 26 November 1914, 2 February 1915, 19 March 1915, and 1 June 1915.

46 A match between Jack Davis, a West Coast grappler, and Patsy Bachant on 18 March 1915, for example, proved to one ringside spectator to be "an exhibition of just how yellow a man can be" when Davis stalled and repeatedly tried to make jokes with the spectators. Choruses of boos greeted his attempts at humour. See Manitoba *Free Press*, 19 March 1915.

47 The Second Battle of Ypres (Canadian involvement 22–24 April 1915) was the CEF's first major foray into armed combat and produced 6,035 casualties. The staggering losses sobered the unbridled patriotic jingoism so apparent during the first eight months of the war. See Granatstein, *Canada's Army*, 71. For an examination of contemporary accounts of Canadians' growing understanding of the war's gravity, see Terry Copp and T.D. Tait, *The Canadian Response to War, 1914–1917* (Vancouver: Copp Clark Pittman, 1971), 19–22. On public attitudes toward civilian sport during the period in Canada, see Horrall, "Keep-a-Fighting," 29.

48 Fort William *Daily Times Journal*, 27 August 1917.

49 Eklund, *Forty Years of Wrestling*, 18.

50 In 1914, the Winnipeg YMCA had a total membership of 4,200. By 1918, the number had decreased to 1,600. It was estimated that 3,000 YMCA members joined the CEF. See Archives of Manitoba, P 3812, Young Men's Christian Association, YMCA—History Sketch and Material 1883–1935, "Y—One Hundred: A Winnipeg Commemorative Publication," 17.

51 See Thomas Dickinson's Attestation Paper and *Casualty Form*, Library and Archives Canada, RG 150, Accession 1992–93/166, Box 2513–10.

52 Concerning the 1915 Manitoba Amateur Wrestling Championships, see Manitoba *Free Press*, 4 June 1915. One of the few amateur wrestling competitions known to have been staged in Winnipeg after June 1915 occurred on 4 February 1916, when the YMCA hosted an exhibition boxing and wrestling event in the Vaughan Street gymnasium featuring former dominion middleweight champion George Akins (158 pounds). See Manitoba *Free Press*, 4 February 1916.

53 Archives of Manitoba, P 3812, Young Men's Christian Association, YMCA—History Sketch and Material 1883–1935, "Y—One Hundred: A Winnipeg Commemorative Publication," 17.

54 Horrall, "Keep-a-Fighting," 29.

55 As Wakefield demonstrates in *Playing to Win*, 19–20, however, once the United States entered the war, similar debates over the efficacy of civilian sport during wartime ensued.

56 Wrestling aficionados in Manitoba, for example, were regularly informed of the exploits of rising heavyweight wrestling star Joe Stecher, who became the heir to Frank Gotch's legacy as the top professional heavyweight wrestler in the United States. Speculation about a match between Stecher and Gotch was regular fodder for newspaper columnists, though Gotch's premature death in December 1917 prevented any such contest from taking place. With America's entry into the war in 1917, the nation's top heavyweight wrestlers, including Joe Stecher, Earl Caddock, and Ed "Strangler" Lewis, all enlisted in the military. See Manitoba *Free Press*, 5 February 1916, 25 May 1916, 5 July 1916, 23 February 1917, 17 December 1917, and 18 September 1918.

57 Brown and Loveridge, "Unrequited Faith," 57.

58 G.E. Hewitt, *The Story of the Twenty-Eighth (North-West) Battalion, 1914–1917* (London: Canada War Records Office, 1918?), 2–3.

59 Morton, *When Your Number's Up*, 79. As Craig Leslie Mantle notes in "Loyal Mutineers: An Examination of the Connection between Leadership and Disobedience in the Canadian Army since 1885," in *The Unwilling and the Reluctant: Theoretical Perspectives on Disobedience in the Military*, ed. Craig Leslie Mantle (Kingston: Canadian Defence Academy Press, 2006), 43–45, problems with discipline in the CEF were consistently linked to soldiers' perceptions of their leaders' command competence and fairness. Failure by leaders to provide sufficient amusement for soldiers was recognized during the First World War as one cause of inappropriate behaviour and poor morale.

60 On 1 May 1916, for example, the *"New Church" Times* noted, concerning esprit de corps, "though the division may be separately all that can be desired, yet perhaps it would be of immense advantage if units knew each other better.... Not only will it give us greater confidence in each other in circumstances which will most certainly arrive one day, but it would make the work much smoother if one were doing the job with ... friends rather than chance acquaintances." See also Wakefield's observations concerning the development of sporting competitions among troops stationed in non-combat settings in *Playing to Win*, 5.

61 Evidently, several of the participating soldiers were well versed, by that time, in the sport, for the winners in each weight division earned victories with well-defined wrestling holds such as the body scissors and half nelson and crotch. See Manitoba *Free Press*, 12 January 1915.

62 Ibid.

63 Toronto *Evening Telegram*, 30 March 1916; 15 March 1916, Library and Archives Canada, RG 24, Vol. 4365, 34-7-23-19, vol. 1.

64 28 March 1916; Library and Archives Canada, RG 24, Vol. 4365, 34-7-23-19, vol. 1.

65 Manitoba *Free Press*, 31 December 1915.

66 24 June 1917, Library and Archives Canada, RG 9, Vol. 4135, folder 22, file 9.

67 Brown and Loveridge, "Unrequited Faith," 60.

68 Quoted in Manitoba *Free Press*, 29 April 1916.

69 Ibid. The MAAUC's commitment to junior sports was reaffirmed at the annual meetings in 1917, when the association secretary was urged to write a letter to the local school board asking that better use be made of school buildings for organizing sports. See the MAAUC's annual report in Manitoba *Free Press*, 28 April 1917.

70 See Manitoba *Free Press*, 24 March 1916, 25 March 1916, 31 March 1916, and 1 April 1916; Winnipeg *Telegram*, 1 April 1916, 3 April 1916, and 4 April 1916; and Winnipeg *Tribune*, 1 April 1916 and 4 April 1916.

71 Manitoba *Free Press*, 1 April 1916.

72 Winnipeg *Telegram*, 8 April 1916.

73 Martha McCarthy, *Camp Hughes: A Summary Report* (Winnipeg: Historic Resources Branch, 1989), 7.

74 Morton, *Manitoba*, 340; Manitoba *Free Press*, 14 August 1916.

75 Winnipeg *Tribune*, 19 August 1916.

76 Manitoba *Free Press*, 16 August 1915.

77 The 90th (Winnipeg Rifles) Battalion staged the April 1916 Winnipeg Garrison meet. See Manitoba *Free Press*, 8 April 1916.

78 Quoted in March 1916, Library and Archives Canada, RG 24, Vol. 4365, 34-7-23-19, vol. 1.

79 During the Great War's early stages, the YMCA's relationship with the CEF overseas was tenuous, its numbers small, and its efforts modest. However, as the war progressed, its activities became more numerous, and its relationship with the military authorities became formalized. By the last year of the conflict, YMCA officials held official staff postings on brigade, division, and corps levels. The Canadian YMCA operated seventy-six centres in England; by 1917, 133 secretaries working overseas had honorary CEF commissions, the majority of whom (seventy-three) received their pay from the Canadian government. YMCA physical education authority Fred J. Smith was enlisted to devise athletic programs for troops overseas during the summer of 1916. See H. Burstaff, ed., *Canada in the Great World War* (Toronto: United Publishers of Canada, 1921), 137–38, 146; J. Castell Hopkins, *Canada at War: A Record of Heroism and Achievement, 1914–1918* (Toronto: Canadian Annual Review, 1919), 254–55; and Charles W. Bishop, *The Canadian YMCA in the Great War: The Official Record of the Activities of the Canadian YMCA in Connection with the Great War of 1914–1918* (Toronto: Canadian National Council YMCA, 1924), 89.

80 Thomas Duncan Patton, general secretary for the Winnipeg YMCA, became the YMCA area supervisor for military work in Military Districts 10 and 11 (Saskatchewan, Manitoba, and northwest Ontario) in 1915. Herbert R. Hadcock, Winnipeg YMCA physical director, likewise resigned his position with the local "Y" to work with the Military Department, as did W.H. Moor, boys' work secretary. See 2 April 1917, Library and Archives Canada, RG 24, Vol. 4289, file 34-1-45; and Archives of Manitoba, P 3812, Young Men's Christian Association, YMCA—History Sketch and Material 1883–1935, "Y—One Hundred: A Winnipeg Commemorative Publication," 17.

81 Bishop, *The Canadian YMCA*, 161–62.

82 Ibid., 163.

83 Ronald G. Haycock, *Sam Hughes: The Public Career of a Controversial Canadian, 1853–1916* (Waterloo: Wilfrid Laurier University Press, 1986), 146.

84 2 April 1917, Library and Archives Canada, RG 24, Vol. 4289, file 34-1-45.

85 Burns, *Physical Culture Wrestling*, 16.

86 Bishop, *The Canadian YMCA*, 168. See also Steven Pope, "An Army of Athletes: Playing Fields, Battlefields, and the American Military Sporting Experience, 1890–1920," *Journal of Military History* 59, 3 (1995): 442.

87 Wakefield, *Playing to Win*, 13.

88 In some instances, aggressive street recruiting tactics led to harassment not only of civilians but also of other units deemed "unmanly." For example, in December 1915, the Canadian Army Medical Corps complained that its men were being verbally accosted in the streets: "Why don't you join a men's battalion?" The Medical Corps expressed concern that its members were being confused with the Red Cross and that such remarks could lead to transfers from the unit. See 9 December 1915, Library and Archives Canada, RG 24, Vol. 4594, file MD10-20-10I.

89 Library and Archives Canada, RG 24, Vol. 4602, file MD10-20-10-54W.

90 *WUB: Western Universities Battalion, 196th* 1, 1 (1916): 12.

91 Ibid.

92 Manitoba *Free Press*, 25 March 1916.

93 Toronto *Evening Telegram*, 6 May 1916. Ongoing problems with his vision were documented in the Manitoba press prior to 1914. The Manitoba *Free Press* noted on 5 April 1910 that his right eye, injured in New York in 1907, was further damaged, along with his left eye, in an effort to make weight for a wrestling match in Winnipeg.

94 Quoted in the Toronto *Evening Telegram*, 6 May 1916.

95 His enlistment records, predictably, neglect to mention his poor eyesight, though a medical examination did note his slightly deformed, "cauliflower" ear. See his Attestation Paper, Library and Archives Canada, RG 150, Accession 1992–93/166, Box 2827–45.

96 Hatton, "Winnipeg's 'Quiet' Man," 24, 25.

97 Toronto *Evening Telegram*, 26 May 1916.

98 Ibid.

99 Thompson, *Harvests of War*, 74; Donald Avery, "Ethnic and Class Relations in Western Canada during the First World War: A Case Study of European Immigrants and Anglo-Canadian Nativism," in *Canada and the First World War*, 288.

100 Thompson, *Harvests of War*, 74–81; Avery, "Ethnic and Class Relations," 272.

101 Artibise, *Winnipeg*, 165; Donald Avery, *"Dangerous Foreigners": European Immigrant Workers and Labour Radicalism in Canada, 1896–1932* (Toronto: McClelland and Stewart, 1979), 14; Thompson, *Forging*, 77. Scholars looking at western Canadian immigration history typically assert that an informal racial hierarchy existed in the region, with ethnically British people occupying the top stratum. Various other peoples were judged by their ability to assimilate to the Anglo-Canadian norm, with northern Europeans being the most desirable in this regard, followed by central and eastern Europeans. Orientals, blacks, and Middle Easterners were commonly deemed unassimilable and therefore wholly undesirable. See Howard Palmer and Tamara Palmer, *Alberta: A New History* (Edmonton: Hurtig Publishers, 1990), 76–78; and Thompson, *Forging*, 76–77.

102 Gulbrand Loken, *From Fjord to Frontier: A History of the Norwegians in Canada* (Toronto: McClelland and Stewart, 1980), 187, 189.

103 Library and Archives Canada, RG 24, Vol. 4602, file MD10-20-10-54X.

104 Ibid.

105 See Manitoba *Free Press*, 12 August 1916, 15 August 1916, and 16 August 1916; Winnipeg *Telegram*, 15 August 1916, 17 August 1916, and 18 August 1916; and Winnipeg *Tribune*, 16 August 1916 and 18 August 1916. Although Gustafson and Sundberg brought the 197th Battalion and by extension Scandinavian Canadians positive press, their fame did not inspire substantial enlistment. The battalion was never able to recruit to full strength, likely in part because of the availability of high-paying jobs in the agricultural sector after 1915. See Brown and Loveridge, "Unrequited Faith," 61.

106 Cosentino, "A History of the Concept of Professionalism," 134, 169.

107 Toronto *Evening Telegram*, 17 March 1916; Winnipeg *Telegram*, 27 March 1916.

108 Quoted in Toronto *Evening Telegram*, 17 March 1916.

109 Ibid.

110 Quoted in the Toronto *Evening Telegram*, 18 March 1916.

111 March 1916, Library and Archives Canada, RG 24, Vol. 4365, file 34-7-23-19, vol. 1.

112 Quoted in Manitoba *Free Press*, 27 March 1916; Winnipeg *Tribune*, 27 March 1916; and Winnipeg *Telegram*, 27 March 1916.

113 Manitoba *Free Press*, 3 April 1916; Winnipeg *Tribune*, 4 April 1916.

114 Winnipeg *Telegram*, 4 April 1916.

115 Manitoba *Free Press*, 3 April 1916.

116 Quoted in Manitoba *Free Press*, 29 April 1916. On 26 May, the Amateur Athletic Union of Canada unanimously affirmed the right of enlisted amateurs and professionals throughout the Canadian Forces to compete together in military-sanctioned events. For a copy of the amended resolution, see Winnipeg *Telegram*, 26 May 1916.

117 Manitoba *Free Press*, 14 June 1916.

118 Ibid.

119 French wrestler Salvador Chevalier, for example, earned the Croix de Guerre and military medals from both France and England for heroic deeds under heavy artillery fire. See Winnipeg *Tribune*, 18 March 1920.

120 Manitoba *Free Press*, 18 May 1915.

121 Records of McLaglen's death are available through the Commonwealth Graves Commission at http://www.cwgc.org/search/casualty_details.aspx?casualty=383974.

122 Quoted in Toronto *Evening Telegram*, 23 May 1916.

123 During the MAAUC's annual meeting in 1918, for example, a reduction in amateur sporting activity during the past year was evident, with reports from various committees being "necessarily brief owing to the small number of events conducted during the past year." See the MAAUC's annual report in Manitoba *Free Press*, 28 April 1917.

124 Wakefield, *Playing to Win*, 21.

125 For example, catch-as-catch-can wrestling competitions were staged at Winnipeg's Minto Barracks during the winter months. See Manitoba *Free Press*, 20 January 1917.

126 5 January 1917, Library and Archives Canada, RG 24, Vol. 2604, file 20-10-80, vol. 1; 8 January 1918, RG 24, Vol. 2604, file 20-10-80, vol. 1. As close a relationship as the YMCA enjoyed with the CEF, it nevertheless remained acutely sensitive to guarding its reputation against criticism. Numerous testimonials and positive reviews concerning the YMCA's work both at home and overseas were forwarded to District 10 command to reinforce its favoured status with the CEF. See, for example, "Re: The YMCA in France," RG 24, Vol. 4604, file 20-10-80, vol. 1; 27 September 1917, RG 24, Vol. 4604, file 20-10-80, vol. 1; and 18 October 1917, RG 24, Vol. 4604, file 20-10-80, vol. 1.

127 Manitoba *Free Press*, 13 December 1917.

128 Horrall, "Keep-a-Fighting," 34.

129 Wrestling matches, along with boxing bouts, were held before 4,000 people at Pond Hill in Shorncliffe during the summer of 1916. Embankments formed a natural theatre for spectators. 5 March 1917, Library and Archives Canada, RG 9 III-B-1, Vol. 816, file S-1-2. Concerning horseback wrestling, see, for example, "Canadian Cavalry Depot Gymkhana Programme, 29 July 1916," Library and Archives Canada, RG 9 III-D-4, Vol. 5081, Sports Programmes file; "Canadian Engineers' Training Depot Military Athletic Sports, 2 September 1916," Library and Archives Canada, RG 9 III-D-4, Vol. 5081, Sports Programmes file; "Canadian Field Artillery Reserve Brigade Sports Programme, 16 September 1916," Library and Archives Canada, RG 9 III-D-4, Vol. 5081, Sports Programmes file; and "Canadian Reserve Cavalry Regiment Grand Military Display, 6 August 1917," Library and Archives Canada, RG 9 III-B-1, Vol. 816, file S-1-2. See also *"Action Front!,"* May 1917, 25–26.

130 27 December 1917, Library and Archives Canada, RG 9 III-B-1, Vol. 612, file C-75-2.

131 *A Guide to Military Sports and Recreational Training*, December 1917, Library and Archives Canada, RG 9 III-B-1, Vol. 612, file S-75-2. Under the CMAA, six areas were designated for sporting competition: Shorncliffe, Bramshott, Seaford, 5th Canadian Division, Bexhill, and London, which included troops not stationed in any of the other five. 4 January 1918, Library and Archives Canada, RG 9 III-B-1, Vol. 612, file S-75-2.

132 While making no distinction between amateurs and professionals in military ranks, the guide nevertheless prohibited money prizes, instead advocating trophies and medals. Wrestling matches were arranged in five weight classes, from featherweight (126 pounds) to heavyweight (over 175 pounds). The official rules advocated a stand-up form of wrestling that allowed holds to be taken only from the waist up. No ground wrestling was permitted, and a match ended when any part of a contestant's body, other than his feet, touched the ground. It does not appear that the rules were followed, for future competitions were conducted according to the more familiar catch-as-catch-can method. See pages 2 and 10 of the guide. For a further discussion of the guide, see Horrall, "Keep-a-Fighting," 34.

133 Elimination matches preceded the finals during the weeks beforehand, and the championships were conducted under catch-as-catch-can rules. 2 March 1918, Library and Archives Canada, RG 9 III-B-1, Vol. 612, file S-75-2; 19 March 1918, Library and Archives Canada, RG 9 III-B-1, Vol. 612, file S-75-2; 22 March 1918, Library and Archives Canada, RG 9 III-B-1, Vol. 612, file S-75-2.

134 In total, approximately 70,000 athletes in all sports participated in preliminary meets, with 750 earning the right to compete in the finals. As had been the case with military sporting competitions throughout the war, the YMCA played a significant role in the Canadian Corps Championships, and following the event Commander Arthur Currie offered his appreciation for their work in helping to facilitate "what was perhaps one of the largest meetings of the kind which has been held in France." See "Canadian Corps Championships," Library and Archives Canada, RG 9 III-D-4, Vol. 5081, Sports Programmes file; and 15 July 1918, RG 9 III-B-1, Vol. 1017, file S-20-3, vol. 1.

135 "Canadian Corps Championships," Library and Archives Canada, RG 9 III-D-4, Vol. 5081, Sports Programmes file. To be expected, not all military personnel were able to attend the Canadian Corps Championships on 1 July 1918. Smaller-scale events, such as the gymkhana staged in Shevevingen, Holland, also featured wrestling in their festivities. See "Official Programme of Gymkhana, 1 July 1918," Library and Archives Canada, RG 9 III-D-4, Vol. 5081, Sports Programmes file.

136 Horrall, "Keep-a-Fighting," 36.

CHAPTER 6: PROFESSIONAL WRESTLING'S "GOLDEN AGE"

1 Toronto *Globe*, 21 November 1918.

2 Manitoba *Free Press*, 25 December 1918.

3 Ibid.; Manitoba *Free Press*, 12 November 1918.

4 Shortly after the decade ended, the 1920s were being referred to as a "golden age" for sport. See, for example, Alison Brandwein and Peter Brandwein, *Sport's Golden Age: A Close-Up of the Fabulous Twenties* (New York: Harper Brothers, 1948).

5 Hatton, *Rugged Game*, 154–59.

6 Manitoba *Free Press*, 25 January 1919.

7 Fort William *Daily Times-Journal*, 10 January 1920. Concerning his professional debut, in which Walker defeated grappler Peter Bazukos in Vancouver, see Vancouver *Sun*, 10 October 1912 and 11 October 1912.

8 Fort William *Daily Times-Journal*, 12 January 1920.

9 Concerning Johnstone's enlistment with the Winnipeg police and place of birth, see the Winnipeg Police Museum, *Police Commission Books*. Concerning his military enlistment and activities, see his Attestation Paper, RG 150, Accession 1992–93/166, Box 4903–33. See also Manitoba *Free Press*, 20 December 1910, 5 August 1916, and 23 March 1920; and Winnipeg *Tribune*, 23 March 1920 and 24 March 1920.

10 Manitoba *Free Press*, 26 March 1920; Winnipeg *Tribune*, 26 March 1920.

11   Concerning attendance, see Winnipeg *Tribune*, 26 March 1920.

12   Manitoba *Free Press*, 7 August 1920.

13   Dauphin *Herald*, 30 June 1921 and 14 July 1921.

14   Wrestlers appearing at the Willis Theatre during late 1920 and early 1921 included Ernie Arthur, Young Gotch, Charles Olson, Lorne C. Curtis, Nels Moe, Harry McDonald, and the well-known Hollywood motion picture "heavy" Bull Montana.

15   These and several other explicit ethnic references were included in the newspaper coverage prior to their bout. See Brandon *Sun*, 5 February 1921 and 12 February 1921.

16   See, for example, Brandon *Sun*, 4 November 1920; 15 November 1920; 7 December 1920; 9 December 1920; 13 December 1920; and 7 January 1921.

17   Brandon *Sun*, 2 September 1920.

18   Brandon *Sun*, 4 November 1920; 8 December 1920; 17 February 1921.

19   Brandon *Sun*, 30 December 1920.

20   Ibid.

21   Melita *New Era* and Napinka *Herald*, 24 February 1921.

22   Melita *New Era* and Napinka *Herald*, 3 February 1921; 10 March 1921.

23   Melita *New Era* and Napinka *Herald*, 10 March 1921.

24   Melita *New Era* and Napinka *Herald*, 24 March 1921.

25   Manitoba *Free Press*, 6 May 1922.

26   For Gustafson's obituary, see Winnipeg *Free Press*, 2 November 1956.

27   Mark Dyreson, "The Emergence of Consumer Culture and the Transformation of Physical Culture: American Sports in the 1920s," *Journal of Sports History* 16, 3 (1989): 271–72; Howell, *Blood, Sweat, and Cheers*, 91.

28   Dyreson, "Emergence," 261.

29   Putney, *Muscular Christianity*, 200; Dyreson, "Emergence," 269.

30   Cosentino, "A History of the Concept of Professionalism," 252–53.

31   Putney, *Muscular Christianity*, 199.

32   "An Act to Regulate and Control Boxing and Wrestling Exhibitions," in *Statutes of Manitoba 1921* (Winnipeg: King's Printer, 1921), 7.

33   Ibid., 7–8.

34   In November 1923, for instance, the commission levied a fine against Wladek Zbyszko for his actions during a match in Winnipeg. After winning the first fall, the Pole refused to continue, complaining of a boil on his knee. When the commission forced him to do so, he lost the second fall because he kicked his opponent, Jack Taylor, in the face, resulting in a bloodied nose. During the third period, after being forced to return to the ring a second time, Zbyszko surrendered after Taylor grabbed his injured limb. The incident generated considerable public uproar, and as a result of his actions Zbyszko was forced to pay $250. See Manitoba *Free Press*, 6 November 1923 and 8 November 1923; and Winnipeg *Tribune*, 6 November 1923 and 8 November 1923.

35   Manitoba *Free Press*, 27 July 1922; 29 July 1922; Winnipeg *Tribune*, 27 July 1929. *Pehlwani* is a folk wrestling style practised in present-day Pakistan and India.

36   Manitoba *Free Press*, 29 July 1922; Winnipeg *Tribune*, 1 August 1922.

37   For census data on Taylor and his family, see Canadian Census 1901, Ontario, District 48 East Bruce, Sub-District 4, Polling Sub-Division 5, Greenock Township, 2. Concerning Taylor's employment with the Pigeon River Timber Company, see Fort William *Daily Times-Journal*, 2

November 1923. References to Taylor as an "ex-cop" were numerous during his early career. See, for example, Lethbridge *Herald*, 12 April 1912; and Medicine Hat *Daily News*, 4 January 1913 and 9 January 1913.

38   Eklund-Odegard, *Wyoming's Wrestling Rancher*, 13. See Lethbridge *Herald*, 25 March 1912, concerning Taylor's first match against Jack Ellison in Raymond, Alberta. As early as 1913, Taylor also received wrestling instruction from Burns. See Medicine Hat *Daily News*, 21 February 1913.

39   Eklund-Odegard, *Wyoming's Wrestling Rancher*, 13–14; Casper *Tribune*, 21 December 1920, 1 March 1921, 1 November 1921, 15 December 1921; New York *Times*, 9 May 1919; Oakland *Tribune*, 10 March 1920.

40   Manitoba *Free Press*, 27 July 1922.

41   Winnipeg *Tribune*, 2 August 1922.

42   Manitoba *Free Press*, 2 August 1922.

43   Ibid.

44   Howell, *Blood, Sweat, and Cheers*, 91–92; Beekman, *Ringside*, 62.

45   Rader, *American Sports*, 133, 134.

46   Quoted in Manitoba *Free Press*, 3 October 1922.

47   Manitoba *Free Press*, 6 October 1922, 10 October 1922.

48   In November 1914, during his second appearance in the city, Taylor wrestled before 1,600 spectators at the Walker Theatre in a match against Charles Cutler, who claimed the world's heavyweight title following one of several "retirements" by champion Frank Gotch. The Canadian won the match because of a controversial decision by referee Alex Stewart to disqualify Cutler for using an illegal stranglehold. For a brief period after the contest, Taylor asserted his right to the world's heavyweight championship, though the claim went completely unrecognized. For a detailed account of his match with Cutler as well as an earlier encounter between the two in Saskatoon, see Hewitt, *Catch Wrestling Round Two*, 79–84.

49   The Great War had curtailed Zbyszko's sporting activities, and the Pole was first detained by the Russian czar and later imprisoned following the Bolshevik Revolution in 1917. Having lost much of his money during the war, Zbyszko returned to North America in February 1920 aboard the Danish steamer *Oscar II* to resume his mat career. His fame once more renewed with the public, Manitobans were kept frequently abreast of his wrestling exploits, which culminated in winning the world's heavyweight wrestling title from Ed "Strangler" Lewis on 6 May 1921 at New York's Madison Square Garden. Although Lewis regained his title on 3 March 1922, Zbyszko's recent turn as champion made the Pole, next to Lewis himself, the most recognized wrestler on the continent. On Zbyszko's activities overseas during the war period, see Graham Noble, "'The Lion of the Punjab'—Part IV: Aftermath," *In Yo: Journal of Alternative Perspectives on the Martial Arts and Sciences* (2002), http://ejmas.com/jalt/jaltframe.htm; and Thomas Van Vleck, "Zbyszko: Passing the Baton," *Milo: Journal for Serious Strength Athletes* 8, 3 (2000): 93. For reports on Zbyszko's wrestling activities between his arrival in North America and his winning the world's heavyweight championship, see, for example, Manitoba *Free Press*, 25 February 1920, 27 February 1920, 1 March 1920, 13 April 1920, 20 April 1920, 31 May 1920, 10 July 1920, 15 October 1920, 10 December 1920, 9 February 1921, 15 March 1921, and 7 May 1921. Record of his title reign is available in Duncan and Will, *Wrestling Title Histories*, 9.

50   Regarding both the announcement and the use of the term "greatest of all wrestlers" in reference to Zbyszko, see Manitoba *Free Press*, 20 September 1922.

51   Manitoba *Free Press*, 23 September 1922.

52   Quoted in Manitoba *Free Press*, 3 October 1922.

53   Quoted in ibid.

54   Manitoba *Free Press*, 6 October 1922.

55   Ibid. and 10 October 1922.

56   Manitoba *Free Press*, 10 October 1922.

57   Ibid.

58   Manitoba *Free Press*, 18 October 1922.

59   Manitoba *Free Press*, 20 October 1922.

60   Winnipeg *Tribune*, 20 October 1922.

61   See, for example, *Czas*, 11 October 1922 and 25 October 1922.

62   Manitoba *Free Press*, 18 October 1922, 19 October 1922.

63   Manitoba *Free Press*, 20 October 1922.

64   Ibid.

65   Manitoba *Free Press*, 24 October 1922. Hazel Eklund-Odegard provides brief commentary on Taylor's relocation to Winnipeg during 1922. She notes in *Wyoming's Wrestling Rancher*, 14, that, "when the Taylors left, it was just a 'walk out' deal. There were dishes still on the table, food in the cupboards and clothes in the closet."

66   During his residency in Winnipeg, Taylor lived at 200 Smith Street in downtown Winnipeg. The 1923 *Henderson's Directory* lists him at the address under the occupation "champion wrestler."

67   See, respectively, Brandon *Sun*, 23 January 1923; Saskatoon *Phoenix*, 31 March 1923; Regina *Leader*, 28 February 1923; Swift Current *Sun*, 4 March 1924; Saskatoon *Star*, 31 January 1924; Edmonton *Bulletin*, 5 March 1924; Lethbridge *Herald*, 26 February 1924; and Saskatoon *Star*, 10 July 1923. Notably absent from Taylor's touring schedule was Calgary, perhaps because of the poor impression that Taylor had left with fans in October 1915 when he had knocked out long-standing rival Charles Cutler with a punch to the jaw. It had been his last match in Canada before relocating to the United States.

68   Bill Waiser, *Saskatchewan: A History* (Calgary: Fifth House, 2005), 240, 244.

69   Morton, *Manitoba*, 273, 296; Bellan, *Winnipeg First Century*, 94–95.

70   Coates and McGuinness, *Manitoba*, 83.

71   Morton, *Manitoba*, 356.

72   Bellan, *Winnipeg First Century*, 145; Thompson, *Forging*, 111; Coates and McGuinness, *Manitoba*, 100.

73   Thompson, *Harvests*, 85–86; Burnet and Palmer, *Coming Canadians*, 33.

74   Friesen, *The Canadian Prairies*, 354; Bercuson, *Confrontation at Winnipeg*, 186.

75   Avery, *Reluctant Host*, 82.

76   Ibid. Even Clifford Sifton, frequently criticized during his tenure as minister of the interior for his "open" immigration policy, became more restrictive in his views. In 1920, he stated that "Canada should bar her door against the German, the Austrian, the Turk and the Bulgarian, and no person of any of these nationalities should be admitted to Canadian citizenship." Quoted in Hall, *Clifford Sifton Volume Two*, 295.

77   Woodsworth, *Strangers*, 169.

78   See, for example, Manitoba *Free Press*, 14 July 1915, 2 September 1915, 16 December 1915, 21 December 1915, 26 August 1915, 21 April 1916, 22 April 1916, 27 June 1916, and 8 August 1916.

79   Concerning the headline "Horror Unequalled in [a] Thousand Years," see Manitoba *Free Press*, 7 October 1915. For other reports in Manitoba newspapers on what is now commonly termed the

"Armenian Genocide," see Manitoba *Free Press*, 24 February 1915, 29 May 1915, 12 August 1915, 18 September 1915, 17 December 1915, and 19 January 1918; Minnedosa *Tribune*, 7 January 1915 and 9 August 1915; and Portage la Prairie *Weekly Review*, 2 June 1915.

80 Manitoba *Free Press*, 30 December 1914 and 1 January 1918.

81 Manitoba *Free Press*, 12 February 1916.

82 Quoted in Manitoba *Free Press*, 16 August 1915.

83 Harriet A. Walker, "Behind the Throne: A Dream of the Kaiser's," Manitoba *Free Press*, 31 August 1915.

84 Manitoba *Free Press*, 8 January 1923, 18 January 1923; Winnipeg *Tribune*, 4 January 1923, 9 January 1923, 13 January 1923, 19 January 1923.

85 Winnipeg *Tribune*, 12 January 1923, 15 January 1923.

86 Winnipeg *Tribune*, 8 January 1923. On 8 January, the Manitoba *Free Press*, likely referring to the same contest, stated that Plestina "received the beating of his life" at Hussane's hands.

87 Winnipeg *Tribune*, 9 January 1923.

88 Winnipeg *Tribune*, 4 January 1923.

89 Winnipeg *Tribune*, 18 January 1923.

90 Winnipeg *Tribune*, 8 January 1923, 11 January 1923.

91 Winnipeg *Tribune*, 20 January 1923.

92 Manitoba *Free Press*, 20 January 1923.

93 Manitoba *Free Press*, 20 January 1923; Winnipeg *Tribune*, 20 January 1923. The *Free Press* reported Taylor's weight as 214 pounds and Hussane's as 193 pounds.

94 Manitoba *Free Press*, 19 April 1923.

95 David Sulz, "Transnational Relations: Japanese Immigration and the Suian Maru Affair, 1900–1911," in *Contradictory Impulses: Canada and Japan in the Twentieth Century*, ed. Greg Donaghy and Patricia E. Roy (Vancouver: UBC Press, 2008), 56.

96 Joseph Svinth, "Professor Yamashita Goes to Washington," *Aikido Journal* 114 (1998), http://www.members.akido.com/public/professor-yamashita-goes-to-washington; Hewitt, *Catch Wrestling*, 49; Portage la Prairie *Semi-Weekly News*, 17 January 1905.

97 K. Koyama and A. Minami, *Spalding's Athletic Library No. 233: Jiu Jitsu* (New York: American Sports Publishing Company, 1904); K. Saito, *Jiu-Jitsu Tricks* (New York: Richard K. Fox Publishing Company, 1912); Svinth, "Professor Yamashita." On 9 April 1907, the Winnipeg *Telegram* noted that M. Matsuo, recently from Tokyo, had joined the University of Minnesota's staff as a "professor of jiu-jitsu."

98 Svinth, "Professor Yamashita."

99 Statements by Annapolis Naval Academy Commander James H. Sands, which appeared in Winnipeg during the "jiu-jitsu craze," reinforced the art's apparent danger, as did occasional reports of near-fatal injuries sustained during jiu-jitsu bouts. See Winnipeg *Telegram*, 17 March 1906 and and 9 March 1905, respectively. Curiously, none of the reports cited, in comparison, the physical damage incurred in catch-as-catch-can wrestling matches during the same period.

100 Manitoba *Free Press*, 6 June 1907.

101 For a general examination of self-styled "World Jiu-Jitsu Champion" Leopold McLaglen's career, see Graham Noble, "Early Ju-Jutsu: The Challenges Part II," *Dragon Times* 6 (n.d.), http://seinenkai.com/articles/noble/noble-jujutsu2.html. The Manitoba *Free Press* reported McLaglen's victory over Yagamata in a jiu-jitsu match in Minneapolis on 13 April 1906. See also Leopold McLaglen, *Police Jiu-Jitsu* (London: Police Review Publishing Company, 1918).

102 Manitoba *Free Press*, 30 March 1910.

103 Winnipeg *Voice*, 13 November 1914.

104 Sulz, "Transnational Relations," 47. For a detailed examination of Anglo-Canadian attitudes toward Oriental immigration in British Columbia, see Peter W. Ward, *White Canada Forever: Popular Attitudes and Public Policy toward Orientals in British Columbia* (Montreal: McGill-Queen's University Press, 1990).

105 Sulz, "Transnational Relations," 47; Ward, *White Canada Forever*, 55.

106 The situation in Manitoba can be contrasted with that in British Columbia, where thousands of Japanese immigrants lived. Substantial numbers allowed traditional Japanese sport to gain a purchase on the West Coast. For instance, 500 Japanese spectators witnessed a sumo tournament featuring thirty-two visiting athletes at Vancouver's Horse Show Building during September 1915. See Manitoba Japanese Canadian Citizens' Association, *The History of Japanese Canadians in Manitoba* (Winnipeg: Manitoba Japanese Canadian Citizens' Association, 1996), 1; Dominion Bureau of Statistics, *Sixth Census of Canada, 1921 Volume I: Population* (Ottawa: King's Printer, 1924), 355; and Vancouver *Sun*, 16 September 1915.

107 Manitoba *Free Press*, 27 May 1914; Minnedosa *Tribune*, 30 January 1908; Winnipeg *Telegram*, 30 April 1907; Woodsworth, *Strangers*, 189.

108 Manitoba *Free Press*, 19 May 1923.

109 Winnipeg *Tribune*, 5 May 1923.

110 Ibid. and 17 May 1923.

111 See, for example, Manitoba *Free Press*, 14 May 1923, 16 May 1923, and 18 May 1923; and Winnipeg *Tribune*, 5 May 1923 and 18 May 1923.

112 Winnipeg *Tribune*, 10 May 1923.

113 Winnipeg *Tribune*, 12 May 1923. Although there were many *ryu*, or "schools," of jiu-jitsu, most of the Japanese wrestlers operating in North America were judo practitioners. As historians Allan Guttman and Lee Thompson indicate in *Japanese Sports: A History* (Honolulu: University of Hawaii Press, 2001), 100–01, judo developed during the Meiji period (1868–1912), and its founder, Jigoro Kano, drew heavily on his Western education in formulating the system. Additionally, many other Japanese instructors, including Taro Miyake, whose primary training was in the *Horzun-ryu*, offered practical written lessons to the English-speaking public with no apparent attempt to perpetuate the notion of "Oriental mystery." See Taro Miyake and Yukio Tani, *The Game of Ju-Jitsu for the Use of Schools and Colleges* (London: Hazell, Watson, and Viney, 1906).

114 Manitoba *Free Press*, 14 May 1923.

115 For a compendium of known wrestler versus jiu-jitsu contests, see Hewitt, *Catch Wrestling*, 257–75; and Hewitt, *Catch Wrestling Round Two*, 399–404.

116 Winnipeg *Tribune*, 19 May 1923; Manitoba *Free Press*, 19 May 1923.

117 Ibid.

118 Manitoba *Free Press*, 12 June 1923.

119 Manitoba *Free Press*, 15 June 1923.

120 Manitoba *Free Press*, 16 June 1923.

121 Quoted in *Cosmopolitan*, May 1905. A copy of the article, with annotations, is available in *Journal of Combative Sport* (2002), http://www.ejmas.com/jcs/jcsframe.htm.

122 Quoted in Montreal *Star*, 20 December 1904.

123 Burns, *Lessons in Wrestling and Physical Culture*, Book No. 6, 4.

124 Quoted in Manitoba *Free Press*, 11 December 1906.

125   Based upon an examination of the matches provided in Hewitt's *Catch Wrestling* and *Catch Wrestling Round Two.*

126   Winnipeg *Tribune*, 10 May 1923

127   Manitoba *Free Press*, 17 September 1910.

128   Manitoba *Free Press*, 17 October 1910.

129   Manitoba *Free Press*, 12 December 1913.

130   Ibid. and 15 December 1913.

131   Manitoba *Free Press*, 16 December 1913.

132   John Boyko, *Last Step to Freedom: The Evolution of Canadian Racism* (Winnipeg: J. Gordon Shillingford Publishing, 1998), 163.

133   Robin W. Winks, *The Blacks in Canada: A History* (Montreal: McGill-Queen's University Press, 1997), 308–09.

134   Ibid., 311–12.

135   Boyko, *Last Steps to Freedom*, 165.

136   Avery, *Reluctant Host*, 8; Boyko, *Last Steps to Freedom*, 164. In 1921, there were only 491 blacks living in Manitoba. See Dominion Bureau of Statistics, *Sixth Census of Canada, 1921 Volume I: Population*, 355.

137   Manitoba *Free Press*, 5 July 1910.

138   Manitoba *Free Press*, 10 December 1923, 15 December 1923, 27 December 1923, 28 December 1923; Winnipeg *Tribune*, 27 December 1923.

139   Manitoba *Free Press*, 15 December 1923.

140   Manitoba *Free Press*, 29 December 1923.

141   Manitoba *Free Press*, 10 December 1923.

142   Manitoba *Free Press*, 29 December 1923.

143   Manitoba *Free Press*, 2 January 1924; Winnipeg *Tribune*, 2 January 1924.

144   Manitoba *Free Press*, 2 January 1924.

145   Ibid.

146   Taylor's first match with L'Heureux was a ten-minute exhibition at the Winnipeg police gymnasium on 5 December 1922. Although warmly received for his performance, L'Heureux was incapable of mounting any effective offence against his veteran opponent. The two were then pitted against one another in Dauphin a few weeks later, with advertising for the event openly acknowledging that "while it is not expected that Taylor will lose his crown the Frenchman has many admirers that think he will make Taylor extend himself." The wrestlers staged a second exhibition before Winnipeg audiences at the One Big Union Hall on 25 April 1924, with the French Canadian once more "giving a good account of himself" in the face of Taylor's superior grappling acumen. Taylor also defeated L'Heureux in matches in Morris, Moose Jaw, and Swift Current. Taylor wrestled Tom Johnstone in a match for the Canadian Heavyweight Championship in October 1923. Johnstone went into training several months in advance. However, the Winnipeg policeman proved to be utterly outclassed and was unable to apply a single hold before being pinned twice in under four and a half minutes. See Manitoba *Free Press*, 6 December 1922; Dauphin *Herald*, 21 December 1922; Saskatoon *Star*, 10 July 1923; One Big Union *Bulletin*, 1 May 1924; and Swift Current *Sun*, 18 December 1923 and 21 December 1923 concerning Taylor's matches with L'Heureux. On his match with Johnstone, see Manitoba *Free Press*, 16 October 1923 and 19 October 1923.

147   Montreal *Star*, 8 April 1905; *La Presse*, 9 May 1905.

148 Thompson, *Harvests*, 71, 72, 169–70. Historians have not universally accepted Thompson's contention that the western provinces contributed disproportionately to the war effort. Christopher A. Sharpe, for example, has demonstrated that, while Manitoba contributed a greater percentage of its total available manpower to the Canadian Expeditionary Forces than did Ontario, Saskatchewan's total enlistment number was significantly lower than that of either province. Alberta's total military enlistment was roughly equal to that of Ontario. With respect to the Victory Loan Campaigns of 1917 and 1918, per capita contributions in both Saskatchewan and Alberta were less than half that of Ontario, and even Manitoba lagged significantly behind Canada's largest province. However, Sharpe's study of Imperial Munitions Board contracts between 1915 and 1919 strongly supports Thompson's argument that western industry accrued little benefit from wartime production. See Christopher A. Sharpe, "The Great War," in *Historical Atlas of Canada Volume III*, Plate 26.

149 John Herd Thompson and Allen Seager, *Canada 1922–1939: Decades of Discord* (Toronto: McClelland and Stewart, 1985), 103.

150 Friesen, *The Canadian Prairies*, 343; Palmer and Palmer, *Alberta*, 54–55.

151 W.L. Morton, *The Progressive Party in Canada* (Toronto: University of Toronto Press, 1950), 8, 11. Western Progressivism did not represent a single ideologically unified movement. Although typically divided into the "Alberta" and "Manitoba" branches of the Progressive Party, at least four distinct "progressive" ideological movements held political sway in the west during the 1920s and early 1930s. Despite such differences, however, all advocated the move toward a decentralized Canadian state. See David Laycock, *Populism and Democratic Thought on the Prairies, 1910 to 1945* (Toronto: University of Toronto Press, 1990), 3–4, 19–22, 282.

152 See, for example, Manitoba *Free Press*, 2 June 1923.

153 Manitoba *Free Press*, 6 June 1923.

154 Winnipeg *Tribune*, 4 June 1923.

155 Winnipeg *Tribune*, 6 June 1923.

156 Manitoba *Free Press*, 7 June 1923. The match between Maupas and Taylor proved to be one of the last in Maupas's professional career. That year Maupas purchased property on Raymond Lake near Val Morin, Quebec, where he later opened a well-known athletic training camp, appropriately named Camp Maupas. Numerous athletes from a variety of disciplines trained at his facility until his accidental death in 1948. See Berthelet, *Yvon Robert*, 35–40; and Oliver, *The Pro Wrestling Hall of Fame*, 155–56.

157 In September 1923, Taylor was matched against Frank Simmons, "Champion of England," in a bout for the Championship of the British Empire. Unlike most of the matches staged by the Empire Athletic Club, however, the event was poorly received both by the public and by the press. Newspaper reports, generally complimentary throughout Taylor's homesteading tenure in Winnipeg, described the match as a "fizzle," "the most disappointing card yet offered by the Empire Athletic [C]lub." The Canadian completely outclassed Simmons, proving to be "faster, defter, and stronger" than his overweight adversary, characterized by the *Free Press* as "weighing 257 pounds, much of which was superfluous." His credentials as a national champion were likewise called into question, with skeptical qualifiers including "billed as" and "alleged" accompanying reports after the match. In actuality, Winnipeg's residents were justified in their skepticism of Simmons, for he was neither a British champion nor British at all, being instead a New Yorker whose real name was Frank Simmons Leavitt. Leavitt served with the US Army in the First World War, during which time he began wrestling under the name Soldier Leavitt. Although limited in actual wrestling ability, Leavitt later became a popular attraction during the 1930s when, following the advice of his wife and manager, Doris Dean, he grew a long beard and adopted the hillbilly persona Man Mountain Dean. Nevertheless, Taylor's victory served to bolster his bid for a match against the world's champion, Ed "Strangler" Lewis, the *Free Press* noting before the match that "a win for Taylor would put the local boy in a position where Lewis would have to give him a chance." See Manitoba *Free Press*, 17 September 1923 and 19 September 1923; and Griffin, *Fall Guys*, 114–15.

158 Lethbridge *Herald*, 17 April 1924; Manitoba *Free Press*, 21 April 1924.

159 For biographical information on Daviscourt, including references to his matches with Lewis, see Greg Oliver and Steven Johnson, *The Pro Wrestling Hall of Fame: The Heels* (Toronto: ECW Press, 2007), 130–32.

160 Lethbridge *Herald*, 17 April 1924; Manitoba *Free Press*, 26 April 1924.

161 Mott, "Flawed Games," 182.

162 Manitoba *Free Press*, 21 April 1924. For similar comments, see One Big Union *Bulletin*, 15 May 1924.

163 Manitoba *Free Press*, 9 May 1924.

164 Ibid.

165 The trust's formation, organization, and operation are well documented in the existing literature on wrestling during the period. See, for example, Beekman, *Ringside*, 53–57; and Griffin, *Fall Guys*, 42–43.

166 Beekman, *Ringside*, 60; Griffin, *Fall Guys*, 59–60; Hewitt, *Catch Wrestling*, 121, 152; Hewitt, *Catch Wrestling Round Two*, 243.

167 Beekman, *Ringside*, 61; Hewitt, *Catch Wrestling*, 153.

168 Griffin, *Fall Guys*, 47. Concerning the "Gold Dust Trio" and the power that they exercised over heavyweight professional wrestling, see also Beekman, *Ringside*, 57; Hornbaker, *National Wrestling Alliance*, 67–68, 96; and Thesz, *Hooker*, 51.

169 Manitoba *Free Press*, 22 March 1924.

170 May, *The Central Canadian Professional Wrestling Almanac*, 2–3.

171 Taylor began actively pursuing a match with Lewis during the winter of 1916–17. However, the first confirmed encounter between the two did not occur until 1932 in Seattle. On Taylor's challenges to Lewis, see Lincoln *Daily Star*, 9 November 1916, 18 March 1917, and 19 March 1917. On his first known match with Lewis, see Calgary *Herald*, 4 July 1933.

172 One Big Union *Bulletin*, 15 May 1923.

173 Manitoba *Free Press*, 19 May 1924, 21 May 1924.

174 Taylor had appeared two months earlier as the penultimate attraction on an Empire Athletic Club boxing card featuring Tommy Gibbons, former contender to Jack Dempsey's heavyweight boxing title. See Manitoba *Free Press*, 15 March 1924; and Winnipeg *Tribune*, 15 March 1924. For Taylor's matches with Harold "Hangman" Cantonwine, see Saskatoon *Star*, 16 January 1924; Regina *Leader*, 5 February 1924; and Medicine Hat *Daily News*, 26 February 1924.

175 Manitoba *Free Press*, 26 May 1924.

176 Manitoba *Free Press*, 18 June 1924.

177 Poddubny and Zbyszko wrestled one another three times prior to their meeting in Winnipeg. Their first encounter, in Paris in 1906, resulted in a two-hour draw. A second contest, staged in London on 12 December 1907 at the London Pavilion, occurred when both men were widely considered to be the best Greco-Roman wrestlers in Europe. The match was essentially a stalemate in which Poddubny was disqualified after thirty-five minutes for unfair tactics. Their third meeting occurred almost two decades later in New York on 8 March 1926 and resulted in a draw. Zbyszko ultimately defeated his long-time rival when they met in Winnipeg one month later. The Winnipeg match received extensive coverage in the local Polish-language press. A detailed examination of Zbyszko and Poddubny's London match is provided by Graham Noble in "'The Lion of the Punjab'—Part II: Stanislaus Zbyszko," *InYo: Journal of Alternative Perspectives on the Martial Arts and Sciences* (2002), http://ejmas.com/jalt/jaltframe.htm. See also New York *Times*, 9 March 1926; Manitoba *Free Press*, 10 April 1926; Winnipeg *Tribune*, 10 April 1926; and *Czas*, 14 April 1926. For more information on Poddubny's career, see Dmitri Zukhov, "The Champion of Champions:

Ivan Poddubny," in *Their Way to the Top: Stories about Sportsmen*, ed. Vladimir Anokhin (Moscow: Progress Publishers, 1978), 15–46.

178 Regionally based professional wrestlers such as Mike Bilinsky, Tommy Elder, Vic Jussack, and Archie McLaughlin participated in matches at Plebs Hall. See, for example, One Big Union *Bulletin*, 17 December 1925, 7 January 1926, 14 January 1926, 16 December 1926, 20 January 1927, 10 March 1927, 10 November 1927, and 14 November 1929. See also May, *Central Canadian Professional Wrestling Almanac*, 3–4.

179 *Ukrains'ki robitnychi visty*, 28 February 1929.

180 See the 1927, 1928, and 1931 Brandon *Henderson's Directory*.

181 Brandon *Sun*, 27 October 1928, 3 November 1928, 5 November 1928, 5 April 1929, 6 April 1929.

182 Brandon *Sun*, 16 October 1929.

183 Brandon *Sun*, 6 November 1929.

184 Brandon *Sun*, 29 October 1928.

185 Brandon *Sun*, 24 January 1929.

186 Brandon *Sun*, 2 November 1929.

CHAPTER 7: AMATEURISM EXPANDS

1 Manitoba *Free Press*, 21 September 1918. In July 1916, Dickinson injured his chest after falling into a shell hole carrying a loaded stretcher. He did not initially tend to his injuries and several days later began coughing up blood. He was later admitted for medical care on 24 August and diagnosed with bronchitis before returning to duty. Dickinson was readmitted on 7 September and spent most of the remaining year under medical care. See his Casualty Form, Medical Case Sheet, and Medical History Sheet, Library and Archives Canada, RG 150, Accession 1992–93/166, Box 2513–10.

2 Classes for the year began on 2 October. See Manitoba *Free Press*, 2 October 1918. A detailed analysis of daily newspaper reports in the *Free Press* and Winnipeg *Tribune* reveals that, if any competitions were held, they were not of sufficient note to garner attention from the local press.

3 J.H. McKinnon, who had won the 1914 Dominion Championships in the welterweight (145 pound) division, participated in the 1920 Dominion Championships in Toronto. However, during this period, McKinnon, defeated in the 154 pound class during the second round by eventual champion H. Adams, was wrestling out of Fort William, Ontario. See Fort William *Daily Times Journal*, 22 June 1920; and Leyshon, *Of Mats and Men*, 109.

4 Manitoba *Free Press*, 22 October 1920, 15 December 1921.

5 Archives of Manitoba, P 3812, Young Men's Christian Association, YMCA—History Sketch and Material 1883–1935, "Y—One Hundred: A Winnipeg Commemorative Publication," 18–19.

6 Ibid., 19. Concerning Winnipeg's ethnic distribution by district, see Hiebert, "Winnipeg," *Historical Atlas of Canada Volume III*, Plate 31.

7 See Zald, *Organizational Change*, 40.

8 Montreal *Gazette*, 9 May 1905; Montreal *Star*, 9 May 1905. Well-known American and European heavyweight wrestlers who visited Montreal prior to the First World War included Tom Jenkins, Frank Gotch, Fred Beell, Yankee Rogers, Youssouf Mahmout, Raoul de Rouen, Stanislaus Zbyszko, B.F. Roller, Raymond Cazeaux, Jess Pedersen, and Constant le Marin.

9 On 21 January 1901, Louis Cyr wrestled American professional catch-as-catch-can wrestling champion Dan McLeod (appearing under the alias George Little) in a handicap match in which the latter agreed to throw the famed strongman within twenty minutes. Although outweighed by 175 pounds, McLeod succeeded in his task in under four minutes. In an apparent attempt to

save face, Cyr later wrestled and defeated the North-West Territories (later Saskatchewan)-born circus giant Edouard Beaupre, who had a billed height of over eight feet. Cyr's match with Beaupre receives mention in historical treatments of his life, such as Ben Weider's *The Strongest Man in Canada: Louis Cyr* (Toronto: Mitchell Press, 1976), 147, yet the extant literature was, until recently silent on his loss to the diminutive McLeod. Hewitt's *Catch Wrestling: Round Two* and Laparade and Hebert's *Mad Dogs, Midgets and Screw Jobs* have rectified the omission.

10   For an overview of wrestling in Montreal during the period, see Laprade and Hebert, *Mad Dogs, Midgets, and Screw Jobs*, 6–14.

11   Manitoba *Free Press*, 1 December 1913, 6 December 1913, 10 December 1913.

12   *Le Manitoba*, 19 November 1913.

13   Analysis of the YMCA's Board of Directors minutes from before the First World War, which included lists of active and new members, fails to reveal any French surnames. See 12 September 1910 to 12 July 1912, Archives of Manitoba, P 3798, Young Men's Christian Association, Minutes: YMCA Board of Directors 1910–13.

14   "Le Saint Office et la Y.M.C.A.," *Les cloches de Saint-Boniface,*15 January 1921, 2; 15 February 1921, 21.

15   *Les cloches*, 15 February 1921, 24.

16   See, for example, Manitoba *Free Press*, 12 April 1919, 21 April 1919, and 10 May 1919. The Union Canadienne choir also participated in the Winnipeg Festival of Music in 1920, at which it performed a rendition of "Last Words of Christ." See Manitoba *Free Press*, 2 February 1920.

17   On lectures sponsored by the Union Canadienne, see Manitoba *Free Press*, 18 January 1916, 24 February 1919, 26 January 1920, 10 March 1920, and 29 November 1920.

18   Manitoba *Free Press*, 2 October 1917, 13 June 1916, 12 August 1916.

19   Organizational records pertaining to the International Athletic Club remain scarce. Opened in 1919 or early 1920, the club operated a gymnasium at 557 Tache Avenue and held professional boxing and wrestling cards both at its headquarters and across the river in Winnipeg. In 1923, it offered a fourteen-month membership at a cost of five dollars to amateur boxers and wrestlers wishing to train for the Provincial Championships. See Manitoba *Free Press*, 6 May 1922, 9 May 1922, 26 October 1922, 11 November 1922, and 17 January 1923.

20   Manitoba *Free Press*, 26 March 1921. See also Manitoba *Free Press*, 25 February 1921 and 30 March 1921.

21   Both special class (125 pound) champion Albert Leveille and middleweight H. Dussessoye represented the International Athletic Club, and St. Pierre's Leo L'Heureux wrestled under the Union Canadienne banner. See Appendix 1 and Manitoba *Free Press*, 26 April 1921.

22   See Appendix 1.

23   Manitoba *Free Press*, 24 March 1923. For more on Tauno Makela's wrestling career, see Charles Nathan Hatton, "Battles on the Bay: Wrestling in Fort William and Port Arthur before the Great Depression," Thunder Bay Historical Museum Society *Papers and Records* 25 (2007): 59–61.

24   For a further discussion on the matter, see Riess, *City Games*, 92.

25   Hutchison, *Century of Service*, 52.

26   Ibid.; Bercuson, *Confrontation at Winnipeg*, 150.

27   Bercuson, *Confrontation at Winnipeg*, 117, 150; Kenneth McNaught and David J. Bercuson, *The Winnipeg General Strike: 1919* (Don Mills, ON: Longman Canada, 1974), 70; J.M. Bumsted, *The Winnipeg General Strike of 1919: An Illustrated Guide* (Winnipeg: Watson and Dwyer, 1994), 3.

28   D.C. Masters, *The Winnipeg General Strike* (Toronto: University of Toronto Press, 1950), 59.

29   Bercuson, *Confrontation at Winnipeg*, 150.

30   Ibid., 150–51; Hutchison, *Century of Service,* 52; Masters, *Winnipeg General Strike,* 74; McNaught and Bercuson, *Winnipeg General Strike,* 70. A copy of both the Winnipeg City Council's pledge and the police union's response can be found in Norman Penner, ed., *Winnipeg 1919: The Strikers' Own History of the Winnipeg General Strike* (Toronto: James, Lewis, and Samuel, 1973), 82.

31   Bercuson, *Confrontation at Winnipeg,* 152–54; Hutchison, *Century of Service,* 52; Masters, *Winnipeg General Strike,* 83, 96; McNaught and Bercuson, *Winnipeg General Strike,* 74.

32   Penner, *Winnipeg 1919,* 127.

33   Masters, *Winnipeg General Strike,* 136.

34   Jack Templeman, "History of the Winnipeg Police Part Three: The Roaring Twenties," http://www.winnipeg.ca/police/history/history3.stm.

35   Ibid.

36   Robert F. Wheeler, "Organized Sport and Organized Labour: The Workers' Sport Movement," *Journal of Contemporary History* 13, 2 (1978): 194; Joan Sangster, "The Softball Solution: Female Workers, Male Managers, and the Operation of Paternalism at Westclox, 1923–60," *Labour/Le travail* 32 (1993): 192.

37   The organization's purpose was stated in its constitution, formulated on 2 October 1919. See 2 October 1919, Archives of Manitoba, P 1040/1, Winnipeg Police Association, Winnipeg City Police Athletic Association Minutes 1919–31, 5. For an overview of activities conducted by the WCPAA during the spring of 1924, see Manitoba *Free Press,* 5 February 1924.

38   Hutchison, *Century of Service,* 55, 57.

39   For example, the Police Commission provided fifty dollars for a WCPAA smoking concert to be held on 5 March 1920. Similarly, requests for money from the Police Commission appear to have been made occasionally by the WCPAA. See 3 March 1920 and 7 April 1921, Archives of Manitoba, P 1040/1, Winnipeg Police Association, Winnipeg City Police Athletic Association Minutes 1919–31.

40   Manitoba *Free Press,* 9 April 1920.

41   9 April 1920, Archives of Manitoba, P 1040/1, Winnipeg Police Association, Winnipeg City Police Athletic Association Minutes 1919–31.

42   In October 1920, John Albrecht, the Minneapolis police officer who had wrestled Tom Johnstone at the River Park Baseball Grounds on 6 August, wrote to the WCPAA asking it to promote a return engagement. The proposal was denied since "owing [to] the status of the Association as an Amateur organisation the offer of Mr. Albrecht [could not] be accepted." See 12 October 1920, Archives of Manitoba, P 1040/1, Winnipeg Police Association, Winnipeg City Police Athletic Association Minutes 1919–31.

43   The WCPAA staged open meets as well as competitions featuring only their own athletes. For examples of the former, see Manitoba *Free Press,* 17 December 1923, 19 February 1924, 28 February 1924, 15 December 1925, and 3 December 1926. Concerning the latter, see Manitoba *Free Press,* 28 April 1926.

44   Manitoba *Free Press,* 25 December 1926, 18 February 1927.

45   See, respectively, Manitoba *Free Press,* 10 April 1924, 10 January 1925, and 12 April 1929.

46   Winnipeg Police Museum, Police Commission Books.

47   See Appendix 1 and Leyshon, *Of Mats and Men,* 110.

48   McKinnon earned four provincial titles and two dominion titles between 1914 and 1926.

49   Other prominent police wrestlers active during the 1920s included Leon Elfinson, Francis Lawrence Miller, Angus MacIver, Benjamin Cecil Newcombe, and William Ross.

50   Manitoba *Free Press,* 6 December 1922, 11 December 1923, 12 February 1924.

51   Manitoba *Free Press*, 6 December 1922. See also Manitoba *Free Press*, 11 December 1923.

52   18 March 1920, Archives of Manitoba, P 1040/1, Winnipeg Police Association, Winnipeg City Police Athletic Association Minutes 1919–31.

53   Reported expenses included hall rental, printing, and purses for competitors amounting to $831.85, with some costs still to be determined. See 18 March 1920, 27 March 1920, and 9 April 1920, Archives of Manitoba, P 1040/1, Winnipeg Police Association, Winnipeg City Police Athletic Association Minutes 1919–31.

54   9 April 1920, Archives of Manitoba, P 1040/1, Winnipeg Police Association, Winnipeg City Police Athletic Association Minutes 1919–31.

55   15 September 1924, Archives of Manitoba, P 1040/1, Winnipeg Police Association, Winnipeg City Police Athletic Association Minutes 1919–31.

56   12 May 1927, Archives of Manitoba, P 1040/1, Winnipeg Police Association, Winnipeg City Police Athletic Association Minutes 1919–31.

57   On 14 June 1922, the WCPAA executive agreed to consult a crown attorney because of the failure of A.R. Morrison, former secretary of the MAAUC, to submit money from ticket sales for the 1921 Manitoba Amateur Boxing and Wrestling Championships. Both Morrison and the MAAUC were notified of the board's decision. In another instance, well-known Winnipeg boxer Dave Coulter failed to compete after weighing in at the Manitoba Olympic trials in 1924. Coulter was suspended by the MAAUC from competing at the request of the WCPAA executive. See 14 June 1922 and 15 September 1924, Archives of Manitoba, P 1040/1, Winnipeg Police Association, Winnipeg City Police Athletic Association Minutes 1919–31.

58   15 September 1924, Archives of Manitoba, P 1040/1, Winnipeg Police Association, Winnipeg City Police Athletic Association Minutes 1919–31. On 12 May 1927, the WCPAA president reported that $300 had been paid to the widow of officer Harry Talbot, killed in a railway accident at Swift Current, Saskatchewan. During the next meeting, a further $100 was provided for Mrs. Talbot, evidently to pay her coal and tax bills. See ibid., 12 May 1927 and 2 June 1927.

59   On 3 March 1927, for example, the WCPAA executive granted fifty dollars to the wives of officers W. Deegan and W. Cameron, and investigations were initiated concerning a third officer, G. Caughey, also ill for a considerable time. Similarly, in April 1928, $100 was given to ailing officer H.A. Sleeman so that he could go to Rochester for an examination. See 3 March 1927 and 6 April 1928, Archives of Manitoba, P 1040/1, Winnipeg Police Association, Winnipeg City Police Athletic Association Minutes 1919–31.

60   See 26 September 1927 and 7 November 1927, Archives of Manitoba, P 1040/1, Winnipeg Police Association, Winnipeg City Police Athletic Association Minutes 1919–31.

61   In 1945, the WCPAA became the official bargaining organization for the Winnipeg policemen, and in 1972 it was renamed the Winnipeg Police Association, representing all policemen in the greater metropolitan area. See Hutchison, *Century of Service*, 58.

62   Bercuson, *Confrontation at Winnipeg*, 185; Masters, *Winnipeg General Strike*, 129; McNaught and Bercuson, *Winnipeg General Strike*, 30, 32; Tom Mitchell and James Naylor, "The Prairies: In the Eye of the Storm," in *The Workers' Revolt in Canada, 1917–1925*, ed. Craig Heron (Toronto: University of Toronto Press, 1998), 178.

63   David Bercuson, *Fools and Wise Men: The Rise and Fall of the One Big Union* (Toronto: McGraw-Hill Ryerson, 1978), 153.

64   Ibid., 166–69. For the most detailed examination of the 1920 OBU convention, see Michel S. Beaulieu, *Labour at the Lakehead: Ethnicity, Socialism, and Politics, 1900–35* (Vancouver: UBC Press, 2011), 65–89. The schism did not just affect the relationship between the OBU and lumber workers in northern Ontario, for workers in British Columbia's forestry sector also withdrew from the union in January 1921. See Manitoba *Free Press*, 17 January 1921.

65 Bercuson, *Fools and Wise Men*, 216.

66 Attacking the OBU as idealistic and unrealistic, by late 1921 the Comintern and Worker's Party advised workers to reaffiliate with traditional labour unions and "bore from within" to realize a communist mandate. See ibid., 221, 224, and 228; and J. Peter Campbell, *Canadian Marxists and the Search for a Third Way* (Montreal: McGill-Queen's University Press, 1999), 191.

67 Bercuson, *Fools and Wise Men*, 217–18; Kidd, *Struggle for Canadian Sport*, 149–50.

68 Bercuson, *Fools and Wise Men*, 219.

69 See 20 February 1923, Archives of Manitoba, MG10, A 14-2 #17, Robert Boyd Russell Collection: One Big Union, OBU Central Council (Winnipeg) Minutes 1922–23.

70 See 20 March 1923, Archives of Manitoba, MG10, A 14-2 #17, Robert Boyd Russell Collection: One Big Union, OBU Central Council (Winnipeg) Minutes 1922–23.

71 OBU *Bulletin*, 17 January 1924, 24 January 1924. By the end of 1923, the Athletic Committee reported to the OBU Central Council that they had over 100 members. See 18 December 1923, Archives of Manitoba, MG10, A 14-2 #17, Robert Boyd Russell Collection: One Big Union, OBU Central Council (Winnipeg) Minutes 1922–23.

72 OBU *Bulletin*, 31 January 1924.

73 OBU *Bulletin*, 14 February 1924.

74 OBU *Bulletin*, 17 April 1924.

75 Kidd, *Struggle for Canadian Sport*, 150; Howell, *Blood, Sweat, and Cheers*, 56–57. Concerning the club's pay-as-you-go policy, see 4 December 1923, Archives of Manitoba, MG10, A 14-2 #17, Robert Boyd Russell Collection: One Big Union, OBU Central Council (Winnipeg) Minutes 1922–23.

76 See, for example, OBU *Bulletin*, 16 October 1924, 16 December 1926, 29 April 1926, and 8 December 1927.

77 For example, a playbill in the 19 April 1928 edition of the OBU *Bulletin* announced that ticket prices for an upcoming show were twenty-five cents for adults and ten cents for children.

78 OBU *Bulletin*, 1 May 1924.

79 Quoted in Lewis H. Thomas, ed., *The Making of a Socialist: Recollections of T.C. Douglas* (Edmonton: University of Alberta Press, 1982), 37–38.

80 OBU *Bulletin*, 17 January 1924, 21 February 1924, 28 February 1924, 22 September 1927.

81 OBU *Bulletin*, 4 September 1924, 11 September 1924.

82 OBU *Bulletin*, 28 February 1924.

83 OBU *Bulletin*, 11 September 1924.

84 OBU *Bulletin*, 16 October 1924.

85 OBU *Bulletin*, 7 January 1926.

86 Jussack competed in the middle and light-heavyweight classes at the 1926 Manitoba Amateur Boxing and Wrestling Championships, though he failed to win a title in either division. See *Manitoba Free Press*, 6 April 1926 and 7 April 1926. On his ethnicity, see *Brandon Sun*, 18 November 1929 and 30 November 1929.

87 See, for example, OBU *Bulletin*, 6 March 1924, 24 May 1924, 11 December 1924, 22 January 1925, and 26 February 1925; and *Manitoba Free Press*, 16 January 1925, 27 February 1925, and 11 December 1925.

88 OBU *Bulletin*, 27 November 1924; *Manitoba Free Press*, 6 March 1925, 9 March 1925.

89 The OBU *Bulletin*, 14 November 1929, incorrectly identified William Crossley as William Crosby.

90 In March 1924, for example, professional bantamweight boxer Jerry Salter fought city bantamweight amateur champion Billy Ayrton. See OBU *Bulletin*, 13 March 1924.

91 Kidd, *Struggle for Canadian Sport*, 150.

92 For specific use of the expression by the OBUAA in reference to itself, see OBU *Bulletin*, 8 April 1926.

93 Metcalfe, *Canada Learns to Play*, 133–34.

94 OBU *Bulletin*, 8 April 1926.

95 Ibid. Virtually identical sentiments were expressed by the OBUAA in late 1924 when a professional card was staged on the same night as its regular Friday program. In the OBU *Bulletin* of 15 December 1924, the club stated that "we have ... been instrumental to a large extent in helping to pull the game out of the mire where it has been dragged by at least some of the professional promoters of this city in their efforts to hoodwink the public and exploit the local talent in their scramble for easy money."

96 Ibid.

97 OBU *Bulletin*, 16 October 1924.

98 OBU *Bulletin*, 10 March 1927.

99 OBU *Bulletin*, 7 January 1926, 10 March 1927.

100 See, for example, Manitoba *Free Press*, 23 March 1922 and 7 July 1926.

101 Manitoba *Free Press*, 12 January 1929.

102 See, for example, Manitoba *Free Press*, 21 April 1927, 17 November 1927, and 16 December 1927.

103 OBU *Bulletin*, 14 February 1924. For coverage of WCPAA-sponsored events, see OBU *Bulletin*, 10 January 1924, 7 February 1924, 17 April 1924, and 8 December 1927.

104 OBU *Bulletin*, 10 November 1927.

105 See 2 June 1927, Archives of Manitoba, P 1040/1, Winnipeg Police Association, Winnipeg City Police Athletic Association Minutes 1919–31.

106 See 6 November 1923, Archives of Manitoba, MG10, A 14-2 #17, Robert Boyd Russell Collection: One Big Union, OBU Central Council (Winnipeg) Minutes 1922–23.

107 OBU *Bulletin*, 26 February 1925.

108 OBU *Bulletin*, 26 February 1926. For details on the preliminary wrestling matches for the 1925 City Championships, see Manitoba *Free Press*, 14 February 1925.

109 OBU *Bulletin*, 14 February 1924.

110 At the end of the 1925–26 season, the OBUAA stated in the 29 April edition of the *Bulletin* that "we ... would like to thank the two local papers for the publicity they have given us throughout the season, and it speaks well for the sporting editors of the *Free Press* and *Tribune* that they are willing at all times to give space on their sporting pages free of charge in order to boost amateur sport." For coverage of the OBUAA's weekly boxing and wrestling programs during the season, see, for example, Manitoba *Free Press*, 31 October 1925, 6 November 1925, 7 November 1925, 13 November 1925, 14 November 1925, 20 November 1925, 27 November 1925, 28 November 1925, 11 December 1925, 8 January 1926, 21 January 1926, 22 January 1926, 23 January 1926, 5 February 1926, 19 February 1926, 26 February 1926, 5 March 1926, 19 March 1926, and 30 April 1926.

111 OBU *Bulletin*, 2 December 1926; Winnipeg *Tribune*, 7 December 1926.

112 Wrestlers representing each of these clubs in amateur competition during the 1920s included H. Asselin, Lawrence Lang, and Clovis T. Amante (St. Jean Baptiste); W. Ketcheson (Canadian National Railway Police Athletic Association and later OBU); William Crossley (Winnipeg Light Infantry and later OBU and YMCA); Mark McDermott and E.L. Young (Royal Canadian Horse Artillery); Andrew Borg, Frank De Cock, Nate Fenson, William Fray, Bill Handbur, and Teddy

Newman (Pioneer Athletic Club); Joe Walker (East Kildonan Athletic Club); and Stanley Zajac (Beaver Boxing Club). On club affiliations, see Manitoba *Free Press*, 26 March 1923, 11 August 1923, 14 August 1923, 5 April 1924, 9 April 1924, 17 May 1924, 15 December 1925, 19 March 1927, 23 March 1927, and 23 April 1927.

113 The four competitors in the inaugural Brandon City Amateur Boxing and Wrestling Championships were Bray and Dave Willey, Oxenbury (given name not known), and Art Nixon. Bray Willey emerged as the eventual victor. Brandon *Sun*, 3 November 1926.

114 Brandon *Sun*, 7 December 1926, 9 December 1926.

115 Manitoba *Free Press*, 30 November 1926, 20 December 1926, 12 March 1928; Minnedosa *Tribune*, 16 December 1926, 23 December 1926.

116 OBU *Bulletin*, 7 February 1924.

117 OBU *Bulletin*, 14 February 1924.

118 The Manitoba *Free Press* noted that several well-known heavyweights had been approached for matches in Winnipeg, including Joe Stecher, Marin Plestina, Wayne Munn, Dick Daviscourt, Jim Browning, and Allan Eustace, but all demanded fees higher than local promoter D'Arcy McIlroy could afford. Ultimately, former world champion Wayne Munn was pitted against Jack Taylor, but the match proved to be a financial failure. See Manitoba *Free Press*, 12 June 1928 and 4 July 1928.

119 Indicative of participation levels during the period, thirty-four boxers entered the City Championships in 1924 compared with nineteen wrestlers. A typical card offered by the OBUAA, for example, featured between six and eight boxing bouts and between two and four wrestling matches. See OBU *Bulletin*, 14 February 1924, 17 December 1925, 11 February 1926, 18 November 1926, and 7 April 1927.

120 John V. Grombach, *The Saga of the Fist: The 9,000 Year Story of Boxing in Text and Pictures* (Cranbury, NJ: A.S. Barnes and Company, 1977), 54–55; Sam Andre and Nat Fleischer, *A Pictorial History of Boxing* (New York: Bonanza Books, 1981), 96. Interest in Dempsey's exploits was not limited to the United States, as author Max Braithwaite colourfully illustrates in his personal recollection of crowds gathering outside the newspaper office in Prince Albert, Saskatchewan, to hear regular telegraph updates during his match with Georges Carpentier in 1921. Winnipeg photographer L.B. Foote captured a similar spectacle on 4 July 1923 when a large, and conspicuously male, gathering of boxing fans congregated in front of the *Tribune* building to listen to the latest updates from Dempsey's fight with Tommy Gibbons in Shelby, Montana. See Max Braithwaite, *Never Sleep Three in a Bed* (Toronto: McClelland and Stewart, 1975), 110–12; and Archives of Manitoba, L.B. Foote Collection 1072, Negative 1813.

121 Arnold, *History of Boxing*, 59.

122 Manitoba *Free Press*, 12 December 1928.

123 Kidd, *Struggle for Canadian Sport*, 64.

124 Alan Metcalfe, "The Meaning of Amateurism: A Case Study in Canadian Sport, 1884–1970," *Canadian Journal of History of Sport* 36 (1995): 38.

125 Manitoba *Free Press*, 8 May 1924.

126 The Manitoba *Free Press* commented on 4 June that "little talent of real Olympic class was visible at the opening of the Manitoba Olympic boxing and wrestling trials" the previous evening. Conclusions were unchanged after the second and final day of competition, when the *Free Press* noted on 5 June that "as a whole the trials were a failure, as they failed to bring out any outstanding talent." The WCPAA, which hosted the event, credited the absence of entries from the highly regarded Pioneer Athletic Club and the late date at which the event was held for its failure. See 15 September 1924, Archives of Manitoba, P 1040/1, Winnipeg Police Association, Winnipeg City Police Athletic Association Minutes 1919–31.

127 See Howard J. Crocker, ed., *Report: Canadian Olympic Committee 1924 Games* (Ottawa?: Canadian Olympic Committee, 1925), 13, 50.

128 Kidd, *Struggle for Canadian Sport*, 68.

129 Manitoba *Free Press*, 30 June 1928.

130 Ibid.

131 Manitoba *Free Press*, 9 July 1928.

132 Manitoba *Free Press*, 18 July 1928.

133 Ibid.

134 Jim Trifunov, who earned a bronze medal in the 123 pound division, was not initially selected for the team, but he went to Amsterdam with funds provided by the Saskatchewan government. See Leyshon, *Of Mats and Men*, 96; and Manitoba *Free Press*, 11 July 1928.

135 OBU *Bulletin*, 21 February 1924. See also OBU *Bulletin*, 12 June 1924, 1 January 1925, 26 February 1925, 22 September 1927, and 2 February 1928.

136 Manitoba *Free Press*, 20 April 1920.

137 Endelman competed for the YMCA between 1924 and 1929 and Romalis between 1923 and 1927. See Manitoba *Free Press*, 18 December 1923, 15 February 1924, 10 March 1925, 23 March 1925, 18 February 1925, 2 May 1927, and 11 April 1929, for references to both men and their YMCA affiliation. Further information on both Endelman and Romalis is contained in Leible Hershfield, *The Jewish Athlete: A Nostalgic View* (Winnipeg: By the Author, 1980), 162.

138 Endelman worked for the Eaton's Company, and Romalis was an agent for Prudential Insurance. See the 1927 Winnipeg *Henderson's Directory*.

139 See 26 September 1929, Archives of Manitoba, P 3798, Young Men's Christian Association, Minutes: YMCA Board of Directors.

140 Winnipeg's Young Men's Hebrew Association was originally founded in 1895 as the Young Hebrew Social Assembly Club. By 1899, it had been renamed according to its more familiar designation. Although Winnipeg's Jewish residents were not able to secure their own gym facility until 1936, interest in boxing and wrestling within the wider community was evident more than a decade earlier. In 1924, the Winnipeg Hebrew Free School secured the MAAUC's permission to stage boxing and wrestling in conjunction with a "Jubilee Carnival," staged on 1 and 2 September. Among the features was a match between Joe Romalis, brother of Lou, and the OBU's Harry Vernon. Over 1,000 people attended the event. Arthur A. Chiel, *The Jews in Manitoba: A Social History* (Toronto: University of Toronto Press, 1961), 110–11; Manitoba *Free Press*, 12 July 1924, 2 September 1924.

141 Manitoba *Free Press*, 27 September 1919. During the AAUC's 1919 national convention, the Manitoba delegates put forward the resolution that "any professional who has stayed out of professional sport for two years may be reinstated." Although it was supported by representatives from Alberta and Saskatchewan, eastern delegates defeated the motion. See Library and Archives Canada, MG 28 150, Vol. 20, Amateur Athletic Union of Canada Minutes 1919, 20–21.

142 Manitoba *Free Press*, 27 September 1919.

143 Manitoba *Free Press*, 7 May 1920.

144 Fort William *Daily Times-Journal*, 7 July 1920; Library and Archives Canada, MG 28 150, Vol. 20, Amateur Athletic Union of Canada Minutes 1920, 12.

145 Manitoba *Free Press*, 3 May 1921, 2 December 1921.

146 Manitoba *Free Press*, 29 April 1926.

147 Kidd, *Struggle for Canadian Sport*, 56.

148 Ibid., 60; Metcalfe, "Meaning of Amateurism," 41.

149 Kidd, *Struggle for Canadian Sport*, 60; Manitoba *Free Press*, 7 May 1930.

150 Manitoba *Free Press*, 5 March 1923.

151 See 14 June 1922, Archives of Manitoba, P 1040/1, Winnipeg Police Association, Winnipeg City Police Athletic Association Minutes 1919–31.

152 See 6 April 1928, Archives of Manitoba, P 1040/1, Winnipeg Police Association, Winnipeg City Police Athletic Association Minutes 1919–31.

153 See 31 July 1929, Archives of Manitoba, P 1040/1, Winnipeg Police Association, Winnipeg City Police Athletic Association Minutes 1919–31.

154 On the AAUC's financial problems, see Kidd, *Struggle for Canadian Sport*, 65.

155 Manitoba *Free Press*, 25 September 1924. See also Manitoba *Free Press*, 19 August 1924.

156 Manitoba *Free Press*, 23 August 1924.

157 Manitoba *Free Press*, 1 January 1925.

158 Manitoba *Free Press*, 16 April 1929.

159 Manitoba *Free Press*, 17 April 1929, 18 April 1929; Port Arthur *Daily News-Chronicle*, 19 April 1929, 20 April 1929, 22 April 1929.

160 Based upon an examination of the championship rosters provided by Leyshon, *Of Mats and Men*, 109–10.

161 See 6 April 1928, Archives of Manitoba, P 1040/1, Winnipeg Police Association, Winnipeg City Police Athletic Association Minutes 1919–31.

CONCLUSION

1 Morton, *Manitoba*, 416; Skene, "C.P. Walker," 147.

2 Stuart, *Prairie Theatre*, 75, 76; Skene, "C.P. Walker," 146.

3 Skene, "C.P. Walker," 148.

4 The Manitoba *Free Press* reported on 3 February 1923 that A. Taylor, a "local radio fan" residing in Waskada, Saskatchewan, had intercepted a detailed radio broadcast of a match between Ed "Strangler" Lewis and Allan Huston in Wichita.

5 Manitoba *Free Press*, 16 June 1931.

6 During the early 1930s, access to electricity was still largely confined to areas with higher population densities. However, those living in rural settings utilized batteries to power their radios. See Jackson, *Centennial History of Manitoba*, 224.

7 Donald G. Wetherell, "Some Aspects of Technology and Leisure in Alberta," *Prairie Forum* 11, 1 (1986): 58.

8 Morton, *Manitoba*, 413; Bellan, *Winnipeg First Century*, 203; Coates and McGuinness, *Manitoba*, 116.

9 Morton, *Manitoba*, 421; Bellan, *Winnipeg First Century*, 191.

10 Bellan, *Winnipeg First Century*, 193.

11 Several historians of Manitoba, among them Coates and McGuinness, and Bellan, emphasize that the services provided by relief organizations in Winnipeg were decidedly superior to those offered in smaller communities or rural regions in the province, resulting in considerable migration to the city. Other historians, such as Doug Smith, however, have been more expressly critical of Depression-era relief programs for the unemployed, stating that "the official reaction to the suffering of the thirties was one of distrust and hostility." See Coates and McGuinness, *Manitoba*, 116; Bellan, *Winnipeg First Century*, 205; and Smith, *Let Us Rise!*, 75.

12　Don Bailey, "The Lost Decade," in Shilliday, *Manitoba 125: A History Volume 2*, 219.

13　Ticket prices at the Paradise Gardens Dance Pavilion, for example, at fifty cents, were roughly equivalent to the larger movie palaces in Winnipeg. See Winnipeg *Tribune*, 1 June 1931. See also Bailey, "Lost Decade," 218, concerning the popularity of Depression-era dance halls.

14　Morton, *Manitoba*, 415–16.

15　Ibid., 416.

16　Motion picture ticket prices, listings, and theatre locations can be found in any daily newspaper from the period. In this instance, see Manitoba *Free Press*, 2 February 1931; and Winnipeg *Tribune*, 23 May 1931 and 2 June 1931.

17　During the spring of 1931, a Minerva electric radio could be purchased outright for $99.75 or with a cash deposit of ten dollars followed by ten monthly payments of ten dollars. The less expensive King battery-operated model could be purchased for $59.50 or with a deposit of six dollars and ten more payments of six dollars. Five years later a Viking electric mantel radio cost $29.95 or a down payment of three dollars and ten monthly payments of $2.80. See, respectively, the 1931 *Timothy Eaton's Spring–Summer Catalogue* and the 1936–37 *Timothy Eaton's Fall–Winter Catalogue*.

18　Manitoba *Free Press*, 16 June 1931.

19　The Amphitheatre Boxing and Wrestling Club's members included Alderman L.F. Borrowman (Borrowman and Jamieson Engineer), C.E. Hayles and H.E. Riley (Canadian Consolidated Grain Company), C.H. McFayden (with ties to local football), Dyson P. Smith (manager, Empire Coal Company), and Arthur Burrows (Burrows Lumber Company). Matches were promoted by Amphitheatre Rink manager Jack McVicar. See Manitoba *Free Press*, 13 June 1931; Winnipeg *Tribune*, 13 June 1931 and 20 June 1931; and 1931 Winnipeg *Henderson's Directory*.

20　Manitoba *Free Press*, 13 June 1931.

21　Griffin, *Fall Guys*, 49–50; Hornbaker, *National Wrestling Alliance*, 96.

22　On Sonnenberg's rise to wrestling fame and the measures taken by promoters such as Philadelphia's Paul Bowser to ensure that Sonnenberg remained protected from legitimate wrestlers who sought to expose his limited ability on the mat, see Hewitt's detailed account in *Catch Wrestling Round Two*, 151–75.

23　Manitoba *Free Press*, 13 June 1931.

24　Michailoff staged his first wrestling card in Toronto's Arena Gardens on 4 May 1929 with Jack Taylor in the main event. His promotion initially attracted small crowds, with attendance being boosted by the availability of free tickets. By 1931, however, thousands of paying spectators were regularly patronizing his programs. Wrestling's dramatic revival in Toronto was elegantly chronicled by Henry Roxborough in the 15 October 1931 edition of *Maclean's* magazine. Michailoff later promoted wrestling in Winnipeg during 1933. Concerning his first wrestling card in Toronto and his tenure as a Winnipeg wrestling promoter, see, respectively, Toronto *Globe*, 6 May 1929; and Nevada, *Wrestling in the Canadian West*, 17–18.

25　Manitoba *Free Press*, 24 June 1924. Taylor wrestled in Calgary for promoter Josef Zabaw before making his return to Winnipeg. See Calgary *Herald*, 17 April 1931 and 6 June 1931. For more information on Zabaw's Calgary-based wrestling promotion, see Nevada, *Wrestling in the Canadian West*, 14–16.

26　Manitoba *Free Press*, 25 June 1931.

27　Ibid.

28　Manitoba *Free Press*, 27 June 1931.

29　Ibid.

30　Winnipeg *Tribune*, 26 June 1931.

31　Ibid.

32   Winnipeg *Tribune*, 9 July 1931.

33   Quoted in Winnipeg *Free Press*, 28 April 1936.

34   Morris Markey, a reporter who investigated professional wrestling's growing popularity in New York for the 18 April 1931 edition of the *New Yorker*, likewise observed that "in the game itself there has been gradual changes toward showmanship. No longer was it a glum tussle on the mat—two interminably long falls out of three, with all the fine points hopelessly concealed from the spectators."

35   See also Rickard, "Spectacle of Excess," 136.

36   Tickets for the initial Amphitheatre wrestling card were priced at $1.75 (ringside), $1.25 (reserved), and $0.75 (rush), making them considerably less expensive than the "high-class" bouts at the Walker Theatre prior to the First World War. See Manitoba *Free Press*, 24 June 1931.

37   Manitoba *Free Press*, 23 June 1931, 6 August 1931.

38   See also Hatton, *Rugged Game*, 137.

39   Manitoba *Free Press*, 1 May 1931.

40   Winnipeg *Free Press*, 5 December 1931.

41   Manitoba *Free Press*, 4 May 1931.

42   In the finals of the 1931 Provincial Championships, for example, five of the eight athletes represented the OBUAA, one represented the WCPAA, and one came from Pine Falls. Neither the YMCA nor commercial clubs submitted participants. See Winnipeg *Tribune*, 20 April 1931.

43   Beekman, *Ringside*, viii.

Bibliography

PRIMARY SOURCES AND COLLECTIONS

Newspapers and Periodicals

"Action Front!"

Bell's Life in London and Sporting Chronicle

Boston Globe

Brandon Sun

Calgary Herald

Casper Tribune

Chillicothe Constitution

Cosmopolitan

Czas (Winnipeg)

Daily Nor'Wester (Winnipeg)

Dauphin Herald

Edmonton Bulletin

Edmonton Journal

Fort William Daily Times-Journal

Heimskringla (Winnipeg)

Klondike Nugget

La Liberté (Winnipeg)

La Presse (Montreal)

Le Manitoba (Winnipeg)

Lethbridge Herald

Lincoln Daily Star

Lloyd's Weekly News

Logansport Journal

Logansport Pharos

Lowell Sun

Maclean's

Manitoba Free Press

Marshfield Times

Medicine Hat Daily News

Melita New Era and Napinka Herald

Minnedosa Tribune

Montreal Gazette

Montreal Star

National Police Gazette

New Church Times

New Yorker

New York Herald

New York Times

Norwood Press

Oakland Tribune

One Big Union Bulletin

Ottawa Journal

Portage la Prairie Daily News

Portage la Prairie Semi-Weekly Review

Port Arthur Daily News-Chronicle

Regina Leader

Ring Magazine

Salt Lake Daily Tribune

Saskatoon Phoenix

Saskatoon Star

Swift Current Sun

Toronto Evening Telegram

Toronto Globe

Ukrains'ki Robitnychi Visty (Winnipeg)

Vancouver *Sun*

Voice (Winnipeg)

Winnipeg *Free Press*

Winnipeg *Real Estate News*

Winnipeg *Siftings*

Winnipeg *Sun*

Winnipeg *Telegram*

Winnipeg *Tribune*

WUB: Western Universities Battalion, 196th

Yukon *Sun*

Library and Archives Canada

Canadian Census

Canadian Expeditionary Forces First World War Attestation Papers (RG 150)

Department of Militia and Defence (RG 9)

Department of National Defence/Library and Archives Canada Photographic Records

Records of the Department of National Defence (RG 24)

Manitoba Archives

Amateur Athletic Union of Canada Manitoba Section Collection

Edward Ernest Best Collection

Edward W. Low Collection

Frederick Phillips Collection

L.B. Foote Collection

Manitoba Sports Hall of Fame Collection

Robert Boyd Russell Collection: One Big Union

Scottish Amateur Athletic Association of Manitoba Collection

Winnipeg Boy's Club Files

Winnipeg City Police Court Records

Winnipeg Police Association Files

Winnipeg Young Men's Christian Association Collection

Manitoba Legislative Library

Journals of the Legislative Assembly of Manitoba

Manitoba History Scrapbooks

Statutes of Manitoba

Manitoba Sports Hall of Fame

Jim Trifunov File

Untitled Scrapbooks

St. Boniface Historical Society Archives

Le cloches de Saint-Boniface

St. Boniface Museum

École Provencheur Archives

Organizations Sportives File

University of Alberta Library

Peel's Prairie Provinces Online Collection

University of Manitoba Archives

Tribune Collection

Winnipeg City Archives

Bylaws, City of Winnipeg

City of Winnipeg Municipal Manuals

Minutes of Council (Winnipeg)

Winnipeg Police Museum

Police Commission Books

Other Private Collections

Randy Rostecki Card File

Other

Brandon *Henderson's Directory* 1927, 1929, 1931

Timothy Eaton's Company Catalogues 1901, 1911, 1931–36

Winnipeg *Henderson's Directory* 1880–1930

SECONDARY SOURCES (PUBLISHED)

Abel, Kerry. *Drum Songs: Glimpses of Dene History.* Montreal: McGill-Queen's University Press, 1995.

Adam, G. Mercer, ed. *Sandow on Physical Training.* New York: J. Selwin Tait and Sons, 1894.

——, ed. *Sandow's System of Physical Training.* London: Gale and Polden, 1894.

Andre, Sam, and Nat Fleischer. *A Pictorial History of Boxing.* New York: Bonanza Books, 1981.

Anokhin, Vladimir, ed. *Their Way to the Top: Stories about Sportsmen.* Moscow: Progress Publishers, 1978.

Archer, Jeff, and Joseph Svinth. "Professional Wrestling: Where Sports and Theatre Collide." *Electronic Journal of the Manly Arts and Sciences* (2005), http://www.ejmas.com/jalt/jaltframe.htm.

Archer, Jeff. *Theatre in the Squared Circle: The Mystique of Professional Wrestling.* Lafayette, CO: White Boucke Publishing, 1999.

Armstrong, Walter. "Wrestling." In *The Badminton Library.* London: Longmans, Green, and Company, 1889.

Arnold, Peter. *History of Boxing.* Secaucus, NJ: Chartwell Books, 1985.

Artibise, Alan F.J. *Winnipeg: A Social History of Urban Growth 1874–1914.* Montreal: McGill-Queen's University Press, 1975.

——, ed. *Gateway City: Documents on the City of Winnipeg 1873–1913.* Winnipeg: University of Manitoba Press, 1979.

——, ed. *Town and City: Aspects of Western Canadian Urban Development.* Regina: Canadian Plains Research Center, 1981.

Avery, Donald. *"Dangerous Foreigners": European Immigrant Workers and Labour Radicalism in Canada, 1896–1932.* Toronto: McClelland and Stewart, 1979.

Baker, William J. *Sports in the Western World.* Totowa, NJ: Rowman and Littlefield, 1982.

Ball, Donald W., and John W. Loy. *Sport and the Social Order: Contributions to the Sociology of Sport.* Reading, MA: Addison-Wesley Publishing Company, 1975.

Barthes, Roland. *Mythologies.* New York: Farrar, Straus, and Giroux, 1972.

Barton, George A. *My Lifetime in Sports.* Minneapolis: Lund Press, 1957.

Beaulieu, Michel A. *Labour at the Lakehead: Ethnicity, Socialism, and Politics, 1900–35.* Vancouver: UBC Press, 2011.

Bederman, Gail. *Manliness and Civilization: A Cultural History of Gender and Race in the United States, 1880–1917.* Chicago: University of Chicago Press, 1995.

Beekman, Scott M. *Ringside: A History of Professional Wrestling in America.* Westport, CT: Praeger, 2006.

Bellan, Ruban. *Winnipeg First Century: An Economic History.* Winnipeg: Queenston House Publishing, 1978.

Bercuson, David J. *Confrontation at Winnipeg: Labour, Industrial Relations, and General Strike.* Montreal: McGill-Queen's University Press, 1974.

——. *Fools and Wise Men: The Rise and Fall of the One Big Union.* Toronto: McGraw-Hill Ryerson, 1978.

Berger, Carl. "William Morton: The Delicate Balance of Region and Nation." In *The West and the Nation: Essays in Honour of W.L. Morton,* edited by Carl Berger and Ramsay Cook. Toronto: McClelland and Stewart, 1976.

Berthelet, Pierre. *Yvon Robert, le lion du Canada français: Le plus grand lutteur du Québec.* Montréal: Editions Trustar, 2000.

Berton, Pierre. *Klondike: The Last Great Gold Rush, 1896–1899.* Toronto: McClelland and Stewart, 1986.

Betts, John R. "Mind and Body in Early American Thought." *Journal of American History* 54, 4 (1968): 787–805.

Bishop, Charles W. *The Canadian Y.M.C.A. in the Great War.* Toronto: Canadian National Council Y.M.C.A., 1924.

Blaikie, William. *How to Get Strong and How to Stay So.* New York: Harper and Brothers Publishers, 1879.

Blair, B. Brian. *Smarten Up! Say It Right!* Tampa: Kayfabe Publishing Company, 2001.

Blanchard, Jim. *Winnipeg's Great War: A City Comes of Age.* Winnipeg: University of Manitoba Press, 2010.

Bliss, Edwin M. *Turkey and the Armenian Atrocities.* N.p.: J. Coghlan, 1896.

Boness, Kenneth R. *Pile Driver: The Life of Charles "Midget" Fischer.* Bloomington, IN: Xlibris Book Publishing, 2003.

Boring, Warren S. *Science and Skills of Wrestling.* St. Louis: C.V. Mosby Company, 1975.

Bothner, George. *Scientific Wrestling.* New York: Richard K. Fox Publishing Company, 1912.

Bouchier, Nancy. *For the Love of the Game.* Montreal: McGill-Queen's University Press, 2003.

Boyko, John. *Last Step to Freedom: The Evolution of Canadian Racism.* Winnipeg: J. Gordon Shillingford Publishing, 1998.

Brailsford, Dennis. *Sport, Time, and Society.* London: Routledge, 1991.

Braithwaite, Max. *Never Sleep Three in a Bed.* Toronto: McClelland and Stewart, 1975.

Brandwein, Alison, and Peter Brandwein. *Sport's Golden Age: A Close-Up of the Fabulous Twenties.* New York: Harper Brothers, 1948.

Breen, David H. *The Canadian Prairie West and the Ranching Frontier 1874–1924.* Toronto: University of Toronto Press, 1983.

Brown, Jennifer S.H. *Strangers in Blood: Fur Trade Company Families.* Vancouver: UBC Press, 1980.

Brown, R. Craig, and G. Ramsay Cook. *Canada, 1896–1921: A Nation Transformed.* Toronto: McClelland and Stewart, 1974.

Brown, R. Craig, and Donald Loveridge. "Unrequited Faith: Recruiting and the CEF 1914–1918." *Revue internationale d'histoire militaire* 45 (1982): 53–79.

Budnick, Carol. "Theatre on the Frontier: Winnipeg in the 1880s." *Theatre Research in Canada* 4, 1 (1983), http://journals.hil.unb.ca/index.php/tric/article/view/7475/8534.

Bumsted, J.M. *The Red River Rebellion.* Winnipeg: Watson and Dwyer, 1996.

——. *The Winnipeg General Strike of 1919: An Illustrated Guide.* Winnipeg: Watson and Dwyer, 1994.

Burger, Peter. *Charles Fenerty and His Paper Invention.* Toronto: PB Publishing, 2007.

Burnet, Jean R., and Howard Palmer. "*Coming Canadians*": *An Introduction to a History of Canada's Peoples.* Toronto: McClelland and Stewart, 1988.

Burns, Martin. *Lessons in Wrestling and Physical Culture.* Omaha: Farmer Burns School of Wrestling, 1914.

——. *Physical Culture Wrestling.* Omaha: Farmer Burns School of Wrestling, 1914.

Burstaff, H. *Canada in the Great World War.* Toronto: United Publishers of Canada, 1921.

Burstyn, Varda. *The Rites of Men: Manhood, Politics, and the Culture of Sport.* Toronto: University of Toronto Press, 1999.

Busch, Briton C., ed. *Canada and the Great War: Western Front Association Papers.* Montreal: McGill-Queen's University Press, 2003.

Cameron, Dick, ed. *The Science of Wrestling.* Sydney: Scotow Press, n.d.

Campbell, J. Peter. *Canadian Marxists and the Search for a Third Way.* Montreal: McGill-Queen's University Press, 1999.

Campbell, W. Joseph. "1897 American Journalism's Exceptional Year." *Journalism History* 29, 4 (2004), http://academic2.american.edu/~wjc/exceptyear1.htm.

Careless, J.M.S. "Frontierism, Metropolitanism, and Canadian History." *Canadian Historical Review* 35 (1954): 1–21.

——. "'Limited Identities' in Canada." *Canadian Historical Review* 50, 1 (1969): 1–10.

——. "Limited Identities—Ten Years Later." *Manitoba History* (1980): 3–9.

Carnes, Mark C., and Clyde Griffen, eds. *Meanings for Manhood: Constructions of Masculinity in Victorian America.* Chicago: University of Chicago Press, 1990.

Cashmore, Ellis. *Making Sense of Sport.* London: Routledge, 1990.

Chapman, David L. *Sandow the Magnificent: Eugen Sandow and the Beginnings of Bodybuilding.* Urbana: University of Illinois Press, 2006.

Chapman, Mike. *Encyclopedia of American Wrestling.* Champaign, IL: Leisure Press, 1990.

——. *Frank Gotch: World's Greatest Wrestler.* Buffalo, NY: William S. Hein and Company, 1990.

——. *The Life and Legacy of Frank Gotch: King of the Catch-as-Catch-Can Wrestlers.* Boulder, CO: Paladin Press, 2007.

Chiel, Arthur A. *The Jews in Manitoba: A Social History.* Toronto: University of Toronto Press, 1961.

Coates, Ken, and Fred McGuinness. *Manitoba: The Province and the People.* Edmonton: Hurtig, 1987.

Comite du livre de Saint-Pierre-Jolys. *Saint-Pierre-Jolys, Manitoba: Au fil du temps….* St. Pierre-Jolys, MB: Comite du livre de Saint-Pierre-Jolys, 2005.

Connell, R.W. *Masculinities.* Berkeley: University of California Press, 1995.

Connors, Tom. *The Modern Athlete.* Milwaukee: Ed Bulfin, 1890.

Cook, Tim. *At The Sharp End: Canadians Fighting in the Great War 1914–1916.* Toronto: Viking Canada, 2007.

Copp, Terry, and T.D. Tait. *The Canadian Response to War, 1914–1917.* Vancouver: Copp Clark Pittman, 1971.

Corbet, E.A., and A.W. Rasporich. *Winter Sports in the West.* Calgary: Historical Society of Alberta, 1990.

Cosentino, Frank. "A History of the Concept of Professionalism in Canadian Sport." In *Proceedings from the Third Canadian Symposium on the History of Sport and Physical Education, 18–21 August 1974.* Halifax: Dalhousie University, 1974.

——. *A History of Physical Education.* Toronto: Captus Press, 1988.

——. *Afros, Aboriginals, and Amateur Sport in Pre World War One Canada.* Ottawa: Canadian Historical Society, 2000.

Culin, Stewart. *Games of the North American Indians.* New York: Dover Publications, 1975.

De Lottinville, Peter. "Joe Beef of Montreal: Working-Class Culture and the Tavern, 1869–1889." *Labour/Le Travail* 8–9 (1981–82): 9–40.

Department of Agriculture. *Census of Canada 1880–81 Volume II.* Ottawa: Queen's Printer, 1881.

Desbonnet, Edmond. *Le rois de la lutte.* Paris: Berger-Levrault et Cie, 1910.

Dheensaw, Cleve. *The Commonwealth Games: The First 60 Years 1930–1990.* Victoria: Orca Book Publishers, 1994.

Dick, Lyle. "The Queer Frontier: Male Same-Sex Experience in Canada's Western Settlement Era." *Journal of Canadian Studies* 48, 1 (2014): 15–48.

——. "Red River's Vernacular Historians." *Manitoba History* 71 (2013): 2–15.

Dominion Bureau of Statistics. *Sixth Census of Canada, 1921 Volume I: Population.* Ottawa: King's Printer, 1924.

Dor, Jonas. *Islendingadagurinn 1890–1989: Saga Islendingadagsins: An Illustrated History.* Gimli, MB: Icelandic Festival of Manitoba, 1989.

Duncan, Royal, and Gary Will. *Wrestling Title Histories.* Waterloo, ON: Archeus Communications, 2000.

Dyreson, Mark. "The Emergence of Consumer Culture and the Transformation of Physical Culture: American Sports in the 1920s." *Journal of Sport History* 16, 3 (1989): 261–81.

Edwards, Harry. *Sociology of Sport.* Homewood, IL: Dorsey Press, 1973.

Eklund, Clarence. *Forty Years of Wrestling.* Buffalo, WY: By the Author, 1947.

Eklund-Odegard, Hazel. *Wyoming's Wrestling Rancher: Life and History of Clarence Eklund, Champion Wrestler.* Buffalo, WY: Self-Published, 1993.

Eisen, George, and David K. Wiggins, eds. *Ethnicity and Sport in North American History and Culture.* Westport, CT: Greenwood Press, 1994.

Erb, Marsha. *Stu Hart: Lord of the Ring.* Toronto: ECW Press, 2002.

Fleischer, Nathaniel. *From Milo to Londos: The Story of Wrestling through the Ages.* New York: Ring, 1936.

Foster, John E. "Paulet Paul: Metis or 'House Indian' Folk-Hero?" *Manitoba History* 9 (1985): 2–7.

——, ed. *The Developing West.* Edmonton: University of Alberta Press, 1983.

Francis, R. Douglas, and Howard Palmer, eds. *The Prairie West: Historical Readings.* Edmonton: University of Alberta Press, 1992.

Friesen, Gerald. *The Canadian Prairies*. Toronto: University of Toronto Press, 1984.

——. *Citizens and Nation: An Essay on History, Communication, and Canada*. Toronto: University of Toronto Press, 2000.

Garvie, Gordon T. *Wrestling for Young Wrestlers and Instructors*. Don Mills, ON: Collier-Macmillan Canada, 1972.

Gay, Peter. *The Cultivation of Hatred: The Bourgeois Experience, Victoria to Freud Volume III*. New York: W.W. Norton and Company, 1993.

Gerrard, Nelson S. *Icelandic River Saga*. Arborg, MB: Saga Publications, 1995.

Gorn, Elliott J. "Gouge and Bite, Pull Hair and Scratch: The Social Significance of Fighting in the Southern Backcountry." *American Historical Review* 90, 1 (1985): 18–43.

——. *The Manly Art: Bare-Knuckle Prize Fighting in America*. Ithaca, NY: Cornell University Press, 1986.

Goulet, Jean-Guy. *Ways of Knowing: Experience, Knowledge, and Power among the Dene Tha*. Lincoln: University of Nebraska Press, 1998.

Granatstein, J.L. *Canada's Army: Waging War and Keeping the Peace*. Toronto: University of Toronto Press, 2002.

——. *Hell's Corner: An Illustrated History of Canada's Great War, 1914–1918*. Vancouver: Douglas and McIntyre, 2004.

Grant, Madison. *The Passing of the Great Race*. New York: Charles Scribner's Sons, 1924.

Gray, James H. *Red Lights on the Prairies*. Toronto: Macmillan of Canada, 1971.

Green, Thomas, and Joseph R. Svinth, eds. *Martial Arts in the Modern World*. Westport, CT: Praeger, 2003.

——, eds. *Martial Arts of the World: An Encyclopedia of History and Innovation Volumes I and II*. Santa Barbara: ABC-CLIO, 2010.

Greig, Murray. *Goin' the Distance: Canada's Boxing Heritage*. Toronto: Macmillan Canada, 1996.

Griffin, Marcus. *Fall Guys: The Barnums of Bounce*. Chicago: Reilly and Lee Company, 1937.

Grombach, John V. *The Saga of the Fist: The 9,000 Year Story of Boxing in Text and Pictures*. Cranbury, NJ: A.S. Barnes and Company, 1977.

Gruneau, Richard, and David Whitson. *Hockey Night in Canada: Sport, Identity, and Cultural Politics*. Toronto: Garamond Press, 1993.

Guildford, Janet. "Creating the Ideal Man: Middle-Class Women's Constructions of Masculinity in Nova Scotia, 1840–1880." *Acadiensis* 24, 2 (1995): 5–23.

Gulick, Luther. *Spalding's Athletic Library No. 1: Muscle Building*. London: Renwick of Otley, 1916.

Gunn, John J. *Echoes of the Red*. Toronto: Macmillan, 1930.

Guttman, Allan. *The Erotic in Sports*. New York: Columbia University Press, 1996.

——. *From Ritual to Record: The Nature of Modern Sports*. New York: Columbia University Press, 1978.

Guttman, Allan, and Lee Thompson. *Japanese Sports: A History*. Honolulu: University of Hawaii Press, 2001.

Hackenschmidt, George. *The Way to Live*. 1908; reprinted, Farmington, MI: William F. Hinbern, 1998.

Hall, D.J. *Clifford Sifton, Volume One: The Young Napoleon, 1861–1900*. Vancouver: UBC Press, 1981.

——. *Clifford Sifton, Volume Two: A Lonely Eminence, 1901–1929*. Vancouver: UBC Press, 1985.

Hall, Ann, et al. *Sport in Canadian Society*. Toronto: McClelland and Stewart, 1991.

Halm, E.W., ed. *The Life Work of Farmer Burns*. Omaha: A.J. Kuhlman, 1911.

Hanbury, David T. *Sport and Travel in the Northland of Canada*. London: Edward Arnold, 1904.

Hardy, Stephen. *How Boston Played: Sport, Recreation, and Community 1865–1915*. Boston: Northeastern University Press, 1982.

Hargrave, Joseph James. *Red River*. Montreal: J. Lovell, 1871.

Harmon, Daniel Williams. *Harmon's Journal 1800–1819*. Surrey, BC: TouchWood Editions, 2006.

Hartman, James B. "On Stage: Theatre and Theatres in Early Winnipeg." *Manitoba History* 43 (2002): 15–24.

Hatton, C. Nathan. "Battles on the Bay: Wrestling in Fort William and Port Arthur before the

Great Depression." Thunder Bay Historical Museum Society *Papers and Records* 25 (2007): 50–66.

——. "A Little Diversion to Dispel the Gloom: Sport at the Lakehead during the Great War, 1914–1918." Thunder Bay Historical Museum Society *Papers and Records* 42 (2014): 45–66.

——. *Rugged Game: Community, Culture, and Wrestling at the Lakehead to 1933.* Thunder Bay: Lakehead University Centre for Northern Studies, 2012.

——. "Winnipeg's 'Quiet' Man: The Early Public Life of Film Star Victor McLaglen." *Manitoba History* 67 (2012): 22–28.

Haycock, Ronald G. *Sam Hughes: The Public Career of a Controversial Canadian, 1853–1916.* Waterloo, ON: Wilfrid Laurier University Press, 1986.

Healy, W.J. *Winnipeg's Early Days.* Winnipeg: Stovel Company, 1927.

Hearne, Samuel. *A Journey from Prince of Wales's Fort, in Hudson's Bay, to the Northern Ocean in the Years 1769, 1770, 1771, 1772.* Toronto: Champlain Society, 1911.

Heine, Michael. *Inuit Style Wrestling: A Training Resource Manual.* Yellowknife: Sport North Federation, 2002.

Heron, Craig. *The Canadian Labour Movement: A Short History.* Toronto: James Lorimer and Company, 1989.

——, ed. *The Workers' Revolt in Canada, 1917–1925.* Toronto: University of Toronto Press, 1998.

Hershfield, Leible. *The Jewish Athlete: A Nostalgic View.* Winnipeg: By the Author, 1980.

Hewitt, G.E. *The Story of the Twenty-Eighth (North-West) Battalion, 1914–1917.* London: Canada War Records Office, 1918.

Hewitt, Mark S. *Catch Wrestling: A Wild and Wooly Look at the Early Days of Professional Wrestling in America.* Boulder, CO: Paladin Press, 2005.

——. *Catch Wrestling Round Two: More Wild and Wooly Tales from the Early Days of Pro Wrestling.* Boulder, CO: Paladin Press, 2009.

——. "John McMahon." *Journal of Manly Arts and Sciences* 2 (2002), http://ejmas.com/jmanly/jmanlyframe.htm.

Heydenkorn, Benedykt, ed. *From Prairies to Cities: Papers on the Poles in Canada.* Toronto: Canadian-Polish Research Institute, 1975.

Hornbaker, Tim. *National Wrestling Alliance: The Untold Story of the Monopoly that Strangled Pro Wrestling.* Toronto: ECW Press, 2007.

Horrall, Andrew. "'Keep-a-Fighting! Play the Game!' Baseball and the Canadian Forces during the First World War." *Canadian Military History* 10, 2 (2001): 27–40.

Howard, Gary. *The Rassler from Renfrew: Larry Kasaboski and Northland Wrestling Enterprises.* Renfrew, ON: General Store Publications, 2007.

Howell, Colin D. *Blood, Sweat, and Cheers: Sport and the Making of Modern Canada.* Toronto: University of Toronto Press, 2001.

——. *Northern Sandlots: A Social History of Maritime Baseball.* Toronto: University of Toronto Press, 1995.

Howell, Maxwell L., and Nancy Howell. *Sport and Games in Canadian Life: 1700 to the Present.* Toronto: Macmillan of Canada, 1969.

Howell, Maxwell L., and Reet A. Howell, eds. *History of Sport in Canada.* Champaign, IL: Stipes Publishing Company, 1981.

Huggins, M., and J.A. Mangan. *Disreputable Pleasures: Less Virtuous Victorians at Play.* New York: Routledge, 2004.

Huizinga, John. *Homo Ludens: A Study of the Play Element in Culture.* Boston: Beacon Press, 1955.

Hutchison, Robert. *A Century of Service: A History of the Winnipeg Police Force 1874–1974.* Winnipeg: City of Winnipeg Police Force, 1974.

Isaac, Rhys. *The Transformation of Virginia, 1740–1790.* Chapel Hill: University of North Carolina Press, 1982.

Isenberg, Michael T. *John L. Sullivan and His America.* Chicago: University of Illinois Press, 1988.

Jackson, James A. *The Centennial History of Manitoba.* Toronto: McClelland and Stewart, 1970.

Jares, Joe. *Whatever Happened to Gorgeous George?* Englewood Cliffs, NJ: Prentice-Hall, 1974.

Jenness, Diamond. *A Report of the Canadian Arctic Expedition 1913–18 Volume XIII: The Life of the Copper Eskimos.* Ottawa: F.A. Ackland, 1922.

Jhally, Sut. "The Spectacle of Accumulation: Material and Cultural Factors in the Evolution of the Sports/Media Complex." *Critical Sociology* 12 (1984): 41–57.

Jolys, J.M., and J.H. Cote. *Pages de souvenirs et d'histoire: St. Pierre-Jolys Manitoba 1872–1972*. St. Pierre-Jolys, MB: La Paroisse de St. Pierre-Jolys, 1974.

Joyce, C.A. Tony. "Sport and the Cash Nexus in Nineteenth Century Toronto." *Sport History Review* 30 (1999): 140–67.

Jukola, Martti. *Athletics in Finland*. Helsinki: Werner Soderstrom Osakeyhtio, 1932.

Kasson, John F. *Houdini, Tarzan, and the Perfect Man: The White Male Body and the Challenge of Modernity in America*. New York: Hill and Wang, 2001.

Kenney, Harold E., and Glenn C. Law. *Wrestling*. New York: McGraw-Hill Book Company, 1952.

Kent, Graeme. *A Pictorial History of Wrestling*. London: Spring Books, 1968.

Kerr, Donald, and Deryck W. Holdsworth, eds. *Historical Atlas of Canada Volume III: Addressing the Twentieth Century, 1891–1961*. Toronto: University of Toronto Press, 1990.

Kidd, Bruce. *The Struggle for Canadian Sport*. Toronto: University of Toronto Press, 1996.

Kimmel, Michael. *History of Men: Essays on the History of American and British Masculinities*. New York: SUNY Press, 2005.

——. *Manhood in America: A Cultural History*. New York: Free Press, 1996.

Koyama, K., and A. Minami. *Spalding's Athletic Library No. 233—Jiu Jitsu*. New York: American Sports Publishing Company, 1904.

Knudson, Jerry W. "Late to the Feast: Newspapers as Historical Sources." American Historical Association *Perspectives* (1993), http://www.historians.org/perspectives/issues/1993/9310/9310ARC.cfm.

Kristjanon, W. *The Icelandic People in Manitoba*. Winnipeg: By the Author, 1965.

Lappage, Ronald S. "The Physical Feats of the Voyageur." *Canadian Journal of History of Sport* 15 (1984): 30–37.

Laprade, Pat, and Bertand Hebert. *Mad Dogs, Midgets, and Screw Jobs: The Untold Story of How Montreal Shaped the World of Wrestling*. Toronto: ECW Press, 2012.

Laycock, David. *Populism and Democratic Thought on the Prairies, 1910 to 1945*. Toronto: University of Toronto Press, 1990.

Leah, Vincent. *Alarm of Fire: 100 Years of Firefighting in Winnipeg 1882–1982*. Winnipeg: Fire Fighters Burn Fund, 1982.

——. *Pages from the Past*. Winnipeg: Winnipeg Tribune, 1975.

Lehmusto, Heikki. *History of Wrestling*. Helsinki: By the Author, 1939.

Leyshon, Glynn A. *Of Mats and Men: The Story of Canadian Amateur and Olympic Wrestling from 1600 to 1984*. London, ON: Sports Dynamics, 1984.

——. "Wrestling in Canada II, 1860–1914." *Journal of Manly Arts* (2001), http://ejmas.com/jmanly/articles/2001/jmanlyart_leyshon2_0701.htm.

Lindaman, Matthew. "Wrestling's Hold on the Western World before the Great War." *Historian* 62 (2000): 779–97.

Liponski, Wojciech. "Still and Unknown European Tradition: Polish Sport in the European Cultural Heritage." *International Journal of the History of Sport* 13, 2 (1996): 1–41.

Loken, Gulbrand. *From Fjord to Frontier: A History of the Norwegians in Canada*. Toronto: McClelland and Stewart, 1980.

Lorenz, Stacy L. "'A Lively Interest in the Prairies': Western Canada, the Mass Media, and the 'World of Sport,' 1870–1939." *Journal of Sport History* 27, 2 (2000): 195–227.

Lundin, Hjalmir. *On the Mat and Off: Memoirs of a Wrestler*. New York: Albert Bonnier Publishing House, 1937.

Luschen, G. "The Interdependence of Sport and Culture." *International Review of Sport Sociology* 2 (1967): 127–41.

MacFadden, Bernarr. *Muscular Power and Beauty*. New York: Physical Culture Publishing Company, 1902.

Mackenzie, David, ed. *Canada and the First World War: Essays in Honour of Robert Craig Brown*. Toronto: University of Toronto Press, 2005.

Mangan, J.A., ed. *Militarism, Sport, Europe: War without Weapons*. New York: Frank Cass, 2004.

Manitoba Historic Resources Branch. *Manitoba's Boundaries*. Winnipeg: Queen's Printer, 1994.

Manitoba Japanese Canadian Citizens' Association. *The History of Japanese Canadians in Manitoba*. Winnipeg: Manitoba Japanese Canadian Citizens' Association, 1996.

Mantle, Craig Leslie, ed. *The Unwilling and the Reluctant: Theoretical Perspectives on Disobedience in the Military*. Kingston: Canadian Defence Academy Press, 2006.

Marks, Lynne. *Revivals and Roller Rinks: Religion, Leisure, and Identity in Late-Nineteenth Century Small Town Ontario*. Toronto: University of Toronto Press, 1996.

Masters, D.C. *The Winnipeg General Strike*. Toronto: University of Toronto Press, 1950.

May, Vern. *The Central Canadian Professional Wrestling Almanac*. Winnipeg: Canadian Wrestle-Media, 1999.

McCarthy, Martha. *Camp Hughes: A Summary Report*. Winnipeg: Historic Resources Branch, 1989.

McCoy, Heath. *Pain and Passion: The History of Stampede Wrestling*. Toronto: ECW Press, 2007.

McKillop, Ingibjorg Sigurgeirsson. *Mikley the Magnificent Island: Treasure of Memories Hecla Island 1876–1976*. Steinbach, MB: By the Author, 1979.

McLaglen, Leopold. *Police Jiu-Jitsu*. London: Police Review Publishing Company, 1918.

McNaught, Kenneth. *A Prophet in Politics: A Biography of J.S. Woodsworth*. Toronto: University of Toronto Press, 1959.

McNaught, Kenneth, and David J. Bercuson. *The Winnipeg General Strike: 1919*. Don Mills, ON: Longman Canada, 1974.

McWhinnie, J.W. *Modern Wrestling: Graeco-Roman and Catch-as-Catch-Can Styles*. London: Health and Strength Magazine Company, 1901?

Mendoza, Daniel. *The Modern Art of Boxing*. N.p.: By the Author, c. 1789.

Menke, Frank G., rev. Suzanne Treat. *The Encyclopedia of Sports*. South Brunswick, NJ: A.S. Barnes and Company, 1975.

Metcalfe, Alan. *Canada Learns to Play: The Emergence of Organized Sport, 1807–1914*. Toronto: McClelland and Stewart, 1987.

——. "The Meaning of Amateurism: A Case Study of Canadian Sport, 1884–1970." *Canadian Journal of History of Sport* 36 (1995): 33–48.

Meyers, John C. *Wrestling from Antiquity to Date*. St. Louis: By the Author, 1931.

Mitchell, Elisabeth B. *In Western Canada before the War: Impressions of Early Twentieth Century Prairie Communities*. Saskatoon: Western Producer Prairie Books, 1981.

Miyake, Taro, and Yukio Tani. *The Game of Ju-Jitsu for the Use of Schools and Colleges*. London: Hazell, Watson, and Viney, 1906.

Mondak, J.J. "The Politics of Professional Wrestling." *Journal of Popular Culture* 23, 2 (1989): 139–50.

Morris, Phillip H., ed. *The Canadian Patriotic Fund: A Record of Its Activities from 1914 to 1919*. Ottawa: Canadian Patriotic Fund, 1919.

Morrow, Don. "Canadian Sport History: A Critical Essay." *Journal of Sport History* 10 (1983): 67–79.

——. "A Case Study of Amateur Conflict: The Athletic War in Canada, 1906–1908." *British Journal of Sport History* 3 (1986): 173–90.

Morrow, Don, and Mary Keyes, eds. *A Concise History of Sport in Canada*. Don Mills, ON: Oxford University Press, 1989.

Morrow, Don, and Kevin B. Wamsley. *Sport in Canada: A History, Third Edition*. Toronto: Oxford University Press, 2005.

Morton, Arthur S. *A History of the Canadian West to 1870–71*. Toronto: University of Toronto Press, 1973.

Morton, Desmond. *A Military History of Canada*. Toronto: McClelland and Stewart, 2007.

——. *When Your Number's Up: The Canadian Soldiers during the First World War*. Toronto: Random House, 1993.

Morton, Gerald, and George O'Brien. *Wrestling to 'Rasslin': Ancient Sport to American Spectacle*. Bowling Green, OH: Bowling Green State University Popular Press, 1985.

Morton, Suzanne. *At Odds: Gambling and Canadians 1919–1969*. Toronto: University of Toronto Press, 2003.

Morton, W.L. *Manitoba: A History*. Toronto: University of Toronto Press, 1957.

——. *The Progressive Party in Canada*. Toronto: University of Toronto Press, 1950.

Moss, Mark. *Manliness and Militarism: Educating Young Boys in Ontario for War.* Don Mills, ON: Oxford University Press, 2001.

Mott, Morris. "The Anglo-Protestant Pioneers and the Establishment of Manly Sports in Manitoba, 1870–1886." In *Proceedings, Fourth Canadian Symposium on the History of Sport and Physical Education.* Vancouver: University of British Columbia, 1980.

—. "Flawed Games, Splendid Ceremonies: Hockey Matches of the Winnipeg Vics, 1890–1903." *Prairie Forum* 10, 1 (1985): 169–85.

—. "One Solution to the Urban Crisis: Manly Sports and Winnipeggers, 1900–1914." *Urban History Review* 2 (1983): 57–70.

—, ed. *Sports in Canada: Historical Readings.* Toronto: Copp Clark Pittman, 1989.

Mott, Morris, and John Allardyce. *Curling Capital: Winnipeg and the Roarin' Game, 1876–1988.* Winnipeg: University of Manitoba Press, 1989.

Nelson, Robert K., and Kenneth M. Price. "Debating Manliness: Thomas Wentworth Higginson, William Sloane Kennedy, and the Question of Walt Whitman." *American Literature* 73, 3 (2001): 497–524.

Nevada, Vance. *Wrestling in the Canadian West.* Gallatin, TN: Crowbar Press, 2009.

Newman, Peter C. *Company of Adventurers.* Markham, ON: Penguin Books, 1985.

Nichols, M. Bennett. *Glima: Icelandic Wrestling.* New Orleans: By the Author, 1999.

Noble, Graham. "Early Ju-Jutsu: The Challenges Part II." *Dragon Times* 6 (n.d.), http://seinenkai.com/articles/noble/noble-jujutsu2.html.

—. "The Life and Death of the Terrible Turk." *Journal of Manly Arts* 1 (2001), http://ejmas.com/jmanly/articles/2001/jmanlyart_noble_0501.htm.

—. "'The Lion of the Punjab'—Part II: Stanislaus Zbyszko." *InYo: Journal of Alternative Perspectives on the Martial Arts and Sciences* (2002), http://ejmas.com/jalt/jaltframe.htm.

—. "'The Lion of the Punjab'—Part IV: Aftermath." *InYo: Journal of Alternative Perspectives on the Martial Arts and Sciences* (2002), http://ejmas.com/jalt/jaltframe.htm.

Nute, Grace Lee. *The Voyageur.* St. Paul: Minnesota Historical Society, 1955.

O'Brien, Mike. "Manhood and the Militia Myth: Masculinity, Class, and Militarism in Ontario, 1902–1914." *Labour/Le travail* 42 (1998): 115–41.

Oliver, Greg. *The Pro Wrestling Hall of Fame: The Canadians.* Toronto: ECW Press, 2003.

Oliver, Greg, and Steven Johnson. *The Pro Wrestling Hall of Fame: The Heels.* Toronto: ECW Press, 2007.

Oswalt, Wendell H. *This Land Was Theirs: A Study of the North American Indian.* New York: John Wiley and Sons, 1966.

Overman, Steven J. *The Influence of the Protestant Ethic on Sport and Recreation.* Suffolk: Ipswich Book Company, 1997.

Owram, Douglas. *Promise of Eden: The Canadian Expansionist Movement and the Idea of the West.* Toronto: University of Toronto Press, 1980.

Page, William, ed. *A History of the County of Middlesex Volume 2.* Suffolk: Boydell and Brewer, 2004.

Palmer, Howard, and Tamara Palmer. *Alberta: A New History.* Edmonton: Hurtig, 1990.

Pannekoek, Fritz. *A Snug Little Flock: The Social Origins of the Riel Resistance of 1869–1870.* Winnipeg: Watson and Dwyer, 1991.

Park, Roberta J. "'Mended or Ended?' Football Injuries and the British and American Medical Press, 1870–1910." *International Journal of the History of Sport* 18, 2 (2001): 110–33.

Parr, Joy. *Gender of Breadwinners: Women, Men, and Change in Two Industrial Towns, 1880–1950.* Toronto: University of Toronto Press, 1990.

Payne, Michael. *The Most Respectable Place in the Territory: Everyday Life in Hudson's Bay Company Service York Factory, 1788 to 1870.* Ottawa: Minister of Supply and Services Canada, 1989.

Pearl, Bill. *Getting Stronger: Weight Training for Men and Women.* Bolinas, CA: Shelter Publications, 1986.

Pellegrini, Anthony D., and Peter K. Smith. *The Nature of Play: Great Apes and Humans.* New York: Guilford Press, 2005.

Pence, Owen E. *The YMCA and Social Need: A Study of Institutional Adaptation.* New York: Association Press, 1939.

Penner, Norman, ed. *Winnipeg 1919: The Strikers' Own History of the Winnipeg General Strike.* Toronto: James Lewis and Samuel, 1973.

Pfrenger, Ken. "Wrestling in Celtic Culture." *Grappling Arts International Newsmagazine* 2, 2 (2000): 32–36.

Plato. *The Republic.* Translated by Benjamin Jowett. Minoela, NY: Dover Publications, 2000.

Podruchny, Carolyn. *Making the Voyageur World: Travelers and Traders in the North American Fur Trade.* Toronto: University of Toronto Press, 2006.

Pope, Steven W. "An Army of Athletes: Playing Fields, Battlefields, and the American Military Sporting Experience, 1890–1920." *Journal of Military History* 59, 3 (1995): 435–56.

Powers, Madelon. *Faces along the Road: Lore and Order in the Workingman's Saloon, 1870–1920.* Chicago: University of Chicago Press, 1998.

Price, Edmund E. *Science of Self Defense.* New York: Dick and Fitzgerald, 1867.

Putney, Clifford. *Muscular Christianity: Manhood and Sports in Protestant America, 1880–1920.* Cambridge, MA: Harvard University Press, 2001.

Quill Lake Historical Society. *Reflections by the Quills.* Wynyard, SK: Quill Lake Historical Society, 1981.

Radecki, Henry. *Ethnic Organizational Dynamics: The Polish Group in Canada.* Waterloo, ON: Wilfrid Laurier University Press, 1979.

Radecki, Henry, and Benedyky Heydenkorn. *A Member of a Distinguished Family: The Polish Group in Canada.* Toronto: McClelland and Stewart, 1976.

Rader, Benjamin G. *American Sports from the Age of Folk Games to the Age of Televised Sports.* Englewood Cliffs, NJ: Prentice Hall, 1996.

Ray, Arthur J., et al. *Bounty and Benevolence: A History of Saskatchewan Treaties.* Montreal: McGill-Queen's University Press, 2000.

Redmond, Gerald. *The Sporting Scots of Nineteenth Century Canada.* Toronto: Associated University Press, 1982.

Reed, Nancy B. *More than Just a Game: The Military Nature of Greek Athletic Contests.* Chicago: Ares Publishers, 1998.

Rich, E.E. *The Fur Trade and the Northwest to 1857.* Toronto: McClelland and Stewart, 1967.

Rickard, John. "The Spectacle of Excess: The Emergence of Modern Professional Wrestling in the United States and Australia." *Journal of Popular Culture* 33 (1999): 129–37.

Riess, Steven A. *City Games: The Evolution of American Urban Society and the Rise of Sports.* Urbana: University of Illinois Press, 1989.

——. "Sport and the Redefinition of American Middle-Class Masculinity." *International Journal of the History of Sport* 8, 1 (1991): 5–27.

Roberts, Julia. "The Games People Played: Tavern Amusements and Colonial Relations." *Ontario History* 52, 2 (2010): 154–74.

——. *In Mixed Company: Taverns and Public Life in Upper Canada.* Vancouver: UBC Press, 2009.

Robidoux, Michael A. "Historical Interpretations of First Nations Masculinity and Its Influence on Canada's Sport Heritage." In *Native Americans and Sport in North America: Other People's Games,* edited by C. Richard King, 130–47. New York: Routledge, 2008.

Ross, Murray G. *The Y.M.C.A. in Canada: The Chronicle of a Century.* Toronto: Ryerson Press, 1951.

Rotundo, E. Anthony. "Body and Soul: Changing Ideas of American Middle Class Manhood, 1770-1920." *Journal of Social History* 16 (1983): 23-38.

——. *American Manhood: Transformations in Masculinity from the Revolution to the Modern Era.* New York: Basic Books, 1993.

Roxborough, Henry. *One Hundred—Not Out: The Story of Nineteenth Century Canadian Sport.* Toronto: Ryerson Press, 1966.

Rutherdale, Robert. *Hometown Horizons.* Vancouver: UBC Press, 2004.

Saito, K. *Jiu-Jitsu Tricks.* New York: Richard K. Fox Publishing Company, 1912.

Sangster, Joan. "The Softball Solution: Female Workers, Male Managers, and the Operation of Paternalism at Westclox, 1923–60." *Labour/Le travail* 32 (1993): 167–99.

Saxon, Arthur. *The Development of Physical Power.* 1908; reprinted, Farmington, MI: William F. Hinbern, 1998.

Schrodt, Barbara. "Problems of Periodization in Canadian Sports History." *Canadian Journal of History of Sport* 21, 1 (1990): 65–76.

Seaman, Holly S. *Manitoba Landmarks and Red Letter Days, 1610 to 1920.* Winnipeg: By the Author, 1920.

Shannon, Jake. *Say Uncle! Catch-as-Catch-Can Wrestling and the Roots of Ultimate Fighting, Pro Wrestling, and Modern Grappling.* Toronto: ECW Press, 2011.

Sharpe, Henry S. "Asymmetrical Equals: Women and Men among the Chipewyans." In *Women and Power in Native North America,* edited by Laura F. Klein and Lillian A. Ackerman, 46–74. Norman: University of Oklahoma Press, 1995.

Shilliday, Greg, ed. *Manitoba 125—A History Volume 1: Rupert's Land to Riel.* Winnipeg: Great Plains Publications, 1993.

——, ed. *Manitoba 125—A History Volume 2: Gateway to the West.* Winnipeg: Great Plains Publications, 1994.

Silver, James, and Jeremy Hull, eds. *The Political Economy of Manitoba.* Regina: Canadian Plains Research Center, 1990.

Smart, James H. *Smart's Manual of Free Gymnastic and Dumb-Bell Exercises.* Cincinnati: Wilson, Hinkle, and Company, 1863.

Smith, Doug. *Let Us Rise! An Illustrated History of the Manitoba Labour Movement.* Vancouver: New Star Books, 1985.

Snowden, Jonathan. *Shooters: The Toughest Men in Professional Wrestling.* Toronto: ECW Press, 2012.

Sokol Polish Folk Ensemble. *Historia Zespolu Piesne I Tanca Sokol, History of the Sokol Polish Folk Ensemble 1906–1990.* Winnipeg: Sokol Polish Folk Ensemble, 1990.

Stoddart, Brian. "Sport, Cultural Imperialism, and Colonial Response in the British Empire." *Comparative Studies in Society and History* 30, 4 (1988): 649–73.

Stuart, E. Ross. *The History of Prairie Theatre.* Toronto: Simon and Pierre, 1984.

Svinth, Joseph R. "Japanese Professional Wrestling Pioneer: Sorakichi Matsuda." *In Yo: Journal of Alternative Perspectives on the Martial Arts and Sciences* 1 (2000), http://ejmas.com/jalt/jaltframe.htm.

——. "Professor Yamashita Goes to Washington." *Aikido Journal* 114 (1998), http://www.aikidojournal.com/article?articleID=43.

Templeman, Jack. *From Force to Service: A Pictorial History of the Winnipeg Police Department.* Winnipeg: Bunker to Bunker Books, 1998.

——. "History of the Winnipeg Police Part Three: The Roaring Twenties." http://www.winnipeg.ca/police/history/history3.stm.

Tester, Jim, ed. *Sports Pioneers: A History of the Finnish-Canadian Amateur Sports Federation 1906–1986.* Sudbury: Alerts AC Historical Committee, 1986.

Thesz, Lou. *Hooker: An Authentic Wrestler's Adventures inside the Bizarre World of Professional Wrestling.* Norfolk, VA: By the Author, 1995.

Thomas, Lewis G., ed. *The Prairie West to 1905: A Canadian Sourcebook.* Toronto: Oxford University Press, 1975.

Thomas, Lewis H., ed. *Essays on Western History.* Edmonton: University of Alberta, 1976.

——, ed. *The Making of a Socialist: Recollections of T.C. Douglas.* Edmonton: University of Alberta Press, 1982.

Thompson, John Herd. *Forging the Prairie West.* Toronto: Oxford University Press, 1998.

——. *Harvests of War: The Prairie West, 1914–1918.* Toronto: McClelland and Stewart, 1978.

Thompson, John Herd, and Allen Seager. *Canada 1922–1939: Decades of Discord.* Toronto: McClelland and Stewart, 1985.

Todd, Terry. "Muscles, Memory, and George Hackenschmidt." *Iron Game History* 2, 3 (1992): 10–15.

Toombs, Frederick R. *How to Wrestle.* New York: American Sports Publishing Company, 1912.

Trachtenberg, Henry. "Ethnic Politics on the Urban Frontier: 'Fighting Joe' Martin and the Jews of Winnipeg, 1893–1896." *Manitoba History* 35 (1998): 2–14.

Turek, Wiktor. *Poles in Manitoba.* Toronto: Polish Alliance Press, 1967.

——. *Polish-Language Press in Canada.* Toronto: Polish Alliance Press, 1962.

Turner, Victor. *Blazing the Trail.* Tucson: University of Arizona Press, 1992.

—. "Liminal to Liminoid, in Play, Flow, and Ritual." *Rice University Studies: The Anthropological Study of Human Play* 60, 3 (1974): 53–92.

Umbach, Arnold W., and Warren R. Johnson. *Wrestling.* Dubuque, IA: William C. Brown Company Publishers, 1966.

Van Every, Edward. *Muldoon: The Solid Man of Sport.* New York: Frederick A. Stokes, 1929.

Van Kirk, Sylvia. *Many Tender Ties: Women in Fur Trade Society, 1670–1870.* Winnipeg: Watson and Dwyer, c. 1980.

Van Vleck, Thomas. "Zbyszko: Passing the Baton." *Milo: Journal for Serious Strength Athletes* 8, 3 (2000): 91–95.

Waiser, Bill. *Saskatchewan: A New History.* Calgary: Fifth House, 2005.

Waite, P.B. *Canada 1874–1896: Arduous Destiny.* Toronto: McClelland and Stewart, 1971.

Wakefield, Wanda. *Playing to Win: Sports and the American Military, 1898–1945.* Albany: SUNY Press, 1997.

Wamsley, Kevin B., and Robert S. Kossuth. "Fighting It Out in Nineteenth-Century Upper Canada/Canada West: Masculinities and Physical Challenges in the Tavern." *Journal of Sport History* 27, 3 (2000): 405–30.

Wamsley, Kevin B., and David Whitson. "Celebrating Violent Masculinities: The Boxing Death of Luther McCarty." *Journal of Sport History* 25, 3 (1998): 419–31.

Ward, Peter W. *White Canada Forever: Popular Attitudes and Public Policy toward Orientals in British Columbia.* Montreal: McGill-Queen's University Press, 1990.

Warkentin, John, and Richard I. Ruggles. *Historical Atlas of Manitoba, 1612–1969.* Winnipeg: Manitoba Historical Society, 1970.

War Office. *Manual of Physical Training.* London: King's Printer, 1908.

Webster, David. *Donald Dinnie: The First Sporting Superstar.* Aberdeenshire, UK: Ardo Publishing, 1999.

Weider, Ben. *The Strongest Man in Canada: Louis Cyr.* Toronto: Mitchell Press, 1976.

West, John. *The Substance of a Journal during Residence at the Red River Colony, British North America in the Years 1820–1823.* Vancouver: Alcuin Society, 1967.

Wetherell, Donald G. "Some Aspects of Technology and Leisure in Alberta." *Prairie Forum* 11, 1 (1986): 51–67.

Wheeler, Robert F. "Organized Sport and Organized Labour: The Workers' Sport Movement." *Journal of Contemporary History* 13, 2 (1978): 191–210.

White, Philip, and Kevin Young, eds. *Sport and Gender in Canada.* Don Mills, ON: Oxford University Press, 1999.

Wiess, Paul. *Sport: A Philosophic Inquiry.* Carbondale: Southern Illinois University Press, 1969.

Wilson, Charles Morrow. *The Magnificent Scufflers: Revealing the Great Days When America Wrestled the World.* Brattleboro, VT: Stephen Greene Press, 1959.

Wilson, J.J. "Skating to Armageddon: Canada, Hockey, and the First World War." *International Journal of the History of Sport* 22, 3 (2005): 315–43.

Winks, Robin W. *The Blacks in Canada: A History.* Montreal: McGill-Queen's University Press, 1997.

Wolf, Kirsten. "Emigration and Mythmaking: The Case of the Icelanders in Canada." *Canadian Ethnic Studies* 33, 2 (2001): 1–14.

Woodsworth, James S. *Strangers within Our Gates: Or, Coming Canadians.* Toronto: Mission Society of the Methodist Church, 1909.

Wyke, Maria. "Herculean Muscle! The Classicizing Rhetoric of Bodybuilding." *Arion* 4, 3 (1997): 51–79.

Zald, Mayer N. *Organizational Change: The Political Economy of the YMCA.* Chicago: University of Chicago Press, 1970.

Zeller, Suzanne. *Inventing Canada: Early Victorian Science and the Idea of a Transcontinental Nation.* Toronto: University of Toronto Press, 1987.

FILMS

Catch: The Hold Not Taken. DVD. Directed by Mike Todd and Ian Bennett. Manchester: Riverhorse Productions, 2005.

Night and the City. DVD. Directed by Jules Dassin. Hollywood: Twentieth Century Fox, 1950.

SECONDARY SOURCES (UNPUBLISHED)

Cosentino, Frank. "A History of the Concept of Professionalism in Canadian Sport." PhD diss., University of Alberta, 1973.

Hatton, Charles. "Headlocks at the Lakehead: Wrestling in Fort William and Port Arthur, 1913–1933." MA thesis, Lakehead University, 2007.

Joyce, Charles A. "From Left Field: Sport and Class in Toronto, 1845–1886." PhD diss., Queen's University, 1997.

McKay, Donald Stewart. "The Cultural Ecology of the Chipewyan." MA thesis, University of British Columbia, 1965.

Mott, Morris. "Manly Sports and Manitobans: Settlement Days to World War One." PhD diss., Queen's University, 1980.

Rostecki, Randy. "The Growth of Winnipeg, 1870–1886." MA thesis, University of Manitoba, 1980.

Tripp, Michael. "Persistence of Difference: A History of Cornish Wrestling." PhD diss., University of Exeter, 2009.

Index